THE UNCONSCIOUS
IN SOCIAL RELATIONS

THE UNCONSCIOUS
IN
SOCIAL RELATIONS

An analysis of unconscious processes in
personality, society, and culture

OTAKAR MACHOTKA

Professor of Sociology, Harpur College

PHILOSOPHICAL LIBRARY
New York

TO MY WIFE, JARMILA

INTRODUCTION

There are several reasons why I welcome the opportunity to write an introduction to the present book. First, it allows me to stress the importance of the profound problem which Dr. Machotka has addressed—a problem which social scientists have scarcely recognized, much less studied. Second, it enables me to comment on the place, the propriety and the value of Dr. Machotka's general method of study. And, third, it permits me to widen familiarity among my American colleagues with the thought of a distinguished Czech sociologist who, although now in our midst for several years, is regrettably not well known among us.

Dr. Machotka has identified the purpose of his volume as pointing out "the role of the unconscious in social life in almost all of its breadth." This breadth is represented by the three major topics of personality, society, and culture. He seeks to explain and to emphasize that the organization of experience and action in all of these three areas depends to a large extent and in a profound way on unconscious processes. It should be made clear immediately that in referring to this "unconscious" dimension of group and personal life, Dr. Machotka is not thinking of the "unconscious" as it is conceived in psycho-analytic theory or in other psychiatric approaches. This latter notion of the "unconscious," which centers in the notion of hidden motives, is only a narrow part of a much wider conception which Dr. Machotka develops. Allowing his thoughtful scrutiny to move freely from one to another aspect of personal and social life he perceives multitudes of instances of the unconscious formation of conduct and of organization. Thus, he directs our attention to the unnoticed and unwitting processes which are at work in such diverse areas as the interaction between people, the formation of impressions, the development of attitudes and judgments, the organization of feelings, the formation of norms and values, the origin of cultural innovations, and the transmission of a social heritage. The reflective reader will come to realize the profound extent to which both group life and personal life are shaped by processes and runs of experience that are not perceived by the participants, or identified or understood by students.

Let me, following the lead of the author, point specifically to a few of the more crucial instances of personal or group happenings in which unknown and unconscious processes are dominant. Perhaps the most important of all is the "acquisition" of a language by the young child; we have essentially no knowledge of how this miraculous development takes place. Similarly, we are devoid of real understanding of how people who are in interaction come to grasp each other's intentions and understand each other; the nature of communication still remains a great mystery. Again, the formation in personal experience of such seemingly simple things as objects, attitudes, or judgments is largely *terra incognita;* "learning theory" may make noisy pretensions but is actually very silent on the mechanisms responsible for such kinds of personal formation. On the collective side we know next to nothing about the processes involved in the origin of cultural patterns; we have advanced little beyond the recognition voiced a half century ago by Sumner that the origin of the folkways is lost in the mist of collective interaction. Finally, we have little knowledge of the processes involved in the selection and rejection of competing forms of group behavior; contemporary group life in particular changes and grows through such unwitting choices between competing patterns. These few references to crucial happenings in personal experience and group life should convey some realization of the wide extent to which unconscious processes are at work at key points in the formation of personality, society and culture. Without misrepresenting what our critical gaze perceives, we can say that most of what is important in these areas remains submerged and undetected.

Such a conclusion would likely be regarded by most present day social and psychological scientists as trite and essentially meaningless. They would say that the presence of large areas of ignorance is natural in the life of any science at any given time; such areas of ignorance merely signify the need of extending to them the perspectives, methods and forms of inquiry of the given science. Thus, the "unconscious" in the formation of personality, society, and culture merely represents those areas in which scientific inquiry has not been undertaken; the "unconscious" in these areas would vanish to the degree to which psychologists and social scientists would bring their concepts, their techniques of research and their forms of analyses to bear on the problems.

If the presentation made by Dr. Machotka could be covered by the above argument there would be, on the whole, little merit to his volume. The merit would be confined to the fact that he had designated certains areas of problems to which psychology and social science were giving little attention. However, Dr. Machotka's position and contribution go considerably beyond calling attention to areas of ignorance in the study of personality, society, and culture — to matters which psychology and the social sciences have so far not approached with their armament. Instead, he is calling attention to the fact that the "unconscious" exists not so much in the sense of the "unknown" as in the sense of matters that are different from what psychology and social science are currently equipped to handle. The "unconscious" refers to processes and lines of happening which elude the mere extended application of current concepts, theories, and methods of sophisticated research. Thus, one does not come to grips with the area of the "unconscious" by merely extending current theories of learning, or by introducing new variations in stimulus-response schemes, or by undertaking some new lines of conventional experimentation in the area of social interaction, or by adding some new variables in survey research. What is called for, instead, is an identification of new lines of happening and an isolation of new mechanisms to explain them. The "unconscious" in personal organization and group life represents the play of new and different processes from those that are dealt with in contemporary theories and research procedures.

This leads me now to comment on Dr. Machotka's general method of inquiry which he follows in approaching the study of "the unconscious in social relations." He does exactly what seems to me to be called for by the nature of his task, namely to use a flexible exploratory inquiry into varieties of empirical happenings in which unconscious processes are seemingly in play. His procedure is to select diverse instances, especially those which arise in his own experience and hence are under his immediate observation. These instances then become objects of scrutiny and of reflection, in which persisting imaginative thought leads to the detection of some feature or relation that would otherwise elude notation. This is not the method that is represented by sophisticated and standard research procedure today in the psychological and social sciences. Standard research procedure calls for rigid research design — the specification of a precise problem, the proposal of a definitive hypothesis, the clear cut identification of independent and dependent variables, and the setting up of the study in such ways as to disengage the relations between these variables. The use of such standard research procedure would be odd, indeed, when one's problems are vague and sketchy, when one's leading ideas are halting and immature, when one's data are uncertain and hazy, and when significant relations are only dimly sensed. To impose rigid research procedure on studies concerned with such undefined problem areas is mere slavish ritual. What is needed, instead, is flexible and imaginative observation — an observation which grows in sensitivity and form through countless instances of thoughtful application to empirical instances. In short, the type of procedure which we note in a Charles Darwin.

Dr. Machotka has wisely followed this flexible, imaginative, and probing form of scrutiny of what catches his attention as suggesting the play of unconscious processes in empirical social life. Accordingly, his discussion is sketchy, incomplete and lacking in the ritualistic forms of contemporary social research techniques. The student who expects to find in this volume a treatment showing the application of "research design," the drawing of representative samples, the construction of a neat hypothesis, and the identification of independent and dependent variables will be disappointed. This book is not for him. The book holds out rich rewards, however, for the student who realizes that Dr. Machotka is addressing a highly important yet markedly uncharted problem. Such a student will benefit greatly if he brings to the reading of this book the kinds of scholarly abilities which have gone into its writing — genuine scholarly dedication, a persisting and troubled preoccupation with an intriguing and slippery problem, a patient and unhurried reflection on diverse aspects of the problem, a readiness to turn to very different kinds of data including the use of personal experience, and the continuing sincere effort to develop insightful understanding. Such a reader will discover that he is in touch with a genuine scholar and a genuine student of human group life.

I wish to close with a few words about the author. Dr. Machotka follows a distinguished tradition of sociological scholarship that dates back to Thomas Masaryk, the eminent president of the Republic of Czechoslovakia following the first World War and that is represented subsequently in the academic work of President Beneš. After early training in his own country and subsequently in the United States and France

Dr. Machotka advanced rapidly in university life in Czechoslovakia, becoming full professor of sociology at Charles University in Prague — actually succeeding to the chair held by President Beneš. The author of seven important books and of many scientific articles, he occupied a distinguished position in learned circles in his country. As a devoted patriot of his country and an unflinching adherent to the principles of Democracy, Dr. Machotka was forced to flee from Czechoslovakia following the Communist coup. His career in both its academic and patriotic lines follows the spirit of Masaryk and Beneš. These few biographical details may lead the reader to realize that the present book comes from a distinguished and unusual person.

Herbert Blumer

Department of Sociology
University of California (Berkeley)

CONTENTS

Part Two

PSYCHOLOGICAL FACTORS AND PROCESSES

Part Three

SOCIAL-PSYCHOLOGICAL CONFIGURATIONS

Part Four

PERSONALITY AND CULTURE

PREFACE

The unusual conditions under which we lived during the German occupation of Czechoslovakia in the last war unveiled some of the often concealed relations between the human personality and its social environment. In this respect I had a number of striking experiences. While more than 99 per cent of the Czech people stood firm in their opposition to the Nazi occupants, a small number turned to collaborate with them. Most of these were opportunists whose abject motives were easily understood. But some of the collaborators were of a different kind. They were not led by motives of personal profit; on the contrary they considered themselves faithful to their nation. As a matter of fact, they even claimed that their ardent patriotism was the main motive for the change of their attitude toward Nazi occupiers.

When you spoke to these people, you had the impression that they tried to explain the deep and often sudden change in their behavior not only to you but also to themselves. They did not know how it happened. Their patriotic reasons were mere rationalizations, and they felt it.

The changes were produced by certain processes which went on without the awareness and perhaps even against the will of the individuals concerned, who became aware of them only after new attitudes, values, norms, and loyalties developed. The additional rationalizations supported them, but they did not bring them into existence.

It was surprising to notice how elaborate and well-defined these new configurations were from the beginning and how well they applied to a number of situations of daily life. These new, well worked out, political conceptions appeared almost without hesitation, fumbling, or internal conflicts. They were ready-made products of spontaneous processes, originating in new conditions in which the individual lived, which needed only a few additional retouchings.

The unconscious and unwitting nature of these changes was extremely interesting for the sociologist and the social psychologist. They indicated how some of the basic adaptations of the personality to new social conditions may occur without any intention, plan, or even awareness; they showed that personality under their pressure may change or

xvii

may be reorganized in the same unconscious and unwitting way. They further taught him that some fundamental cultural changes may be produced by these unconscious processes and that all people do is take cognizance of them and perhaps support them by a few rationalizations.

How was all this possible? How could this happen? These crucial questions appeared not only important but also perhaps basic to our understanding of social life because it was soon evident that the unconscious processes, and often also their unconscious products, were not an exception, but rather a rule in the changes of personality, of culture, and even of social structure. I found such processes in certain unexplainable changes in literary tastes; in the seemingly unfounded acceptance of certain unreasonable fashions; in the changes of attitudes of a poor young man married to the daughter of a rich businessman; in some religious, artistic, or political conversions, as well as in the slower changes of our personality and culture of which we become aware only when many years later we meet our old friends or read an old newspaper.

The more I pondered the socially relevant unconscious processes of adaptation and adjustment to new social conditions, the more I became convinced of their basic importance for social life. I wrote a brief analysis of some of them shortly before the communist coup in Czechoslovakia in 1948. I published its first part in the Czech sociological journal, *Sociologie a Sociální Problémy*. Its second part, the proofs of which I had corrected, was never allowed to be published.

After my arrival in the U. S., I paid more attention to references to unconscious processes in the writings of sociologists. I did not find many, but those I found were encouraging. While I disliked their often incidental nature and their brevity, I was heartened by the fact that they were found in the writings of people belonging to different schools of sociological thought. Let me mention some of them.

It is well known what role has been ascribed by Gustave LeBon to the unconscious emotional and intellectual processes of individuals in the crowd. He says that in the crowd the conscious personality vanishes, that "the individual forming part of a psychological crowd . . . . . is no longer conscious of his acts."[1] Tarde spoke about unconscious imitation,[2] Durkheim, and Hollingshead and Redlich, about unconscious judgments.[3] Thomas and Znaniecki[4] and Mannheim[5] mentioned unconsciously occupied standpoints. Thomas and Znaniecki discussed the unconscious modification of culture.[6] Cooley was convinced that we may be wholly unaware of the existence of certain values as well as of their motivating power on our behavior. He believed that values may be generated by unconscious processes.[7]

E. Faris wrote about unconscious attitudes.[8] More recently Burgess and Cottrell recognized the role of partly or wholly unconscious reaction patterns in the marriage situation.[9] They considered unconscious trends, factors and strivings of the personality, as well as unconscious influences, as the important part of these patterns. Burgess and Locke claim that the parental influence upon mate selection is largely unconscious and includes family expectations in terms of culture, class, and conceptions of qualities of the desirable person. Falling in love is determined by motivations below the conscious level. The person tends, generally unconsciously, to fall in love with a person similar to his parent. One's conception of the ideal mate may likewise function unconsciously.[10] Greenwood speaks about unconscious biases and about the unconscious use of the method of agreement.[11] Piaget discusses the unconscious assimilation of feelings and thoughts concerning the rules of a game;[12] Simmel, unconscious interests,[13] Max Weber, unawareness of motives,[14] and Sorokin, unconscious activities.[15]

These examples are taken from books which study certain sociological problems without any explicit interest in unconscious processes, motives or patterns. The authors simply felt it necessary to use the concept of the unconscious in order to explain the discussed phenomenon. In all these cases they did it briefly, without adhering to any existing theory of the unconscious and without having any such theory of their own. This made their statements especially valuable for us.

Similarly, a number of anthropologists felt that they had to use the concept of the unconscious in order to explain certain cultural phenomena. They speak about unconscious imitation, adaptation, assimilation, projection, and selection. They discuss unconscious learning, conditioning, or acceptance of culture, its unconscious tendencies, activities, or recasting. They use the concepts of unconscious linguistic rules, social structure, cultural patterns, sanctions, prototypes, and others.[16]

Thus, two groups of social scientists felt equally the necessity of using unconscious processes and configurations of the human mind in their explanations of the life of society and culture. They found them in so many aspects of social life that it is rather surprising that no attempt has been made to present them in a more systematic and complete way. The present study is wholly devoted to them, but it is very far from being complete or systematic. I felt that I could not be more inclusive without making the book too lengthy. Thus, for instance, I will not discuss unconscious motives, interests, and ideals; and I will mention empathy, roles, solidarity, status and identification as well as some other unconscious psychic phenomena only very incompletely.

A systematic approach to the problem has been hampered by several factors. I must mention one of them in particular. Some chapters are based on psychological concepts, others on sociological, socio-psychological, and anthropological concepts. Although I feel how much the unity of the study suffers by it, I was not able to remedy it. In some respects some of these concepts complement each other, but in other respects they do not fit together well at all.

The mere fact that I had to use facts from four different scientific fields was a serious difficulty in coping with the problem satisfactorily. It is almost impossible to master all these four fields equally well. I am aware of the shortcomings of the study in this respect.

In spite of this, I have the feeling that its results are not without value. For one, it became apparent that so broad and basic is the role of the unconscious mind that social life is unthinkable or rather impossible without its participation. Secondly, I was able to trace more precisely the role of some unconscious phenomena in social life and to point to the existence of some others which have not yet been discussed by either the students of society or those of the unconscious.

Besides that, personality, social structure, culture, and the culture process appeared in a rather new light. The number of unconscious, spontaneous processes that produce social adjustments, adaptations, innovations, and other social behavior patterns, as well as processes that maintain culture, was revealed to be enormous. The human mind is a much more complex, efficient, and less self-conscious agent in the culture process than has generally been thought. Many puzzles of culture change and of the mere existence of culture are better explained by the stream of unconscious processes of the human mind than by any other previous theory.

Unfortunately, the nature of most of the unconscious psychic processes is so poorly known that the present study, instead of bringing forth a satisfactory explanation of their role in social and cultural life, often only points to the problems which are to be solved in the future.

By stressing the role of unconscious factors and processes in the life of society and culture, we do not want to underestimate the importance of the fully conscious and purposeful human activities. They, too, play an indispensable role in social life and culture but are no more basic than unconscious processes.

The concept of "unconscious" will be used in the broadest meaning. Certainly the psychoanalytic understanding of the term represents only a fraction of what we consider necessary to include in it. From the sixteen meanings of unconscious listed by J. G. Miller,[17] we include the following (in addition to the psychoanalytic use): unresponsive, undiscriminating, conditioned, subliminal, unattending, insightless, unremembering, unlearned, unrecognizing, ignored, and unavailable to awareness.

The aim of the book is to point to the role of the unconscious in social life in almost all its breadth. To my knowledge, no such attempt has yet been made. As a rule, the studies concerning the problem have dealt with some aspects of social life only; or, more frequently, they mention the role of the unconscious only occasionally. This book attempts to remedy both shortcomings.

In every such attempt, the problem of method is a very difficult one. If you want to point to a broad field which should be open to systematic research, you cannot use the method of experiment. You have to proceed rather summarily, and your conclusions have necessarily the nature of general hypotheses rather than that of painstakingly-established truth.

I use this method with hesitation. I consider empirical research as the only method whereby the empirical sciences establish new knowledge. But in many stages in the development of science, it is also necessary to outline the problems, to point to the future paths of research; to formulate the hypotheses; and to clarify, at least partly, certain basic issues. There is a difference between speculation satisfied with its own results and speculation which tends to lead to new facts by later empirical research. It is the latter that I had in mind when writing this book. I expect the empirical research to follow.

In order to make my hypotheses clear, I use a number of examples. But I have to stress that my examples are not given as proofs of my explanations, as used to be the practice in early sociological texts. They really are mere examples, supposed to ease the understanding of my hypothetical explanations; and they do not prove anything by themselves. Nor does my quoting modern students of the unconscious intend to prove the correctness of my approach. I quote them rather to point to the importance of the concept of unconscious in the field that they study.

Although I will discuss most of the areas of social life, I will give more detailed attention to culture. In the future, similar attention should be given to groups and to social structure and possibly to social movements.

The plan of the book is such that the unconscious experiences, factors, and processes pertinent to social life will be discussed first. Then I will pay attention to the configurations unconsciously produced by the human mind from these experiences, factors, and through these processes, again as far as they are socially shaped and accepted. Consequently my interest turns to the ability and limits of the human mind to produce such configurations and to the importance of such unconscious configurations for the existence and changes of culture.

An analysis of the unconscious experiences, factors, and processes in social life necessarily leads to a new approach to personality, to its complexity, flexibility and creativity. These are rather logical and unavoidable consequences of our basic approach and its development. If I succeed in stimulating some of my readers to use this approach in their own research, even if some of my hypotheses might be discarded and replaced by better ones, then I shall think that this book has not been written in vain.

When writing the book I enjoyed the help of my colleagues at Harpur College and of many friends. Dr. Enrico L. Quarantelli and Dr. Thomas P. Makres of Broome County Mental Health Clinic read the whole manuscript and commented on it from the sociological and psychological points of view respectively. Dr. Harold T. Fagin advised me on the chapters discussing the personality and Dr. Jack Richardson on the chapter on learning. I am very much aware that I could not live fully up to their advice.

Mrs. Alice Penfield devoted much of her time to the linguistic and stylistic improvements of the whole manuscript, while Mrs. Josephine Downey, Mrs. Ada Wexler and Mr. Harold E. Rockwell did the same to some portions of it. Dr. Bernard F. Huppé answered many of my questions pertaining to the linguistic problems I encountered when preparing the text. Miss Mary A. Randar helped with its editing. My son Dr. Pavel Machotka read the manuscript in its final stage and Dr. Peter Dodge read the galley proofs. Both contributed much to the correctness and smoothness of the text. My wife Dr. Jarmila Machotka helped very much with the final work on the book, especially with proofreading and preparation of the index. I wish to express my heartfelt gratitude to all of them.

O. M.

Harpur College
State University of New York

FOOTNOTES TO PREFACE

1. G. LeBon, *The Crowd,* Macmillan, New York, 1947, p. 31; see also pp. 22, 28, 29, 32, 36.
2. See p. 74.
3. E. Durkheim, *The Rules of Sociological Method,* Free Press, Glencoe, Ill., 1950, p. XXXVII; A. B. Hollingshead and F. C. Redlich, *Social Class and Mental Illness,* J. Wiley & Sons, New York, 1958, p. 6.
4. W. I. Thomas and F. Znaniecki, *The Polish Peasant in Europe and in America,* A. Knopf, New York, 1919, vol. I, p. 23.
5. K. Mannheim, *Ideology and Utopia,* Harcourt, Brace and Co., New York, 1949, p. 177.
6. *Op. cit.,* V, p. XIII.
7. C. H. Cooley, *Social Process,* C. Scribner's Sons, New York, 1924, pp. 284, 290.
8. E. Faris, *The Nature of Human Nature,* McGraw-Hill, New York, 1937, p. 128.
9. E. W. Burgess and L. S. Cottrell, *Predicting Success or Failure in Marriage,* Prentice-Hall, New York, 1939, pp. 175, 335, 334.
10. E. W. Burgess and H. J. Locke, *The Family,* American Book Co., New York, 1960, pp. 365, 369.
11. E. Greenwood, *Experimental Sociology,* King's Crown Press, New York, 1945, p. 77.
12. J. Piaget, *The Moral Judgment of the Child,* The Free Press, Glencoe, Ill., 1948, p. 41.
13. K. H. Wolff, ed., *The Sociology of Georg Simmel,* The Free Press, Glencoe, Ill., 1950, p. 41.
14. Max Weber, *The Theory of Social and Economic Organization,* Oxford University Press, New York, 1950, p. 97.
15. P. A. Sorokin, *Social and Cultural Dynamics,* American Book Co., New York, 1937-41, vol. I, p. 3.
16. See pp. 259, 289 and footnote No. 89 on pp. 296-7.
17. J. G. Miller, *Unconsciousness,* J. Wiley & Sons, New York, 1942, pp. 21-44.

PART ONE

UNCONSCIOUS EXPERIENCES

I

SUBLIMINAL EXPERIENCES

The unconscious experiences affecting our social behavior may be divided into two groups: experiences which are (1) unconscious while occurring and (2) conscious while occurring but later dropped into unconsciousness. To the first group belong subliminal and partly marginal perceptions, to the second, some marginal perceptions, and forgotten and unrecollected experiences.

Stimuli which are below threshold intensity are considered subliminal. Miller says that "through the years it has been demonstrated that they can affect behavior directly."[1] Many psychologists have tried to prove this and their results have been most convincing. Hansen and Lehmann, for instance, proved that correct guesses of what had been subliminally whispered were better than chance when the cues were whispered in the same room as the receiver. Also, geometric figures projected at an intensity below the limen produced recognition above chance frequency. As early as 1904 Dunlap reported that subjects perceived the interruption of inaudible sounds.[2]

Recently there has been an increase in interest in subliminal perception and its influence on human behavior. Goldiamond[3] lists 198 articles and books in this field. The influence of subliminal perception on human behavior is strongly supported by a number of experiments.

Murphy says: "The rapid, unanalyzed evaluation of a person or situation (constituting part of what is meant by 'intuition') may be due to . . . multiple elements, or to their configurations, which are not consciously noted."[4] In most of the impressions of this kind we find subliminal as well as possibly marginal perceptions.

Speakers often assess the reaction of an audience by subliminal stimuli coming from very slight actions of the individuals in the audience. Certain very weak noises and certain contractions of facial muscles of the persons relatively far from the speaker may be perceived subliminally, especially if they are many and if they are repeated. Psychologists know about summations of similar subliminal stimuli. This probably is what happens to the speaker; undoubtedly numerous repeated and simultaneous subliminal perceptions are summed into a final strong conviction about the reaction of the audience.[5]

1

People who have many contacts with others and who have to depend on their own judgment develop a startling use of subliminal perceptions to evaluate them. The trust or distrust of a businessman in a newcomer, the evaluation of his sincerity, good will, real intentions, financial background, interests, and other important characteristics are probably evaluated on the basis of partly subliminal perceptions and their summations.

Most frequent amongst the subliminal perceptions of the behavior of a person are probably the very slight movements of the eyes and of the facial muscles. Also, slight shades and incoherences of gestures, as well as certain very short hesitations, may be perceived this way, as may some inflections of voice, differing slightly from the usual ones.

There are three kinds of summations of subliminal experiences. We summate a number of successive similar or identical subliminal experiences (like the impression a person made on us after we talked to him for a while) or a number of simultaneous impressions (like the impression a speaker forms from hundreds of people in his audience). Finally, we may summate a number of successive or simultaneous subliminal experiences of different nature such as gestures, inflections of voice, movements of the eyes, and facial expressions of a person.

The process of summation and organization of the subliminal perceptions is itself generally unconscious. Only the result sometimes becomes conscious. There are differences in the clarity and intensity of the resulting idea or feeling. It may be a vague and uncertain feeling or a very positive conviction.

Subliminal impressions are summated even if we do not need them and are not interested in them at the time. For instance, we may not be interested and we do not need to have a judgment about people we have incidentally met. But, later on upon having unexpectedly to co-operate with one of them or upon having business with one of them, the total impression we have of him (including subliminal experiences) emerges in our mind.

The importance of subliminal impressions in social life seems to me to be twofold. Many of our reactions and adaptations to persons may be based on subliminal experiences. The avoidance of certain persons; the development of friendliness; the hesitation to accept friendly help; co-operation; the acceptance of convictions and attitudes of other people; the adjustment to their moods, interests, and goals, may be cases in point. The adjustments of speakers or soloists to their audiences, as well as our reactions and adjustments to small groups, naturally seem to be greatly helped by subliminal impressions. The cues we often use to recognize that our friends or co-workers do not

2

approve of what we do, that their mood is less enthusiastic, less friendly, more determined, or uncertain, probably are in a large degree subliminal. How often do we feel that way, without being able to say why! We may be convinced of our impression even if the known facts indicate that the opposite is the case.

Subliminal cues undoubtedly seem to help our adjustments to culture and to its changes, too. These cues give us information about whether certain norms, values, attitudes are still equally as strong as before or whether they are weaker or stronger. They may also provide information about how much and in what way they changed. Either by our reactions to these changes or by our adjustments to them, we participate actively in the changes of culture.

FOOTNOTES TO CHAPTER ONE

1. J. G. Miller, *Unconsciousness*, p. 145.
2. All three experiments quoted by J. G. Miller, *ibid.*, pp. 149, 151, 152.
3. Israel Goldiamond, "Indicators of Perception: I. Subliminal Perception, Subception, Unconscious Perception: An Analysis in Terms of Psychophysical Indicator Methodology," *Psychological Bulletin, 55*, 1958, pp. 373, 411.
4. G. Murphy, *Personality, a Biosocial Approach to Origins and Structure,* Harper, New York, 1947, pp. 233, 234.
5. Recently there have been attempts to use subliminal perception in advertising. See *The New York Times Magazine,* January 12, 1958, pp. 22, 59-60.

II

MARGINAL EXPERIENCES

The conscious life of men living in society is so basic and so conspicuous that marginal stimuli have almost completely escaped the attention of the students of society, even though, because of their number and importance, they are responsible for a considerable portion of our social behavior.

Let us take a simple example of a businessman who usually finishes work in his office at 5:00 P. M. and walks home through the city. The problems connected with his work generally continue to occupy his mind so that he does not notice many of the objects and people whom he passes in the streets. He perceives them through the fringe of consciousness and almost immediately forgets all about them. When talking with his wife at dinner, however, after being asked about events in the city, he knows that people were walking as usual; they were rushing neither more nor less, and they looked just the same as on other days. They were no more excited, worse or better dressed, nor were they paying more attention to some objects than ordinarily. Does he remember any of the numerous people he passed? Does he remember any of the expressions of faces he met, any of the paces set by the numerous passersby? No. Despite that, he "knows" that nothing has changed. This general impression of a normal life was chiefly based on a great number of marginal perceptions. How many similar general impressions we have all the time! We know that everything is normal in our family; in our office; in our club; in our church; in the economic situation of our friends; or in our neighborhood.

Our businessman also knew, for instance, that in the summer during vacations, the mood of the city was lighthearted, that it was tense when the international situation was getting dangerous; he knew that it was joyful before Christmas. Hundreds of marginal impressions were unconsciously organized into a picture of a real Christmas atmosphere.

Modern psychologists do not pay much attention to marginal perceptions (with the exception of incidental learning). Few of them use the term.[1] More attention was given to them by psychiatrists such as Sullivan[2] and Prince. In Prince's opinion, marginal perceptions are to

5

be classified into two groups: Those of which we are dimly aware and those which "belong to an ultra-marginal zone and are really subconscious.[3] Evidence of their being present can only be obtained through memories recovered in hypnosis, abstraction, and by other methods."[4] In any case it seems that the line of demarcation between the focus and the margin of attention is not sharp.[5] This seems to be supported by the experiments of Guratzsch[6] and others.[7]

Prince says that perceptions of all kinds (fully conscious, marginal, ultra-marginal) leave traces. He supports this by the following observation: "I asked B. C. A., (without warning and after having covered her eyes) to describe the dress of a friend who was present and with whom she had been conversing for perhaps some twenty minutes. She was unable to do so beyond saying that he wore dark clothes. . . . B. C. A. was then asked to write a description automatically. Her hand wrote as follows (she was unaware that her hand was writing): 'He has on a dark greenish gray suit, a stripe in it—little rough stripe; black bow cravat; shirt with three little stripes in it; black laced shoes; false teeth; one finger gone; three buttons on his coat. . . .' The written description was absolutely correct. The stripes in the coat were almost invisible."[8] This points to the fact that under certain circumstances marginal experiences are available to us.

We are interested in the extent to which traces of marginal experiences influence our behavior. Unfortunately, we find only bits of knowledge concerning this field. We know, for instance, from the experiments of Coover that objects attended to by peripheral vision are more often named, if we ask the subject to name objects of this kind, than could be accounted for by chance. The subjects evidently do not know where the idea of those objects comes from.[9]

Many of us have, for instance, had an experience similar to the following: while working on a task fully occupying our attention, we suddenly stopped and looked around attentively without knowing why we did so. A certain noise which we were not conscious of hearing (because we were concentrating on the work at hand) caused that reaction.

We have statements of hunters who, being occupied by something else, suddenly knew that a bear or elk was close by. They were not aware of having heard a twig snap or some other similar noise. In other similar cases,[10] we may have reacted in a more specific, well-adjusted way without a conscious reason.[11]

In all such cases the reaction of the person seems to be based on one or several marginal or ultramarginal perceptions. These were able to start the appropriate action. This happens especially when we are set to perceive certain things.

6

Imagine the following case. We are accustomed to visiting the family of a friend, and we are thoroughly familiar with all the objects of his living room. One day the usual and well-known impression of this living room seems to us to be changed. The well-used and almost shabby room looks almost elegant. We cannot ascertain the specific change. Finally, we are told that the curtains have been washed and ironed and that there is a new cut glass vase instead of the old one. Those two objects were sufficient to change the total impression. Our eyes certainly received the sensation of those two objects; but only after we had been told, did we really become aware of these changes and understand the causes of the new impression.[12]

Here also belongs what Linton[13] and Horney[14] call "registry." Linton says that ". . . the individual may register several situations and produce the habitual responses to them as they arise without knowing that he has done so and without interrupting the flow of his conscious psychological processes."

Some psychologists discuss the very weak but perceptible cues as a separate category. They call them "very weak," "reduced," or "slight" cues.[15] As long as they are fully perceptible but not perceived consciously, they must be considered as marginal.

MARGINAL EXPERIENCES IN SOCIAL SITUATIONS

APPROPRIATE REACTION TO THE SITUATION

Miss E. K. had the following experience: She was reading in the parlor, and her parents were sitting in the kitchen. Without knowing why, she suddenly stopped reading. "I began to be disturbed by my parents conversing in the kitchen. I could not hear exactly what they were saying, but I judged that something was wrong. When I went into the kitchen, I learned that my aunt was quite seriously ill and that my mother had not wanted me to know about it until I had taken my exam that day." When I asked her why she had stopped reading, she told me that she did not know. Without any doubt, the change in tone of the parents' voices that was perceived by the fringe of attention did not enter into her consciousness, which was fully occupied by the content of the book; but she reacted in a perfectly fitting way.

PERCEPTION OF CONCEALED THOUGHTS

Marginal perceptions help us very much in understanding the thoughts of other people if they are not clearly expressed or even if they are concealed by them. Suppose, for instance, that we ask a favor

7

of an official whom we had previously met through our friends. We expect that he will use some good will in the consideration of our case, but we do not know just how far he will go. Finally, after having discussed the whole problem with us he says: "We will do everything we can for you." Is his answer mere politeness? Or does he mean to do something special for us? Or can we expect a real endeavor or even a very great determination to bring our problem to a satisfactory conclusion? We understand the real meaning from his voice expression, small movements of head (firm, tense, hesitating, uncertain), eyes (long and sincere look or only short meaningless glance), or hands (decisive, energetic, unexpressive), perceived in part consciously, in part marginally or ultramarginally. These marginal perceptions are fundamental in our final conviction as to whether the gentleman will or will not do something for us and to what extent. Frequently our impression is clear and correct.[16] Thus judges often develop a correct opinion about the guilt of a defendant before it has been proved. Teachers similarly may know if a student is sufficiently prepared for the examination often even before they finish asking questions.

UNDERSTANDING OF EMOTIONAL STATES

Marginal impressions also help us understand emotional states of other people. Miss M. G. reported about an experience of this sort: "One evening I was in the room of another girl who lives on my floor. My roommate came upstairs while I was there and poked her head in the door to say hello. She was only in the room for a minute, but after she left I had the feeling something was wrong. Later, I discovered that she had had an argument with her boy friend and that my feeling was correct." The affliction of the friend had been understood without any particular changes of behavior being consciously perceived. We may suppose that certain changes in gestures, vitality, voice, and expression of eyes were marginally noticed.[17]

Gestalt psychologists[18] point to the fact that we directly perceive emotional states like pomposity, modesty, friendliness, and coldness. Estes[19] found that people who judged correctly the emotional states of other persons (from motion picture records) were not able to explain how they did it. All they could say was: "I let myself go," "I gave myself over to it." Our "feelings" of this kind are based chiefly on marginal perceptions.

Marginal impressions are also sometimes very useful in our understanding of emotional states of groups or crowds. Mr. C. K. reports about the following case: "A year or so ago, I attended a symphony concert. They played through the program to the intermission. As soon

8

as they came back in and began to play the second half of the program I knew, somehow, that something was wrong — just what it was I couldn't figure out — but something wasn't right. Well, after the concert I found that during the intermission the bassoon player was taken ill."

A politician who is in contact with the masses knows very much about their feelings toward pending political problems and personalities. He is able to give a rather dependable report about their loyalty, determination, resentments, often without having a sufficient factual basis for it.

Surprisingly enough, even in very rationally organized and controlled groups marginal impressions often must be taken into account. Let us think of a general inspecting an army. When thousands of soldiers marched before him, he had thousands of impressions of face, eyes, and body movements. Consciously, he could pay attention only to a fraction of them; others undoubtedly were perceived marginally. Both together were organized into direct "feelings" about the morale, discipline, courage and willingness to fight of the inspected army.

The American General Van Fleet,[20] former commander-in-chief of the allied forces in Korea in 1951-53, reports a similar experience from casual talks with soldiers. "If you have lived with troops, as I have in World War I, World War II, and in Greece, you can actually just take a fairly fast jeep ride through its installations, stop for a word or two here and there, and at the end of the day have a pretty accurate idea of how well it will do in combat." He speaks about a "feel," which he considers pretty accurate, an irrational product of many small casual experiences, some of which certainly were marginal.

GRASPING OF CHARACTER

Marginal perceptions play an equally important role in our judgments concerning the character of other people. "Feelings" about character are probably more complex than the "feelings" about intentions and emotional states. Let us take two examples.

Miss W. L. L. says about rushing parties: "Each fall the sororities hold what are known as the rushing parties. The new girls on the campus are invited to attend. After the party there is always the comment about a certain number of the girls, that for some reason a person can't put a finger on, the girls will not fit into the atmosphere of the sorority. Yes, the girl behaves as we would want her to, is dressed in a pleasing manner and her tone of voice and conversation is as desired; but several girls still don't feel that she would make a good member of our particular sorority. They cannot explain why they feel this way."

G. W. Allport[21] published an appraisal of a new professor by a

9

student. The appraisal was detailed, long, and elaborate. Yet Allport says that the student was "unable to tell the entire basis for her judgments." They seem, he says, to be due to intuition. Although there is no generally accepted explanation of intuition, the undoubted fact is that intuitive knowledge of a person's character may come about chiefly through unconscious perceptions of appropriate clues. In many cases the perceptions are marginal.

Even animals and infants often understand intuitively other people's attitudes toward them,[22] sometimes better than adults.[23] This may be improved by experience and training. Lawyers, ministers, and practical people develop a highly dependable ability to judge people's character.

DIFFERENT WAYS OF USING MARGINAL EXPERIENCES

It seems to us that the ways in which the marginal perceptions are used are basically four. First, we "register" marginally the known, often repeated clues to which we react automatically. Second, we marginally perceive some new small clues (see the case of the girl noticing that something unpleasant happened because of some unknown change in the conversation of her parents sitting in the kitchen). Third, we notice marginally even large new clues to which we do not pay attention; and we are affected by them without knowing what these are (for instance, newly washed-and-ironed curtains). Fourth, we notice marginally small clues which indicate a condition to which we pay full attention without knowing what these clues are (changes in the appearance of the patients, see Ch. II, footnote 11).

In the cases we discussed, sometimes one or two marginal experiences were sufficient (greater elegance of the living room); in other cases there were hundreds (the mood of the street) or thousands of them (the general). The ability of the human mind to perceive hundreds or perhaps thousands of facts, marginally, in a relatively short time and to organize them unconsciously into a meaningful impression is genuinely amazing. The process of organization begins at the onset of the series of impressions and the result generally is ready with the last perception. Sometimes such a result is rather provisional, and it will appear in its final form perhaps on the next day or after a longer time.

Paying full attention to a person or event possibly creates more marginal perceptions and induces a better selection, organization, and increased readiness of these to be used. Yet if we think of the experiments of M. Prince showing the surprising precision and completeness of incidental marginal perceptions in which we are not interested, we are inclined to believe that with focused attention the number of marginal perceptions does not increase substantially, although their selection, organization, and availability for use is probably improved.

The reaction to marginal perceptions may be immediate or postponed. In the first case the reaction may be slow and gradual or rapid and energetic. The girl hearing her parents talking in the kitchen stopped studying and went to ask them what was the matter. Marginal perceptions that arouse no immediate physical or mental reaction are either stored and wait for a future use; or they change our present attitudes, opinions, or knowledge — sometimes also values, norms, and expectations. They may stay as material for possible adaptations or adjustments or they may produce adaptive or adjustive changes which perhaps one day will show up in actual behavior.

* * *

The importance of marginal perceptions in the socialization of the personality, in its adaptations and adjustments to social life, and in the creation and maintenance of social and group structure, as well as in culture, seems unquestionable. If our preliminary analysis proves correct, we would summarize their importance as follows.

First, marginal perceptions help us to carry out our routine social activities. In personal contacts or in social gatherings, we react with a large number of automatic reactions, part of which are based on marginal perceptions. Being with a group of friends and feeling that everything is as usual we react with accustomed gay, casual, and friendly talk.

Marginal perceptions also keep us informed about many new developments in the life of society. They help to keep us ready to react in a well suited way to current social changes. Thus, for instance, we know quite a bit about the present state of public opinion in our locality; about the prevailing feelings and interests; or about the momentary social atmosphere of a certain place.

Further, constant information about the social happenings around us makes us sure about the unchanged validity of social values (or about their changes). A marginally perceived smile or knowing look may tell us that the value in question is still formally maintained, but not taken too seriously, and that a slight deviation will be accepted rather well. A stern facial expression, when a case of non-observation of a value is discussed, assures us of its full validity, even if noticed furtively by the margin of attention. The proportion of marginally noticed, strongly positive, weakly positive, negative, or other reactions gives us rich information about the extent and degree of acceptance and observance of the value.

This applies also to norms. A man may not be at all interested in women's fashions and not pay attention to them. But when travelling abroad, for instance, he knows, without being able to say why or how, that the fashions in the respective countries are different. Also, in his own locality, when meeting a girl, he has the feeling that she is dressed in an old-fashioned way again without knowing the reasons for his feeling. In both cases he noticed, marginally, certain differences of which he is not clearly aware.

Such incidental, marginal perceptions are important for our continuous, up-to-date information on the state of social conditions in which we live. All this plays a considerable role in our smooth contacts with people; in our working out a way between their interests and ours, as well as between the accepted norms and values and their wishes and ours. Imitations; the working out of the appropriate frames of reference and adjustment to them; the shaping of new common ideas, plans, feelings, opinions, attitudes, values, social movements, or new cultural traits are to a large extent possible with the help of incidental marginal perceptions. Most of the occupations dealing with people or groups of people can be carried on only with the help of such perceptions.

A minister who enforces certain moral and religious values also receives continuous information about the results of his endeavor from incidental marginal perceptions. Likewise, the information of a dressmaker about the reactions of her customers to her products is partly due to them. An army commander needs them to evaluate the state of mind of his staff, of his aids, the attitudes of the population in the occupied territory, and so on. A hostess uses them to evaluate how pleased the guests are in her house in order to make them more happy. A comedian needs to know what kind of jokes suits the audience of the evening in order to please them.

Our knowledge about the mood of a reception, of a dance, of a celebration, of a concert, about the enjoyment of musical or theatrical performance by the audience is partly or chiefly based on marginal perceptions.

Marginal perceptions have another special importance. In numerous social contacts and complex situations, we can pay full attention only to one or two, or perhaps alternately to several things. All other parts of the social situation would escape us, and we could not adjust to them without marginal perceptions.

Marginal perceptions enable the individual to become a full member of his society, a better equipped and better integrated participant. He has more contacts with other members, has more participation in social life, and is better integrated into it. They are one of the means of continuous socialization and resocialization of the individual.

12

FOOTNOTES TO CHAPTER TWO

1. Marginal perceptions are discussed for instance by E. R. Guthrie and A. L. Edwards in their *Psychology* (Harper & Brothers, New York, 1949). E. B. Newman in his "Perception" in E. G. Boring, H. S. Langfeld and H. P. Weld, *Foundations,* p. 218 says: "The focus of your attention is occupied by the words you are reading on this page. The margin of your experience is filled with such things as the table on which this book is lying, the sound of people moving near by, perhaps a pressure from your stomach which reminds you of lunch or a slight pain in your foot from an ill-fitting shoe. You have been quite unaware as you read this of the touch of your clothes, of slight strains in your eyes as they move back and forth over the lines of print, of the sounds of your own breathing, of the color of the paper on which this is printed. You were unaware of them, that is, until reading the preceding sentence made you attend to them!" W. E. Vinacke speaks about the more peripheral, more indefinite part of consciousness (*The Psychology of Thinking,* McGraw-Hill, New York, 1952, p. 33). N. L. Munn without using the term marginal gave a similar description of these: "While reading these words, you are only vaguely, if at all, aware of your surroundings. But suppose you now attend to a piece of furniture in front of or to the side of you. Its image may have been falling upon your eye while you were reading, but it either elicited no conscious reaction or, at best, only a vague perception . . . Although receptor adjustment plays a part in clarifying perception, it is not solely responsible. One may have a perfectly clear retinal image, yet—especially if he is preoccupied with his thoughts—fail to have a corresponding visual perception." (N. L. Munn, *Psychology,* Houghton Mifflin Co., New York, 1946, p. 311).
2. H. S. Sullivan, *Conceptions of Modern Psychiatry,* W. A. White Psychiatric Foundation, Washington, D. C., 1947, p. 131.
3. W. E. Vinacke distinguishes three levels of consciousness: central, peripheral and outside of awareness (see W. E. Vinacke *op. cit.,* p. 33).
4. M. Prince, *The Unconscious,* Macmillan, New York, 1924, p. 343.
5. *Ibid.,* p. 351.
6. W. Guratzsch, Das Klarheitsrelief der Gesichtsempfindungen unter dem Einfluss der willkürlichen Aufmerksamkeit, *Arch. f. ges. Psychol.,* 70, 1929, 257-310 (quoted by J. G. Miller in *Unconsciousness*).
7. J. G. Miller, *op. cit.,* p. 171.
8. M. Prince, *op. cit.,* pp. 53, 54.
9. Quoted by J. G. Miller, *op. cit.,* p. 179.
10. K. Young recognized the influence of marginal perceptions in the following lines: "Frequently the marginal impressions of an experience determine our response, because these tangential stimulations seem to touch off the

13

deep-lying attitudes." (See K. Young, *Personality and Problems of Adjustment*, Appleton-Century-Crofts, New York, 1940, p. 104.)

11. Interesting examples are quoted in literature from the field of medical practitioners. H. Hankin speaks about cases of a very rapid diagnosis by some medical doctors who cannot give satisfactory reasons and have no conscious reasons for their diagnosis which is nevertheless correct. He says: ". . . a medical man gave me a detailed account of a doctor, at a hospital where my informant had been a student, who had a power of this kind that was little short of marvelous. A child arrived one day at the hospital very ill. Several members of the staff examined the child carefully, but were unable to discover what was the matter with it. Afterwards the doctor in question came to the hospital, and, not knowing of this failure in diagnosis happened to walk through the ward where the child was lying. While walking slowly past the child's bed, but without stopping, he remarked, 'That child has pus in his abdomen.' This rapid diagnosis was afterwards found to be correct. It is easy to say that this was a lucky guess. But the doctor in question so frequently made lucky guesses of this nature that it was impossible to ascribe them to chance. My informant, who was then at the head of a large hospital, had similar power. He told me that he is sometimes unable to tell the students the reasons for his diagnosis, despite his attempts to call his reasons to mind. The case of another physician has been related to me whose habit of intuitive diagnosis went so far that he was useless as a teacher. Frequently when asked why he had made a particular diagnosis he had to reply, 'I am sure I don't know.'" (J. G. Miller, *op. cit.*, p. 60).

A diagnosis of this kind is undoubtedly based on some marginal and ultra-marginal or in some cases even subliminal perceptions of the color of skin; of the expression of eyes; of some contractions of muscles; or, on the contrary, on the lack of tension in muscles which are normally tense; on the position of limbs and maybe on other changes that are perceived by the fringe of attention and of the existence of which the doctor is unaware. J. F. Dashiell knew another such case: "A physician who had had years of general practice once assured the present writer that frequently as he first stepped into a sickroom he would be possessed by a conviction that the patient's illness was of a certain particular order, then after careful diagnosis would find the conviction confirmed. And he maintained that he was often quite unable to say what it was about the patient that had shaped his guess. But he was not guessing; he was being guided subtly by perceptible signs too weak to be explicitly recognized by him." (See J. F. Dashiell, *Fundamentals of General Psychology*, Houghton Mifflin Co., New York, 1949, p. 459).

12. Experiments which were conducted at Harpur College in 1961 seem to fully confirm this kind of impression based on similar marginal experiences.

13. R. Linton, *The Cultural Background of Personality*, Appleton-Century-Crofts, New York, 1945, pp. 87-89, 94.

14. K. Horney, *The Neurotic Personality of Our Time*, W. W. Norton and Co., New York, 1937, p. 69: ". . . I shall use the term 'register' when I mean that we know what is going on without our being aware of it."

15. See, for instance, J. F. Dashiell, *op. cit.*, 458, N. L. Munn, *Psychology*, Houghton Mifflin Co., Boston, 1956, pp. 270, 332; L. E. Cole, *General Psychology*, McGraw-Hill Co., New York, 1939, p. 442.

14

16. We do not consider necessary here to enter the discussion about how we can understand the psychic processes of another person if in reality we can only hear sounds or see movements but not the psychic processes themselves. Although we accept the gestaltist explanation through direct perception as basic and the inference through analogy with our own psychic life, as well as conditioning, as complementary, we do not doubt that all three ways of understanding the personality are based partly or fully on marginal perceptions. See for instance G. W. Allport, *Pattern and Growth in Personality*, Holt, Rinehart and Winston, New York 1961, pp. 523-548; K. Lewin, *Field Theory in Social Science*, Harper and Bro., New York, 1951, pp. 83, 156-9; S. E. Asch, *Social Psychology*, Prentice-Hall, New York, 1952, pp. 144-161; H. A. Murray, *Explorations in Personality*, Oxford Univ. Press, New York, 1938, pp. 243-58; K. Koffka, *Principles of Gestalt Psychology*, Harcourt, Brace and Co., New York, 1935, pp. 654-61; W. Köhler, *Gestalt Psychology*, Liveright Publ. Corp., New York, 1947 pp. 206-248.

17. H. A. Murray gives a similar case: "One may pass a man in the street and immediately think: He appears anxious . . . The conscious perception of the man's face as a physical schema, however, may have been so indefinite that one is utterly unable to describe the feature which contributed to the apperception of his inner state." (H. A. Murray, *op. cit.*, pp. 50-51).

18. K. Koffka, *op. cit.*, pp. 655-661; W. Köhler, *op. cit.*, pp. 217, 237-247.

19. S. G. Estes, Judging Personality from Expressive Behavior, *J. Abnormal Soc. Psych.*, 33, 1938, p. 234.

20. James Van Fleet, The Truth About Korea, *Life*, May 11, 1953.

21. G. W. Allport, *op. cit.*, pp. 502-504.

22. S. E. Asch points to the "vivid social understanding among chimpanzees and babies" (S. E. Asch, *op. cit.*, p. 148). K. Lewin says that "Within three or four years, the child . . . is not likely to be fooled by the superficial friendliness of a hostile or uninterested aunt . . . Frequently he seems to perceive more clearly than an adult the character of certain social interrelations . . ." (K. Lewin, *op. cit.*, p. 156).

23. E. Fromm says about this (*Escape from Freedom*, Rinehart and Co., New York, Toronto, 1941, p. 243): ". . . children have a capacity for noticing such negative qualities [hostility and insincerity] without being so easily deceived by words as adults usually are. They still dislike somebody 'for no good reason' — except the very good one that they feel the hostility, or insincerity, radiating from that person . . .; it does not take long for the child . . . to lose the sense of discrimination between a decent person and a scoundrel . . ."

III

FORGOTTEN EXPERIENCES

Sigmund Freud was one of the first to point with a certain depth and consistency to the existence and operation of some of the forgotten experiences in the life of normal people. These are the ideas which were forgotten through repression. Nevertheless, the repressed ideas continue to exist and to influence our life. They appear in dreams; they cause slips of tongue and errors in reading and writing; and of course, they cause a number of different mental difficulties.

The repressed ideas may produce slips of tongue which are completely opposite to our intentions. They generally have a meaning — it is the meaning of the repressed idea. Freud was convinced that "repressed memory traces . . . suffer no changes even in the longest periods."[1] Prince claimed that traces of many other forgotten experiences, such as perceptions, as well as of the emotions and all the inner life,[2] are preserved.

It seems to us that some of Freud's suppressed ideas may also be considered as forgotten, although more often they have to be considered rather as unrecollected.

The quantity of traces of the forgotten experiences which are conserved seems to be enormous. Prince says: "Just as our vocabulary is memory, though we do not remember how and where it was acquired, so our judgments, beliefs, and opinions are in large part made up of past experiences which are forgotten but which have left their traces as integral parts of concepts ingrained in our personalities."[3] The full conservation of traces of forgotten experiences enables us to recover them by automatic writing, in the state of abstraction, in hypnosis, by visual or auditory hallucinations, by free association, and in dreams. Let us give examples of some of these methods (automatic writing has been discussed in the previous chapter).

"For instance, a young woman . . . had lost some money several days before the experiment. . . . In abstraction, she remembered with great vividness every detail at the bankteller's window, where she placed her gloves, purse and umbrella, the checks, the money, etc. Then there came memories of seating herself at a table in the bank, placing her umbrella here, her purse there, etc., of writing a letter, and doing other

16

things . . .; of other later incidents including lectures, exercising in the gymnasium, etc. . . . until the moment came when, looking into the purse, she found one of the five-dollar gold pieces gone."[4]

In a dream we can also bring back memories that have been forgotten while we are awake. "A relative of mine gave me a very accurate description of a person whom she had never seen from a dream in which he appeared. After describing his hair, eyes, contour of face, mouth, etc., she ended with the words, 'He looks like a cross between a Scotchman and an Irishman.' After she had most positively insisted that she had never . . . heard him described . . . I reminded her that I had myself described him to her only a few days before in the identical words. . . . Even then she could not recall the fact."[5]

Prince thinks that the memory traces are of physiological[6] nature. K. Koffka's hypothesis accepts them rather as chemical changes;[7] others stress rather their physical or psychic nature. Nevertheless, since K. S. Lashley's work we know that their nature is more complex than was previously assumed.

A new importance has been given to the concept of traces by Gestalt psychologists, especially by Köhler and Koffka. Not far from them seems to be, in a certain respect, the viewpoint of H. S. Sullivan (". . . living beings *fix* . . . meaningful traces of everything they live through, not as 'perceptions' or 'states of excitation of the cortex' . . . but rather as a pattern of how the organism-and-significant-environment existed at the moment").[8] G. Katona[9] distinguishes between structural traces (conserving the meaning of the event or idea) and individual traces (memorized items without meaning, fixed, unchanging visual or verbal images, historical data, poems, etc.). Murray's theory of personality uses the concept of traces frequently. Only a few psychologists are opposed to this widely spread concept (for example, Wheeler and Bartlett).

Freud's repressed ideas and Prince's neurograms (memory traces) constitute what they call "unconscious." It is a storage for these ideas or traces. The comparison of the unconscious to a storehouse is shared by many psychiatrists[10] and some psychologists (for instance Head and Rosenblatt)[11] but opposed by others (Bartlett, Koffka). It seems to be located in the temporal lobes of the brain as well as in the hippocampus (Penfield).[12]

Stout's traces "are not present in the form of actual consciousness" and "we know of their existence through their effects."[13] Similarly, Murray's traces may be unconscious[14], Vinacke's traces may function unconsciously.[15]

Besides the two above mentioned processes, Freud lists distortion and condensation as inducing forgetting. In addition to that, there is

17

organization of the traces with other traces, which means their modification. Reproduction tends to make memories similar to some familiar form (normalizing); to exaggerate some features of the pattern (emphasizing); to simplify them; and to change them according to expectations and opinions of the subjects. Succeeding events inhibit previous events (retroactive inhibition), and new impressions interfere with old traces.[16] All those and other similar processes are part of forgetting.

Whatever was the way through which the experience has been changed or forgotten, the original, unchanged trace of the experience is, according to Freud, still conserved and kept in the storehouse of traces.[17] There is no doubt that some of the traces are not inactive and not without importance to our behavior. They influence our reasoning, imagination, and volition, they cause the slips of tongue (Freud), they also cause different kinds of emotional disturbances, dreams, hallucinations, paralyses, contractures, and vasomotor disturbances (Prince).[18]

Unfortunately, we do not find very much about the influence of forgotten experiences on social behavior in the books either of psychiatrists or of psychologists. Besides Freud's explanation of slips; besides Prince's statement that our vocabulary, judgments, etc., are in large part made up of forgotten experiences; besides similar statements by Cantril concerning attitudes;[19] by Köhler concerning organization;[20] and some other general statements of this kind, we do not find much more that would illuminate the role of forgotten experiences in normal social behavior.

It seems to us that we have to divide forgotten experiences into three groups: the prevailingly emotional experiences; the prevailingly cognitive experiences; and the experiences concerning outward behavior. This classification is basically in accordance with the classification of the influences of forgotten experiences on abnormal phenomena as given by Prince. Nevertheless, we think that it also applies to normal psychic phenomena.

EMOTIONAL EXPERIENCES

We have to deal separately with the influence of a single forgotten emotional experience and with the influence of several similar forgotten emotional experiences.

Some of our likes for people or for a certain type of people, for certain institutions, values, objects, etc. may develop after a single experience. We may, for instance, develop a liking for a certain uniform because we once saw it worn by a very handsome man whom we have completely forgotten. Or we may dislike another uniform because we witnessed some unpleasant behavior on the part of a man wearing

18

it (for instance a member of the Nazi party). Our liking or disliking somebody at first sight has been explained by the followers of the inference theory by the similarity of the person's traits to the traits of someone we knew previously as an agreeable or disagreeable person. The inference psychologists did not suppose any recollection.[21]

More often than shaping a certain emotional reaction, the forgotten past experiences give a certain emotional coloring to our convictions or to our opinions. Thus some of our moral, religious, esthetic, or political convictions, although based chiefly on rational, conscious reasons, may be colored by a certain forgotten emotional experience.

Let us turn now to the sentiments produced by several similar emotional experiences. We may, for instance, develop a liking for an historical era (say the late Middle Ages) because as young students we saw in a museum several impressive objects from that time, because we read a very good magazine article about it, and because of several enthusiastic statements about it by a good friend. Most of these experiences may have been forgotten, but their enduring emotional effects were summated into a sentiment still in existence.[22]

Many of our emotional attitudes toward people, groups, institutions, and cultural products, or at least their emotional part, are chiefly due to summations of this kind. Yet a question could be raised whether the explanation by summation is satisfactory and complete. Similar successive experiences may easily induce learning processes; and our sentiments, resulting from these experiences, could be explained perhaps by learning, too. Some sentiments may be chiefly or perhaps fully developed by learning, others may result from summation. Whenever a sentiment is produced chiefly by learning it can hardly be dropped immediately after a new experience is clearly opposed to it. On the other hand, a mere summation may be undone without delay as soon as there is such a new experience.

Let us discuss several examples. Our emotional attitudes toward distant nations or races often have no known rational basis. We might have heard something about them in childhood, or we might have read something. Several similar experiences of this kind, all of which perhaps have been forgotten for years, formed an attitude — the reasons for which are completely unknown. Surprisingly enough, this is sometimes true about our feelings toward near-by, personally well-known nations or races, too. Studying the origins of the race prejudice toward Negroes in the South, Hartley and Hartley found that their youngest subjects responded naïvely that Negro children were nasty or dirty or might hit them and that "their mothers had told them so." By the time they had reached the seventh or eighth grade, they had "forgotten" the sources of these attitudes and claimed that they had always thought as they did because it was obviously so.[23]

Another example of the development of a strong emotional attitude arising from summation of many forgotten and some unrecollected and conscious experiences is the growth of hatred toward Nazis in the occupied countries during World War II. I witnessed the formation of such an attitude in Bohemia; I observed its growth in my friends, in the masses of people, and in myself, too.

Naturally, a strong negative attitude towards Germans started with the very beginning of the occupation. The hatred, however, grew with growing persecutions, humiliations, brutalities and executions. And these probably increased the hatred, although many of them were forgotten. I have forgotten many widows of executed men I met; many victims of the Nazi regime I helped; many children whose parents were in jail or executed and whom our underground took care of. Likewise, I have forgotten many cases of insolence and arrogance of my Nazi superiors or of army officers in the streetcar or other public places. But most of them, undoubtedly, joined each other and also other remembered and unrecollected similar experiences to yield the final product — a deep general hatred of Nazis. In any individual reaction to the German people, the German flag, uniform, language, this hatred showed up. It strengthened every reaction to any new German misdeed.[24]

The summation of forgotten emotional states often leads to a good social adaptation or adjustment. It is good if the cause of resentment still exists and is to be removed, or if the cause of the liking is to be kept. But whenever the social situation is ambiguous or complex, the summated forgotten emotional experiences may not lead to a satisfactory result. They may, for instance, break down the desirable patience, they may prevent using more refined and complex methods; or they may oppose certain social values, or bring other inconveniences.

The effect of forgotten emotional experiences leads more often to desirable adaptations or adjustments when it is combined with an unconscious judgment. Thus the growing hatred of Nazis during the war helped the Czechs in the final revolution against them and in the recovery of Czech independence. It helped them to resist the Germanization during the occupation, too. On the other hand, if not kept under cover, it would have brought fatal consequences to a number of people.

Forgotten emotional experiences are also important in the change of culture and social structure. They may induce the individual to produce an invention or to accept it. They may also bring culture change by changing some parts of the personality. If similar configu-

20

rations develop in many individuals and the individuals share them, they may be instrumental in starting a social movement leading to a social change. Finally, the forgotten emotional experiences are useful in producing energy and in making the reactions of the individual faster and more effective.

COGNITIVE EXPERIENCES

Forgotten experiences of cognitive content also affect our social behavior. We may forget everything about what happened and how it happened, but our behavior may be affected by it in the future.

One of the simple cases of the influence of a forgotten cognitive experience is, for instance, the "feeling" that our idea, knowledge, or information about certain people, situations, or objects is not correct. Although the idea seems logical and we cannot find anything wrong with it, we cannot get rid of our feeling either. This may be due to a forgotten experience which cannot be brought back to our consciousness through normal ways and which exercises its influence unconsciously.

Many students had an experience similar to that of Mr. J. P. B.: "The examinations might be of the true-false type or the multiple choice. I will come to a question which looks to be true, but something within me tells me that it is false. I look at the question again, check my first answer to see that it is true. Everything seems to be true; I mark the answer as 'true.' But I still feel that the answer is false. After I hand in my paper, I suddenly realize that the answer was false and that I should have changed it."

A case of this kind may be explained in two different ways: by a seemingly logical but false judgment, or by the impossibility of recalling the pertinent piece of knowledge. The trace of this knowledge, of which we are not aware, is so strong that it protests against the given answer by arousing the feeling that the answer is not correct.

Another type of effect of the forgotten experience on our behavior is not infrequent when we are looking for something. A misplaced book, manuscript, or fountain pen, for example, may be found after we seemingly without reason come to a place where it is but where we never keep it. If this is not because of mere chance, we were led by the forgotten idea that we put it there. Probably a certain part of our social behavior is due to this type of influence of forgotten experiences. Mature artists, scientists, medical doctors, salesmen, politicians, certainly are guided in their professional activities by many such accumulated forgotten experiences. Of course habit, learned behavior, or unrecollected experiences may also co-operate.

21

Another type of influence of forgotten experiences is that of bringing the cognitive content of the forgotten experience to our mind without any other accompanying circumstance or happening. All the rest of such an experience is so forgotten that we may consider the revived ideational content as our own. Often one hearing or reading of an idea is sufficient for our using it, whenever it suits the situation, without sometimes knowing that it is our own. Our speech, our letters, and our writings are full of such ideas or phrases, the source of which has been completely forgotten. They help to increase the uniformity of cultural patterns of behavior, enhance mutual understanding, and smooth social relations. They help our adaptations and adjustments.

More important for social life are the "summations" or configurations of several similar forgotten experiences concerning a certain problem, social fact, or social situation. I may quote the following case from my own experience. When at the end of 1947 I came for five weeks to the U. S., the men's hats had a larger brim than European hats. They seemed to me funny; and looking at such a hat, I always had the feeling that its brim was just about half an inch larger on each side than it should be. I almost saw the strip of felt that should be cut off. But this feeling did not last long. It disappeared after two weeks of my sojourn. Every day during these two weeks I saw many more hats until, finally, the mass of these almost identical impressions completely changed my taste. Looking incidentally in a mirror at the end of the second week I felt to my great surprise that the brim of my own hat, till now just as wide as it should be, seemed to me about half an inch narrower on each side than it should be. It looked funny, and I was embarrassed on going into the street.

I certainly forgot practically all my experiences with the individual hats of thousands of men I saw. Perhaps I would have been able to recall two or three concrete cases at the most. Yet my forgotten experiences changed my taste[25] and I was not able to remove their influence even if I would have liked to have done so.

What happened to my taste against my will? First, my mind worked out unconsciously an average picture or central tendency of the thousands of forgotten hats I saw. Second, this new average model replaced, unwittingly, the old one and was accepted (a) as a frame of reference[26] and (b) as a social norm. Third, some of the individual experiences of seeing especially smart looking hats becoming to an attractive face, left more impressive traces. All together they produced a new, well-organized configuration.

22

When we go to southern Italy, the people we see in the streets seem to us small. After we come back to our mother country, most people seem to be tall. We have forgotten almost all the individual impressions; we can remember at best only a few of them. But the forgotten impressions entered the final product, the new frame of reference which served as the basis of the unconscious comparisons.

A similar change occurs twice a year to the ladies of the western world. Every spring and fall the fashions of the last year seem outmoded, drab, sometimes ugly; and the new fashions seem beautiful. The feeling of beauty generally develops after repeated exposure to the new fashions.

If we say about somebody that he is scrupulous, punctual, straightforward, etc., our judgment is based on thousands of forgotten experiences with scrupulous and unscrupulous, punctual and impunctual, straightforward and deceptive people.

The tendency of the personality to establish a point of reference (or a scale of points of reference) from a series of successive stimuli is well known to psychologists since the pioneering work of Wever, Zener, Sherif, and further experimental work by Wedell, Cohen, Beebe-Center, Volkman, Rogers, Tresselt, and others. These writers were interested chiefly in points of reference[27] drawn from series of present or very recent stimuli which were presented to the individual in the laboratory.

In this chapter we are interested in the establishment of a point of reference from the past forgotten experiences. It may be objected that here the establishment of the point of reference is rather a matter of learning how to make estimates. This is partly correct. But forgotten experiences and unconscious judgments play their role, too. When estimating the weight of different objects, we lift and hold a baby, a barrel, a package, a bushel of apples, or a blanket differently. Although in each case our muscles may be differently involved in the process of learning, we are able to make our estimates more or less well. There is no simple comparison based on learning. The process also involves unconscious judgments based on forgotten experiences with previous lifting of different objects.

If we compare the different examples of the influence of forgotten experiences, we find that in each one of them there is a different proportion of factual information and of normativity. A low degree of normativity would be found in judgments about the height of people; but in the correct width of the hat brim and in the beauty of new fashions, the normative element is much stronger. It may be still stronger in the norms of good behavior and in moral norms derived from a number of forgotten experiences.

The central tendency gets its normative coloring, first, because of its equidistance from extreme positions, the adoption of which might involve the risk of inciting opposition.

The second normative element comes from the fact that the average pattern generally is used by more people than are the extreme patterns. There is a well-known tendency toward assimilation to the majority patterns. The experiment with canaries singing their individual tune when alone and assimilating it to the tune of others when put together with them;[28] the experiments of F. Allport pointing to the assimilation of the judgments of odors to the average judgments of other people;[29] Sherif's experiment with the convergence of the judgments of autokinetic movements,[30] and several others point clearly to this tendency.

The third normative element may come from the unwitting summation of the normative content of the gathered facts. The wider brim was considered as good, desirable, fashionable by millions of Americans. Each new view of such a hat (generally without awareness) conveyed again and again this evaluation.

The fourth element of normative feelings may come from insight. Certain internal organization, mutual relations of parts, and certain meanings of their mutual relations are grasped by the mind and considered as logical, well-balanced, well-suited to the present conditions, and so forth.

All this points to the importance of forgotten cognitive experiences in social life. These may make the individual's behavior congruent with the conditions of life and with the accepted behavior patterns. By doing so, they support conformity to culture. Also very important is the tendency of the personality to produce points of reference from the forgotten experiences. This activity is spontaneous (does not depend on our decision or will), is extremely rich, and covers practically all the fields of an individual's life. Its continuity and automatic character make it very effective.

The mere unconscious production of points of reference from forgotten experiences is the first step in working out an acceptable pattern of behavior which serves in most cases as a good adaptation or adjustment to the social situation.

The normative components, accompanying the configuration produced by cognitive forgotten experiences, constitute an important raw material in the formation of social norms of all kinds. Many of the existing social norms would not have come into existence without the use of similar forgotten experiences of millions of people.

The conformity produced partly by spontaneous and unconscious

24

establishment of points of reference from the same past experiences is in turn basic for the existence of any culture, society, or group.

OUTWARD BEHAVIOR

Certain linguistic patterns, ways of doing things, gestures, or facial expressions may be completely forgotten by the person who perceived them, but despite that, they may be used by the same person if needed.

Sapir saw in language a good example of a network of patterns of behavior which are "preserved and transmitted with a minimum of consciousness."[31] One means by which they are preserved is, according to our understanding, the keeping of traces of forgotten linguistic experiences, which are used as soon as needed. The words, their meaning, and their complex relations have been heard somewhere from somebody; but we know neither where nor from whom. Evidently in the mastery of any language there is also a great deal of learning as well as recalled and unrecollected experiences.

In the case of the first use of a new word, which we have heard only once before, without knowing when and from whom, it may be objected that this is not really a case of a forgotten experience. Of course, there is a memory of the word. But we use it with a certain meaning, in connection with certain other words, with a certain accent and inflection of voice—all of which characteristics we are not able to remember, although we imitate them correctly. Thus, at least an important part of the word structure has been forgotten; but it is correctly used.[32]

Similar is the influence of forgotten experiences in the development of our style. It is a well-known fact that extensive reading of good authors improves one's style. Do we remember anything from the specific parts of the texts we read which improved our style and which we now use? In most cases not at all. The forgotten experiences again influenced our behavior.

The use of certain gestures is also to be explained by the influence of forgotten experiences. If we reproduce the ideas of a speaker we have heard recently, we may use the same gestures as he. We may use them although we forgot them, not having really paid attention to them. In imitating a well-known personality, the actor may successfully imitate the posture of the body, the gait, the total physical impression the personality makes, without being able to say anything (or very much) about these characteristic details.

More basic elements of outward behavior may likewise enter into our actions from the traces of forgotten experiences. Reaction to a certain proposition with a slight smile (instead of the usual serious facial expression) may result from an unconscious use of a trace of a similar reaction we witnessed weeks ago in a similar situation and have completely forgotten. Even if we know about the event, we may not know anything about the smile. Similarly, we may take a firm or charitable stand in imitation of another person whose behavior in a similar situation we do not remember. Any reaction to a certain situation or any solution of a problem witnessed years ago and completely forgotten may, in a similar situation, possibly induce a similar reaction or solution, especially if the forgotten behavior pattern was successful (see pp. 41-42).

The number of imitations (and self imitations) of this kind is relatively high in all fields of the life of society. They give the individual ready solutions in difficult situations. They make the individual better adjusted and more efficient as a member of society. Again, they help to keep social life in line with given cultural norms, make it more consistent and stable.

CREATIVE ACTIVITY

A great deal of our creative activity is reproduction of forgotten ideas or experiences we consider as our own new original ideas. This is true of scientists and writers, as well as of composers, painters, sculptors, and practical people.

As writer and speaker, I know how many times I have found in my articles, studies, or speeches certain ideas that I read or heard elsewhere and which I considered as my own. This happens to every creative mind. Even in most original creations there often are more forgotten experiences and ideas of others than truly and fully new ideas.

To support my analysis I will quote several examples of young persons, partly my students. Miss J. B. C., student of art, says: "My high school girl friend and I were assigned to make an Easter poster design for art class. Hers came surprisingly easily and was very attractive. That day to the surprise of both, as we walked down to the stores, we saw in one of the windows a design identical with the one my girl friend thought she had originated."

A young virtuoso and composer, J. Y. says about his composing: "In composition it is difficult to escape the music you are familiar with. At the conclusion of some of my compositions I have noticed traces of one or another composer. I find myself sounding occasionally like Bartók, the most modern influence of our day." It is very interesting to notice how this young composer was fully aware of the inescapable necessity of using forgotten (and unrecollected) ideas, and of the impossibility of being fully original despite the best intentions.

This is true to a certain extent of outstanding creators in other fields, too. Lowes[33] undertook the task of discovering the sources of images and phrases of an outstanding poet, S. T. Coleridge. He found that a large number of these come from Coleridge's readings. Coleridge apparently did not know it in most instances.

* * *

Our tentative analysis of forgotten experiences shows how these help us to get integrated into our cultural heritage and how they are available for use whenever the situation seems to need them. Often they readily offer to the individual the needed pattern of adjustment. If there is no such suitable pattern, a series of forgotten experiences may help to produce a new scheme of adjustment.

The adaptations of society and of groups to the changing conditions are strongly helped by the provision of forgotten experiences common to a large number of people. Think how important this is for the eventual common reaction to a new event, for working out or accepting a new culture pattern, as well as for the maintenance of the unity of culture. Such are, for instance, common experiences from a war or depression, from farm life or artistic life. How difficult it is to maintain a common culture if two parts of a nation have lived for a certain time in different conditions can be seen, for instance in the difficulties of co-operation of politicians of Central European nations after World War II, some of whom lived during the war in London and others in Moscow.

With the help of forgotten experiences, we understand better the conformity of religious, philosophical, artistic, and scientific schools, as well as of schools of cooking, gardening, and others. The common background of identical and similar forgotten experiences considerably complements the common principles and ideas accepted by the school. On the other hand, foreign students who lack most of the common forgotten experiences from the same social environment find great difficulty in developing the full adherence to the school and, still more, in developing a real creative activity in the accepted line.

Social structure and the structure of groups are also greatly helped by forgotten experiences. How much do they mean for the unity of the family, for the informal structure of a platoon, a group of factory workers, an orchestra!

FOOTNOTES TO CHAPTER THREE

1. S. Freud, *The Basic Writings of Sigmund Freud*, Psychology of Everyday Life, The Modern Library, Random House, Inc., New York, 1938, p. 174.
2. To the inner life "belong the hopes and aspirations, the regrets, the fears, the doubts, the selfcommunings and wrestlings with self, the wishes, the loves, the hates, all that we are not willing to give out to the world, and all that we would forget and would strive not to admit to ourselves. All this inner life belongs to our experience and is subject to the same law of conservation." M. Prince, *The Unconscious*, p. 85.
3. *Ibid.*, pp. 85, 86.
4. *Ibid.*, pp. 25-26.
5. *Ibid.*, pp. 43-44.
6. *Ibid.*, p. 132.
7. K. Koffka, *Principles of Gestalt Psychology*, p. 446.
8. H. S. Sullivan, *Conceptions of Modern Psychiatry*, p. 52.
9. G. Katona, *Organizing and Memorizing*, Columbia Univ. Press, New York, 1949, pp. 193-204.
10. For ex. W. S. Sadler in *The Mind at Mischief*, Funk and Wagnalls, New York, 1929, says: "Thus we come to recognize the unconscious as the final and ultimate repository of human experience. Here are to be found stenciled on the nerve cells of the brain, the real and final records of our thoughts, feelings and emotions . . ." (p. 8).
11. F. Rosenblatt, "The Perception: a probabilistic model for information storage and organization in the brain," *Psychological Review*, 65, 1958, p. 387.
12. W. Penfield, in *Proc. 14th Inter. Congr. Psychol.*, 1955.
13. G. F. Stout, *A Manual of Psychology*, W. B. Clive, London, Univ. Tutorial Press Ld., 1913., pp. 21, 24.
14. H. A. Murray, *Explorations in Personality*, pp. 52-53.
15. W. E. Vinacke, *The Psychology of Thinking*, p. 5.
16. J. G. Miller, *Unconsciousness*, pp. 220-227.
17. S. Freud, *op. cit.*, pp. 174-175.
18. M. Prince, *op. cit.*, pp. 107, 108.
19. H. Cantril, *The Psychology of Social Movements*, J. Wiley and Sons, New York, 1941, p. 13.
20. W. Köhler, *Gestalt Psychology*, p. 191.
21. See for instance G. W. Allport, *Pattern and Growth in Personality*, p. 526.
22. The term "summation" is used in a way similar to ours by W. McDougall and by G. Murphy. McDougall explained the patriotic feelings or the appetizing impression of a dish as clusters of affective disposition. Murphy says that the appeal of an appetizing dish "usually proves to function first of all by summation." (See G. Murphy, *Personality*, p. 629.)

23. E. L. Hartley and R. E. Hartley, *Fundamentals of Social Psychology*, A. A. Knopf, New York, 1952, p. 152.
24. See M. B. Arnold, *Emotion and Personality*, Columbia Univ. Press, New York, 1960, vol. II, p. 266.
25. See W. E. Vinacke, *op. cit.*, p. 60.
26. See M. Sherif, *The Psychology of Social Norms*, Harper and Br., New York, 1936, pp. 43-45, 104-106, 195.
27. Also called frame of reference, anchoring point or anchoring agent.
28. M. Metfessel, "Relationships of Heredity and Environment in Behavior," *J. of Psychology*, 10, 1940, pp. 177-198.
29. F. H. Allport, *Social Psychology*, Houghton Mifflin, Boston, 1924, pp. 274-78.
30. M. Sherif, *The Psychology of Social Norms*, pp. 98-112. See also H. T. Moore, "The Comparative Influence of Majority and Expert Opinion," *Am. J. Psychol.*, 32, 1921. pp. 6-20, H. G. Sperling, *An Experimental Study of Some Psychological Factors in Judgments*, M. A. Thesis (quoted by S. E. Asch. *op. cit.*, p. 487) and S. E. Asch, "Effects of Group Pressure Upon the Modification and Distortion of Judgment," in *Groups, Leadership and Men* (ed. by H. Guetzkow), Pittsburgh, The Carnegie Press, 1951.
31. E. Sapir, "The Unconscious Patterning of Behavior in Society," in *The Unconscious, A Symposium*, ed. by E. S. Dummer, A. A. Knopf, New York, 1927, p. 136.
32. See L. Krasner, "Studies of the Conditioning of Verbal Behavior," *Psychological Bulletin*, 55, 1958, pp. 148-170.
33. J. L. Lowes, *The Road to Xanadu*, Houghton Mifflin, Boston, 1927.

IV

UNRECOLLECTED EXPERIENCES AND IDEAS

By unrecollected experiences and ideas we understand those which can be brought back into our consciousness on call, but which, when being used, are out of our consciousness. Psychologists do not speak of unrecollected experiences and ideas as being a special category of unconscious influences on our behavior, but some of them have studied phenomena which can be so labeled. It seems that some of the well-known slips of pen or tongue studied by Freud are very close to what we have in mind. The suppressed tendencies which caused such a slip were later on recognized by some subjects as their own. They did not recall them at the moment of the slip, yet these tendencies produced the slip.

Here should be mentioned the above quoted studies of the "frame of reference" (some of the experiences were not forgotten but unrecollected), studies of context,[1] expectations,[2] as well as those of estimates of weight, size, height, and the like. In all these, the unrecollected experiences play an important role. Sullivan's recall outside of awareness[3] points also to this phenomenon.

Koffka points out two types of influence of experiences which were not in consciousness when affecting behavior. If, for instance, we compare two successive sensations (like two telephone clicks) and find that one is stronger than the other, we do not have the image of the first sensation in our mind.[4] He also gives an example of an unrecollected idea affecting our behavior: ". . . my knowledge that I still have a hundred dollars in my bank account may make me enter a hatter's shop and buy a particularly fine hat and at the same time will drive me away from the temptation of an exhibition of the latest models of a smart motor car."[5] He speaks about knowledge of the amount of money in the bank account, but evidently he means knowledge which was not in his consciousness while affecting his behavior.

The fact that unrecollected ideas may be taken fully into account by our behavior is of basic importance. Let us first take some more

30

cases and then try to find out the fundamental types of social behavior based on this fact.

Every normal individual has the very surprising ability to keep in mind (though not in consciousness) an enormous number of more or less constant basic facts concerning his present personal and social situation. Already Murray has well pointed out: "When of an evening I am conversing with a friend, I am reacting from moment to moment on the basis of a great many realizations and suppositions which are not in consciousness. For instance, that the floor stretches out behind me — I should be anxious if there were a yawning chasm behind my chair — that I will be free to leave at a certain hour, and so forth. Such assumptions, though not conscious, are providing a time-space frame for conscious events and hence are determining their course."[6] Suppositions of this kind are evidently many. For instance, being at home, I unconsciously know that people in the adjoining room cannot understand my conversation with my friend; that it is after dinner and we shall not have to interrupt our conversation by going to the dining room and eating; that my friend and I have about two or three hours to spend together; that the occasion to meet my friend in such a quiet way is rare and that it is to be used fully. Many other assumptions help me to behave in a well-adjusted way.

The unconscious knowledge of all these conditions practically never stops operating (except partly in sleep). Only ill people with a high fever, or very tired people, people completely occupied by an intense activity, or people having a very vivid daydream sometimes may lose this unconscious knowledge for a short time.

Similar is the influence of unrecollected knowledge of a different kind. Our greetings of acquaintances whom we meet daily may be more or less friendly, according to what we know about them. If on the previous day our neighbor's wife was not very kind to our wife, the quality of our voice and our smile may be cooler and less friendly. If, on the contrary, our neighbor rendered a service to our family yesterday, our greeting is more cordial and more friendly than usual. Often, we do not recollect it at the moment of greeting; but our behavior proves that the respective knowledge was active.

The fact that somebody very close to us has died may change almost all our behavior, even if we do not think of it; all our life is "in the shadow" of this fact. We do not laugh; we do not whistle or sing. We are not interested in entertainments, we do not supervise as closely the work of our subordinates; we do not insist so much on perfect order in our home. We cannot enjoy many things we enjoyed before (such as fishing, playing piano, gazing at the woods and flowers);

31

and we are critical of exaggerated entertainments of other people. We also automatically change our behavior toward things and persons close to the deceased (his personal belongings, his office, his friends); and the fact of death is unconsciously taken into account in our own plans.

Of course, our new attitudes and behavior are partly due to depression and sorrow. But the effect of unrecollected experiences may be seen from cases where the death did not cause us any emotional upset. We change our behavior in presence of an acquaintance who has suffered a loss by death: we avoid mentioning the deceased person, the expression of our voice is restrained, we avoid any gay remarks or jokes, and so on. The unrecollected idea of the condition of our friend keeps our behavior well-adjusted without thinking of it.

If we are to represent a given institution on a certain occasion, we unconsciously take on an appearance fitting the character of the institution. Suppose that we have been assigned by our political party to represent it at a local festivity in a middle-sized town. We have to make a speech, to appear publicly with the officials of the town, to be present at a banquet, and so on. Unconsciously, all our behavior will be such as to draw sympathy for the party: smiling; cordial approach to the people; pleasant talk; self-confidence and so on. Unconsciously, we also constantly respect the local religious denominations, the local patriotic feelings of the population, the town's pride in having an outstanding religious leader born in it, the racial and national minorities, and so on. Perhaps only a small part of our behavior is based on a full awareness of these facts.

Partly different is the case of an inexperienced speaker who was asked to make a public address. Feeling that he could not refuse, he accepted and tried to do his best. He did fairly well. When thinking back over the ideas, formulations, and gestures he used, he discovered that some of them had been unconsciously borrowed from the mayor of his town, who was a well-known speaker. The unrecollected impressions of several speeches of the mayor unconsciously helped his adjustment to the new situation.

The influence of unrecollected experiences may be divided into four groups. The simplest case is (1) the adaptation or adjustment of our behavior to a single unrecollected experience or idea (the man greeting his neighbor with a restrained smile). More frequent is the (2) adaptation or adjustment of a number of varied actions or reactions to one unrecollected factor (like the death of a close relative). There is also (3) the adaptation or adjustment of our behavior to several unrecollected factors (politician respecting local interests, pride, mi-

32

nority groups, etc.). Finally, (4) we may make a number of different adjustments to several unrecollected experiences.

All these types of influences of unrecollected experiences, but specially the second, third, and fourth ones, are of basic importance for the life of society. To live in a society means often to meet several conditions at the same time or in a rapid succession. This means keeping in mind physical objects, people, institutions, economic factors, and so forth, while observing a number of specific and general norms, values, or informal obligations. It also means satisfying one's own interests, the interests of the institution we are representing, the interests of our family and of our friends, all without hurting the interests of others. Only some of these factors are conscious; a large number of them remain unrecollected. By the co-operation of both, we are able to satisfy all the requirements of the complex social situation.

Now let us analyze more closely the co-operation of the unrecollected and conscious experiences. Suppose, for instance, that in a political function I have to receive daily forty, fifty, or more people. I can spend only a very limited time with each case. But occasionally I spend more than the very limited time with some cases. Sometimes I do it without clear and rational reasons. Let us discuss such a case.

One day I was visited in my office by a young lady, slightly over thirty, recommended by a personal friend. I paid more attention to her than to the usual cases. I phoned to the employee who was to handle the case (something I did only rarely). Later I promised her that I would speak to him personally the next day when I was to meet him. This was still more unusual help. Then, again without knowing why (the recommendation of my friend was not sufficient reason for it), I asked my secretary to take her into the adjoining room and to write an application for her. This I did only in very rare cases.

At noon, while having my lunch, some of the many cases I saw this morning came back to my mind; and I asked myself what induced me to be so kind toward this person without sufficient reasons. I easily found out. Besides the recommendation of my friend, the lady made a very good impression. Also, before entering my office, I saw her sitting on a bench in the corridor (with some other people waiting for me), speaking with her two beautiful children. She gave the impression of a loving and efficient mother. I did not recollect this later when I spoke to her, but this impression evidently joined the good impression I got from her talk. In addition, the beautiful children aroused my sympathy; and this was another reason for my very good will when handling her case. Two conscious factors (the recommendation of my

33

friend and her charm) joined two unrecollected factors (her devotion to her children and the attractive looks of the children).

In such a co-operation of conscious and unrecollected factors, which is rather frequent, the unrecollected factors may induce both unconscious and conscious behavior. So can the conscious factors.

FOUR MAIN WAYS IN USING UNRECOLLECTED EXPERIENCES

The effects of unrecollected experiences may be classified into four categories. These are different from the above mentioned four groups.

The first category is rather frequent in the above mentioned *unconscious reckoning* with all kinds of relevant realities of the physical and social world. In some situations, we reckon chiefly with one long existing reality (for instance with the financial situation); but probably simultaneously we reckon with other such realities as well (being for instance 40 years old, having a family, being a public servant, and so on).

Into the second category belongs the *drawing of conclusions* from a new unrecollected fact. Here belongs the case of the man whose greetings to his neighbor are less friendly after a recent difficulty between both families.

The third category consists of actions to *attain a certain goal* with the help of unrecollected facts. I may unwittingly use a certain expression which proved very successful with ladies, without thinking of the man whom I heard using it.

Finally, the unrecollected fact helps us to *play a certain role*. The case of the inexperienced speaker imitating the mayor clearly belongs in this category.

A. UNCONSCIOUS RECKONING WITH GIVEN CONDITIONS

This category is not limited to the present personal conditions of the immediate environment, as it would seem from examples given above (pp. 30, 31). Also, less immediate and sometimes very general conditions are unconsciously reckoned with. We unconsciously reckon with the fact that it is now spring; that we live in the twentieth century; that we live in America. But our knowledge about the month or day may be less dependable.

How we reckon constantly with the fact that we are living in the twentieth century and, not only that, but also in a certain year or at least around a certain year, we can see from direct estimates of the space of time which separates us from certain events. If we are shown a picture from 1860, for instance, we may immediately say: "Yes, a hundred years ago the times were very different." We say it without having in our mind that we are now in 1963.

Social Importance of Assumptions

a) Concerning the Present

We constantly reckon with numerous present conditions of the primary and secondary groups of which we are members. We act perfectly according to which members of the family are alive and which have died; what the character of each member of the family is; what their interests are; their age, occupation, relation to us, facial features, stature; and so on.

The conditions of the institution in which we are working are equally at our disposal, even when not recollected. The approximate number of employees or workers, the size of the buildings, the financial situation, the kind of products, and the basic principles of the policy are reckoned with, often without their entering into our consciousness.

Similarly, our behavior reckons with a number of conditions of the city we live in. We behave as if we were conscious of the location of a number of stores and offices; of the main communications; of the special character of certain sections; and so on.

The national situation is reckoned with, in most cases unconsciously, too. We constantly and unconsciously reckon with the democratic mentality of the population; with the present political parties; with the leading industrial plants; with the great number of different Christian denominations; with the prevailing ideology of free enterprise; and with many other conditions.

Internationally, we take into account the exquisite French taste, the good quality of English products, the unsettled international situation, the threat of communism, the United Nations, and so on.

Similarly, unconscious may be our taking into account the generally accepted social values, the basic moral and legal norms, the norms of good taste, the necessity of respecting other people, and other norms and expectations.

b) Concerning the Future

We expect the place where we live to exist next month, next year and ten years from now. Our personal business plans are built on this unconscious assumption. Similarly, we reckon with the future of certain

35

physical conditions, like the existence of the earth and the sun, or of the four seasons of the year. A producer of dresses, swimming suits, skis, and many other seasonal goods unconsciously puts into his plans the reckoning with their recurrence in the future.

There are a number of suppositions of the continuation of present social conditions: practically unlimited existence of the U. S.; continued existence of the competitive economy, democratic government, the particular states of the Union, all the big cities, the institutions of marriage and the family, newspapers and books, libraries, museums, universities and public schools, most of the present occupations, the selfish interest of individuals, and many others.

Likewise, we reckon with certain future changes such as aging; we have a basically different attitude toward projects aimed at a very distant future from that to less remote projects, which we expect will be carried through in our lifetime. Also, we reckon with certain political changes. From 1943 on, we reckoned with the defeat of Germany.

During World War II, my immediate superior was German, and the president of the entire Statistical Office, where I worked, was also German. I often had to discuss with one or both of them certain future dispositions concerning my division. From 1943 on, we always began our work from two different unconscious viewpoints. Our plans, as well as our comments, corrections or additions to them, reckoned unconsciously with opposite expectations for the future. My supposition was that soon the Germans would be defeated, and all the plans would change basically. Their supposition was that they would win the war and that there would be a rapid development of our work under their leadership. Naturally, I was not in the position to reveal my ideas; but in several instances they could have been rather easily understood, and I had to give some acceptable explanation in order not to go to jail.

The expected social changes which enter into the plans of most normal people in the U. S. are probably the following: technical and organizational progress, especially progress in certain concrete fields like those of communication, television, production, more of higher education, increase in population, increase of scientific knowledge, of medical care, prolongation of life, better housing conditions, more labor saving devices in the household, and similar changes.

c) Concerning the Past

If we try to understand the situation of certain historical personalities, we unconsciously suppose fewer means of communications, cruder behavior, inefficient political organization, slow and incomplete news, primitive production, less money, more poverty among low classes, more religious bigotry, less scientific knowledge, and so on.

Some readers will perhaps object, saying that some of the above mentioned unconscious suppositions, according to their experience, were sometimes fully conscious. I do not doubt it. When acting, we are often aware of several such facts, while many other facts which also affect our behavior remain unrecollected. Normally, the number of unrecollected facts we take into account is larger than that of the recollected ones. When, for instance, I am ready to leave in the morning to go to my office, I unconsciously know that I am dressed as is expected of me (not in underwear, or in pajamas, or without coat, necktie, and so on); that I am shaved, washed, combed; I do not check on it and I even do not think of it; but before leaving, I wonder if I have my handkerchief, or my fountain pen.

B. DRAWING CONCLUSIONS FROM RECENT UNRECOLLECTED FACTS

Living in society, we draw conclusions from numerous new un-recollected experiences or ideas all the time. They may refer to a present, past, or future situation.

We will first pay attention to the newly established assumptions concerning the present situation. The fact that a member of the family celebrates his birthday induces a more gay, friendly, and tactful behavior toward him during the whole day, especially when he is a child. We are less restrictive and more indulgent, often without thinking of the fact of the birthday. A different attitude toward a sick member of the family is maintained, again without having it continuously in mind.

If we visit an outstanding neighbor, all our behavior expresses an attitude of respect and admiration. We greet him, as well as the members of his family, more respectfully; we are more kind toward his small grandchildren than we usually are with little tots. Although not thinking of it, we behave all the time as if we were fully aware of his position.

Bad news about the international political situation may make us more cautious in our business decisions; in our plans for the future; in our spending money; it may make us less eager to undertake new things, even if we do not think of the situation. The emotional depression, naturally, is partly responsible for our careful behavior, too; but the rest of it is due to the unrecollected idea.

A good example of the strong influence of an unrecollected fact is shown in the case of a Mr. W. R.: "After my final examinations I bought a secondhand, though nice looking car. The following fall when I started college again, I found that my behavior toward girls was different. Before, I had been shy; but after I got the car, my personality began to change. I talked faster and more confidently than before. I was subtly giving the impression that I had more money than I did. I also began acting more casually toward my dates. Without realizing it, I gave the impression that I could have as many dates as I wanted and that I was very popular."

Mr. W. R.'s statement that his behavior changed and that one of the changes occurred "without his realizing it," points to the unintentional character of the changes. There is no doubt that Mr. W. R. did not think of his ownership of the car all the time he behaved in the new way. But the unrecollected idea kept him behaving that way.

Who does not remember similar changes in his own behavior? We sometimes are surprised by a new tone in our speech and new expression in our gestures, caused by an unrecollected change in our life conditions. We say on such occasions that we did not recognize ourselves, so surprising has been the impact of unrecollected facts on our behavior.

In the above quoted cases, the conclusions drawn from the new fact were not many. There may be more as we shall see from two other examples. They are based on rather occasional observations of several persons. I summarized these observations in two composite cases. Unfortunately this is, at the present time, the only material I can use. A more systematic and complete observation of such changes is necessary to confirm our hypothesis.

The first case is that of Mr. Novak, a lower middle class employee who unexpectedly has inherited a large sum of money. The fact of being so much richer now is certainly one of the most important factors in his consciousness. But it also influences his behavior in many ways he is unaware of. First, we notice that he becomes more self-confident. This may be partly conscious and partly unconscious, or in some situations, fully unconscious. The expression of his eyes, for instance, becomes unconsciously keener and firmer; likewise, the more upright posture of his body and head and his more energetic way of walking. He talks more loudly. He expresses his opinions with more certainty; he more often loses his patience and tries to shorten all unnecessary discussion.

Mr. Novak starts to speak to people more easily; he is more daring in asking service from them, and he is less hesitant and bashful in dealing with public authorities. Even his gestures (for instance,

38

when smoking a cigarette) are more energetic, less hesitant, more abrupt. He is aware of only a few of these changes.

Mr. Novak does not handle his own belongings as carefully as previously. He does not spare paper or pencils; he is less careful of his clothes and shoes. Also his ties and shirts, his hats, coat, and umbrella are no longer objects of the same care. He can easily buy new ones. Nevertheless, this idea almost never emerges clearly in his mind.

Reading newspapers, Mr. Novak is interested in advertisements of more expensive objects. Sometimes, he does it without any purpose in mind. Expensive objects in the show windows also draw his attention. Likewise, he is interested in material possessions which are distinctive of the higher economic class. It is an unconscious way of integrating himself into this class.

Thus a large number of behavior patterns have been changed because of one new factor in his life, which, consciously or unconsciously, produces a number of logical conclusions. Think of the enormous amount of conscious activity which would be necessary to draw all the above mentioned conclusions and to achieve these adaptations. Probably only very intelligent and exceptionally capable people would be able to achieve, consciously, any large portion of them.

We may ask now whether the unconsciously drawn conclusions are as logical and consistent as would be the conscious ones. In some cases, strong, previously unsatisfied, wishes may unconsciously bring more radical changes in behavior of the man who became rich than is desirable. The removal of previous barriers may lead to spending more money for showing off than is reasonable. Likewise, the power of money may be unconsciously overestimated. But most other unconscious conclusions of a well-balanced personality are generally well-suited to the new situation.

Another typical case of the unconscious application of one fact to a large number of life-conditions is exemplified by a great personal misfortune or disaster. Let us take as example the loss of Mr. Brown's permanent, and probably irreplaceable position. The letter announcing the dismissal changes all the values around the occupation itself: all the objects on his office desk; the pictures on the wall; the view from the window; the stack of daily mail; the daily reports of his employees; the visits of customers; the orders of the boss; the business plan for the next year; the possibility that a new boss will take over the department; the improvement of the working conditions of the employees; the efficiency and co-operativeness of the collaborators and subordinates; the good will of his boss, of the janitor sitting at the gate, and that of the cleaning women — all these and many other conditions take on a new coloring, new meaning, and new value. Mr. Brown sees them differently now; he has different feeling reactions toward them and behaves toward them in a different way.

The superiors who seemed to him to be important personalities suddenly became persons of average or even small stature. Mr. Brown sees more of their human weaknesses than before, more of their inefficiency and relative unimportance. Their orders do not seem nearly sacred any longer. His future is somewhere else; the consequences of his not paying attention to them are no longer important for him.

The pen on his desk with which Mr. Brown signed so many letters and decisions no longer is the important instrument of his work but merely a pitiful indifferent piece of plastic and metal. Even his chair is seen in a different light; his future is not connected with it anymore, his physical comfort does not depend on its shape. All these changes were immediate and occurred unconsciously.

This also applies to his new attitudes toward his family and the outside world. When his son mentioned the unsettled problem of getting a new bicycle, Mr. Brown sharply said "no" (although before his dismissal, he was inclined to buy it). Many of the expenses which previously seemed reasonable, now seem to him just a mere waste of money. The old shoes and clothes look much better now, and there is no ground for buying new ones. The economic level of the officials of his category seems to him now quite satisfactory, whereas formerly, he always felt that his salary was shamefully low. In all his personal needs Mr. Brown is now very modest.

There is also a change in many of his attitudes toward public life and toward social problems. Before his dismissal, Mr. Brown was willing to overlook and excuse some of the deficiencies of the political parties. He is much more critical now. They seem to him more irresponsible; their leaders less capable; their interest in the well-being of the citizens insufficient. He is equally critical of the governmental policy, of the inefficiency of governmental officials, of the system of social security, and so on. His attitude toward communism has changed. He still is anti-communist. But, if previously, the communist ideology seemed to him foolish, he understands now why some less intelligent people accept it. Mr. Brown is not aware of the influence of his fateful experience on some of his new opinions; he denies vehemently that he is biased. He thinks that only now does he see clearly and that regardless of his personal condition, he is right.

Likewise, there is a change in Mr. Brown's interests. His love for literature and music has dropped substantially. He feels that these are luxury activities for people who are economically secure and have no worries.

When, later on, Mr. Brown finds a new job and his economic conditions, social status, and security improve, many of his new attitudes change again. Mostly, he comes back to his old ideas. Many of his seemingly objective and logical convictions concerning political and social conditions fade away unconsciously.

C. ACHIEVING GOALS

Imagine a young man who is determined to get rich. Although he is fully conscious of his goal, he unconsciously pays more attention to objects and to people who may help him in achieving it; and he evaluates them accordingly. His energy is unconsciously mobilized at any good opportunity to approach his goal. Also his unconscious thinking aims at it.

Let us take a case of achieving a goal with the help of an unrecollected model. In the last years of World War II, the Germans declared work obligatory for women below forty years of age. To the sociological section of the Institute of Labor, which I was heading at that time, nine women employees were assigned. One of them was Mrs. N. R., an attractive young mother who had been a society leader and whose background was of wealth and culture. She dressed very tastefully and behaved with exquisite sense of correctness. Her son was in the first grade. I never could feel that she was my subordinate as were the other girls. One day I happened to be leaving the office at the same time she was, somewhat earlier than the other employees. Just in front of the gate of the office her husband was waiting for her. I felt pity for these people having to live in such difficult conditions. Both were obliged to work 10 hours a day or more, and there was no one to take good care of their small son. I felt the need of not showing them that I was her superior. I tried to be friendly and gay.

I remember how the idea of not letting these people feel my official position with regard to the lady was insistently coming back to me. I noticed that my voice had become more mellow and gracious, my words more friendly. There was something of the old-fashioned chivalry in my way of speaking. My manner had changed past recognition. The whole event was short and unimportant, and I did not recall it for months.

One day one of my old friends from my previous governmental office came to see me. He mentioned the boss we had had in common. At that moment I suddenly understood that he was the model I unconsciously imitated when talking to Mr. and Mrs. N. R. some months ago. All the old-fashioned chivalry, all the suaveness of voice; all of the very friendly attitude outside the office was just an imitation of his ways. I understood, too, why I imitated him particularly. He used to behave very differently toward his employees inside the office and outside of it, and I was just seeking to make such a difference. He was very formal and strict in the office and very friendly and charming in the unofficial social situation. For me, in my situation, he was the most helpful model my unconscious mind could find. The insistent need to find the right way of speaking to these two people threw all the accumulated energy, mobilized for this purpose, into the pattern which was kept in the storage of traces. There was no question of choice, no time for hesitation, or adaptation of the model.

I have to remark that I used this suitable model although I had no inclination to imitate him otherwise. We were very different; we had different interests and different convictions from each other.

The traces which I used were at least two years old when I used them and had never been used before. It was a sudden jump into a new form of behavior, more or less satisfying the momentary need, but otherwise not suiting very well my personality. That is why it has not been used again and has not changed in the least the organization of my personality. It remained a mere trace again.

This case shows a surprising ability of a human personality to attain a momentary goal by unconsciously picking out the most fitting trace from many available, unrecollected traces and using it as a pattern without any conscious decision.

Use of unrecollected social models undoubtedly helps our understanding of traditions. In political life, for instance, we notice that the governments of constitutional states in Europe traditionally offer certain grounds, different in different countries, for their resignations. The tradition had been started by the early constitutional governments of the country which resigned in a certain difficult situation. In the next similar situation, the feeling that the resignation should be offered develops even if there is no conscious comparison with previous situations. Likewise, a successful revolution induces revolutionary tendencies when, later on, another tense situation develops (see certain South American states).

Very often, old traces are unconsciously used when parents have to handle certain problems in the education of their children. Such is, for instance, the answering of embarrassing questions such as: Why shall we not use certain expressions? Why shall we cover certain parts of the body? Why shall we let ladies go first? Why do parents sleep in one bed?

42

Often, after the answer has been given, the parents remember that they heard the same answer from their own parents. The unrecollected answer may be used even if it is untrue and illogical and even if the parents had a firm intention not to use such impossible explanations.

The parents unconsciously use not only the arguments and basic manners and gestures of their models, but also their accent, their facial expression, their melody of voice, their mannerisms, and so forth.[7]

People who only once have watched how other people have behaved at a diplomatic reception, funeral, wedding, or in battle, are able to behave partly in a similar way, using their unrecollected experiences.

Sometimes unrecollected experiences of our own previous actions are used in a similar way. Sullivan is convinced that "their effects, to however small a degree, remain as a memory, whether conscious or not, and a potentiality for similar situations in the future."[8]

Although we cannot make a clear distinction between the unrecollected idea of a goal and a set, it seems that the set is generally understood as enabling us to continue in a relatively narrow activity or to achieve a rather simple goal or to start such an activity, later on, at the right moment. The use of an unrecollected idea is broader, more flexible, richer, and more creative than the operation of a set.

The unrecollected idea is also different from the mere interest which unconsciously turns our attention toward certain objects. The interest helps us neither by any ready-made pattern of behavior nor by a social model for imitation.

D. PLAYING SOCIAL ROLES

Unrecollected experiences and ideas help us in two different ways to play our social roles. First, we adjust to our role with the help of unrecollected experiences of social models who have played the same role. Second, we shape our behavior according to the unrecollected requirements of the role.

A) UNRECOLLECTED SOCIAL MODELS

The informal roles of a lady, of a gentleman, of a Maecenas, of a spiritual leader, of a sportsman, and so on, generally are played with the help of unrecollected models. But even the well-defined roles, such as those of an army officer, of a civil servant, of a bishop, can be played satisfactorily only with the help of such unrecollected experiences. Where these are lacking, the role is played incompletely or at least clumsily.

Let us analyze some of my experiences from governmental service. My example is again a reconstruction from several concrete cases. Mr. Frost is a minor official who has been promoted. With the promotion goes a new official title, higher pay, and a more responsible kind of work. Mr. Frost now supervises a department in which he worked previously. His behavior has changed in many ways. Some of the changes derived from greater power, higher income and higher social position are similar to those of a man who inherited a large amount of money (greater self-confidence and self-assurance, upright posture of the body, louder talk, etc.). But there are other changes besides. Mr. Frost's whole behavior is decidedly more dignified. He is no longer interested in details like office equipment, supplies, files, mimeographing, and so on. He is less willing to discuss the problems of work, feeling that his job is more to decide than to discuss. He expects his wishes to be accepted as orders. His way of dealing with subordinates shows more unquestioned authority. Mr. Frost also is more intimate with his previous superiors, now his equals, and condescending to his previous colleagues, now in a lower rank than he. He avoids using certain words and replaces them by more suitable expressions; he has likewise dropped certain gestures and accepted new ones. He expresses his opinions more freely and gives them with more authority; his movements are slow. He demonstrates less willingness to be easily contacted. His smile and laughter appear less often and only at the right moments.

In all, hundreds of changes have occurred in the behavior of Mr. Frost. Only a minority of them are really conscious. The unconscious changes are due partly to unconscious projections of his new status into different social situations and partly to the influence of unrecollected and forgotten models.

His proud behavior, for instance, is due to both of these sources. The feeling of pride is unconsciously projected into his movements, tone of voice, and eye expression. But the way how, the degree to which, and the situation where and when this feeling is projected, are due to unrecollected and forgotten experiences.

The unrecollected auditory and visual experiences with social models had been gathered by Mr. Frost for twenty years. During this time he dealt with many superiors; watched many of their reactions to different situations; heard many different qualities and inflections of voice; watched many different gestures and expressions of eyes. He had also experienced how orders were given with a certain authority, clemency, dignity, and firmness, all at the same time. He experienced the emphasis put by his superiors on the interests of the office; he experienced their identification with these interests. He experienced

44

also the interest of his superiors in the personal life of the employees, in their health, and in their families. All these and many other components of behavior were observed in different shades and degrees. All the unrecollected, as well as marginal and forgotten experiences, left traces. For years, they were mostly inactive; there was no use for them. Finally, after the promotion, a number of them were selected and organized into a personally worked-out product. As a matter of fact, the organization of some of the particular components started years sooner and was finished only after the promotion.

The enormous storage of traces has been only partly used. The pressure of new responsibilities and the traits and tendencies of his personality selected and combined only certain of them. Shy and modest people, for instance, choose other models than the formalistic or domineering personalities.

The conscious and unconscious processes shaping a new role often are in good harmony and support each other. However, in some cases, the consciously planned adjustments may be in conflict with the unconscious use of unrecollected models. Not always does the conscious plan win. This, for example, happened to Mr. Frost.

Before the promotion, he sometimes thought about what would he do in certain situations in which he did not like the behavior of his superiors. Perhaps he decided very firmly that he would never deal with people in the way they did. But being in his new position, and assuming new responsibilities, he was only partly able to carry out his intentions. To a large extent, he had to imitate the unwanted models.

In all institutions with an elaborate hierarchy, processes similar to those which we have noticed on the promoted official may be observed. Probably the most interesting are the religious orders and the army. The monks and the army officers have to use numerous specific ways of behavior as expressed by the rules of the institution and by the orders of their superiors. Many others, though, are a matter of transference from living social models. These, for instance, enable the new superior of a monastery to overcome the complex and contradictory requirements of his new position. The Christian humility, modesty, poverty, and readiness to serve, are to be combined with authority, power, and consciousness of superiority; with constant awareness of representing the order publicly; of being a religious authority to the lay population; of being one of the top personalities on social occasions; and so on.

The contradictory requirements of humility and service on the one hand, and of authority, dominance, and high social role on the other, never could have been met by personal original adaptations and

45

by application of certain principles.[9] A satisfactory pattern results from centuries of difficulties, of collisions of ideas, of practical necessities, from personal clashes, group fights, criticism, punishments, discussions. Every individual accepting the new function of a superior is practically compelled to consult, both consciously and unconsciously, the ways of behavior of his predecessors. It does not matter much whether he was critical of some of their decisions or not, whether he disliked some of their ways or not. He necessarily will use their precious help.

Theoretically, the officer's function seems to be defined more fully by the numerous regulations and rules. Nevertheless, there is much space left for the unconscious imitation of social models.

To impose their will on soldiers, the czarist Russian officers used an enormous number of abuses. There was a proverb that a good Russian officer has to be able to call names for a whole hour without repeating a single one of them. In Western armies, the calling of names is rare. The Austrian army officer was an intermediate type. His stock of abuses was rather limited, and he also used them less often than the Russian officers, but more often than the American, French, or English officers.

Regulations forbidding the calling of names were in existence in almost all armies. But the frequency of name-calling was due to the army traditions. It was an accepted means of enforcing the orders, used partly with the help of unrecollected experiences.

Let us now say a word about the use of unrecollected experiences with social models in order to solve a pressing problem when playing a certain social role. In all, there are five general causes or conditions impelling an individual to resolve a problematical situation with the help of unrecollected social models. Besides these, there are three additional social causes. We will summarize first the general causes and then discuss the social causes.

The pressure of the unsolved problem situation and the energy mobilized by it are the first two general causes. The physical impossibility of dealing with all the numerous components of the situation in a conscious way and the necessity of keeping the consciousness free for dealing with other problems are the third and fourth conditions. The fifth general facilitating condition of using the unrecollected models is the ease and rapidity of the wanted solution tried out previously by other people.

Then, there are three additional, specifically social, conditions that facilitate the use of unrecollected models. The first one is that the behavior patterns that imitate the unrecollected models are easily understood by other people, while the chances of original adjustments to be

46

understood are smaller. The second is that adjustments that use social models are generally well-accepted. Finally the necessity to conform to social norms is the third social cause of imitation of suitable models.

These social reasons for using unrecollected models are only rarely conscious. The individual yields to their pressure, in most cases unconsciously, guided only by a vague feeling.

A concrete example will illuminate what we have in mind. Suppose that a foreigner comes to a country marked by a degree of cultural and technical development similar to that of his own country. Suppose that he knows the language of the country well and can deal with people without difficulty. Nevertheless, on some occasions he is not understood nor does he understand the behavior of others. His mere politeness may be accepted as high appreciation, his courtesy toward ladies as flirting; his kindness may be understood as weakness, his normal emotional reactions as deep resentment or strong sympathy, the quiet acceptance of unkindness as lack of courage.

The undesirable reactions of people to personal original adaptations of a non-conformist individual might be similar and might bring similar pressures. Every normal person feels it unconsciously and welcomes wholeheartedly all established patterns of life that are at his disposal as unrecollected experiences. To reach a keener understanding of role playing with the help of unrecollected experiences and of solving the difficulties connected with it, let us discuss the use of unrecollected social models by stage actors.

The actor must adjust to the character and actions of the stage personality, he must fill out the general scheme of the role by numerous characteristics of a living person not given in the text of the play, and finally, he must adjust to the needs and taste of the audience. These three groups of different social adjustments may be achieved only with the help of unrecollected experiences with social models.

Suppose that an actor is to play a role from a different social and cultural milieu, for instance, the role of a Roman emperor. He starts with historical studies of Roman life, Roman habits, mores and gestures, as well as of the life of the particular emperor. He accepts the usual conception of Roman emperors as very powerful and very proud people. We know something about it from literature, and we have such an impression from the statues of Roman emperors. Their head is usually held high, the movement of the hand is dignified and apparently slow, the whole bearing is lofty.

If the actor accepts as granted that the Roman emperors were proud and far above the masses, he fills out his fragmentary conception of his role with the expression of pride as accepted by our culture and

47

as worn by our presidents or kings or possibly by generals and other high officials. Probably he also adds some of the expressions of naturally proud individuals in more modest positions, whom he has had the opportunity to observe, as well as some of his own ways of expressing pride (experienced, for instance, after having achieved notable artistic success).

Some Roman, some personal, and some modern traits (observed in several people of different occupations and different ranks) — all these together with some predominant conceptions and beliefs about Roman life and the life of the respective emperor, blend together into a new personality that is to please the public.

When the actor works on his role, the social models he uses generally are not recollected. The number of different components of behavior he uses on the stage is so large that he can never be aware of all of them.

Despite the seemingly incoherent and unhistorical work, his creation is not an accidental mixture of disparate and incoherent components. A better historical knowledge would probably help to make the role closer to historical reality, but it would harm its theatrical attractiveness. The actor feels what the audience wants. It expects to relieve its own feelings and ponder its own emotional problems while watching the play from Roman life. The actor fully feels this need and uses the unrecollected experiences accordingly, though unconsciously. This is the way we all use them in the real situations. We play the role as it is required by the situation, and we use the unrecollected social models which can help us and we use them to the extent that we need them. We are more interested in satisfying the needs of the situation than in the best possible imitation of the social models. We often combine several models if it suits the needs of the situation.

The unrecollected models are used by actors whether they play historical or modern roles. Stories of the gay imperial Vienna are often presented in movies. The elegance of the army officers, their courtesy, chivalry toward ladies and *savoir-vivre* attract the American and European public. The Central Europeans who knew the specific ways of behavior of Austrian officers recognize immediately the actors who knew Vienna and its social life and those who have only read or heard about it. The younger actors, as well as all American, English, and French actors portray only gay, elegant, lightminded, pleasure-seeking individuals, which remind us of the old Austrian ways more by uniforms than by anything else.

They are not able to do better despite their being given the necessary background of information; despite their study of old pictures and photographs; despite the discussion of their roles with people who knew imperial Vienna; and despite appropriate guidance by a director. All this combined information is not enough. The actors are missing the traces of past experiences which nobody can share with them. Even the careful preparation of each small scene which is shot separately, numerous rehearsals, and high ambition are not of much help. The missing traces of past experiences with proper models, are replaced by less fitting traces of other non-Viennese models. The actor has to use some past experiences even if they are not the correct ones. He uses at least the second best ones.

b) Unrecollected Idea of a Role

Miss W. A. L. says how she was helped by the unrecollected idea of her role: "When I was first appointed to the job of treasurer in my sorority, I did not realize the changes that were coming over me. I unconsciously became much more attentive to all the many things that increase the expenses of the sorority. I noticed lights that should not be on, as well as leaking faucets. I also took on a more sure and definite attitude toward debate about expenses for dances and other social events."

Practically all the social roles we play are helped in a similar way by the unrecollected idea of the role. Such are not only the well-defined roles of policeman, father, mother, boss, reporter, teacher, diplomat, and others, but also less formal roles such as gentleman, conscientious student, friend, lover, writer, and so on.

Of course, the help of the unrecollected idea of the role we are playing often is close to the unconscious idea that helps to achieve a certain goal. Both may be simultaneously part of the same behavior. Both of them also are close to the psychological set. Nevertheless, there are differences between them, and they have to be distinguished from each other as much as possible.

FINAL REMARKS

So far we have paid attention only to unrecollected experiences from observation of social life. But we have to complete our analysis by pointing out that other unrecollected experiences may be equally influential. Unrecollected experiences with literary fictitious personalities may sometimes exercise as extraordinary an influence as unrecollected experiences with living people. Numerous suicides committed in Germany under the influence of Goethe's *Werther* may have been partly due to unrecollected experiences with this literary personality. Historical social models such as we know from books (Edison, Washington, etc.) may also affect our behavior as unrecollected social models.

*   *   *

The most interesting influences of unrecollected experiences on social life have been tentatively given in the previous discussion. Nothing of special importance can be added to them, unless more facts are known to support or possibly deny some of our hypotheses. Besides sociological facts also more psychological knowledge is needed.

FOOTNOTES TO CHAPTER FOUR

1. See, for instance, E. L. Hartley and R. E. Hartley, *Fundamentals of Social Psychology*, pp. 120-127; W. E. Vinacke, *The Psychology of Thinking*, pp. 5, 64.
2. S. E. Asch for instance says in his *Social Psychology*, p. 584, "We expect our neighbor, when he opens his mouth, to speak in English; we would be much surprised if he spoke to us in Latin. When we purchase an article we expect the clerk to wrap it, not to sing us an aria. We walk down the familiar street with full confidence that the grocery store is around the corner . . .; we are often not even aware of the expectations . . .; they function most reliably when they are not present to consciousness."
3. H. S. Sullivan, *Conceptions of Modern Psychiatry*, p. 53.
4. Kurt Koffka, "On the Structure of the Unconscious" in *The Unconscious, A Symposium*, p. 49.
5. *Ibid.*, p. 52.
6. H. A. Murray, *Explorations in Personality*, p. 50. See also H. Cantril, *The Psychology of Social Movements*, p. 26. He speaks about "assumptions . . . taken for granted . . . hidden from consciousness." K. Lewin in his *Field Theory* says " . . . an individual sits in a room trusting that the ceiling will not come down ," p. 58.
7. See D. R. Miller and G. E. Swanson, *Inner Conflict and Defense*, H. Holt, New York, 1960, p. 395.
8. H. S. Sullivan, *op. cit.*, p. 124.
9. E. Goffman says: "When an individual moves into a new position . . . he is not likely to be told in full detail how to conduct himself, . . . he will be given only a few cues . . . and it will be assumed that he already has in his repertoire a large number of bits and pieces of performances that will be required . . ." (*The Presentation of Self in Everyday Life*, Doubleday & Co., 1959, pp. 72, 73).

PART TWO

PSYCHOLOGICAL FACTORS AND PROCESSES

V

MENTAL SET

Psychologists are in general agreement that a set or determining tendency is often unconscious. For instance, there is no doubt that a determining tendency unconsciously guides our attention to baby carriages if we want to buy a carriage or to ladies' handbags if we want to buy one for our wife. This happens even if we have no intention of looking for those objects at the particular moment.

Sets of different kinds (some of them close to attitudes or even habits) guide our behavior practically continuously. Because of an unconsciously operating set, we behave with dignity and restraint in church; with joy and relaxation at a dancing party; quietly in the library; and so on.

A set enables us to carry out our plans without thinking of them constantly. "The lady shopper picks out from all the hats in the store window the hat which matches her new dress; . . . and the student sticks to his lesson despite the lack of intrinsic interest."[1] If we want to do a certain thing at a certain hour, we may forget it. Yet at the right time we stop our activity, and we try to recall what is to be done at the moment.

The operation of a set may also be connected with a certain place. If, for instance, when going downtown we plan to stop at the post office to claim a registered letter and then forget to do so, the psychological set stops us at the corner of the street where the post office is. Only then do we remember that we have to pick up our registered letter.

Perception may also be directed by a set. A detective spotting pickpockets at a football game has a number of perceptions different from the rest of the crowd, even if he is off duty.

A set may maintain certain expectations. R. W. Husband says that ". . . when Mark Twain in his later years tried occasionally to make a serious speech, the set of his audiences was such that they laughed at his most sober and serious observations." Expectations may

55

become unconscious prejudices or biases. Husband says that a "jury often deals with an accused person in terms of a set his past record has given them."[2]

On the other hand, apparently, sets of this sort often help considerably in achieving well-adjusted social behavior. In certain social situations, we expect what we should; and this makes our reaction faster and better. The saleslady in a shop expects the customers to buy the goods; the social worker in his office expects to hear about the needs of his case; and so on. None of these expects such behavior on the street, at home, in a private meeting, and so on. The sets that specialists have are part of the adjustments to their work which make the work more efficient. Of course, learned and automatic behavior, habit, and routine also help.

The appropriate sets keep in continuous operation what Lewin labels as "levels of aspiration." We want, for instance, to achieve a perfect spelling, a high standard of living, or a good mastery of French. These enduring levels of aspiration are worked toward not only when we think of them, but also when we do not, practically most of the time. Even if we are occupied by a very different activity, we generally do not miss the opportunity to take a step forward in order to approach our level of aspiration. For instance, when reading a novel or watching a movie, we notice with a vivid interest an unfamiliar French word said by the hero. A set also may induce a rich mental activity around a new word: we may compare it with other similar words, look for its Latin origin, think of its possible use, and so on.

The set may also be of emotional character. "A grouchy person seems to be looking for any possible insult in the conversation of others, while a happy person derives the more favorable interpretation."[3]

The concept of a "set" apparently covers psychological phenomena of varying natures. Some of them are more of a volitional character, others are more emotional. Still others have a prevailingly cognitive character. Nevertheless, there is always some volitional aspect, varying from a faint desire to a strong determination.

TEMPORARY AND PERMANENT SETS

From what has been said, it is clear that we can divide sets into temporary and enduring ones. The enduring sets may be divided into those operating recurrently and those operating almost continuously. A recurrent enduring set, for example, regularly wakes us in the morning at the proper hour. Some other sets recur less regularly. They operate whenever they are needed. Such are, for instance, the sets that maintain correct spelling, clear and logical style, careful handling of tools, precise manual work, and sets that use correct legal and technical terms.

Temporary sets may be divided into those operating only once for a short time and others operating repeatedly. The first category of temporary sets is to be found in preparing material for a special committee meeting, in looking for a lost object or in writing a special report. The second kind of sets helps in preparing an amateur stage performance, beating a competitor, in taking care of a wound till it heals, and so on. In a particular activity several sets may often be in operation.

If the temporary sets help chiefly in frequently changing social situations, the permanent sets are basic in maintaining our socialized behavior and in satisfying the innumerable requirements of the culture. Our use of language, our morality, personal and civil loyalty, religious beliefs, artistic taste, good manners, attitudes toward people, and many other patterns of cultural behavior operate with the help of an enormous number of permanent sets.

The first help the psychological sets render to us in keeping our well-socialized behavior in operation is to make us perceive in the terms of our culture. From the enormous number of details in our physical and social environment we generally perceive the part our society wants us to perceive. The sets help us, further, to see several things as belonging together and some others as being separate, according to the definitions of our culture. They also help us to put the perceived things into socially established categories, to give them the socially accepted meaning, to put them into socially meaningful relations, and to handle them properly according to the social norms.

Still more important are the psychological sets in reminding us (without our awareness) of culturally and socially expected behavior at the right time and in carrying it through in the expected way.

The great value of sets to a culture is also in their large number and in their simultaneous existence and operation. A well-socialized person is generally guided by several sets at a time. Let us think, for instance, of a small diplomatic dinner, during which diplomats are supposed to tackle a delicate international problem. The behavior of each of these is simultaneously guided by a large number of sets. First is the bearing and manners: sitting upright, smiling, being agreeable, self-confident, friendly, and keeping one's own exterior in perfect condition (the tie well-fixed, napkin on the lap, hair well-combed, the coat sitting correctly on the neck and on the shoulders, limited movements of hands, legs, and of the whole body). The handling of fork and knife follows many strict rules maintained by sets and habits. The food is put into mouth in small quantities, with a polite enjoyment of it. The attention (due to a set) is given largely to the guests rather than to the food.

Our relation toward those seated nearby is that of interest and enjoyment (maintained by a set). Our behavior expresses high appreciation of their persons and high respect for their country. It shows continually the good will to help as much as the interests of one's own country permit. The interests of one's own country are defended with moderation and firmness, without any aggressiveness, stubbornness, or overemphasis. All this behavior is guided by appropriate unconscious sets. Only from time to time may they appear in consciousness, but they disappear again to continue their unconscious work.

The above listed sets, supplemented or supported by learned behavior and by habits, maintain the proper social setting and atmosphere. It is necessary for the diplomatic negotiations, which proceed consciously while the appropriate behavior is unconsciously maintained.

Some of the listed components of behavior include not one but several generally unconsciously operating sets. Take only the table manners. The habit of holding a knife and fork and handling them in a certain way is animated by a set aiming at an elegant appearance, by another set trying to show that the man is well used to similar situations, that he is fully at ease, by a set that he should appear perfectly sure of himself, by sets making him charming, imposing, important, and interesting.

UNCONSCIOUS PROPERTIES OF A SET

What may be unconscious with a psychological set? I should say three things: its coming into existence, its existence, and its operation.

A) UNCONSCIOUS DEVELOPMENT OF A SET

Certain strivings of the personality may induce a set whose development never enters our consciousness. Some puritanic people have high ambitions, although they are convinced they have none. They develop a set helping them into an ambitious career, which may be understood as a service to a lofty goal (as, for instance, the interests of the religion, the nation, peace, science, and so on).

The stress on certain moral values may induce a special set unconsciously, drawing attention to those values in the speeches, sermons, or articles of a politician, priest, or newspaperman.

If a person has behaved thoughtlessly toward us several times in succession, we develop a set of increased watchfulness toward him. Similarly, we may develop sets safeguarding our interests of which we may not be aware. Thus, we may unconsciously establish a set of taking very good care of our rich old uncle, of being especially polite toward our potential boss or toward our influential neighbor.

Another type of set develops unconsciously from conflicting situations. Such a set may unconsciously keep us in the middle between two people, interests, or groups. Mothers, for instance, may develop an intermediate position between their adolescent children or between the father and the son who are in conflict.

b) Unconscious Existence of a Set

Not only the development of a set but also its existence itself may never enter consciousness. In the case of the ambitious Puritan the high value of Christian humility does not allow the man to become aware of it. Other sets may be unrecollected or forgotten. We may not think of the set that maintains our good appearance or logical thinking.

c) Unconscious Operation of a Set

Some sets start to operate automatically, without anybody setting them into operation. Such is, for example, the set of being careful not to spill soup or beverage on the dress or not to drop a bit of food on the lap when eating. These sets start to operate unconsciously as soon as you sit down at the table. Likewise, a number of sets concerning our dealing with people, doing our daily work, or handling money, start to operate without entering our consciousness.[4]

Other sets are put in operation consciously, but then operate unconsciously. Such is, for instance, the set guiding our careful handling of a precious old piece of china or of a valuable violin; the set helping us to play well the difficult role of a chairman of a tense committee meeting; the set of making a good impression on the public by a political speech; and so on.

Finally, there is a type of set which begins with a conscious decision that is to be carried out later in a certain well-known moment or situation and is dropped from our consciousness. We automatically and without awareness pull out our knife when coming back to our desk because we knew, when leaving it half an hour ago, that we should have to sharpen our pencil before starting to work again.[5]

59

SUMMARY: THE ROLE OF SETS IN SOCIAL LIFE

Sets are part of our social adjustments. Enduring sets help the individual to use the adjusted behavior pattern consistently in all appropriate situations. They may induce more flexible behavior than other adjustments (such as habits, routine, etc.). That makes them very valuable for our participation in the changing social situations.

Sets are an especially appropriate means of making the personality an agent of his society, carrying through the desirable social goals and cultural ideals, as well as playing the expected social roles. Many of these are carried through simultaneously and unconsciously. In the meantime, the consciousness is free to be occupied by other pending problems, without dropping for a moment other appropriate kinds of well-adjusted, culturally expected, and continually readjusting social behavior. The sets are indispensable for the smooth operation of social values. Values being more a matter of meaning than of rigid required behavior, they are invaluably helped by the sets. We may say that sets are the main executors and watchdogs of cultural values.

Many other parts of social structure and culture are also maintained and kept operating by permanent psychological sets. The temporary sets are equally important tools for changing them. They help culture in adapting to new conditions, and in producing new culture patterns. The more complex the structure and culture are, the more they depend on the unconsciously established, existing, and operating sets.

The temporary sets are instrumental in the achievement of new adjustments. An example may be our taking part in an afternoon tea, which we attend with the plan of making a good impression on an influential person, whose help we may need in the near future. We are gay, entertaining, witty, attractive. But as soon as we notice that the person shows signs of fatigue, we unconsciously change our present behavior into a more restrained, quiet, less conspicuous one. Thus we carry out our original plan of making a good impression on the important person by using different means which suit the situation better.

Unconscious and unconsciously operating sets help the individual's participation in group life. They help him in respecting the interests of other members of the group, in carrying through the special patterns of behavior developed by the group, and in achieving the goals of the group.

FOOTNOTES TO CHAPTER FIVE

1. J. R. Butler and T. F. Karwoski, *Human Psychology*, Pitman Publ. Co., New York, 1936, p. 266.
2. R. W. Husband, *General Psychology*, Farrar and Rinehart, New York, 1940, p. 492.
3. R. W. Husband, *op. cit.*, p. 492.
4. See A. S. Luchins, "Mechanization in problem solving," *Psych. Monogr.*, 248, 1942, and N. R. F. Maier, "An Aspect of Human Reasoning," in *Brit. J. of Psychology*, 1933, *XXIV*, pp. 144-155.
5. S. E. Asch is convinced that sets function most reliably when not present to consciousness (*Social Psychology*, p. 584).

VI

AUTOMATIC BEHAVIOR, ROUTINE, HABIT

Automatic behavior is a non-reflective, involuntary, and unconscious reaction; for instance, when approaching the door of our house, we unconsciously and involuntarily put our hand in the pocket of our coat and pick up our housekeys. Automatic behavior is to be distinguished from reflexive reactions, as well as from reactions of instinctive nature.

The second type of behavior to be dealt with in this chapter is routine. We understand with Muenzinger[1] that it is a sequence of behavior repeated from day to day in the same succession without previous oral instruction. After we wake up in the morning, we first wash, then shave, brush our teeth, dress, comb our hair, eat breakfast, look into the newspaper and regularly do other things before leaving for the office.

The understanding of habit is not uniform, habit being connected with learning, on the one hand, and with automatic reactions and even routine on the other. To some writers it covers partly all three of these. For the purpose of this book, we shall discuss as habits only such behavior patterns as produced by certain stable conditions, which finally become physical or psychic needs. We may have the habit of eating salted meals, having many social contacts, dealing with educated people, reading novels, using certain words, or thinking in a certain way.

AUTOMATIC BEHAVIOR

Of the three types of personality adjustment being considered, probably the most important for our full participation in social life is automatic behavior. It is more closely connected with our culture than routine and habits. While routine is imposed chiefly by the nature of the conditions in which we live (we must first get up, shave, wash our face, and so on), and habits consist in reshaped inborn needs (eating habits, sleeping habits) or newly acquired needs of the organism (need for reading detective stories), automatic reactions are due chiefly to cultural patterns of our society. Therefore, they may be completely different in different cultures, more different than routine behavior or habits. If we meet somebody and greet him using the corresponding gestures (removing or tipping the hat, bowing, waving the hand, smiling, nodding the head, and so on), the words we use automatically on that occasion are as different as the cultures are. In some greetings we wish good health or we inquire about it, in others we express our respect, we refer to God, we wish success, and so on. In different social situations we use the expected greetings without hesitation. Both the choice of the greeting and its execution are equally automatic.

Automatic reactions accompany all our daily life from morning to night.[2] Langfeld says that "a day is replete with such semivoluntary acts, acts that hardly touch the conscious level."[3] When we finish the routine morning activities, we pass by the radio, and automatically turn the buttons; when we notice that the coffee is ready, we automatically sit down at the table. We then automatically pour the coffee into our cup, put sugar and cream into it, and take the morning newspaper. Ten minutes later, after having glanced at the clock, we automatically rush into the hall and take our hat and coat. When in the street, we wait for the streetcar and we automatically approach the one which is supposed to take us to our office. In the streetcar, we automatically give the money to the conductor. Looking for a seat, we automatically avoid people. Seeing a free seat, we automatically sit down on it. When we approach the street where our office is, we automatically get up, often without looking out of the window.

Work in our office is also full of automatic behavior. After having automatically greeted our colleagues and our superior, we automatically sit down at our desk and start to work. We prepare our morning report (partly automatically); then automatically go and see our boss; automatically wait until he starts to talk; or we automatically begin our report when he turns to us with the expectation to hear it. Then, after he dismisses us and thanks us, we automatically nod and leave his room.

Reading the daily mail, we automatically put aside certain letters as very urgent. We also automatically set aside the letters which are to be seen by our superior. The answers we dictate to our secretary are automatic to a considerable extent. We have a certain number of polite phrases and phrases which from the legal point of view perfectly fit the usual situations; and we use them automatically. We have standard phrases for rich and important clients; we use appropriate phrases if we are in best relations with him, others if we have to insist that he do something, and still others if we have to warn him. A similar set of different possible phrases is ready, also, for the less important clients and for the unimportant ones, too.

Also, in writing a newspaper article or even a novel, we use a provision of ready-made expressions, phrases, and sentences suiting certain situations. Whenever communism or dictatorship is mentioned, we are ready to use such expressions as "cruel," "authoritarian," "terroristic," "slave labor," "despotism," and so on. A different set of thought reactions is ready at any mention about democracy: rights of men, government of the people, respect for the individual, human dignity, and so on.[4] The use of stereotypes in speech or writing is very often an automatic reaction, which we deliver without thinking.

A great deal of what we say consists partly of automatic mental reactions. Consider only the beginning of a normal conversation of two friends who meet in the street. The first phrases are simply ready-made automatic reactions to each other's utterances. Only then does the conversation become more specific and personal with the use of less standard words and phrases. But even then, we use mental reactions common to the culture in which we live. When, for instance, one person mentions the nice children of the other, the other reacts without thinking of it by saying some flattering words about the children of the first person.

Automatic, conversational reactions may be divided into two groups. The first group are the unimportant reactions, used mostly to keep the conversation going or to be agreeable and sociable; the others are more factual, though not much less automatic.

A religious service (especially the Catholic service) is to a certain extent a series of automatic reactions between the clergyman and the members of the church. When we say grace at home, there again is a series of automatic reactions: a serious expression of face, stopping of conversation, bending of the head, motionless position, and so on. Similar is our behavior at the beginning of a serious concert.

Some of the automatic reactions become so completely unconscious that while performing them, we can carry on simultaneously another very different activity. We automatically read the music and press the corresponding keys on the piano while the emotional expression and phrasing are produced consciously.

When talking, generally, the words come automatically. Automatic is their choice, sequence, and the pronunciation, too. As long as these processes are automatic, our talk is smooth and sure of itself.

Sometimes the automatic reactions enable us to give complicated performances consisting of several simultaneous activities, most of which are unconscious. A lecturing professor consciously develops only his ideas and observes the faces of his students. But his standing behind the desk, his gestures, his correct manners, his dignified appearance, his phrasing, pronunciation of words, the inflection of voice, his emotional involvement in the discussed problem are automatic, unconscious.

ROUTINE

Routine helps us to fulfill social functions in a certain succession and without a conscious effort. It frees us from thinking of the succession of performed acts. We simultaneously do other things which are to be done in the given situation. The routine activities also are quicker and safer.

It takes much more time for a beginning hunter to get prepared for a hunt than it takes an old experienced hunter. People who travel only occasionally have to start hours before the departure of the train. A traveling salesman spends only a small fraction of this time in getting ready for a new trip.

In any work, routine plays an important role in keeping the necessary activities regular and orderly. This applies to a factory, to military service, medical examinations, a visit, a court procedure, the proceedings of a committee, and so on. Routine helps the actor to go from one scene to another without thinking of it; it helps the virtuoso to play one theme of the concerto after another in the due order; the bank clerk to go through the succession of formal acts with his client requesting a loan; the worker to repeat the same succession of performances during his work.

The more the culture is differentiated, the more its operation depends on routine. Getting ready to go to work in the morning requires many more routine acts than the personal morning care of a Greek in the time of Christ or of a bourgeois in the 16th century.

The activities of any organized group or institution, the operation of a number of social norms and cultural patterns, as well as of considerable parts of social structure, are greatly helped by routine.

HABIT

As a relatively stable condition of the personality, habit tends to survive longer than the conditions in which it originated. As long as the conditions are stable, habits are a powerful help to the life of the acculturated individual in society. Most of our habits suit the social and cultural conditions in which we live.

On the other hand, there are other habits irrelevant to the social and cultural adjustments of the individual (wearing the wallet in the left or right pocket, using a pen with a fine or wide point) and habits which are opposed to good social and cultural adjustments of the individuals (disorderliness, lack of punctuality).

Socially suitable habits spare our attention for other needed activities and accelerate the performance of our social roles both physically and psychologically. The school habit of sitting long hours without much physical activity, later on enables us to work intensively in the office or to have long meetings and discussions. The habit of logical thinking and objective analysis enables us to come to an agreement with people having different opinions from ours. The habit of concentrating for hours on a certain problem enables us to do good research work, to write a book, or to work out a solution of a complex problem.

Socially well-adjusted habits are powerful, though in themselves not sufficient supports to the existing culture and social structure. Likewise, subcultures and structures of groups profit greatly from their services. W. James called them the "enormous flywheel of society."

ALL THREE AS UNCONSCIOUS SOCIAL ADJUSTMENTS AND PARTS OF CULTURE AND SOCIAL STRUCTURE

A) ACQUISITION AND EXISTENCE

Least unconscious is the acquisition of a routine because routine generally is imposed by the necessities of life. Our reactions to them, as well as the routine which develops, come to our consciousness as soon as we meet them.

This is also true of the development of some habits. The first acceptance of new conditions is often resented and therefore is fully conscious. But later on, the acceptance gets less and less conscious and may become fully unconscious. Nevertheless, other habits may develop unconsciously. We unconsciously develop the habit of living in climatic and other conditions, which we may miss if we have to live in other conditions. A Norwegian living in Italy would miss snow, and an old professional soldier would miss the discipline of the military life. We may even miss things we did not like such as the noise of our street, the dirty children playing in front of our house, the clanging of the streetcars, political fights, and so on.

Automatic behavior at the beginning is also often conscious.[5] We may acquire it with difficulty, a fact which makes us fully aware of it. Think of the difficulties of making a small European child greet older people. Only many repeated orders and admonitions succeed in making him do it. Every one of them comes into the consciousness of the child.

But some other automatic reactions come into use without any clear knowledge of them. After several weeks in France, E. Faris started to shrug shoulders as Frenchmen do. He discovered it with surprise, apparently after he had already used this special gesture.[6] One is more often unaware of the existence of the three patterns discussed than one is of their acquisition.

B) OPERATION

Generally all three types of adjustment suit the stable conditions in which we live and may operate without awareness. Occasionally, the conditions may change; and then we have to reconsider their use. This is also often done without awareness.

Let us take an example of a routine. The routine of getting up at seven, of shaving, washing, and so on, is really good for the six days in the week and for the eleven months of the year. On Sundays or on holidays we modify it, and we have to change back again on Monday morning or the day after a holiday. We let the routine go on because we unconsciously know that we are at the beginning of another working week. Although much of our behavior depends on routine, a check on the conditions generally precedes its use.

We find the same to be true of automatic behavior. We greet differently the same people in our family, in the street, in the office, or in church. We also greet differently old and young, men and women, important and unimportant people, our boss and our subordinate employees (the differences are more pronounced in Europe). Various combinations of these make up scores of ways of greeting people, some of them not differentiated by words but only by inflexion of voice and by gestures. Now, when we meet a person we have to choose the right greeting. We do it unconsciously and immediately. We automatically use a combination of a certain degree of warmth of the smile, of certain words, of certain quality of voice, of a suitable facial expression, and of certain gestures.

In automatic behavior there is always some room for modifications. If the basic situation is identical but the meaning of the situation is slightly different, we reshape the automatic response; or we do not use it at all. We automatically help our superior when he drops his pen, or we automatically hand to him the object he momentarily needs. Yet we may not do it if his secretary is present (expecting that she will).[7]

The least subject to additional adjustments to the situation are probably the habits.[8] If we are accustomed to eat on plates with fork and knife and on a set table, we miss these if we have to eat without them. Only when we eat in very different conditions (for instance on a hike) is our personality willing to accept the necessary readjustments. In order to avoid many ad hoc readjustments of our habits, we develop (generally unconsciously) what is called "generalized habitual responses" which fit a number of similar, though in certain aspects different, situations.[9] (See p. 89.)

Any of the three discussed types of behavior may co-act with one or two of the others. A performance of a singer in the opera (besides its conscious part) is a complex of routine acts, habits, and automatic reactions. He is used to singing with the accompaniment of the orchestra; with the habitual electric lights blinding his eyes; with side-scenes and decorations; with the unconscious feeling of his responsibility to the audience. He is used to reacting to the other singers' acting. He is used to building up the climax of emotions to the tragic end; to spending a great amount of energy during the performance; to giving all the details of gestures and body movements.

The same is true practically of every job performance, like surgical operations, business deals, school examinations, lectures, or public addresses.

In many of the above given examples of automatic behavior, routine, or habit, we also easily find the other two unconsciously functioning adjustments. In the automatic reaction of greeting, there is, for instance, also an element of habit of encountering people of certain type in certain places and situations. If we unexpectedly find our boss in our home, our greeting will probably be slightly delayed and will be in some ways different from the usual. In the routine of a pianist there is not only the automatic reading of the notes and the automatic pressing of corresponding keys, but also the habit of sitting on a chair of a certain height and shape at a certain distance from the piano.

All the discussed performances are occasionally checked by consciousness. The checking is very short, usually a small fraction of a second. After we automatically put the brush into our mouth and brush one side of it, we often become aware of what we have just done; and we continue again in our routine brushing of the other side.

In both the automatic reactions and in the routine activities, there may be a different frequency of the flashes of the checking consciousness. When the interventions are very frequent, some authors speak of a half-conscious behavior.

Not very different is the role of consciousness in habit behavior. Although our eating habits free our consciousness most of the time, there is some checking from time to time. Less frequent is the checking

68

of some other habitual activities, such as wearing clothes, sitting long hours and concentrating, and others. Some habits may even be almost continuously unconscious and remain so for years, like the habit of living in a certain place.

The co-operation of automatic behavior, routine, and habit multiplies enormously the amount of socially well-adjusted unconscious behavior.

The stability and functioning of culture, of social structure, and of groups are considerably increased by the unconscious operation of all these three mechanisms. Enabling their richer development and a fuller participation of the individual in them, these three mechanisms increase the fluent operation of accepted cultural and subcultural patterns.

FOOTNOTES TO CHAPTER SIX

1. K. F. Muenzinger, *Psychology, the Science of Behavior,* Harper and Br., New York, 1942, p. 49.
2. R. Linton says in his *The Cultural Background of Personality,* pp. 106-107 that the whole configuration of automatic responses "takes care of nearly the whole business of living, which can thus be carried on."
3. E. G. Boring, H. S. Langfeld and H. P. Weld, *Introduction to Psychology,* J. Wiley and Sons, New York, 1939, p. 269.
4. H. Cantril says that cultural norms provide us with "relatively fixed and limited standards of judgments" (H. Cantril, "Attitudes and Opinions" in E. G. Boring, H. S. Langfeld and H. P. Weld, *Foundations,* p. 563).
5. Linton (*op. cit.,* p. 94) says: "While the emergent responses always involve some degree of consciousness of the situation and of effort to solve the problem which it presents, established responses are automatic and can be produced without either the registry of the situation or the associated behavior attaining a conscious level."
6. E. Faris, *The Nature of Human Nature,* p. 78.
7. Compare D. D. Wickens, "The Transference of Conditioned Excitation and Conditioned Inhibition from one Muscle Group to the Antagonistic Muscle Group," *J. Exp. Psych.,* 22, 1938, pp. 101-123.
8. In a disaster situation the housewives generally attempt to leave through the side-entrance (their habitual way out) though it may be blocked and though the main entrance is free (from unpublished material gathered by E. Quarantelli).
9. See Linton, *op. cit.,* p. 103.

VII

IMITATION

The inconsistent operation of imitation (we imitate certain models but refuse to imitate others; we imitate a model in a certain situation but refuse to imitate him in another) convinced modern students of imitation that neither instinct nor any other inborn[1] property can explain it. If there is any inborn inclination to imitate, it must be very flexible, and there must be other, additional causes responsible for imitative behavior; for instance, learning and conditioning.[2] We learn to imitate a certain type of people (parents, teachers, leaders) and not to imitate others. Through generalization we imitate other persons of similar type in similar situations. But blind imitation due to learning is rare; generally some reasoning, conscious or unconscious, accompanies the operation of learned imitativeness. This has been found by Field,[3] who repeated the experiments of Miller and Dollard.

Thus, learned imitativeness explains at best only a part of social imitation. It seems that Miller and Dollard felt it and therefore accepted rather favorably the well-known reflex circle theory by Holt.[4] But even these two types of imitation explain only some cases of social imitation.

The narrow understanding of imitativeness as a learned behavior pattern is accepted by a number of modern writers, such as, for instance, Crespi[5] or Ogburn and Nimkoff.[6] Similar is the standpoint of F. H. Allport, Folsom, Dashiell, and many others. Murphy[7] and K. Young[8] consider imitativeness as a product of conditioning. A number of writers discuss other types of imitation. Nevertheless, there is no agreement about the number of different kinds of imitation. Some authors recognize two, others three or four types.[9]

In our opinion, it is best to divide the types of imitation according to the basic causes of imitative behavior. The causal types are the only simple ones. If we did not accept this criterion, we would arrive at a large number of different types of social imitation, like imitation of superior people, of people with prestige, imitation of technicians or of intelligent people, crowd imitation, slow, unwitting imitation (like imita-

71

tion of dialect), role-imitation, and many others as found in studies of imitation. If we accept the classification according to basic causes, then all these possible types of imitation will be mixed types.

There are psychological causes, social causes, and physical causes of imitation. With a certain hesitation, we shall label certain causes as psychological, although they operate between two people and thus are social, too. Some of the causes mentioned in the discussion of the use of unrecollected models also operate in the imitation of present models of which we are fully aware.

Learned imitativeness can be considered as the first psychological cause of imitation. *Imitation through empathy* seems to me to constitute another psychological type. Some students of imitation mention the particular imitation by the audience of the movements of football players, wrestlers, tight-rope walkers, flying trapeze artists and other performers. Watching any muscle strain produces tensions in the same muscles of the onlookers and results in imitation of the movement. G. Allport says that the observer "takes into his own muscles the postures and tensions of the person observed. . . ."[10]

Empathy may lead to imitation of animals or even to imitation of inanimate objects. We may empathize with the movements of a hardworking machine and experience "similar" tensions in our arms, legs, or back. Or "we are likely to feel a stretch when we see a tall building. The mountains are likely to exalt us and the valleys to depress us" say Hartley and Hartley.[11]

Imitation by physical empathy is much more frequent in daily social life than would seem at first glance. G. Allport says that the "imitative assumptions of the posture and facial expressions of other people play a greater part in ordinary life than is commonly realized."[12] Imitation of mental processes through empathy is equally frequent. But the accompanying factors resulting from learning, past experiences, personal goals, understanding of the situation, as well as from the establishment of the frames of reference and from social pressures, influence it generally more than they influence the prevailingly physical empathy.

Different from the above mentioned types is *imitation under the internal pressure of too much energy* (accumulated or naturally overflowing). Natural overflow of energy is common in healthy, strong children, especially after sleep, rest, or eating. In such a condition, children feel the impulse to do something without knowing sometimes what it should be. We may hear them asking "What shall I do now?" They ask for a way to spend their pressing energy, and they are willing to imitate almost any available social model in order to do it.[13]

In adults a surplus energy develops after long repeated trials to solve a difficult problem or after a stimulating experience. Imitation partly relieves the pressure of the surplus energy.

Imitation by sympathy or love is another basic psychological type. Love for a person makes his behavior patterns so dear and desirable that we may copy some of them without any other reasons. The *imitation by "identification"* as formulated by psychoanalysts may often be included in this type especially if connected with empathy. It is also partly what Hartley labeled differently as *imitation of a "satisfier."*

The last psychological type of imitation which we feel we have to mention is *rational copying,* reasons for which we are not aware of (in opposition to the conscious rational copying which we do not consider as a special type needing further study).[14] Its reasons may be so thoroughly unconscious that sometimes we do not even know that we imitate, and we may even be convinced that we do not. This may happen, for instance, when we imitate a profitable method of our competitors, our subordinates, or other people whom we do not like to imitate.

The general social causes of imitation arc less numerous. Basically, there are only four. First to be listed and probably the one most frequently encountered is *social pressure.* Every society develops a strong pressure toward a high degree of conformity of its members. The numerous imposed imitations start with the education of children in the family and in the school: imitation of speech, of table manners, food habits, imitation of letters printed in the schoolbook or written on the blackboard, imitation of spelling, and so forth. They continue throughout the life of adolescents, as well as of adults.

The opposite of pressure is a voluntary, *enthusiastic adherence* to the group and to its values. Our strong adherence to certain moral standards, to our language, to certain religious ideas, to certain political convictions makes us follow certain accepted models.

Perhaps in between these two social causes of imitation lies the third one—imitation due to a *feeling of social uneasiness* when we are different. Visiting with rich people, we put on our Sunday best in order to be similar to them. But visiting with poor people, we dress modestly in order not to be too different from them. In both cases the difference would be harmful to a smooth and satisfactory social intercourse.

Another social reason for imitation is the *necessity for being understood,* a necessity which develops a strong incentive toward imitating certain generally accepted behavior patterns. If our gesture is to convey the meaning we have in mind, it must follow a generally accepted pattern.

Pressure of physical needs may also lead to imitation. Although it seems similar to social pressure in its influence on individuals, there is a considerable difference. Physical pressure (hunger, cold, fatigue) does not directly impose any social conformity in the solution of the difficulty. But if somebody else finds a desirable solution, we easily imitate it.

Of all the numerous older and more modern studies of imitation only some speak about unconscious imitation; and practically none of them study it in detail. Generally they mention it only incidentally and very briefly. Typical in this respect is the statement of the great old protagonist of the role of imitation in social life, Tarde:". . . imitation may be conscious or unconscious."[15] Also, G. Allport mentions "conscious or unconscious imitation,"[16] as well as Reuter and Hart,[17] Ogburn and Nimkoff,[18] Cantril, Fredericksen[19] and others. Unconscious imitation of attitudes is mentioned by G. H. Mead[20] and by W. H. Whyte[21] (who mentions unconscious adopting of political outlook). Faris, as we know (see Ch. VII, footnote 9), has two "unwitting" types of imitation. He is the only one to give at least a description of several cases as well as an attempt at an explanation.

LEARNED IMITATIVENESS

As all learned behavior, learned imitativeness may become automatic and in that way, unconscious. The handwriting, pronunciation, and intonation of the teacher in school are unwittingly imitated by the pupils, who learned to imitate her in more consequential matters. Similarly, methods of a foreman are imitated by workers, the moves of an officer during military exercises by the soldiers. We automatically rise or sit down when a lady or superior does.

The number of pure instances of learned imitativeness inducing unconscious imitation is probably smaller than we would surmise. In the majority of cases an unconscious judgment checks the suitability of our behavior and supports, modifies, or hampers the incentive to imitate.

EMPATHY

Imitation which is produced by physical empathy is often unconscious. As examples we may take much of the imitation of facial expression, movements of the body, manipulation of different objects, and so on.

Somewhat different is the imitation of the singing and partly the acting of an opera star when we come home and report to our family

74

what we had heard at an opera. At the beginning, we only talk, then hum, and later stand up and start some movements imitating the singer. This spontaneous imitation was partly conscious (singing), partly unconscious (some of the gestures).[22]

Psychic empathy, likewise, induces unconscious imitation. We empathize with and we imitate reasoning, judgments, emotions, feelings or moods, often without being aware of it. The experiments conducted at Harpur College in 1960 support the importance of empathy for imitation. Subjects who empathize more often and more strongly are more inclined to imitate.

Imitation of this kind may not be only unwitting, but also against our will. There is much of such imitation on the borderline of two hostile nations.[23]

If the imitated pattern makes use of large muscles, it generally enters into consciousness immediately. But smaller movements, as well as imitation of feelings, volitions, and ideas, often escape our awareness. In the case of more complex patterns of behavior, only a part of them may become conscious; and the other parts cannot enter the consciousness because we cannot pay attention to them.

OVERFLOW OF ENERGY

Many imitations of this kind in children often are playful. Children play father and mother and different occupations,[24] putting into the conscious role a number of unconsciously imitated details. The same applies to the early attempts to play games. The facial expression, the talk, the gestures, the gait, etc., are imitated unconsciously.[25]

Still more unconscious elements are to be found in mimicking. A schoolboy may imitate his teacher to make the class laugh. The mass of details of a good imitation of this kind is completely unconscious.

In adult people, a natural overflow of energy is more rare. If a group of men discuss a difficult business problem for hours and cannot come to a solution acceptable to all, they become restless, impatient; and the internal tensions increase. If at that moment one of them fixes his tie nervously or adjusts his glasses, often another of the group imitates him. Such imitations are mostly unconscious, and people often notice them only after they have performed them. The accumulated energy easily accepts any such harmless pattern of behavior as a welcome way of discharging itself.

In critical situations producing strong tensions, we may often notice people imitating blindly, or almost blindly, those who started to do something about the tensions. Fires, floods, automobile accidents always show the same picture: several people unnecessarily do what another one has already begun to do. Certain imitative actions of people in a mob may be so far unconscious that, as is well-known, those who committed them or helped to commit them later may not know anything about it and may deny it sincerely.

In many committee meetings, social parties, theater, and concert audiences, a part of the actions and reactions of certain people is of this kind. I know of temperamental people who were so carried away by a singer and by the enthusiastic applause after his performance that they applauded vigorously without noticing it. The aching palms awakened them from their frenzy.

In professions requiring immediate and very energetic decisions the imitations of this type are frequent. Commanding a platoon, directing a stage play, leading a mass meeting, one is prone to copy social models. Most frequently, the imitator uses an old model which he had the opportunity to watch previously. A trace picked out by the aroused energy will yield the needed pattern. My above quoted experience of the unexpected imitation of my boss (see pp. 41, 42) is a case in point. Actors, singers, and other soloists when performing, may unwittingly bring an unexpected new element into their performance, which is due to an unrecollected or forgotten model, the trace of which has been revived by the energy aroused by multiple stimulation from the audience.

LOVE AND SYMPATHY

It is generally known that a young wife in love may accept the opinions of her husband and defend them vigorously. Such an imitation is often partly and sometimes chiefly, unconscious. It may concern mannerisms, political, religious, and moral views, taste for certain music or literature, and so forth. Some of the young ladies I knew were aware of their acceptance of some of their husband's views, but did not know about others.

This type of imitation is very frequent in children, although it is hard to establish how far the imitations of parents by children are due to love and how far to social pressure, unconscious but rational reasons, learned imitativeness, or other causes. But children who love their parents generally imitate them more than those who do not love them. The majority of imitations by love and sympathy is unconscious. Practically none of us knows that the inflexion of his voice is similar to that of his beloved father. Still less do we know when and how we developed this imitated inflexion of voice.[26]

Similarly, a great deal of imitation of great masters by their followers is caused by love and remains unconscious. As students at the

76

university, we acquired a deep, passionate love for science and for scientific work. We somehow took this devotion for granted and as natural for every real scholar. Only after some of us came to certain foreign countries, did we notice that people may be deeply interested in scientific work without any such passionate devotion. It appeared to be a specific cultural pattern of certain European countries (including my mother country), transmitted to us by several beloved teachers. It certainly developed in their lectures and seminars, through their remarks, from their sacrifices for science, from watching their whole dedicated pesonalities.

UNCONSCIOUS REASONING

The number of reasons of which we are not aware but which induce us to imitate may be surprisingly high. The unconscious reasons for imitation may be similar to the conscious ones. But not all unconscious reasons for imitation would be accepted if conscious. We know something about it from psychoanalysts. The repressed and suppressed ideas cannot be accepted consciously as reasons for our imitations, but they can be accepted unconsciously. The large proportion of imitation is, however, based on both conscious and unconscious reasons.

The unconscious reasoning inducing imitation probably starts operating in childhood with the first imitations which are rewarded. Not all the prospective rewards come to the mind of the child at the moment when the imitative behavior of a desirable pattern starts. In many cases the child feels only a vague impulse to imitate, without any clear reason. This happens to adults, too. A new dress of a leading actress or princess may appear very attractive in the eyes of thousands of young ladies. The majority of them are convinced that it really is beautiful in itself; the real reason for having a similar one — the high prestige of the person wearing it — may not be thought of at all.

In the other cases, the imitation itself may also be unconscious. When buying a new dress, handbag, piece of furniture or picture, we may have in mind a desirable kind we want to have. It may be completely unknown to us that what we like is a copy of an article seen in an exhibition, in a fashionable journal, in the home of rich friends, and so on. We imitate a social model without knowing it, because of its prestige.

A literary style in vogue is often imitation of a leading successful writer. The younger writers may not know that in certain aspects of their own writings they are imitating the noted author. Some may even be deeply convinced that they have not imitated him because they had striven for the most individual and original style. Also unconsciously imitated are the type of literary plot, the type of leading personalities, the setting of the story, and so on. Painters, sculptors, and musicians are in danger of similar unconscious imitations (see pp. 26, 27).

Success in economic life may produce unconscious imitations of a like type by people active in the same branch. Business methods are copied often consciously; but the habits, type of house, automobile, hobbies of a successful businessman may be imitated partly or completely unconsciously. Certain behavior patterns of oustanding speakers, singers, actors, inventors are imitated equally unconsciously by people who have good reasons for it, of which they may be unaware.

SOCIAL PRESSURE

A) DIRECT PRESSURE TO IMITATE

Social pressure to imitate sometimes meets opposition, which necessarily becomes conscious. Only after many instances of imitation, under pressure, may the imitated pattern become automatic and finally unconscious.[27]

The number of behavior patterns imitated under pressure which are used without awareness is evidently enormous. A great deal of our socialized behavior from speech and writing to mannerism, economic behavior, and technique of playing the piano consists of automatic and often fully unconscious imitations of this kind. Most of the imitated cultural patterns have been accepted so thoroughly that we feel them as a vital part of our own personality.

Some pressures are rather mild and do not meet any real opposition.[28] When dealing with people of different interests and professions or belonging to different groups, we often hear them using their special technical vocabulary. Such groups are, for instance, musicians, painters, businessmen, hunters, and mechanics. At the beginning of our association, we use colloquial expressions when speaking about their problems. But later on, unwittingly and without thinking of it, we may start using their professional expressions. Sometimes we are surprised by it ourselves. The inconspicuous pressure of the group of specialists induces us to use the specialized language.

B) PRESSURE TO SOLVE A PROBLEM BY IMITATION

We saw before that we solve certain pressing problems by using suitable unrecollected social models (pp. 41-43). Of course, we do

78

the same when watching social models who just found a satisfactory solution to a problem similar to ours.

As an example, let us take a man who came to a church bazaar conducted for the profit of a charitable organization. A young church lady offers him combs, vases, brushes, and other articles he really does not need. He understands that the young lady is anxious to make a transaction and to sell to other people. The tension increases, and he feels that now he must do something. At that moment another man approaches and, without hesitation, picks out a brush. Our guest unwittingly reaches for a brush, too, and pays for it. The pressure of the situation was such that he preferred to follow blindly the available social model rather than wait to make a more suitable choice. The internal tension aroused by the social pressure threw its energy into the pattern of an incidental social model.

In any social party, we may face situations in which we are expected to say something or to react in a certain way; but we may not know how. How often are our smiles, looks, laughs, gestures, an unconscious imitation of other people, whom we consider as safe social models! How often do we look around, sit, rise, turn, speak about a certain object in unconscious imitation of other people in order to overcome a moment of uneasiness, embarrassment, or lack of an idea as to what to do next!

ADHERENCE TO THE GROUP
AND TO ITS CULTURAL PATTERNS

A large part of the behavior patterns of our culture or subculture are voluntarily adhered to by all normal, well-socialized individuals. The warm or enthusiastic adherence to a gang of boys often produces voluntary imitation of the patterns of behavior accepted by the gang. Religious people imitate the religiousness of an evangelist; an enthusiastic piano player imitates the brilliance and charm of a great master. The imitators adhere to the religious or artistic values these people achieved and imitate them.

How far may such imitation be unconscious? I should say that the stronger the adherence and enthusiasm, the more likely is the imitation unconscious. In some cases, the main elements of the imitated patterns may be conscious while a host of other elements is imitated unconsciously.

Certain schools of modern painting adhere not only to certain formulated principles of beauty, but also to disrespect for bourgeois ways, defiance of regularity in daily life, carelessness about one's own appearance, loose sexual morality, night life, lack of interest in family life, contempt for money, and so on. The members of the school imitate, partly unconsciously, these and many other details of behavior patterns of leading social models.

Some readers will probably think of another similar case — that of specialists in a certain foreign culture. Historians, especially literary historians, linguists, orientalists, and sinologues generally love the culture they study. Often, they are inclined to imitate unconsciously some of the characteristic behavior patterns created by that culture, such as their smile, jokes, approach to people, handwriting, pleasures of life, interests, and habits. For instance, some specialists in French language and literature like to charm the ladies, to make spirited jokes, and so on, without any conscious imitation.

FEELING OF UNEASINESS

There are a number of cultural or subcultural patterns which are neither imposed nor expected and which we, moreover, may not like. But we imitate them for the sake of easy, efficient, and pleasant social contacts. We say the small, meaningless, agreeable phrases when talking with people who like this kind of conversation. We are more stern and factual with scientific people.

Most of such imitations are unconscious. Perhaps the reader would say that these are based on an unconscious judgment or empathy. Certainly this is often the case. But sometimes there is positively no empathy — we may dislike the people and be very different from them — and the unconscious judgment could in some cases speak equally as well against imitation as for it. We may be very formal, formal, or only slightly formal on a certain formal occasion. But we choose rather to imitate the more formal people in order to avoid all uneasiness.

In some cases, new behavior may be a combination of imitation with assimilation to group standards, or to points of reference unconsciously established from the behavior of the members of the group.

The last two causes of imitation, the need to be understood (see p. 73) and the pressure of physical needs do not need more detailed discussion.

COMBINED CAUSES OF IMITATION AND THE CONFLICT AMONG THEM

Imitations due to several causes are probably much more frequent than imitations arising from one cause only. As we know already, we very often combine learned imitativeness with unconscious reasoning, which approves the behavior we are ready to imitate. The unconscious reasoning checks equally the imitations due to empathy, love, overflowing energy, as well as physically and socially caused imitations.

Both main social causes of imitations co-operate very often. The imposed cultural patterns of behavior frequently are voluntarily accepted and beloved. Also, two or more psychological causes of imitation, such as empathy and overflowing energy, may co-operate.

Social causes of imitation generally co-operate with the psychological ones. As a matter of fact, they must co-operate very often; otherwise, there would be too many frustrations, too many split, disorganized personalities. Thus, the learned imitativeness is very often supported by social pressure and in later years of life, by adherence to social values as well. Love and empathy are generally directed toward well-accepted social models so that there is more harmony between them than discord.

On the other hand, empathy, overflowing energy and love may be in conflict with social causes of imitation. Boys often imitate behavior of their close mischievous friends or admired gang leaders. Whenever there is such a conflict, generally the psychological causes have to give up. Established cultural norms and social values generally must prevail.

Combination of conscious and unconscious causes is frequent. Only rarely are all the co-operating causes fully conscious, and equally rarely are all of them unconscious. Such an unusual case would be imitation of manly manners and appearance by a youngster because he unconsciously compensates for his own physical inferiority, unconsciously wants to gain the favor of a girl, and to equal his successful friend. All of these reasons may be sincerely denied by the youngster.

*   *   *

The unconscious imitations of all types are so frequent that they probably help the individual in most of his adaptations and adjustments to social environment.

The unconscious imitations are also a powerful means that help the assimilation of the individual to group standards. They are basic to the group conformity; they are one of the conditions making groups possible.

Unconscious imitations are one of the basic conditions enabling the individual to master a substantial part of the complex and refined culture. The existence of culture itself is made possible largely by them. They give an extraordinary power to the human personality, multiplying the number of its activities while keeping them in the expected line of behavior and leaving the consciousness free for other activities. They run the millions of actions of masses of individuals participating in social life smoothly and dependably.

Linton says about the importance of imitation: "There seems to be a strong tendency on the part of many writers on the subject to accord first place to intellectual processes and second to those of trial and error. Actually, the initial response of any individual who has to develop a new pattern of behavior to meet a new situation usually depends more on imitation than on either of these."[29]

FOOTNOTES TO CHAPTER SEVEN

1. Imitation was considered as inborn without any specifications of its character by W. Bagehot, G. Tarde, R. S. Woodworth, A. Courtnot, C. Wissler and others. To E. A. Ross it was due to suggestion, to C. L. Morgan, W. McDougall, and C. A. Ellwood it has instinctive character.
2. N. E. Miller and J. Dollard, *Social Learning and Imitation,* Yale University Press, New Haven, 1941.
3. See S. E. Asch, *Social Psychology,* pp. 393-395.
4. E. B. Holt, *Animal Drive and the Learning Process,* H. Holt and Co., New York, 1931, pp. 37-43.
5. L. P. Crespi, "Social Relations of the Individual" in E. G. Boring, H. S. Langfeld and H. P. Weld, *Foundations,* p. 591.
6. W. F. Ogburn and M. F. Nimkoff, *Sociology,* Houghton Mifflin, Cambridge, 1950, p. 219.
7. G. Murphy, *Personality,* p. 221.
8. K. Young, *Personality,* p. 88.
9. E. Faris distinguishes three types of imitation: immediate unwitting (as in a crowd), slow and unwitting (as imitation of dialect), and conscious, rational imitation. Similarly C. L. Morgan recognizes three types: instinctive, intelligent and reflective imitation. L. P. Crespi under the influence of Miller-Dollard classifies imitation into: simple, matched dependent behavior and copying. G. Allport recognizes again three types of imitation: the echo principle, mimicry of muscle tensions and deliberate copying. Hartley-Hartley has four types: imitation due to suggestibility, superiority, imitation of satisfier, and imitation as method of mastering. On the other hand J. F. Dashiell distinguishes only the habitual and intentional imitation, W. E. Vinacke the "echo" imitation and "copying."
10. G. W. Allport, *Personality, A Psychological Interpretation,* H. Holt and Co., New York, 1937, p. 156.
11. E. L. Hartley and R. E. Hartley, *Fundamentals,* p. 285.
12. G. W. Allport, *op. cit.,* p. 530.
13. Of course there also are other causes of play behavior and other explanations of play.
14. See p. 42.
15. G. Tarde, *The Laws of Imitation,* H. Holt and Co., New York, 1903, p. 192.
16. G. W. Allport, *Personality,* pp. 156, 185.
17. E. B. Reuter and C. W. Hart, *Introduction to Sociology,* McGraw-Hill, New York, 1933, p. 271.
18. W. F. Ogburn and M. F. Nimkoff, *op. cit.,* p. 219.
19. E. G. Boring, H. S. Langfeld and H. P. Weld, *Introduction,* p. 12.
20. G. H. Mead, *Mind, Self and Society,* University of Chicago Press, Chicago, 1934, p. 69.

21. W. H. Whyte, *The Organization Man*, Doubleday, Anchor Books, Garden City, New York, 1957, p. 332.
22. Psychologically, this kind of imitation is not yet understood; see G. W. Allport, *Personality*, p. 156.
23. See A. L. Kroeber, *Anthropology*, Harcourt, Brace and Co., New York, 1948, p. 263 and M. J. Herskovits, *Man and His Works*, A. A. Knopf, New York, 1950, p. 531.
24. Probably there are additional causes of such imitations like empathy, love and others. Hartley and Hartley consider such imitations as not completely understood (See Hartley and Hartley, *op. cit.*, p. 284).
25. A. L. Kroeber recognizes the extent of unconscious imitations by children: ". . . the actual imitating of the young is mostly done without much specific awareness" (*op. cit.*, p. 347).
26. Of course, some of the similarity is to be explained through biological inheritance.
27. Compare pp. 286-289.
28. See p. 142.
29. R. Linton, *The Cultural Background of Personality*, p. 96.

VIII

LEARNING

The appraisal of the importance and function of unconscious learning in the life of society naturally must be based on the psychology of learning. Unfortunately, this basis is not fully satisfactory yet. Hilgard, a specialist in learning, acknowledges this openly.[1]

First, it is not clear what is to be considered as learning. The narrowest definition of learning is: the acquisition of skills. On the other hand, a very broad definition of learning says that it is the processes "by which an activity originates or is changed through reacting . . ." with exception of "native response tendencies, maturation or temporary states of the organism."[2] Another very broad delineation sees in learning the modifications of behavior resulting from activity (excluding fatigue and sensory adaptation).[3]

Still broader is the definition by Wheeler, for whom learning is stimulation-induced maturation which, after the stimulation occurred, depends on internal laws of maturation and not on exercise.[4] For Pronko the study of the field of learning is as broad as psychology itself.[5]

It is more and more accepted that learning includes several different types of processes. Certain authors are satisfied with two,[6] some others with three, four,[7] or seven[8] types of learning. Each classification has a different basis and uses different concepts.

There is also doubt about the validity of the laws of learning. Hilgard says: "There are no laws of learning which can be taught with confidence."[9] The agreement between psychologists is limited to certain fundamental, relatively few, concrete concepts and to some experimentally established facts.

When we turn to the special, narrow problems in the field of learning (such as transfer, practice, performance, motivation, reasoning), we are again at a loss. In the case of transfer, different theoretical conceptions even lead to different names of this one single phenomenon, like generalization, transposition, and assimilation. Repetition itself is generally no longer considered as necessary to learning. Guthrie's theory claims (as do Miller, Dollard[10] and Koffka[11]) that a single trial is sufficient.

Performance was generally considered as a substantial part of learning. Tolman was the first to claim that his rats learned to know the maze without any performance. The difference between performance and learning has been emphasized also by Lashley.[12] R. E. L. Faris reminds us that many of the finest golfers learned as young caddies by observing the first-class golfers.[13] New words or new opinions may be learned by hearing only; new gestures or new attitudes may be learned by mere observation.

The problem of motivation is another point in the theory of learning, the solution of which is very needed. Psychologists, by means of numerous animal experiments, studied motivation of learning by physical, inborn drives. But learning without motive also seems to take place; it is discussed by a number of authors as incidental learning.[14] So far, results of numerous experiments seem to indicate that it often is less efficient than intentional learning.[15]

The role of reasoning in learning is considered by some as minimal, in many instances as non-existent (connectionists, behaviorists, reflexologists, stimulus response theorists), yet basic by others (gestalt, neogestalt, organismic and sign-significate theorists).

UNCONSCIOUS LEARNING

The problem of unconscious learning, so important in social life, has not drawn much attention from psychologists. Thorndike[16] thinks that connections may be strengthened without awareness. Shaffer finds unconscious learning especially frequent in small children, who cannot be fully aware of it.[17]

Köhler likewise points to the fact that much of the children's learning is unconscious;[18] K. Young is convinced that much of the involuntary learning is unconscious[19] (he draws on Baker's study concerning subliminal auditory stimuli). G. W. Allport speaks about unconscious conditioning.[20]

McGeoch, as well as Shaffer, on the basis of the experimental studies, found good factual reasons for unconscious learning without being basically influenced by any psychoanalytical theories of the subconscious. More experimental evidence for learning without awareness has been secured in recent years (Sidowski, Hirsch, Philbrick and Postman, Eriksen, Kuethe and Sullivan).[21]

The unconscious processes of learning according to McGeoch are: the "spread of effect," the "strengthening influence of irrelevant rewards," "learning complex acts of skill," much of the "transfer" and "the learning of the manifold subtle attitudes and other responses of the daily life."[22]

86

Seemingly close to the problem we are studying is the theory of "latent-learning" (derived chiefly from experiments with animals).[23] Tolman's and Honzik's rats that were not hungry learned something from the plan of the maze by merely walking through it. But this has been denied by a number of psychologists.[24]

The theory of latent learning, however, can hardly contribute anything to a better understanding of human unconscious learning because human learning in similar conditions can be known to the learning individual and reported.

KINDS OF UNCONSCIOUS LEARNING

Lacking any other more satisfactory classification, we have to accept the kinds of unconscious learning as given by McGeoch and complement them as it seems necessary.

A) Spread of Effect

According to the law of spread of effect, which may operate unconsciously, any established association irradiates to the adjacent associations. McGeoch claims that the spread of effect accounts "for many instances of learning . . . in daily life."[25]

What may these be? Halbwachs noticed that many of our personal memories are preserved because they happen close to an important social event.[26] We remember, for instance, who visited us or what we did the day when World War II broke out, although we forget similar unimportant events which happened the day after or the day before.

Likewise, many of our attitudes, values, and feelings are consequences of the spread of effect. Everything belonging to the church shares partly its sacred character; everything connected with places of sin loses part of its real value. In Prussia everything connected with the army had a higher value. Patriotic feelings spread to everything characterizing our country.

B) Irrelevant Rewards

The second unconscious learning process listed by McGeoch, is the "influence of irrelevant rewards." This means that sometimes our actions have effects which were not intended, but which prove to be satisfactory and are therefore learned. "A child motivated to obey a parent or to make a good impression on a stranger, but not specifically to smile, to be courteous, or to act interested in the stranger, may do these things, receive satisfying consequences . . . and have these ways of acting strengthened as a result."[27] The amount of this kind of unconscious learning in daily social life seems to be considerable. Any incidental social behavior which suits the situation and which is well accepted may be acquired by such learning as a social adjustment. Adjustments of speakers, clergymen, actors, entertainers, and other soloists to the audience develop partly by unconscious learning of this kind. Similarly, part of our adjustments in meeting people, entertaining people, persuading people, teaching people, asking favors from people, and the like, belong here. In all such cases, the "incidental" successful reactions are often learned unwittingly and unconsciously.

In unconscious learning of this kind, six different components (besides the nature of the learning process itself) may be unconscious. First, if the cause of the response (first component) is unconscious, the first performance itself (second component) may be unconscious. Third, the person may not be fully aware of the good reception of his action. Fourth, the repetition during which the person learns may be unwilled and unconscious. Fifth, the fact that there was learning may not penetrate the consciousness of the person. Sixth, the fact that a new behavior pattern has been acquired may not be known either.

Many successful salesmen or diplomats have very attractive manners, of which they are not always aware. These were in part unconsciously learned owing to irrelevant rewards and were automatized by many repetitions. By a simultaneous and similarly unconscious process the unattractive elements of behavior have been removed.

c) TRANSFER

Murphy defines transfer as the "effect of training in one function upon performance in another function or upon performance of the same function in another part of the body."[28] Transfer is probably more often unconscious than any other process connected with learning.

Practically each new social adaptation and adjustment is unconsciously facilitated by certain previously learned patterns. A child adjusted to school adjusts more easily to other situations of organized group life outside the school as well. The family develops certain social adjustments, which may be transferred to many other social situations in later life. If one of these two basic social adjustments were lacking, we would miss a very important basis for our behavior in other social groups. If both of them were lacking, we would possibly fail in many other social situations.

Agreeable appearance and speech, together with self-confidence, as developed in his professional duties, help other social adjustments of a lawyer, while a priest adjusts on the basis of his friendly and paternalistic manners learned in his profession.

In connection with transfer, we must mention generalization, which is basically an extended form of transfer. Generalization may be defined as a tendency for the same or similar patterns of cues to elicit the same responses.[29] Generalization is more often unconscious than conscious. Precisely its unconscious character (enabling people to pay attention to other things and to act immediately and appropriately in all similar situations, without losing time), makes it socially so valuable. If the psychologists stress the immense value of generalization for the life of the organism,[30] we have to do the same for the socialized personality in its participation in the life of society.

The variety of social phenomena is much richer than that of the physical or biological realm. In the life of society we do not find stable species but varied and everchanging human personalities, social situations, values, institutions, and social movements. Human personalities differ much more than non-human specimens of the physical or biological realm. Their inborn differences are deepened by different education, interests, ambitions, different economic and social status, different family backgrounds, different social contacts, different religious or political convictions, different social ties, and so on. The same applies to groups and institutions.

Thus social situations require a very frequent use of generalizations, especially in certain social positions. Politicians, for instance, or other people with many social contacts easily use their usual smiles, their handshakes, their greetings, and their phrases upon meeting people for the first time or in new situations. In a majority of cases, this use is automatic and unconscious. It is part of their political skill.

D) COMPLEX ACTS OF SKILL

McGeoch gives a new tennis stroke as an example of a complex act of skill learned unconsciously. I understand it in this way: When we learn a new tennis stroke, we know only its rough scheme. We do not know the detailed movements of each particular muscle nor their coordination. Often a single incidental little change in the movement of one particular muscle brings the success. We do not know where and how the expected improvement has been achieved. But we can repeat it; and finally we master it well.

The unconscious achievement of complex acts of skill evidently applies also to psychic skills. Unconscious social adjustments of this kind may be divided into two groups: the culturally patterned skills and the original personal skills.

1) *Culturally Patterned Skills*

Here belongs much of the learning of speech by children, a great deal of their learning of gestures and body movements with a social meaning, of acting and reacting in different social situations, of acquiring certain male or female behavior patterns, and so forth.

A long mispronounced word is one day pronounced correctly by the child. The change may be sudden, without transition. It may be an unexpected success, and the child does not know how he achieved it. An immigrant similarly has to learn a number of new skills in a new country. As an adult person, he must learn not only the language but, for instance, new approaches to the solution of certain personal problems, organization of his work, use of certain methods of work, making decisions, maintaining his dignity, dealing with people, and making friends. After several years, he drops many of the old ways and acquires the ways of the country of residence. Most of them have been learned unconsciously. He does not even know about many of these changes; and when told about them by a visiting countryman, he naturally is not able to say one word about how or even that he learned them.

As for language, Sapir was one of the first to recognize the learning of complex linguistic patterns (see p. 25) "with minimum of consciousness." This minimum is considerable not only in illiterate nations, but also in most advanced, modern nations which teach their children the grammar of their language.

As a matter of fact, only certain aspects of the language are scientifically known; other aspects are still reserved for the unconscious learning. Certain shades of the meaning of many words, certain mutual relations of the words, as well as their relations toward objects, uses of certain words in a certain connection, and some other peculiarities of the style are guided by unknown rules. Especially the dialects and neologisms of modern languages have many, yet unknown unconsciously learned rules.

The unconscious learning of the mother tongue before the child comes to school produces the basic mastery of a language. Adults who never went to school, although unaware of rules, speak their mother tongue fluently, while people who consciously learned a foreign language with all its rules, seldom speak it perfectly.

Later on, equally unconsciously, people learn the meaning of a word in connection with certain adjectives, verbs, adverbs, and so on. We also learn, for the most part unconsciously, that certain other combinations are impossible, while still others are funny, clumsy, pejorative, or indecent. We even do not know that we mastered these before we use them. This mastery may be so unconscious that when we are in doubt as to the use of a certain word or phrase when writing a letter, or when we question the meaning of a sentence we wrote, we often have to turn to our unconsciousness. We depend on our feeling (which is not based on any clear reasons) that the pertinent text is (or is not) satisfactory, possibly queer, or not quite suitable. If the feeling does not appear, we may encourage it by reading the relevant passage two or three times aloud. Only after having dug out from our unconsciousness what has been kept as an unconscious skill, do we have a feeling for what to do.

Sapir also insisted on the unconscious use of learned rules of language: "Perhaps there is a far-reaching moral in the fact that even a child can speak the most difficult language with idiomatic ease but that it takes an unusually analytical type of mind to define the mere elements of that incredibly subtle linguistic mechanism which is but a plaything of the child's unconscious."[31] And again: "Here are found determinations of bewildering variety, concerning which few even among the sophisticated have any clarity, though the lowliest peasant or savage head-hunter may have control of them in his intuitive repertoire."[32]

The high mastery of linguistic skills by famous writers or speakers also remains mostly unconscious. Sapir says in this connection: "It is needless to say that no normal speaker has an adequate knowledge of these submerged sound configurations. He is the unconscious and magnificently loyal adherent of thoroughly socialized phonetic patterns . . ."[33]

Language appears as a mostly unconsciously learned, complex, social skill whose learned patterns are equally unconsciously used. This also applies to a large number of other social skills such as skillful conversing, using properly the accepted concepts, and all other patterns of thought common to the given culture. It applies also to a large part of the chivalrous behavior toward ladies, to businesslike manners, to good salesmanship, and to many other behavior patterns accepted by the culture.

2) Original Personal Skills

New, personal adaptations and adjustments fitting the specific situation of the individual may also be learned unconsciously. This may be, for instance, a personal gesture, or the skill to express one's own mental and emotional responses, drives, and intentions in such a way as to fit in with the momentary social situation, with the social values, obligations, other people's interests and rights, and also with one's own interests. Educators, after years of teaching, unconsciously develop a specific smile expressing at the same time friendly understanding of faults, encouragement to further effort and hope for improvement in the future. The smile of a medical doctor expresses the will to help, sympathy with the troubles of the patient, the confidence in his medical knowledge, with perhaps the warning that it will take some time to cure the illness. The smile of a salesman expresses several (partly fictitious) components: the pleasure in selling to the customer, the willingness to satisfy his wishes, as well as the conviction of selling excellent goods at attractive prices.

Those who master such skills cannot be of great help to the beginners since they do not know how they learned them or even of what they consist.

When skillful writers and speakers develop new linguistic achievements, they make the language richer, more beautiful, more precise, and also find new ways of expressing certain new social realities. These additional features of their mastery of the language are partly acquired by the unconscious learning of original linguistic skills. Only parts of this process are occasionally conscious.

E) ATTITUDES

It is not clear why McGeoch speaks only about "subtle" attitudes and not about attitudes in general. We think that both subtle and other attitudes may be learned unconsciously. McGeoch probably means those attitudes which are not formulated in words and norms, which are not derived from recognized principles or values, or are not so strong as to be conspicuous.

We may learn attitudes not only unconsciously, but also against our own will. As we know, we sometimes learn from our enemies, whom we dislike, an attitude which we do not want to accept. Despite a constant attempt to keep their national culture pure from influences of the disliked neighboring culture, people living in the borderline area acquire many of its attitudes. They may be so unaware of it that they notice it only after coming back to the interior of the country where the differences between their own new attitudes and those of their countrymen become conspicuous. But even then, they cannot recall anything about how and when they learned the neighbor's attitudes.

92

Another case in point are the colonial officers who learn unconsciously and against their will certain attitudes of the colonial people among whom they live. The continuous, unconscious empathies with the points of view of the persons we deal with daily, with their tensions and strivings, in co-operation with the understanding of their situation, teach us their attitudes whether or not we want or value them. Of course, even well-formulated attitudes also may become automatic and thus, possibly, unconscious.

Attitudes of strictly personal character may likewise be learned unconsciously, either by repetition or by one single experience. We may not know about such an attitude and we consequently may be surprised after it shows up.

f) OTHER RESPONSES

McGeoch listed "other responses" without saying more about what they are. Evidently, he meant neither attitudes (which were listed separately) nor values, sentiments, or norms since none of these are responses. It seems to us that this category could possibly include responses such as avoiding unnecessary disagreements with colleagues, smiling at people, turning toward people with whom we speak, overcoming embarrassment by a smile or rapid talk, and so on. These responses are small parts of our daily social techniques, learned mostly unconsciously by unconscious imitation of social models or by unconsciously perceived rewards of such reaction. Some of them, though, may be consciously learned partly in school and in the family. But the details of such responses generally are learned without teaching and without any awareness of it.

Very often our unconsciously learned responses are complex. Let us take, for instance, such a very simple reaction as a "yes" when somebody asks us if we agree with him in an unimportant matter discussed at an afternoon party. This "yes" may be different according to the situation, the person to whom we say it, consideration of who else hears it, what our real attitude is toward the subject, what we want or have to achieve, and so on. There are dozens of different "yeses" having dozens of meanings differentiated by accent, by inflexion of the voice, by length, hesitation involved, or melody used with it. The expression of eyes and face, as well as gestures, achieve further differentiation. A certain "yes" may express, for instance, the following reactions, attitudes and intentions: "Although my attitude is not very positive, I finally agree because I don't want to disagree with the hostess, and I want to maintain an amiable atmosphere. Finally, I agree because the matter is unimportant and because, anyway, in a given situation nobody is really bound by such an agreement. I can agree also because my wife, who is strongly opposed to such an opinion, is sitting in the next room and can not hear me." Only people who have learned certain social skills are able to express these meanings in one single word. People without necessary social skills would be embarrassed or would react inappropriately, clumsily.

g) OTHER BEHAVIOR PATTERNS

The unconsciously learned behavior patterns as listed by McGeoch are certainly not complete. There are many other patterns which should be added to McGeoch's list. Such are, for instance, sentiments, feelings, values, norms, obligations, taste, and some others. We shall deal with them in special chapters.

LEARNING BY WATCHING

Tolman and his followers consider insight as learning without performing. Koffka's understanding of mathematical demonstrations and Faris's learning of golf by watching fine golfers also indicate that such learning exists. But we really do not know enough about this neglected aspect of learning.[34]

We learn a new word by hearing it (our first use of it is perfect); we learn a new gesture by seeing it. We learn how to use a simple tool by watching a craftsman working with it. We learn simple calisthenics by watching our teacher perform them.

How far may learning by watching be unconscious? First, the observed behavior pattern may be perceived unconsciously, marginally, or possibly subliminally. Watching the behavior of an interesting social model, we generally perceive a part of it consciously and the rest unconsciously. We may learn both the consciously and the unconsciously perceived parts of the model's behavior equally well.

Second, we may be completely unaware of the learning processes which are taking place, even if we are fully aware of the learned behavior pattern. Third, we may not know that we acquired a certain new skill. We may know of the process later on, by inference after we had first used the new pattern unwittingly. Finally, the fourth unconscious component may be the performance. E. Faris speaks about his acquiring of the gesture of African Negroes of pointing by lips. He was not aware of using it and when told he denied it sincerely. Only later did he notice it.[35]

94

Learning of unconsciously perceived behavior patterns may occur, as we know, in two different ways. First of all, the new elements of behavior may be inconspicuous. Some manners of very fine modest people may not be noticed, although they may be finally learned and used by another person. Second, we may not consciously notice a rather conspicuous behavior if we are paying attention to something else. If we talk with a person about a business proposition, we may not pay attention to his manners, to some of his gestures or words. Despite that, we may learn some of them after we have watched them marginally several times. I learned quite a number of English words to which I did not pay any conscious attention, being only interested in the content of what was being said. I noticed the result of learning after I had used the acquired words.

An interesting case of such learning is used in some old theatrical pieces from the 17th or 18th century. The plot of this type of play consists in the disguise of a servant (or a maid) as his lord (or her lady) and in behaving so well as not to be recognized. The servant (maid) succeeds on the first try. In a feudal society this was a much more difficult achievement than we would be inclined to imagine because the differences of manners and behavior between servants and noblemen at that time were enormous.

In all these cases of learning by watching (despite the lack of performance during the time of learning), there often is at least a partial abortive acting[36] by direct empathy and by empathy in recollection. At first, when watching or when recollecting, some of the learners occasionally imagined themselves to be in the position of their master and were co-acting with him in their imagination. In addition to this, there was an initial, rudimentary motor reaction, a beginning of physical performance in the form of slight muscular feelings and contractions. One may go so far as to open the mouth when the watched model speaks or in some cases to silently move the lips.

The co-acting is generally more complete in the psychological field than in the physical field. There is a full familiarity with the performance, a complete understanding, as well as learned mastery of intellectual and emotional components of the role (strengthened often by admiration or love for the model); there is an association of the pertinent behavior patterns with the conditions in which they occur, with the expected reactions of other people; and there is a temporal, spatial, and logical organization of it with the previous experiences, with interests, attitudes, and values, of the imitator. There is also a frequently experienced connection between the psychological reactions and the initial motor reactions. Only the complete physical execution is lacking.

95

Of all kinds of learning, learning by watching is the least conspicuous, the least systematic, and the least known. On the other hand, it probably is the most frequent and the most responsible for the conformity of culture. It goes on uninterruptedly during the whole life of the individual[37] and covers all the fields of social life. It accompanies all our participation in social life.

DIFFERENCE BETWEEN UNCONSCIOUS LEARNING AND THE INFLUENCE OF UNCONSCIOUS EXPERIENCES

Unconscious learning through observation reminds us, in a way, of the influence of the unconscious experiences with social models analyzed in the preceding chapters. What is the distinctive characteristic of their effect on behavior as compared with the effect of a pattern learned by the silent and motionless watching of a model?

Learned behavior is acquired more actively than the unconscious past experience. Also, the empathy in learned behavior probably is stronger. The learned patterns affect strong interests of the personality and influence the personality structure, while the experiences which left traces often belong only to the outward, storage part of the personality.

LEARNING THROUGH A SINGLE EXPERIENCE

Let us start first with a frustrating experience. After we have been "taught a lesson" by a frustrating experience (such as by a failing grade or by loss of money in stocks), our behavior may be changed enduringly. The connection established between the stimulus and response is strong, immediate, and may be used automatically.

Often, both the existence of the process of learning as well as its result are unconscious. In some instances, we are amazed at changes in our behavior, and we have to search in our past to discover their causes. A slight mocking smirk on the face of a person in a given delicate situation may cause us to avoid meeting this person on other occasions. We may deny it sincerely at first and may not believe it. Then we may acknowledge that we avoid the person, but still perhaps not know why the change occurred.

Social adjustments secured by unconscious learning through a single experience may be divided into three types. In the first one are the adjustments to a personal, specific social situation. A very bad, unexpected reaction of our superior may have taught us to avoid a certain kind of behavior which he dislikes.

The second type is unconscious adjustments to conditions prevailing in our society. We may become very cautious in writing the address correctly after the non-delivery of a vitally important letter because of an incomplete address.

The third type of unconscious learning adjusts people to generally accepted norms, values and to social currents and movements. The following distinction may be made in this third group. After the pertinent experience 1) we may carefully maintain certain generally accepted norms or values, or 2) we may accept new specific (minority) social values or movements (like communism).

Certain moral obligations, the respect for religion, the respect for patriotic feelings and for other social values are sometimes taught efficiently through a single experience. Also hatred of another race, as found in racism, may originate in a single painful experience with a member of this race.

In the above mentioned cases, the fact that we learned, what we learned and what new behavior we acquired were unconscious, while the object of learning was often conscious. How far the fact of learning and the result of learning may be unconscious is to be seen clearly from the fact that people, after a bad experience caused by their own behavior, often do not know whether they will improve or, on the contrary, become still more determined in their ways. They may not know it for months until a new critical situation appears, and they react in one or in the other way.

UNCONSCIOUS LEARNING OF SOCIALIZED BEHAVIOR

If we think of the innumerable adjustments we have to learn before we are able to behave in a well-adjusted manner in a simple social situation (imagine a "caveman" at an afternoon tea!), we will understand that probably only a relatively small number of these have been learned consciously through teaching and a relatively large number in an unconscious way through social experiences.

It would be practically impossible to list all the kinds of special patterns acquired by unconscious learning. Nevertheless, we may possibly get a very incomplete idea of their enormous number if we watch a man who has lived for several years in a foreign country. Let us discuss such a case drawn from my experiences.

Imagine the case of a man who has returned to his mother country after having spent several years in Paris. Before leaving France, for instance, our man is probably aware that he dresses in a more sophisticated way, that his conversation is lighter, that he is able to formulate his ideas in a clearer way than previously. After his coming back, he becomes aware of further changes due to incidental comparisons with his old friends. But his old friends certainly notice still further changes in his behavior, which remain unknown to him. These probably are the following: more gestures with hands when talking; some new gestures; more vivacity in gestures; more verbal reactions; more jokes and especially more complicated and rather literary jokes; more compliments toward persons present and more interest in being charming; greater appreciation of art, especially of painting; greater flair for refined and tasty food; more enjoyment of sophisticated and precise style; more explicit appreciation of the beauty of women, of buildings, of nature; more definite judgments about everything; more generalizations, more respect for big ideas; more stress on original thinking and personal form of thoughts; less planning and more improvising in certain situations; more yielding to moods; less inclination to practical and business activities; less patience with painstaking empirical or experimental procedures; more open criticism of public affairs and also of private affairs of persons who are not present; less clinging to the same subject when conversing; and some other changes which cannot be so easily noticed as those we listed.

Evidently the list of changes is extremely incomplete. Also many expressions we used for individual changes, in fact, often cover a whole set of changes. If, for instance, the man had now a greater appreciation for art, this is not a single but a number of changes of attitudes, knowledge, values, judgments, emotional reactions, and other elements of behavior which could be described on dozens of pages if we would like to be precise and complete.

A substantial proportion of the changes we mentioned is due to unconscious learning by repetition of the performance or by repeated watching — a smaller part, to unconscious learning through single experiences. Evidently, too, there was some conscious, though informal learning by paying attention to certain things considered as necessary or desirable.

A child, of course, learns much more from his own culture without awareness than does an adult who spent several years in a foreign country. It is just impossible to master all the cultural, subcultural, and group patterns he has to use, in a conscious way. The conformity of culture is achieved in a high degree through unconscious acquisition of culturally accepted patterns.

FOOTNOTES TO CHAPTER EIGHT

1. E. R. Hilgard, *Theories of Learning*, Appleton-Century-Crofts, New York, 1956, p. 457. Similarly M. Sherif says: "It will not help a social psychologist (as yet) to take sides with a learning theory . . ." (*An Outline of Social Psychology*, Harper and Brothers, New York, 1948, p. 213).
2. E. R. Hilgard, *ibid.*, p. 3.
3. N. L. Munn, *Psychology* (1946), p. 89.
4. R. H. Wheeler, *The Science of Psychology*, T. Y. Crowell Co., New York, 1940, pp. 208-274.
5. N. H. Pronko, J. W. Bowles and others, *Empirical Foundations of Psychology*, Rinehart and Co., New York-Toronto, 1951, p. 374.
6. K. F. Muenzinger, *Psychology*, pp. 63, 105, 130; G. Katona, *Organizing and Memorizing*, pp. 5-9; B. F. Skinner, *The Behavior of Organisms*, Appleton-Century-Crofts, New York, 1938, pp. 18, 19.
7. See E. R. Hilgard, *op. cit.*, (1948), pp. 295, 296; K. Lewin, *Field Theory in Social Science*, pp. 65, 66.
8. H. L. Kingsley, *The Nature and Conditions of Learning*, Prentice-Hall, New York, 1946, p. 32; E. R. Hilgard, *op. cit.*, p. 320.
9. *Ibid.*, p. 326.
10. N. E. Miller and J. Dollard, *op. cit.*, pp. 26-27.
11. K. Koffka, *Principles of Gestalt Psychology*, pp. 549-550.
12. K. S. Lashley, "Learning: Nervous Mechanism in Learning," in C. Murchison ed., *The Foundations of Experimental Psychology*, Clark Univ. Press, Worcester, Massachusetts, 1929.
13. R. E. L. Faris, *Social Psychology*, The Ronald Press Co., New York, 1952, p. 179.
14. J. A. McGeoch and A. L. Irion, *The Psychology of Human Learning*, Longmans, Green and Co., New York, 1952, pp. 210-215; L. Postman, V. L. Senders, "Incidental Learning and Generality of Set," *J. Exp. Psychol.*, 36, pp. 153-165; G. H. Brown, "Factors Influencing Incidental Learning," *J. Exp. Psychol.*, 47, 1954, pp. 163-169.
15. Saltzman and Atkinson found that after 2, 6, or 8 presentations there was no difference between incidental and intentional learning, but after 16 presentations, the scores of intentional learning were higher (I. J. Saltzman, R. L. Atkinson, "Comparison of Incidental and Intentional Learning After Different Numbers of Stimulus Presentations," *Am. J. Psychol.*, LXVII, 1954, pp. 521-524).
16. E. L. Thorndike, R. T. Rock, "Learning Without Awareness of What is Being Learned or Intent to Learn it," *J. Exp. Psych.*, 17, 1934, pp. 1-19. On the other hand the recent experiments of L. Postman and R. F. Jarrett show "only little reliable evidence for learning without awareness" (*Am. J. of Psych.*, LXV, 1952, pp. 244-255).

17. L. F. Shaffer in E. G. Boring, H. S. Langfeld and H. P. Weld, *Foundations*, p. 516.
18. W. Kohler, *Gestalt Psychology*, pp. 79, 80.
19. K. Young, *Personality*, p. 76.
20. G. W. Allport, *Personality*, p. 203.
21. J. B. Sidowski, "Influence of Awareness of Reinforcement on Verbal Conditioning," *J. Exp. Psych.*, 48, 1954, pp. 355-360; J. Hirsch, "Learning without Awareness and Extinction following Awareness as a Function of Reinforcement," *J. Exp. Psych.*, 54, 1957, pp. 218-224; E. B. Philbrick and L. Postman, "A Further Analysis of Learning without Awareness," *Am. J. Psych.*, 68, 1955, pp. 417-424; C. W. Eriksen, J. W. Kuethe, D. F. Sullivan, "Some Personality Correlates of Learning without Verbal Awareness," *J. of Personality*, 26, 1958, pp. 216-228.
22. J. A. McGeoch, *The Psychology of Human Learning*, Longmans, Green and Company, New York, 1942, pp. 590-592; see also J. A. McGeoch and A. L. Irion, *op cit.*, pp. 269-272.
23. Nevertheless, there are some studies of latent learning in humans: H. W. Stevenson, "Latent Learning in Children," *J. Exp. Psychol.*, 47, 1954, pp. 17-21; L. Postman and A. H. Tuma, "Latent Learning in Human Subjects," *Am. J. Psychol.*, LXVII, 1954, pp. 119-123.
24. D. Thistlethwaite gave a list of 76 published studies concerning latent learning ("A Critical Review of Latent Learning and Related Experiments," *Psychol. Bulletin*, 48, 1951, pp. 97-129) and summarized the reasons for the acceptance of this theory. H. Kendler and I. Maltzman summarized in two different articles the opposite point of view (*Psychol. Bulletin*, 49, 1952, pp. 47-60).
25. J. A. McGeoch, *op. cit.*, p. 580.
26. M. Halbwachs, *Les Cadres Sociaux de la Mémoire*, F. Alcan, Paris, 1935.
27. J. A. McGeoch, *op. cit.*, pp. 588-589; see also E. L. Thorndike, "An Experimental Study of Rewards," *Teach. Coll. Contr. Educ.*, No. 580, 1933.
28. G. Murphy, *Personality*, p. 999.
29. N. E. Miller and J. Dollard, *op. cit.*, p. 44.
30. C. L. Hull, "Learning: II, The Factor of the Conditioned Reflex," in C. Murchison, *A Handbook of General Experimental Psychology*, Clark University Press, 1934, pp. 446-7.
31. E. Sapir, in *The Unconscious, A Symposium*, p. 123.
32. *Ibid.*, p. 128.
33. *Ibid.*, p. 134.
34. J. F. Dashiell, *Fundamentals of General Psychology*, pp. 413-414.
35. E. Faris, *The Nature of Human Nature*, p. 78.
36. According to R. E. L. Faris "all perception seems to require a muscular response of some sort . . . which in the case of language appears to be an actual silent repetition or rehearsal of what is said." *Op. cit.*, p. 231.
37. E. T. Prothro and P. T. Teska, *Psychology*, Ginn and Co., Boston, 1950, p. 394.

IX

THINKING

It is difficult to agree about what is to be understood by thinking.[1] Some psychologists see in thinking chiefly the solving of new problems (new for the thinker),[2] others speak rather of reasoning. Still others consider imagination as an equally rightful part of thinking. A still broader conception of thinking includes also the so-called "personalizing processes" expressed in opinions and prejudices.[3] We shall limit our discussion only to some thinking processes which are pertinent to the goal of this book.

For many years, the core of thinking was conceived as covert, symbolic trial and error. But since the Gestaltists revealed the basic importance of insight, these old conceptions of associationists and mechanists can be applied only to a lesser part of our thinking. It is evident that many of the so-called trials and errors include hypotheses, reasonable assumptions, and rational understandings. Often they are not blind — they may have the characteristics of insight and creativeness.

Although some thinking is adaptive and adjustive,[4] it is not always so. We agree fully with G. W. Allport (and others) that thinking is also spontaneous, creative, and that there is active need for thought.

The important question for us is whether or not the thinking processes may be unconscious and the extent to which they may be so. The conviction that there are such processes is more and more accepted by modern writers in the field. The man who first pointed systematically to the existence and operation of the unconscious thinking processes was Hartmann. About three decades before Freud he devoted a whole chapter and portions of other chapters to unconscious thought in his rather metaphysical study of the unconscious.[5] More than a quarter of a century later, the French sociologist LeBon[6] used unconscious thinking processes in explaining the behavior of individuals in a crowd. He was convinced that "conscious life of the mind is of small importance in comparison with the unconscious life."

101

A very strong impetus to the study of unconscious thought was given by Freud. Although using a narrow and sometimes doubtful basis, his approach was new and penetrating. His followers deserve merit for enlarging substantially our knowledge of the unconscious thought. Prince, too, made a valuable contribution. Among the modern students of the thinking processes who gave full attention to the unconscious thought are Montmasson, Blanshard, Miller and a few others. Several authors studying the creative processes in general or creative achievements of certain noted artists or scientists,[7] as well as some creative personalities themselves (like Hadamard[8] and Poincaré[9]), shed much light on certain unconscious thinking processes.

The most frequent attitude of modern experimental psychologists toward unconscious thoughts is either to ignore them completely or to recognize their existence but to give them only unsystematic and mostly incidental attention. Some of them point to some particular unconscious thinking processes; others mention the unconscious thinking processes in general.

The associationist school is responsible for one of the oldest conceptions of an unconscious mental process in the field of psychology proper — the unconscious inference. However, it is doubted by the opposing schools. Another unconscious process, as claimed recently by Vinacke[10] (but previously formulated by Hartmann) is the process of abstraction. M. Sherif and C. W. Sherif are convinced that standardization of norms "need not be conscious or deliberate."[11] Similarly, Sherif and Cantril say that ". . . the scales of magnitudes . . . need not be consciously formed . . ."[12] Claparède came to the conclusion that regulating mechanisms or hypotheses may take place at an unconscious level.[13] Stagner and Karwoski are convinced that most of the linkages between the ideas or images do not reach consciousness. They also discuss unconscious cerebration and creativity.[14] Kluckhohn and Murray speak about regnant unconscious intellectual processes.[15] James had recognized that there is a kind of genius who by intuition, without noticing the bond of identity, comes to new ideas.[16] Lindesmith and Strauss claim that we cannot be aware of all the biases involved in our thinking.[17]

A number of modern authors may be quoted for their general recognition of the existence and operation of unconscious thinking processes. Vinacke, for instance, is convinced that unconscious mental activities exist in everyone.[18] Humphrey writes that thinking "may go on without the person's realizing it".[19] . . . Heidbreder declares that ". . . thinking . . . is too complexly and obscurely determined to be profitably conceived of as essentially a conscious process."[20] Ryan says: "It is a fact that thinking is, for the most part, unconscious."[21] The most inclusive statement in this respect is by Murphy: "All thinking as we have constantly tried to make clear, is in its core unconscious; it is only its shadow which is conscious, and this is true of free as of directed thought."[22]

Experimental evidence for unconscious thinking processes is still very limited. Some of the important experiments in this field will be quoted during the discussion of different kinds of unconscious thought.

In present psychological research, the study of thinking processes is mostly done without any distinction between conscious and unconscious thought. Even the writers who recognize unconscious thought often do not make any effort to analyze it separately. Thus, the knowledge of unconscious thinking we can use in our discussion is rather limited.

AUTOMATIC THINKING

Under automatic thinking we may understand basically two different kinds of thinking processes. The first is the unconscious carrying out of accepted mental tasks; the second is the unconscious use of mental clichés, of habitual mental operations and usual associations.

We already know the extent to which the operation of psychological sets may be unconscious and automatic. An important part of the operation of any set is the appropriate mental processes. For instance, a psychological set in the mind of a public servant applies automatically the administrative rules on a number of cases, as long as he sits in his office. His mind constantly produces new applications in succession, without being reminded to do it.

In a similar way, we consistently and automatically apply the norms and values of our culture to all appropriate situations we face in our daily life. When thinking of our friends and acquaintances, of our superiors, as well as of public personalities, we automatically apply the norms and values of friendship, of good taste, decency, or morality; thinking of novels we read, of paintings we saw, and of music we heard, we automatically apply norms[23] and values of beauty. If a scientist reads a scientific book, his mind automatically picks out the ideas or data which are needed for his present study.

The other type of automatic thinking is equally, if not more, common in our participation in social life. Some of the habitual judgments, usual comparisons, and other mental operations, stereotyped classifications, and generally accepted associations may be used so often that they do not enter consciousness when in operation. B. Blanshard gives the following example of it: "The bankteller can add his columns, the

103

grocer fill his orders, even the judge pass rulings on petty cases, with little of the effort or attention. . . . It may seem impossible that the teller should run down his column as fast as he does and still have noted all the figures; indeed, at the end he may have no memory that he did note certain ones; but the correctness of his result shows that he must have taken account of them."[24] Similar is the statement by T. A. Ryan: "You can read a simple clear prose passage of five hundred words through quickly and understand it perfectly. Perhaps the preposition *by* occurred in the first sentence, and the passage would have been altered throughout in its meaning if the word had been *to* instead of *by*. If quizzed, you have the meaning correct. So you must have perceived *by*. Yet you do not remember the word, you did not pause to pronounce it or to let any imagery arise to indicate its meaning."[25]

Any recurring, social situation produces similar automatic thought processes. Medical doctors, army officers, business managers and engineers perform the repetitious mental operations needed in their job without thinking of them. This we do also when having guests, when lecturing at the college, when meeting people in the street, and so on. Perhaps the mental processes of a receptionist who automatically gives stereotyped answers by applying certain knowledge of the situation to the client's questions is the most typical example.

A careful analysis of both types of automatic thinking processes would perhaps reveal that there are few pure cases of either of them. In most cases both co-operate, supporting each other in the final effect. Thus, an automatic application of a law may be partly habitual, partly due to the operation of a set. The spiritual cultural heritage most often uses both automatically operating tools simultaneously in order to operate fully and dependably. Our religious thought, for instance, is continuously guided by certain psychological sets, which are the substantial part of our striving to be close to God and to please Him, as well as by innumerable habits of religious thoughts.

Even higher, creative mental operations often use both automatically operating tools. The mind of a French novelist working at his writing desk is impelled to seek surprising comparisons, refined literary jokes, and interesting contradictions, automatically and unconsciously. The mind of an American novelist, equally unconsciously and automatically, seeks rather interesting facts, realistic descriptions, adventurous experiences. Both minds are led by habitual thought patterns specific to their own culture, as well as by psychological sets, to appeal to the taste of the public, to express well certain national values, and so on. Scientists, likewise, follow certain cultural patterns of scientific thought which are helped by psychological sets aiming at the achievements of certain scientific goals. European scientists, for instance, tend automatically to develop new, general, systematic knowledge, sometimes without seeking the full support by facts, whereas American scientists, on the contrary, tend to establish new concrete facts, paying less attention to general conclusions and to a systematic presentation. Both groups follow unconsciously the habitual scientific patterns of their country.

Automatically used, mental patterns and sets, including automatic thinking processes, keep us behaving according to the norms of our culture in all fields of social life. They are necessary conditions of a smooth functioning of the culture. Many elements of culture could not be maintained without their help at all. Likewise, the functioning of groups and their adaptation to changing conditions is greatly helped by both kinds of automatic thinking.

UNCONSCIOUS JUDGMENTS ABOUT
THE PRESENT SITUATION

Murphy gives an interesting example: "The bird on the ground 'knows' that it is in danger; at the top of a tree it knows that it is not. But, in the ordinary sense of the term, such knowledge is 'unconscious'." Similarly, he says, that birds "often instantly recognize . . . the attitudes of other birds toward themselves, instantly divining the presence of hostile intentions of a guileful and indirect sort." Thus one "man knows perfectly well that he is in danger, whereas another does not, and neither can define any of the specific cues which make him feel as he does."[26] Murphy explains these unconscious processes through "ordinary conditioning" and through organization of the perceptual activity. This is undoubtedly a correct explanation, although perhaps not a complete one. Certainly in such an intuitive "knowledge" there also is often unconscious judgment.[27] Only cases of repeated and basically identical situations can be sufficiently explained by conditioning. But men and animals recognize danger also in new situations.

Dogs seem to grasp that their master is in trouble without any such previous experience. W. Köhler found that chimpanzees understood facial expressions with which they have not had any experience.[28] Stern established that small children also react appropriately to facial expressions or gestures that they have not experienced.[29] Although psychologists do not agree on the explanation of these facts (whether by direct perception, intuition, inference, empathy, or "verstehen,"), it seems that at least in complex new situations there is organization of the cues, knowledge, and unconscious reasoning. Especially if some signs are perceived later than others, explanation by reasoning seems necessary. G W. Allport says correctly that "perception never reveals the relation between distant causes and present effect."[30] It does not reveal the connection between distant and present impressions either. These can be linked together by reasoning (or possibly by generalization), be it conscious or unconscious.[31]

This conviction is based on the usual, rather narrow conception of perception. But some writers, especially those from the Gestalt school, stretched the concept of perception much farther.[32] It embraces not only the environmental cues and their selection and organization, and the psychic conditions of the perceiver, but sometimes also his relevant previous experiences, the relations between successive events, relevant social values and norms, simple insight, judgments, and the meaning of the whole situation. On the other hand, Senden has a very narrow concept of perception. Even the distinction between the triangles and the squares is a judgment for him.[33] To Bartlett[34] and Humphrey,[35] perception, thought, and judgment are inextricably mingled with each other; this seems to me the most probable.

The cases of unconscious judgments about the present situation may be divided into two groups: a) where the elements of the situation are conscious and only the judgment is unconsciously established, and b) where the elements of the situation, as well as the reasoning, are unconscious.

A) UNCONSCIOUS JUDGMENTS FROM KNOWN FACTS

Teachers, judges, sometimes historians, or appraisers, often unconsciously[36] make judgments on the basis of well-established facts; the unconscious reasoning leading to the judgment sometimes cannot be brought to consciousness. A very good example of such judgments by a governor was given by Hankin.[37] Miller, who quotes Hankin's example, remarks that the unconscious judgments are often more accurate, easier, and more rapid than conscious judgments.

In business and political life, judgments of this type are frequent. Even well-informed businessmen often make intuitive decisions. Experienced politicians are also inclined to make such decisions.

Our judgment about known facts may unconsciously be modified by the influence of the group. People assimilate their judgment[38] to the group opinion; or, if they disagree, they draw strong support from other dissenting persons.[39] The assimilation of the judgment, as well as the stiffening of one's own judgment are unconscious processes which may remain unconscious even after the final judgment has been formulated.

106

B) JUDGMENTS FROM MARGINAL IMPRESSIONS

We have already heard about medical doctors[40] making their diagnosis intuitively (see footnote 11, p. 14). The ones we quoted probably based their intuitive diagnosis chiefly on marginal perceptions.

In the same chapter we quoted similar cases from other walks of life: judgments about the character of a person (for instance of the professor) produced by unconscious reasoning. There were also cases of unconscious reasoning concerning the state of mind of a person, such as the official who promised to do everything in his power for the person who asked his help, or the girl suddenly grasping the state of mind of her parents talking in the kitchen.

Many of our esthetic judgments are based chiefly on marginal impressions. Of course, they are generally supported by some conscious impressions.

JUDGMENTS FROM PAST UNCONSCIOUS EXPERIENCES

Some of the impressions were not recollected when the general we discussed on p. 9 was forming his final judgment the next morning, and some others were already forgotten. But the influence of neither of them was lost. They were included in his judgment concerning the training, discipline, equipment, and morale, of the army unit.

Thus, for instance, the parade strengthened the general's old conviction that there was too much drilling in the army instead of training in warfare. He also was now quite sure that the equipment was too heavy and allowed insufficient freedom of movement to the soldiers.

Although at the end of the parade the final judgments were almost ready, the general felt that he needed some short time to put them into the final form. He decided to "think it over." He did it, as most people do, by dropping the whole thing from his mind and letting it ripen by itself. The next morning he felt sure that the previous day's judgments were basically correct. The unconscious thinking processes checked on them and found them all right. They only added more emphasis to some highlights of his mental picture and put into a dimmer light some other points, while the rest remained unchanged.

Much inspection, supervision, and checking use unconscious experiences in a way similar to the general's. The school superintendent visiting classes, the manager inspecting offices, the engineer visiting the factory shop, the inspectors of playgrounds and parks use unconscious experiences in much the same way. The professor correcting essay-type examination papers or giving an oral examination makes frequent use of them in order to establish, consciously and unconsciously, the correct grade.

Let us now give more attention to the last case. During the relatively short time of an oral examination, the professor hears answers to three or four questions and forms a number of impressions about the personality and knowledge of the student. The latter seems to him bright and intelligent, easygoing, self-confident, but not industrious. He has the impression that the student did not prepare thoroughly for his examination, but that his good judgment makes his answers rather satisfactory. Most of them were good, some were mediocre; and the student made only two serious mistakes. The personal qualities and the answers were mostly unconsciously compared with the unrecollected traits and knowledge of other students he examined that same day, previous days, and previous months (or possibly years), as well as with the appropriate, chiefly unconscious standards.

A regular professor of social sciences or humanities (it is different in physics or in mathematics) generally is unable to remember fully all the details of the answers, and is unable to summate the evaluations of different parts of students' answers consciously into a final judgment. A great deal of this is done unconsciously. The professor's mind works generally so that he reacts to what the student says every few seconds by an often half-conscious judgment: "good . . . very good . . . not quite that . . . you are going in the wrong direction . . . oh, not at all, . . . yes, you finally found it . . . that's clever, but not completely correct . . . you have a keen judgment but you do not know what you should know . . . at least you know the most basic things . . ." Then with the help of unconscious judgments, these reactions are tranformed into quantitative values — grades. Each of the listed reactions adds or subtracts something from a tentative grade, until the desired result — a final grade — is produced.

Now what does the professor remember from what he heard? Probably only some of the basic points. Otherwise, he depends on his general impression produced by the numerous positive and negative judgments. Nevertheless, even those partial evaluations, as well as the factual ground for them, were partly forgotten or unrecollected; but they came somehow into the final product anyway.

How could he establish his final judgment so rapidly and so easily? What are its components? First, there are vague and unformulated (though rather correct) frames of reference, measures of what the students generally know. If the professor's second reaction in the series we listed above was, for instance, "very good," it was due to an unconscious comparison with such a standard. The student's answer at that moment was above it. The other unconscious frame of reference used by the professor was the ideal level of the student's knowledge. The answer was slightly below it.

Of course, there are differences between professors. Those who have a very good memory recall more of the details; the others having a less good memory recall fewer of the details. But both types assign grades without many conscious comparisons and judgments. They simply "know" what grade to give after the student has completed his last sentence.

As far as the unconscious standards are concerned, we have to add that these are also produced without awareness and practically continuously. A higher proportion of very good or very bad students in the last semester lifts or lowers them unconsciously, without any intention of the professor. Even the students who immediately preceded the one being examined affect the frame of reference. The generally unconscious character of these standards is only rarely replaced by an effort for a conscious one. If in case of doubt we ask: "Is this really a very good (grade A) answer?" we seek such a conscious measure. But we do not find it. There is none. We remain with our feeling that "this is" or "is not" a very good answer, a feeling produced by a number of often unconscious comparisons of partly unrecollected impressions with not consciously conceived standards.

There is another reason why certain elements of our final evaluation do not enter clearly into our consciousness. It is the difficulty of conceptualizing them. The precision and clarity of thought and the beauty of style, skillful handling of certain facts, the ease of formulating the ideas, the systematic approach to the subject, the keen insight into certain problems, and the originality of ideas are all difficult to evaluate precisely.

It is rather surprising that even in grading essay-type, written examination papers, with "black and white" answers which the professor can reread if needed, the importance of unconscious judgments is not much smaller.

It is interesting that this kind of work is generally rather correct. In some cases I have gone over the examination papers carefully two or three times. Sometimes the repeated reading brought to my consciousness certain favorable or unfavorable points which seemingly escaped at the first reading and would change the original judgment. But later on, it brought other points which set my judgment back to the original grade. Apparently all these seemingly new points were noticed unconsciously at the first reading and were unconsciously taken into consideration.

But what if we would use quantitative scales for each quality and would assign a weight to each of them? We doubt that despite such a cumbersome procedure the dependability of the grade would increase considerably. In many cases, we would feel that the mechanically produced grade is too low or too high.

There are even cases when conscious, rational thinking is unable to produce a satisfactory judgment despite the extreme effort of the most serious scholars. A minute, thoroughgoing analysis and scientific discussion of certain outstanding novels or poems may not lead to a final and generally accepted judgment about them. Some may remain objects of controversy for decades. After all the qualities of style, originality, beauty, depth of ideas, outstanding expression of human feelings, or of modern conditions of life and other features have been minutely analyzed, the opinion may still be divided: one group of specialists may consider the work as one of the best in the national literature and the other group only as a mediocre work of art.

Unconscious reasoning is a necessary part of our daily judgments about current affairs especially those based on marginal, unrecollected, and forgotten experiences. Generally, unconscious comparisons are involved in each of these judgments. Our judgments about a movie, social party, reception, sermon, or speech are basically founded on them. To a lesser degree, also, our judgments concerning the loyalty of our employees, the friendly or unfriendly feelings of our acquaintances, the mood or feeling of the masses, or the opposing political party depend on them. But even our judgments on certain palpable realities such as new fashions, advertisements, books, articles, paintings, or poems are complemented by unconscious reasoning, using unrecollected and forgotten experiences and frames of reference.

Let us now analyse a concrete example of an unconscious judgment in a different field, for instance, in the field of political life. At the close of the second World War, I saw a very interesting process in the formation of political judgments on the part of the masses of the Czech population. There was a passionate desire for freedom. The underground groups were strong from the beginning of the occupation despite the extreme rigor of the German regime. After the drastic punishment of its initial undertaking, the underground limited its activities to sabotage and to sending news to the government in exile. The population adopted the attitude of an outward compliance which concealed a strongly rebellious mood. Everybody felt that any open action had to be delayed until the situation gave a certain reasonable hope.

The first revolutionary acts were spontaneously committed in several small towns on the second and third of May and in Prague,

110

on the evening of the fourth of May. By noon on the fifth of May the revolution was in full swing. It is interesting how the masses of population felt that the time was ripe and that the first opportunity for a hopeful revolution was imminent. Their evaluation of the situation was basically correct. The revolution was carried out victoriously, and on the eighth of May in the afternoon the commanding general of the German armies signed a full surrender of all German armies in Bohemia. Subsequent analysis revealed that the people of Bohemia actually selected the very first favorable moment.[41]

Their judgment about the situation certainly was not a rational and conscious one. Most of the revolutionaries were simple people who did not check consciously all the present political and military conditions. Some did not even have the intention of starting a revolution. They simply felt there were no longer good reasons to accept a position of inferiority imposed by the German soldiers and SS men. They felt that finally they could oppose the Germans' arrogant behavior, and they began to fight individual German soldiers in the streets.

It is interesting that for more than five years the same individuals had kept their hatred within legal limits. Suddenly they did not. The change occurred simultaneously in thousands of individuals. I take it as chiefly the result of a rather vague but convincing feeling that the probability of being caught and punished rapidly decreased. The revolutionaries, chiefly unconsciously, compiled the numerous bits of international and local news, as well as personal observations. It was rather a gradual process of a continuous, chiefly unconscious, formation of a judgment not dissimilar to the formation of the judgment of a professor reading a student's paper.

The judgment of the people proved to be fairly correct. It could be objected that other similar revolutions have been crushed, for instance, the Polish revolution in Warsaw in 1944. That is true. Only it seems to me that some components of the unconscious judging processes of Polish revolutionaries were different. The latter could not expect that the Red army at the gates of Warsaw would not help them in the least.

The feeling-judgments of masses generally are rather less dependable than the judgments of their leaders because they are based on less information. But although largely unconscious, they lead people who have no time or opportunity to make a more conscious and systematic judgment into a fairly satisfactory course of action.

During the German occupation, it was interesting to follow the successive changes in the development of an unconscious evaluation

111

of what the Czech people could dare and what they could not. Often I admired some of my friends in the office where I worked, who were extremely sensitive to all political and military events and were able to guess very precisely what any particular German in the given situation would tolerate and what he would not stand. These guesses were not founded on rational grounds; these people just felt (using unconscious judgments) what the German state of mind was after the latest developments.

PROBLEM SOLVING BY DIRECT ACTION

Now we have to turn to a still more evasive type of unconscious reasoning, the existence of which may be accepted or denied with almost equally good grounds. We have in mind sudden actions which are not based on any feeling but which at least in some cases are based on unconscious reasoning processes.

A striking example of such unconscious thinking processes is given by the psychologist von Allesch.[42] Koffka reports the following about von Allesch's experience. "During the war he was on a patrol in the Alps. He had to make a descent from a rocky crag by means of a chimney whose upper mouth gaped about ten meters under and far to the side of his position. Having climbed down on a rope he found himself hanging in the air and several meters to the left of the chimney, with no more rope for a further descent which would have landed him on a ledge by which he had hoped to reach the chimney. He determined to reach the opening by swinging on the rope. In doing this the rope slipped from his feet, and his hands were not able to support his weight. He felt 'This is the end.' The next moment the author realized (and this point is absolutely certain in his observation) that he had taken hold of the rope with his teeth. . . . In the next moment his feet waving in the air had caught hold of a projecting piece of a slab (and thus he succeeded in saving himself and reaching the chimney). The important point in the process is that this action, *not* belonging to the technique of mountain climbing, never previously considered, and of course never previously practiced . . . arose spontaneously without any conscious deliberation. The event regulated itself." Koffka adds that ". . . the solution was *not* produced by an act of thought, but . . . the stress between Ego and surrounding field succeeded in finding *that* movement which alone could relieve it."

It is interesting to notice that there was no "conscious deliberation." This expression, Allesch's own, would allow the supposition that there was possibly some unconscious thought. Anyway, our incomplete knowl-

112

edge of thinking process allows for both: that there was either unconscious thought or that there was no thought, but only a direct finding of a solution by the stress between the ego and the environment. I am inclined to believe that there was unconscious thought, since the experiments by Ruger with the so-called thoughtless solutions of mechanical puzzles support the hypothesis of unconscious thought operations even in more complex situations.[43]

Perhaps Allesch's seemingly original solution can also be understood as an imitation of an unrecollected or forgotten model. It could have been, for instance, an old childhood experience of having seen a parrot keeping himself on a perch by its beak. Such an experience could have been unconsciously used and adapted to the present emergency situation.

The unconscious adaptations of Allesch's type may occur, for instance, during races of any kind, in a critical business situation, during an emergency surgical operation, in case of dangerous accidents, floods, fires, when driving a car very fast, when playing a very active game (like tennis, football, basketball), in a critical social situation, and so on. They may save the situation in favor of the individual or group; but they rarely create new social patterns of behavior, new values, norms, or techniques. Half-original adjustments of this type, however, occur frequently.

The chairman of a stormy meeting, who is not able to master it, may start singing the national anthem. It proves to be a successful although unpremeditated, means of calming the stormy situation. Later on, he may find that many years ago he observed the calming effect of the national anthem in a slightly similar situation. An unemployed man, hard-pressed by the needs of a large family, may impulsively start a new economic activity which saves him. This new activity is an adaptation of an old unrecollected experience from childhood.

The reactions stimulated by tense or difficult social situations, which are not really emergency cases, are much more frequent than real emergency solutions.

For instance, we may solve a certain embarrassing social situation by looking for our glasses or keys. Unless such a type of reaction has been learned or imitated from a social model, it may be due to the stress between the ego and the situation or to the unconscious reasoning.

Similar is sometimes the behavior of speakers when they deliver a speech or answer the questions. They may speak without having a clear idea of what they will say. I know from my own experience that not infrequently I have said something in my speeches that did not have any conscious background in my mind. Occasionally I listened to myself as to a third person. It went so far that sometimes I asked myself "What will the fellow say now?" The reasoning, as well as its results, were so far unconscious, that I had to listen to myself to realize it. The verbal behavior was a kind of direct reaction to the situation.[44]

INSIGHT

Wertheimer and Koffka understand insight as the sudden grasping of certain chiefly mathematical, spatial, or social relations. Köhler, on the other hand, was interested in a direct understanding of causal relations between the subject and the outside conditions[45] (the refreshing effect of a glass of cool beer on a warm day is understood as caused by it) or of the possible physical relation between two objects (two sticks put together by a chimpanzee in order to reach a banana). Later students of insight stretched its meaning considerably so that it also includes the solution of a problem which has been deliberately sought for.

The new grasping of certain relations or solution of a problem in insight seems to result from certain unconscious mental operations. Different parts of the sudden new view which opened to our internal sight must have been organized gradually before the last illuminating grasp occurred. The examples given by Wertheimer and Koffka point to it convincingly.[46] The solving of certain mathematical equations, for instance, supposes several steps of thought, some of which are unconscious (see p. 130-131).

Insight may be concerned with a real present situation (as perceived) or an imagined situation, physical or social. In a social situation there are persons, objects, institutional backgrounds, surroundings, purposes of the meeting, personal plans of the people present, possibly orders or wishes of other people; there are laws and regulations, possible dangers, expectations, the behavior of the individuals, and other elements. At the time we enter such a situation, certain of these conditions and relations may be unknown to us. Such a situation is very similar to an equation with several unknowns. There are only two major differences: first, we may not know whether there are any unknowns at all and if so, how many there are; and secondly, in trying to solve the equation, we do not follow any consciously learned rules. We use any suitable mental operations, especially insight.

All of us have sometimes had the experience of suddenly grasping the meaning of a perplexing social situation. This may happen in a business meeting, in political negotiations, in an informal social gathering,

114

or in the classroom. The number of unknowns increases with the number of persons we deal with.

The discovery of the hidden motives of other people is especially difficult when, as it happens, the individuals themselves are not aware of them. The difficulties in achieving a correct insight are then extreme.

The social importance of insight will be more fully understood from a discussion of incubation.

INCUBATION

New grasping of the mutual relation of the different aspects of a situation may sometimes require a certain time. The problem may "intentionally [be] laid on one side, in order to be thought of again. Nevertheless, . . . after days, weeks, or months . . . we find to our great astonishment that we have undergone a mental regeneration" and that new convictions "have already become quietly lodged there."[47] This is what William James labeled "incubation" (after Hartmann's "digestion" and Schopenhauer's "unconscious rumination" had been abandoned). Morton Prince says that when we have a complicated question to decide, but feel that we cannot do it offhand, we . . . "take the matter 'under advisement.' . . . Now what we . . . do is to put the problem into our minds and leave it so to speak to incubate. . . . All happens as if subconscious processes had been at work. . . ."[48]

Incubation may also occur without the seeking of a solution to a problem. Prince says that "stored neurograms may undergo subconscious incubation . . . to finally burst forth in ripened judgment, beliefs, and convictions, as is so strikingly shown in sudden religious conversions and allied mental manifestations."[49] Murphy[50] and many other authors also point to the sudden character of the end phase of incubation.

Blanshard distinguishes two types of incubation. In the first type, the "consciousness supplies a litter of fragments and leaves it to the lower self to introduce order among them." In the second type, the subconscious fills in the framework supplied by the consciousness.[51]

A number of historical cases of incubation of creative minds are well known. Blanshard cites Spencer ("and thus, little by little . . . without conscious intention or appreciable effort, there would grow up a coherent and organized theory", *Autobiography,* p. 401); Henry James (who dropped his main idea "for the time into the deep well of unconscious cerebration: not without the hope, doubtless, that it might eventually emerge . . . with . . . a notable increase of weight"); O. W. Holmes (every new idea of a thinker "will be growing when he is least

115

conscious of it"); R. L. Stevenson ("when a story was brewing in his mind, he could commit the theme of it to his 'Brownies', who would elaborate it for him in sleep"); and Wilamowitz-Moellendorf (who says that "the spirit goes on working in sleep . . .").[52] Wallas,[53] Dewey,[54] Vinacke[55] and others also recognize incubation as a phase of the thinking processes although they sometimes label it illumination. It seems to occur continually during the creative process.[56]

Incubation helps our understanding of social situations. When the relations between the different components of the social situation are not clear, we often drop our conscious efforts for a while until the unconscious incubation brings forth the desirable understanding.

Incubation is useful in understanding personal relations of people. How often are we puzzled about what the feelings and attitudes of one person are toward another, what resentment keeps two people apart, what conflicting elements are behind their mutual reactions! Similarly, sometimes we may wonder about behavior of people toward ourselves. We need to adjust to a puzzling or to a tense situation; but the known facts, overheard utterances, and the noticed gestures do not yield any clear meaning of it. Next morning we may see it clearly. All these have arranged themselves unconsciously in meaningful relations.

Unconscious incubation also helps us to find out the proper place and social consequences of our own plans. It may reveal to us the conflicting and the harmonious points of two or more values, rights, personal interests, groups, or institutions which were not clear to us. It may make clear the mutual relation of two norms, rules, attitudes, and the relation of these toward persons, groups, institutions, and social situations. By producing a clear picture of the social relations, the process of incubation secures for us a necessary basis for a proper reaction. Then we are able to decide which of the norms, rules, values, personal or group interests, and wishes we shall meet and in what degree, which others we shall satisfy only partially or not at all. Incubation is instrumental in keeping our right place in our society and culture.

The second of Blanshard's types of incubation seems to have a more moderate role in social life. When a speaker prepares a speech or an artist a performance, it is sometimes sufficient to work out the main framework of what he intends to do. During the days before the performance, the details may unconsciously fill in so that shortly before the appropriate date the performer is ready.

RECKONING WITH UNCONSCIOUS REALITIES

In the chapter on unrecollected experiences, we discussed the

116

influence of unconscious assumptions on our behavior. They influence our thinking, too. Our plans for the future, our judgments about present conditions or about certain persons take several such realities into consideration. This is recognized fully by certain writers such as Ryan,[57] Dewey, Mannheim, and others. Dewey says: "A person in pursuing a consecutive train of thoughts takes some system of ideas for granted (which, accordingly, he leaves unexpressed, 'unconscious'). . . . Explicit thinking goes on within the limits of what is implied or understood."[58] Those who tried to untie the famous Gordian knot were unsuccessful because of the unconscious assumption that the cord should not be damaged. Alexander the Great was the first to reject this assumption and untied the knot by cutting it with his sword.

The operation of similar unconscious assumptions has been proved experimentally. We cannot solve certain picture puzzles as long as we unconsciously assume that the picture is to be held in the regular position, while it can be solved if we turn it through 90 degrees.[59] In another experiment a young man had been given a corked bottle with a marble inside. Being asked to remove the marble without pulling out the cork he pushed the cork inside. To the question why he did not break the bottle, he answered he didn't think it was allowed.[60]

We saw in the chapter about unrecollected experiences that we consider not only a large number of unconscious assumptions, but also their further existence and changes.

In wars or revolutions most people stop making plans, except for the immediate future. They unconsciously assume that unpredictable changes make planning useless.

This example shows clearly that taking for granted the stability of social phenomena in normal times is not merely a matter of habit. There is also a judgment about the continuation or discontinuation of similar conditions in the future. We express our judgment in many different shades, such as that the situation is safe, certain, shaky, doubtful, dubious, or risky.

The unconscious assumptions of our thoughts are automatically kept up-to-date. Whenever some of the conditions in our surroundings change, we automatically make the desirable corrections in the appropriate assumptions so that our future thinking uses correct unconscious premises. Generally, we do not know that such a change in our assumptions has taken place. Nevertheless, this special service operates fairly dependably.

The importance of the use of unconscious assumptions in our thinking for the participation in social life and for our adjustments to it is basic. To what has been said in the chapter on unrecollected experi-

117

ences we would like to add that assumptions can be classified into general, long-lasting, specific, temporary, short-lived, and possibly other categories.

As examples of general and long-lasting assumptions (in addition to those indicated in our previous discussion) we may mention: the validity of laws, the existence of social classes, and the use of English as the national language.

A list of specific assumptions might include, for instance, interests of people with whom we deal, our physical shortcomings, our economic and social status, as well as that of people close to us, and the like.

When writing an article, I noticed that I used certain temporary assumptions. My daughter who was in high school was doing her homework in the adjoining room. She studied English and occasionally asked me about the meaning of some words. Later in the evening she studied French and asked me about the meaning of some French expressions, without telling me that she shifted into French. Unconsciously, I assumed that she was still in English. I answered that there was no such word in English. The same happened when she shifted into Latin without warning. Assumptions of this kind (although generally correct) are used abundantly at any moment of our daily activities.

Some of the empirical studies analyzed the use of unconscious assumptions in social life. Homans, for instance, discussed the assumptions operating in the minds of the wiremen in the well-known Roethlisberger research. It was assumed that a job carrying higher wages, greater skill, and more seniority than another, even a job that is placed "in front of another," is a better job. Also, a man giving orders has a better job.[61] The ability to use the unconscious assumptions is basic in our participation in social life. They are an important part of the existing social structure, social movements, and other social realities. Without them the major part of culture and social structure would not exist. The unconscious assumptions are especially important in the observance of social values and norms. We assume their validity and thus have the reason for their observance. They are equally necessary for the life of social groups.

The use of a large number of assumptions in our thinking generally increases the stability of the social phenomena. We keep the old assumptions as long as we can, unless there is good reason to replace them by new ones.

UNCONSCIOUS COMPARISONS

Already by 1868 Hartmann had claimed that comparisons of two objects are generally carried through unconsciously.[62] Let us discuss more thoroughly the thinking processes involved in them. First, we have to recall that associationists claimed that in such comparisons the image of the previous experience must be aroused, while the Gestalt psychologists claimed that the trace itself with the new stimulus may yield the gradient effect.

Koffka's explanation by gradient effect of our buying a fine hat because we have one hundred dollars in a bank account seems, however, less probable than that of the two telephone clicks (see p. 30). In both of these cases, the two compared items were simultaneous or almost simultaneous. The effect of the first click was almost still in our ears when we heard the second one; the knowledge of the amount of money operates as a steady assumption which is continuously taken into account. But what about the stimuli which succeeded each other after a long interval? Do we compare them again by mere gradient effect? It certainly is very doubtful. In the meantime, we could have heard so many different stimuli that the comparison is probably impossible. We know from the experiment by Wever and Zener[63] that it is difficult to keep the original stimulus as a point of reference after 20 or 25 intervening stimuli.

We are still more inclined to find unconscious thinking in unconscious comparisons of stimuli which occurred years ago and which we did not compare when the second stimulus occurred. We are able, for instance, to tell that a certain object we used five years ago was about one fourth heavier than a similar object used ten years ago.

And what about comparing a physical stimulus with an idea (for instance, that I have $100 in the bank account) or a perceived object or behavior with ideals of beauty, with moral norms, and norms of good taste or other social norms and values, or with our aspirations and plans? It seems to me doubtless[64] that they can be compared only by unconscious thinking.

Now what about unconscious comparisons of two ideas? Is it possible to explain these by mere gradient effect? We do not think so. If we know immediately, without hesitation or deliberation, which one of the two ideas is more original, clear, complex, or perhaps more daring, revolutionary, or systematic, it is due to unconscious comparisons. Nevertheless, our knowledge of thinking processes is not sufficient to claim this with certainty.[65]

Not only rapid and immediate, but also slow comparisons may be due to unconscious thinking processes. If the difference in the value of two men or objects is not clear, we concentrate for a brief moment; and the result of the unconscious comparison emerges into the consciousness. For instance, after someone has asked you which of two of your employees, two opera singers, violinists, speakers, or perhaps hunting dogs is better, and you do not know, you hesitate for a short moment, and after two or three seconds you tell which one is better. During these few seconds your conscious mind may remain blank, but the needed comparison has been produced. The feeling indicating which one of the two compared individuals was better had developed unconsciously.

Our use of unconscious comparisons in social life is practically continuous. They make possible our immediate, appropriate reactions to each of the compared persons, or cultural products and institutions, whether these be books, newspapers, paintings, school class morale, religious meetings, moral deeds, or artistic creations.

Thus, two different unconscious comparing processes, one of them a thinking process, the other a gradient effect, keep us continuously informed about the differences of socially relevant facts. They are helpful in creating new social values and norms by continually producing fairly dependable distinctions. The unconscious, comparing processes also keep us ready to correctly apply the appropriate social norms to all the happenings in social life around us.

ABSTRACTION AND GENERALIZATION

Abstraction and generalization, two related thinking processes, very often go on together. First, we notice a similar property in all individuals of a certain type (abstraction); and then we expect to find this property in all other individuals of this type (generalization). Some psychologists recognize their frequently unconscious character. Although the experiments in abstracting did not aim to illuminate this unconscious character, it is hard to imagine that the experimental subjects proceeded only consciously.[66]

Observations of our daily social life strongly substantiate this conviction. Participation in social life gives rise to a number of ideas about the common properties of people, groups, and institutions. Whether we have the intention of securing such ideas or not, our mind produces them anyway. Even, for instance, if we are not teachers or parents, we unconsciously develop certain knowledge of children. If asked, we are able to give many approximately correct ideas about children, which were produced unconsciously from incidental impressions and marginal observations. If on our trip to Europe we stop only for a day in Paris, we develop in a few hours a number of abstractions about Frenchmen without any intention or awareness. We would probably say that they are vivacious, temperamental, talkative, responsive, and so on.

120

It is hard to overestimate the importance of the unwitting and unconscious abstractions and generalizations in our participation in social life. They reduce the enormous number of various impressions and experiences to a relatively small number of general ideas which are applied successfully, although mostly unconsciously, to new similar situations and facts. They enable our mind to master the enormous complexity of social life to a large extent without engaging our consciousness.

The continuous changes in social life make them a basic tool in our adaptation to it. Although not always correct, the unconsciously produced abstractions are fairly dependable. Considering their rather casual character, they are surprisingly often correct. Their merit consists also in their large number. We would never be able to produce as many of them by conscious thinking.

Unconscious abstractions and generalizations are fundamental for the establishment and operation of social obligations, norms, values, and attitudes.

UNCONSCIOUS COMPUTING SERVICE

In a way similar, although more complex, are the summative processes we label as a computing service. Each object, person, or institution we come in contact with has something like an open account in our mind. The traces of previous experiences with a person or object seem to be added automatically and unconsciously, as has been partly illuminated by the discussion of unrecollected and forgotten experiences.

The computing service is maintained primarily for persons or objects in which we are interested. Yet it seems that in many cases such a computing service operates even without any special interest.

The computing service adds positive instances and subtracts the negative ones; it also weighs them and organizes them. The computing service does not handle only one "currency" as the bank account does. It takes care of prestige, fame, importance, bad or good behavior, intentions, attitudes, moral, artistic, and other values of the persons or institutions, as well as of their emotional experiences, interests, plans, or wishes. All the changes occurring in any of these fields are noted and the total picture retouched accordingly.

The work of the unconscious computing service is so efficient that generally we are able to tell at any time its complicated balance, without giving it additional thought. It certainly is a special kind of social-psychological process which is to be handled separately and to which the psychologists have not yet given due attention.[67]

121

The simplest kind of computing service provides us with an approximate knowledge of how many times we did certain things, how many times we saw or heard certain events. We know, for instance, that we were at the dentist's this winter about four times, that we went to the neighboring city about seven or eight times, that we went to the swimming pool this summer about ten times. Such statements are generally close to the correct figure, although we can give them without delay, without recalling the individual instances, without counting them, and even without being able to recall any of them. The preliminary experiments at Harpur College revealed that 37.4% of students at the end of a semester knew precisely how many times they had skipped class; and 15.7% almost correctly (within the range of 20%). Thus more than half (53.1%) had practical, immediately available information without counting the instances and in most cases without either recall, or the ability to recollect the specific occasions.

Let us take a more complex example. A friend of ours, who plans to buy the same make of fountain pen as we have, asks us how good it is. As a matter of fact it writes nicely, holds a lot of ink; its point does not get dry easily, and it seldom picks up fiber from the paper. Only two or three times in the year did the pen leak a little bit and slightly soil our hands. At the unexpected question of our friend, we say without hesitation that it is a fairly good pen. We feel clearly that it is neither an excellent, very good, nor a very bad pen. On its account there are many good or very good experiences, but also some not very good ones. Nevertheless, before we answered the question, we did not recall them; and we did not subtract the latter from the former either. Our judgment was ready all the time; we did not fabricate one for the present use.

The open account took under consideration also what are the technically achievable qualities of a fountain pen and what we can expect from it. Our present judgment about the fountain pen would necessarily be different from such a judgment ten years later. We know that at the present time every pen must pick up a fiber from the paper once in a while (no better points are produced yet), that it must get dry if not protected by the cap for a while, and that there are very few pens which never leak.

Our unconscious computing service takes into consideration the experiences with the object, as well as with the general circumstances relevant to our judgment about the object. It also uses a frame or rather scale of reference, unconsciously established from a number of previous experiences with other similar objects.

In the statement concerning our fountain pen, we probably summarized most of the forgotten experiences (for instance, the daily satisfaction it gave us), as well as of unrecollected experiences. If we were asked further why we do not think that our pen is an excellent one and what trouble we had with it, then and only then would we bring to our consciousness some of the unrecollected experiences. Usually, we are not able to recall all the troubles we had, and we feel that our judgment looks rather exaggerated (although we know that it is not). Therefore we add "and some other troubles like that." In this way we summarize the forgotten, unrecollected, and perhaps marginal experiences; it is the only possible way to tell the full truth. If, occasionally, we recall further experiences, we feel very happy that we can help remove our embarrassment caused by the discrepancy between our bad memory and our good computing service.

If we are interested in a certain object, person, or institution, or if the social situation impels us to watch it, our computing service probably is more complete and dependable. The teacher, for instance, knows all the time whether a certain pupil is excellent, good, fairly good or rather weak. Similarly, an officer has a ready-made judgment about each of the soldiers of his company and the nurse about her patients. Even unexpected questions can be answered promptly. When, for instance, a parent comes to see his child's teacher, the teacher generally can give his opinion without delay.

The computing service also greatly helps our judgment about the frequency of certain kinds of behavior of people we deal with. Thus, we know the proportion of witty reactions of a friend and say that he is witty, sometimes witty, or not very witty; about a lady we may say that she is a very elegant person, or perhaps that she is usually well-dressed or rather old-fashioned. Comparing the unconsciously established balances of the accounts, we are also ready to say that a person is more elegant or less witty than another.

If we compare the products of the computing service with the conscious judgments, we cannot say that the latter are generally more dependable. Each of the two kinds of judgments has its own advantages and disadvantages. The unconscious summations often include more experiences (for instance, marginal or forgotten) than the conscious ones. They generally have a broader, richer basis. Let us illuminate the point with an example. Suppose that a teacher has a clear and firm intuitive judgment about one of his pupils and wants to check it on factual material. He looks over the results of tests, quizzes and oral examinations, as well as the grades on papers. When he averages the grades, the teacher may feel that the averaged grade overrates or underrates the pupil. Actually, later on, he realizes that some of the good (or bad) qualities of the pupil were not revealed well in his work. They were not taken into consideration in the teacher's conscious judgment; but his computing service used them fully, although unconsciously. This certainly was the reason for his trust in his intuitive judgment.

On the other hand, the consciously established judgments are more systematic; and their often less complete, factual basis is more dependable. Only rarely do they take into account certain conditions omitted by the computing service.

With the help of the computing service we are able to follow the constant changes in the character of institutions, social currents, personalities, and social values; and we can react in a suitable manner. We are socially up-to-date, ready for well-adjusted participation in social life. The great advantages of the computing service, which cannot be secured by any other means are: 1) immediate availability of the balance, 2) the inclusion of instances we cannot recall, 3) the inclusion of events over a long period of time, 4) the relative dependability of the service, 5) the full preparedness of the individual for the well-adjusted actions and reactions, 6) the large number of such judgments which cannot be equaled by any conscious effort.

Another product of the computing service is the development of the feeling that a certain kind of behavior is expected or obligatory. The more frequent it is and the more generally it is accepted, the stronger is its normative character. We grant that in some instances this same phenomenon may also be conceptualized as learning; the fact that it depends on repeated encounters with certain events gives it, however, the special character akin to computing.

The normative coloring of the results of the computing service may have the meaning of physical necessity, social desirability, or social obligation. The mildest degree of social desirability is, for instance, the feeling that on a particular occasion it would be good to wear a certain kind of tie, that we should be able to discuss a certain topic currently popular in social conversations, that we should avoid mentioning a certain rather ticklish question, and so on. The degree of formality in dress and speech may be more binding. Still more binding in a certain group may be the avoidance of certain words. A strong feeling of obligation also develops from the fact that certain objects are always kept in a certain place.

A rather complex example of normative products of the computing service may be given from the postwar, political life in Czechoslovakia in 1945-48. Many Czech and Slovak communist leaders lived in exile after 1939, chiefly in Moscow and in London. After more than five

124

years, they returned to Czechoslovakia and became members of the government and of different governmental bodies. The disorganization of political, social, and economic life at that time raised a great number of problems; and it was interesting to watch the differences in attitudes and approaches of these two communist groups to these problems. The differences were consistent. The Moscow group always proposed and defended hard, ruthless, and inhuman measures, use of terrorism, of lies, and frauds. It did not respect human rights, or even human life. The London group was consistently milder and more often used democratic methods.

The London group was under the strong influence of democratic ways of political life in England. Its members were more inclined to feel unlawful measures or injustice as such; in their speeches they appealed more to the moral basis of socialism and communism, while the Moscow group preached strict revenge and violence.

If we take into consideration that both groups had the same ideology, obeyed the same general orders from Moscow, and followed the same political aims, we may be rather astonished. Evidently the difference in the experiences of the previous five or more years, which were unconsciously computed, gives a satisfactory explanation.

Unconscious normative summations (as we may label these balances of computing service) greatly aid our adjustments to social situations whenever social expectations, norms or values are not formulated or clearly established. They are the basis of our feelings that a certain behavior is or is not in good taste, decent, becoming, just, that it belongs or does not belong to a certain position, office, situation, etc.

If we are asked to give money for a charitable goal, we find our decision in the unconscious knowledge of what we and other people have generally donated in similar situations. It appears as a feeling that a certain amount of money is not enough, is too much, or is just right. A foreigner in a similar situation feels completely lost, without any basis for making a reasonable decision.

The amount of work we expect from our subordinates, the way we formulate our orders, organize our work, all this is partly, or sometimes chiefly, based on such directive, unconsciously established computations. They continuously help to direct our social behavior, often only by inconspicuous hints, inclinations or preferences.

In this way also many of our moral and esthetic feelings find their rather safe basis. Even our scientific methods are partly the result of unconscious directive summations. The number of facts necessary for a valid induction is often brought out not only by rules of scientific method, but also by the unconscious summations of the working standards of our teachers, colleagues, great masters of the field, and other scientists. The normative summations help us also to find out the degree to which the accepted norms are to be observed. There are many possible degrees of laxity or strictness in the observance of different norms by different persons, social classes, occupations, and localities. Think only of cleanliness, honesty, truthfulness, good appearance, friendliness, in connection with various social classes, with New England, with the South and the West; think also of these norms in connection with different situations like formal dinners, camping, hunting, or military life.

The degree to which certain norms are observed changes in a matter of years. We believe that since the war, respect for the flag has increased spontaneously in the U. S. On the other hand, the amount of the surface of the body we have to keep covered in public has decreased. In all these cases, the basic norms remain practically the same, only the degree of observation varies.

Besides giving a correct and up-to-date degree of validity to the accepted norms, the normative summations establish the groundwork for the change of norms. The feeling that certain behavior should be more accepted than before or that certain tolerated behavior is no longer suitable may become accepted norms.

Sherif[68] was the first to point to the origin of social norms in the frame of reference established spontaneously from the behavior of the members of the group, by some of the processes we labeled as unconscious computing. Only he did not include both positive and negative experiences and their balance; he did not study the influence of experiences over a long range of time and he did not study the forming of frames of reference from experiences in which the individual is not interested. Although he recognized their unconscious character, he did not stress it enough. The unconscious computing service covers a very broad area, often encompassing simultaneously many different events in all relevant fields, and operates practically continuously.

CONCEPT FORMATION AND USE

From the experiments by Hull and Smoke, we know that we form certain concepts without awareness.[69] Hull, in fact, considers the conscious formation of concepts spurious; for him, they are rather an artifact.[70] The importance of the unconscious formation of concepts for social life naturally is enormous. It is probably greater in the establishment of practical concepts than in the establishment of scientific concepts. The ability to form concepts unconsciously helps the average individual to understand what is fair play, what is loyalty and solidarity. It helps him in conveniently (although unconsciously) grouping people, institutions, objects and their properties in order to deal with them accordingly. It is a continuous process.

We know that some objects or people do or do not belong together if we think of them from the point of view of their usefulness, moral standard, interests, hopes, friendliness, and so on. We know many of their common and different properties, even if there is no concept in our culture for them. Sometimes we even give them a new name. But the use of such unconsciously established concepts does not depend on the name given to them. We use them anyway. Thus, we distrust people of a certain kind, although we cannot say clearly what kind of people these are. Similarly, we like or avoid books, places, and social affairs that have certain properties we rather "feel" than really know.

It is easy to understand the importance of the unconsciously produced concepts for social life. Some personal, as well as social attitudes, values, norms, and other similar configurations are based on them. Concepts are used whenever these are applied. And the application pertains only to a certain type of people and not to other people. Likewise, application of normative summations is based on the unconsciously established concepts.

PRODUCTIVE AND CREATIVE THINKING

Productive and creative thinking brings new solutions, approaches, methods and concepts. They may be new only for the individual himself. The first understanding of certain mathematical operations by a grade school pupil may have a productive character.

At the present time, creative thinking is one of the few fields of the psychic life, the unconscious character of which is recognized rather generally. Although some psychologists do not speak of its unconscious aspects (for instance, Wertheimer, who wrote a book about productive thinking), there is no doubt that certain creative processes, as described by them, are unconscious.

Let us discuss, first, what is called productive thinking. Max Wertheimer sees in it a special type of thinking processes which are barely included in the thinking processes as given by formal logic, or in those described by associationists. He mentions chiefly reorganization, centering, grouping, segregation, and structural transposability of items, data, or relations in a certain situation.

Productive thinking is initiated by vectors originating in strains, stresses, and tensions produced by the problem situation. In other cases, intentions or desires may be the source of productive thinking.[71]

127

Wertheimer gives a number of examples of productive thinking. Interesting for us is the case of two boys playing badminton. The older boy is much better; he wins all the games. The younger boy has no chance. He resents it and finally refuses to play. The older boy insists that he continue playing. He conceives the situation only from the point of view of the winner, who is pleased by winning. After his vain attempts to make the younger boy play again, he finally starts to view the situation from the point of view of the other boy. He understands now the bad feelings of his opponent; he starts also to understand the situation from the point of view of the game itself; he understands that some reciprocity is necessary. Finally, in order to satisfy his wish to play again, the wish to play a nice game and to keep the friendly relations with the other boy, he finds a solution: he proposes to play by keeping the bird going between the two boys as long as possible and counting how many times it goes back and forth without falling. Wertheimer says that he "spoke happily like someone who discovered something. It was a new idea to him . . ." The solution "involved the transition from a superficial attempt to get rid of a trouble . . . to dealing with it in a productive way."[72]

In all, four different changes were achieved: 1) transition from a onesided view to the centering required by the objective structure of the situation, 2) a change in the meaning of the parts in accordance with their structural place, role, and function, 3) a view of the situation in terms of "good structure," and 4) a trend to face the issues honestly and to draw the conclusions from it.

The question is now how far these processes are or may be unconscious. Wertheimer says that the older boy did not have thoughts, he only "felt his way through." This points to the unconscious aspects of his thinking processes.

In these processes, says Wertheimer, "past experiences, previous knowledge and orientation" are often involved. The use of these may, of course, also be unconscious. It seems to us that Wertheimer was aware of their unconscious use, although he did not say so. Closer analysis of his examples of the understanding of certain mathematical or geometrical relations points to it rather convincingly.

Nathan Israeli supplemented Wertheimer's types of productive thinking by additional factors: emotions and drive factors, as well as social influences.[73] These may, likewise, operate unconsciously or possibly be totally unconscious (compare pp. 162, 164 and 211-214).

Unconscious recentering from our own personal interests and situation to the interests and situation of other persons or groups is a basic mental operation in the life of every member of society. It occurs first during the process of socialization of children. The long and hard way of small children from the strongly egocentric orientation to the co-operative and morally autonomous stage (so well analyzed by Piaget[74]) is basically a process of prevailingly unconscious recentering. A similar recentering process, together with reorganization and grouping, occurs in conversions of all kinds. Less dramatic and conspicuous are these processes in the development of adherence to a new group and in assimilation of the members of the group to it.

Other examples of recentering in social life are: falling in love, developing adherence to a social value, becoming an enthusiastic follower of a new idea or a new leader, worshipping a new hero, developing a love for a foreign culture, and so forth. Some adjustments of a shopkeeper to his customers, of a lawyer to the viewpoints of the jury, or of a public servant to the people he serves, may be achieved with its help. Also, the adjustments to the members of the family, or the fraternity; the adjustments of a political leader to the members of the party, or the teacher to his pupils; and many others are often based on unconscious recentering.

A wealth of material has been gathered about the creative processes of outstanding creative minds. Some of it comes from autobiographical sources (like writings by J. S. Hadamard, H. P. Poincaré, H. Helmholtz; see also p. 115), some from letters (for instance, by W. A. Mozart), from persons close to the creative person (like Eckermann), from specialists who have studied the creative activity of an outstanding mind (as have J. L. Lowes, B. C. Squires, A. H. Nethercot, C. F. E. Spurgeon, A. E. Armstrong), as well as from students of creativity and inventiveness. Blanshard, who gathered the pertinent information from books of this kind, says: "Mozart wrote, 'When I am, as it were, completely myself . . . my ideas flow best and most abundantly. *Whence* and *how* they come I know not nor can I force them. . . .' 'Gluck said thoughts flowed to him, and he knew not whence they came . . .' Goethe said of *Werther* that he had written it 'somewhat unconsciously, like a sleepwalker.' Milton, after a long drought, would sometimes call for his daughter in the middle of the night and ask her to seize a pen to help him catch the verse that was descending in unexpected floods. . . . 'Ce n'est pas moi qui pense,' wrote Lamartine; 'ce sont mes idées qui pensent pour moi.' "[75] Fr. Nietzsche wrote: "If one had the least vestige of superstition, one could hardly refrain from supposing himself to be . . . merely the medium of higher forces . . . One hears, one does not search; one receives, one does not ask who gives; like lightning an idea flashes out, appearing as something necessary . . . "[76] "The creative magic that united all these particles into

129

integral works of art, which give no signs of being mosaics, was unconscious" is Miller's[77] comment on Coleridge's work while Dashiell
ends his discussion of Coleridge and others by saying that ". . . rational
processes commonly go on in a person without his being conscious of
them."[78]

As for scientists, Blanshard summarizes the known cases in the
following lines: "A well-known case is the discovery of the method of
'quaternions' by Sir W. Rowan Hamilton . . . For fifteen years, he says,
he had been haunted by the problem which this method finally solved.
When at last the solution came, it came abruptly and unannounced;
it 'started into life, or light, fullgrown, on the 16th of October, 1843, as
I was walking . . .; all that was necessary was to seize a note-book
and jot down the new equations . . .' Gauss had been trying to prove
a theorem in arithmetic for four years. 'As a sudden flash of light
the enigma was solved. For my part I am not in a position to point
to the thread which joins what I knew previously and what I have
succeeded in doing.' Most of the original work of Henri Poincaré
seems to have been done in the same way . . . On one occasion after
two weeks of fruitless effort on a problem of great technicality, he went
sleeplessly to bed, when suddenly

> 'the ideas came surging up in a crowd; I could feel them jostl-
> ing each other until two of them would lock together, so to
> speak, and form a stable combination. By morning I had estab-
> lished the existence of a class of Fuchsian functions.' 'I now
> wished to represent these functions by the quotient of two
> series; this idea was fully conscious and reflective. . . . At this
> point I left Caen . . . The events of the journey drove my
> mathematical work from my mind; but, arriving at Coutances,
> we were getting into an omnibus for some excursion or other
> when, at the moment of putting my foot on the step, and with-
> out anything, so far as I could see, in my previous thoughts to
> prepare me, it struck me that the transformations I had used
> to define the Fuchsian function were identical with those of
> non-Euclidian geometry. . . .' His further progress in this field
> was of the same sort, an alternation of intense but apparently
> fruitless application and sudden bursts of insight. 'It is needless
> to multiply instances; the reports I should have to make about
> my other researches would be entirely similar . . . the role of
> this unconscious work in mathematical invention seems to me
> incontestable.' "[79]

Hartmann, who likewise, considered the work of mathematicians as an outstanding example of intuitive, unconscious solution of problems, points especially to the fact that they make intuitive leaps, omitting a number of terms so that from the premises the conclusion springs into consciousness. He gives chessplayers as another good example. They do not consider a hundred thousand possible moves, but only five or six. The good chessplayer, when looking at the chessboard, sees immediately the only two good moves.[80]

Many professional inventors declare that their best ideas occurred to them while they were doing something else, like conversing, listening to a sermon, dressing, bathing, or something other than working on their invention.[81]

In agreement with William James, Blanshard distinguishes two different types of unconscious creative processes. The first type is used by creative minds who notice the bond of identity and the other by those who merely obey it. The first are men of science and philosophers, the latter are artists, men of intuition.

According to Blanshard,[82] the creative processes may be unconscious in four different degrees. The first degree is very light, and the processes may become conscious by a mere shifting of attention. In the second degree, the final steps seem fully conscious while the hidden stepping stones by which they are reached cannot be discovered by introspection. In the third degree not only the materials, but also the process of inference are unconscious. The fourth degree is, so to speak, doubly unconscious: the conscious processes (succession of images) are mere symbols of further unconscious processes like those, for instance, in dreams or in mathematical operations under hypnosis.

The social adjustments of a creative personality, through unconscious creative thinking, lead to new, original patterns of behavior. These often are not strictly personal adjustments. Speaking for himself, the poet in reality speaks for the reader, for his nation, for humanity, or at least for his class or group.

Still more impersonal are the creations of scientists. Their problems are basically problems of the whole society; they make them part of their own life, but the chief meaning of the solution of the problem is social.

Creative thinking is not only artistic and scientific: it is used in many other fields such as political, economic, administrative, educational, and so forth.

Unconscious creative thinking is a substantial part of the creative thinking process. Thus it is to be credited with a considerable part of the development of culture. It contributes equally to the development of subcultures of special groups (religious, artistic, hobby groups, and others). The social structure is partly its product, too.

Unconscious thinking accompanies most of our participation in and adjustment to social life. It is one of the powerful means of the application of the existing social and cultural norms and, still more, of the carrying through of social and cultural changes. Likewise, the life of groups depends on it to a high extent.

FOOTNOTES TO CHAPTER NINE

1. T. A. Ryan in F. G. Boring, H. S. Langfeld and H. P. Weld, *Foundations,* p. 185.
2. See, for instance, T. A. Ryan, *op. cit.,* p. 197; E. R. Guthrie and A. L. Edwards, *Psychology,* p. 294; J. F. Dashiell, *Fundamentals,* p. 547; J. Dewey, *How We Think,* Heath, Boston, 1910, p. 15.
3. For instance, W. E. Vinacke, *The Psychology of Thinking,* p. 7.
4. G. W. Allport says that thought "facilitates adjustments" (*Personality,* p. 555). E. Heidbreder says that "thinking, as a psychological activity, is some kind of adjustive activity . . ." (in T. G. Andrews, *Methods of Psychology,* J. Wiley and Sons, New York, 1948, p. 97). W. E. Vinacke thinks that "as behavior, then, thinking can fruitfully be treated in terms of adjustment" (*op. cit.,* p. 7. See also pp. 6 and 21).
5. Eduard Hartmann, *Philosophy of the Unconscious,* Harcourt, Brace and Co., New York, 1931, I., pp. 301-324. First German edition in 1868.
6. Gustave LeBon, *The Crowd,* esp. pp. 28, 64.
7. See, for instance, J. Rossman, *The Psychology of the Inventor,* Washington D. C., The Inventors Publ. Co., 1931; G. Wallas, *The Art of Thought,* Harcourt, Brace and Co., New York, 1926; J. L. Moreno, *The Theatre of Spontaneity,* Beacon House, New York, 1947; J. L. Lowes, *The Road to Xanadu;* C. F. E. Spurgeon, *Shakespeare's Imagery,* The University Press, Cambridge, 1936; S. Freud, *Leonardo da Vinci,* Random House, New York, 1947.
8. J. S. Hadamard, *An Essay on the Psychology of Invention in the Mathematical Field,* Princeton Univ. Press, 1949.
9. H. Poincaré, "Mathematical Creation," in *The Foundations of Science,* The Science Press, New York, 1913.
10. *Op. cit.,* p. 92.
11. M. Sherif and C. W. Sherif, *Groups in Harmony and Tension,* Harper and Br., New York, 1953, p. 233.
12. M. Sherif and H. Cantril, *The Psychology of Ego-Involvements,* J. Wiley and Sons, New York, 1947, p. 43.
13. See W. E. Vinacke, *op. cit.,* p. 187.
14. R. Stagner and T. F. Karwoski, *Psychology,* p. 417.
15. C. Kluckhohn and H. A. Murray, *Personality in Nature, Society and Culture,* A. A. Knopf, New York, 1959, p. 8.
16. W. James, *The Principles of Psychology,* Dover Publ., Inc., New York, 1950, II, p. 361.
17. A. R. Lindesmith and A. L. Strauss, *Social Psychology,* H. Holt and Co., New York, 1956, p. 254.
18. W. E. Vinacke, *op. cit.,* p. 289.

19. G. Humphrey, *Directed Thinking*, Dodd, Mead, and Co., New York, 1948, p. 129.
20. E. Heidbreder, *op. cit.*, p. 121.
21. T. A. Ryan, *op. cit.*, in E. G. Boring, H. S. Langfeld and H. P. Weld ed., *Foundations*, p. 201.
22. G. Murphy, *Personality*, p. 411.
23. S. Körner even claims that we may accept without awareness any rule logically following from accepted rules (*Conceptual Thinking*, Publ. of the University of Bristol, Cambridge, 1955, p. 6.)
24. B. Blanshard, *The Nature of Thought*, G. Allen and Unwin, London, 1948, *II*, p. 175.
25. T. A. Ryan in E. G. Boring, H. S. Langfeld and H. P. Weld, ed., *Foundations*, p. 201.
26. G. Murphy, *op. cit.*, pp. 357, 358.
27. M. B. Arnold says: "The appraisal that arouses an emotion . . . is not the result of reflexion . . ." Such "judgments are direct, immediate, non-reflective, non-intellectual, automatic, 'instinctive,' 'intuitive.'" (*Emotion and Personality*, Vol. I, pp. 172, 175.)
28. W. Köhler, *The Mentality of Apes*, Harcourt, Brace and Co., New York, 1927, pp. 322, 323.
29. W. Stern, *Psychology of Early Childhood, up to the Sixth Year of Age*, H. Holt and Co., New York, 1930, p. 138.
30. G. W. Allport, *Personality*, p. 534. In complete harmony with our standpoint, Allport says also: ". . . it is scarcely accurate to speak of the perception of personality; for personality is not all given at any one time." (p. 545).
31. K. Young says: "We can define intuition as a method of formulating beliefs, postulates and hypotheses, or of drawing conclusions or generalizations, in which not all the steps in the mental processes are known to the individual." (*Personality*, p. 268.) G. Murphy defines intuition as a product of "organized activity of which only a small fragment flashes meteor-like through a corner of the conscious field" (*op. cit.*, p. 357). E. Hartmann thinks that "in intuition the same logical links are present in the Unconscious" and that "only the last term comes into consciousness" (*op. cit.*, I, p. 316).
32. We know from experiments with chimpanzees and from experiences of blind people who recovered their vision that it takes time before they learn to organize their visual field and that therefore this organization is not inborn or spontaneous but learned. This learning at the beginning certainly includes much thinking (A. H. Riesen, "Arrested Vision," *Scientific American*, July, 1950, pp. 16-19).
33. Quoted by R. E. L. Faris, *Social Psychology*, p. 184.
34. F. C. Bartlett, *Remembering: A Study in Experimental and Social Psychology*, Cambridge, Univ. Press, 1932, especially p. 31.
35. G. Humphrey, *op. cit.*, p. 78.
36. See E. Hartmann, *op. cit.*, I., pp. 310, 311.
37. The newly appointed governor of a West Indian island who didn't feel competent to serve as judge, complained about his worries to his friend Lord Mansfield, one of the greatest English lawyers of the 18th century. Lord Mansfield gave him the advice ". . . to mistrust his formal reason" and to rely "in legal matters on his subconscious judgment." He

invited him to decide according to his notions of common sense but never to give his reasons: " 'For,' said he, 'your judgment will probably be right, but your reasons certainly will be wrong.' . . . Some years afterwards, Lord Mansfield, while sitting on Privy Council appeals, had a judgment of this Governor brought before his court, which seemed . . . absurd in its reasons . . . . It was found, however, that the decision itself was perfectly right. It appeared that, at first, the Governor had acted on Lord Mansfield's advice by deciding without giving reasons; and, finding that he acquired a great reputation thereby, began to think himself a great lawyer, and then at length, took to giving his reasons with the above-mentioned result." (J. G. Miller, *Unconsciousness*, pp. 197, 198).

38. M. Sherif and C. W. Sherif, *Outline of Social Psychology*, Harper and Bros., New York, 1956, pp. 135-140.
39. S. E. Asch, *Social Psychology*, p. 478.
40. Psychiatrists also sometimes make their appraisals unconsciously (see N. W. Ackerman, *The Psychodynamics of Family Life*, Basic Books, Inc., New York, 1958, p. 174).
41. I know it from my own experience, since I served as vice-chairman of the revolutionary committee.
42. G. J. Allesch, *Zur nichteuklidischen Struktur des phenomenalen Raumes*, Jena, 1931, pp. 148-9, quoted by Koffka, *Principles of Gestalt Psychol.*, pp. 626-27.
43. A short summary of their results is "that new and better ways of dealing with a puzzle often appeared as variation in motor reactions *before* the subject was aware of changing his procedure." (E. Heidbreder, *op. cit.*, p. 105).
44. H. S. Sullivan noticed something similar to it. When somebody speaks publicly, there is in his mind an illusory auditor I_1 then the "talking organism" and finally, another illusory auditor I_2. Thus one sees the incompleteness of exposition and possibilities of misunderstanding, while the talking organism and the auditor I_1 see to the matters of the formulation, vocabulary, grammar, rhetoric and elocution. I_1 is . . . that which is going on in the center of awareness, while I_2 is only marginal, the fringe of awareness. "If I were not rather secure in my ability to function with I_1, if I were 'nervous' . . . most of the I_2 phenomena would receive no attention." (*Conceptions of Modern Psychiatry*, p. 99).
45. The existence of the unconscious grasping of causal relations has been recognized already by E. Hartmann (*op. cit.*, I., p. 308).
46. Although not well understood, insight certainly should not be considered as a mysterious force. Koffka says that it is neither a force nor an explanatory principle. It is neither mechanical nor a consequence of a vitalistic principle. It is a fact containing a problem (*op. cit.*, pp. 628, 631). Some authors use the expression of illumination instead of insight.
47. E. Hartmann, *op. cit.*, I, p. 322.
48. M. Prince, *The Unconscious*, p. 227.
49. M. Prince, *op. cit.*, p. 263.
50. G. Murphy, *op. cit.*, p. 462.
51. B. Blanshard, *op. cit.*, II, p. 192.
52. *Ibid.*, pp. 184, 190, 191.
53. G. Wallas, *op. cit.*, pp. 86-93.
54. J. Dewey, *op. cit.*, p. 284.

55. W. E. Vinacke, *op. cit.*, pp. 243, 245, 248-9, 254.
56. J. E. Eindhoven and W. E. Vinacke, "Creative Processes in Painting," *J. General Psychol.*, 47 (1952), pp. 139-164.
57. T. A. Ryan in E. G. Boring, H. S. Langfeld and H. P. Weld, *Foundations . . .*, p. 209.
58. J. Dewey, *op. cit.*, p. 281. Similarly, K. Mannheim speaks about the unconscious influence of presuppositions on one's point of view (*Ideology and Utopia*, p. 169).
59. T. A. Ryan, *op. cit.*, p. 208-209.
60. G. Humphrey, *op. cit.*, p. 17.
61. G. C. Homans, *The Human Group*, Harcourt, Brace and Co., New York, 1950, pp. 128, 139.
62. E. Hartmann, *op. cit.* I., p. 305.
63. E. G. Wever and K. E. Zener, "The Method of Absolute Judgment in Psychophysics," *Psychol. Review*, 35, 1928, pp. 466-493.
64. See M. Sherif and H. Cantril, *op. cit.*, p. 41; M. Sherif, *Psychology of Social Norms*, p. 85.
65. See L. Long, "A Study of the Effect of Preceding Stimuli upon the Judgment of Auditory Intensities," *Arch. Psychol.*, 209, 1937, p. 55. He says that although the existence of contrast judgments cannot be doubted "an explanation of why contrast operates or what processes (either psychological or physiological) underlie it, must be postponed. . . ."
66. N. L. Munn, *Psychology* (1956), pp. 297-302.
67. One of the very few who discussed at least a narrow part of this unknown field is S. E. Asch. He studied the organizational properties of group impressions. Unfortunately, he did not make the desirable distinction between the spontaneous, unconscious summations and the results of intentional observations (*op. cit.*, p. 235).
68. See pp. 22, 24.
69. C. L. Hull, "Quantitative Aspects of the Evolution of Concepts," *Psychol. Monogr.*, 123, 1920; K. L. Smoke, "An Objective Study of Concept Formation," *Psychol. Monogr.* 191, 1932.
70. *Ibid.*, pp. 81, 85. See also J. S. Bruner, J. J. Goodnow and G. A. Austin, *A Study of Thinking*, J. Wiley & Sons, New York, 1956, pp. 234, 241.
71. M. Wertheimer, *Productive Thinking*, Harper and Br., New York, 1945, p. 198.
72. M. Wertheimer, *op. cit.*, p. 131.
73. Nathan Israeli, "Set Theory Models for Research concerning Creative Thinking and Imagination," *J. of General Psychology*, 60, 1959, pp. 63-96.
74. Jean Piaget, *The Moral Judgment of the Child*.
75. B. Blanshard, *op. cit.*, II, pp. 166-167.
76. A. R. Chandler, *Beauty and Human Nature*, Appleton-Century-Crofts, New York, 1934, p. 329.
77. J. G. Miller, *op. cit.*, p. 184.
78. J. F. Dashiell, *op. cit.*, p. 567.
79. B. Blanshard, *op. cit.*, II., pp. 169-171.
80. E. Hartmann, *op. cit.*, I., pp. 316-318. In a similar way, K. Mannheim speaks about unconscious steps in our thinking (*op. cit.*, p. 92.)
81. See H. G. Barnett, *Innovation, the Basis of Cultural Change*, McGraw-Hill Book Co., New York, Toronto, London, 1953, p. 128.
82. B. Blanshard, *op. cit.*, II., p. 172.

PART THREE

SOCIAL-PSYCHOLOGICAL CONFIGURATIONS

X

EMOTIONS AND FEELINGS

In some previous chapters the emotions and feelings toward people, groups, and institutions appeared to be produced by unconscious processes. We have to supplement what has been said and to give a more systematic picture of it.

Unfortunately, there is no generally recognized definition of emotions and feelings; there is no generally accepted terminology, and there is no generally accepted theory either.

We rather feel that the standpoint of some psychologists who do not make a distinction between emotions and feelings, but use these terms interchangeably is well-founded.[1] The strong emotional states, however, are generally more often called emotions by some psychologists, and the milder emotional states are labeled rather as feelings.[2]

We do not consider as well-founded the distinction which considers emotions as states having an object, while feelings are limited to emotional states without an object;[3] and we do not consider feelings as conscious experiences either.[4]

We do not think that theories considering emotions as arising from a meaning, and feelings from stimulation of sense organs,[5] would prove helpful to us. Similar is our attitude toward theories classing emotions as finished products and feelings as raw material,[6] considering emotions as organized feelings, or, on the contrary, considering feelings as educated emotions.[7]

We will not unnecessarily complicate our situation by speaking of affective states. But we feel free to use, if convenient, the term of sentiment for enduring emotional configurations.

Some of the theories limit the concept of emotions and feelings, as it seems to us, without a satisfactory reason. We do not think (as Stagner does), for instance, that tension-feelings lie out of the field of emotional life. We rather accept the opposite standpoint.[8]

We cannot accept the reduction of emotional states to pleasantness and unpleasantness (as proposed by E. B. Titchener and F. Allport) either. This reduction excludes some tension-feelings and also feelings where there is a strong excitement without a clear tone of pleasantness or unpleasantness. Some of the authors[9] exclude from the category of feelings the vaguely perceived sensations like, for instance, the feelings of emptiness or insecurity. We will not include them in our discussion either.

On the other hand, some writers consider emotional components as being present in every experience, which seems very probable. According to others, they accompany all overt learning and intellectual processes.[10]

Fortunately, we do not need to take any decisive position in regard to the theory of emotions and feelings (such as the excitement theory of Bridges and Stratton, emergency theory of Cannon, theory of pleasantness and unpleasantness, shock theory, strain theory, startle, upset, amazement, and other theories).

Our analysis is based on the conception that emotional life is shaped or in some cases even produced by culture and that social interaction produces certain emotional states. Although not many psychologists share this conception,[11] it is the theory developed by modern sociologists, anthropologists, and social psychologists. Moreover, psychologists indirectly give a helping hand to the cultural explanation of emotions by their insistence that the rich emotional life of an adult individual develops from a small number of original emotions.[12] An explanation of this differentiation of emotions may partly lie in their socialization. Then, too, the rather widely accepted hypotheses that emotions are conditioned and/or learned,[13] that they are organized,[14] integrated,[15] or even that they are quasi topological structures,[16] open another way to their socialization. Kardiner's basic personality also is created by the prevailing requirements of culture. Finally, the sublimation, transference, displacement, and reaction formation of psychoanalysts may often have a social causation.

The basic manifestations and causes of the influences of social life and culture on emotions may be briefly expressed in the following way:

a)
1. Emotions are alike in one culture and different in different cultures;[17] some of them are missing in certain cultures completely;
2. The differences between the emotions in different cultures are clearly expressed by the differences in the dictionaries[18] of respective languages;
3. Emotions are different in different social classes;[19]
4. Emotions change in the history of culture;[20]

b)
  1. Higher emotions (such as religious, moral, esthetic) are more influenced by culture[21] (or even completely produced[22] by the group) than lower emotions based on instinctive drives;
  2. Emotions are imposed by society through (sometimes unrecognized) pressure;[23]
  3. Personal emotions may be changed under social pressure into other, acceptable emotions;[24]
  4. Emotions are solidified by being given a name;[25]
  5. Emotions decay in isolation;[26]
c)
  1. Emotions are stimulated by the group;[27]
  2. They are refreshed by participation in group life.

It seems necessary to distinguish between emotional states of short duration and enduring sentiments.[78] Sentiments often produce emotional states when we get into contact (factual or imaginary) with the object of sentiment.

Let us turn now to the problem of unconscious acquisition, existence, and operation of emotions and feelings. Unconscious acquisition is recognized by Cattell (partly through suggestion).[29] Others also speak about unconscious learning,[30] generalization,[31] formation,[32] and conditioning.[33] Psychoanalysts know about unconscious sublimation, transfer, displacement of emotions, about reaction formation, etc.

The whole field of unconscious acquisition of emotions is, of course, broader. Besides suggestion, learning, and development of emotional habits, generalization, sublimation, transfer, displacement, and others, there is, it seems to us, also unconscious summation and imitation, as well as unconscious organization of several elements into one emotional configuration.

The unconscious existence of certain feelings and emotions has been recognized already by LeBon.[34] The anthropologist Kroeber,[35] speaking about esthetic emotions, says that they spring from the unconscious portions of the mind. Naturally, many psychiatrists recognize the unconscious existence of emotional states, but only a few psychologists like Hart, Pear, Murray,[36] Hartley and Hartley,[37] Miller,[38] Cattell,[39] and French speak of them. French[40] found that sentiments cannot be entirely conscious. They have some unconscious components. The unconscious operation of emotional states, fully recognized by psychiatrists of different schools, is mentioned by psychologists in only exceptional cases.[41]

We will turn our attention first to the temporary emotional states and then to the enduring emotional structures.

UNCONSCIOUS EMOTIONAL STATES

A) ACCEPTANCE

It is well known that a group may produce a variety of emotional states in its members. This happens in small face-to-face groups, as well as in larger ones (audiences). Individuals may also produce emotional states in other individuals as, for instance, a preacher arousing his congregation.

1) By Suggestion[42]

Cattell considers the greater part of sentiments acquired by suggestion as unconscious. Nevertheless, the suggestive word or gesture is generally consciously perceived. Many appeals to feel in a certain way reach us through our consciousness. But despite our awareness of the suggestion, we may not notice the emotional changes induced by it.

We may be fully aware of a newspaper propaganda and be sure that we will not succumb to it. In reality our feelings change gradually and unconsciously, without our noticing it. Possibly, we discover this change later on when we have to react to the pertinent person or nation. If such an occasion does not occur, the effects of the suggestion remain possibly unconscious.

Only in a small number of instances may we not notice consciously that there is pressure on us to feel in a certain way. This happens, for instance, when certain truthful news is selected and arranged in such a way as to arouse a certain emotional reaction without our noticing the arrangement. A great deal of propaganda uses suggestion of this kind. The marginal and subliminal perceptions may also produce certain feelings without the suggestive word or gesture entering the consciousness. Several authors, like Durkheim,[43] Cartwright and Zander,[44] Hartley and Hartley,[45] Gorden[46] and Sherif,[47] claim that the individual may not be aware of the social pressure and of its effects on his behavior; and some of them support their contention by experimental evidence. This probably applies also to emotional states.

The inflection and expression of voice, for instance, is suggestive; but the audience may not be aware of it. Despite that, it often induces the expected feelings very efficiently.

Luchins pointed to some of the conditions increasing the effectiveness of the suggestion (like truthfulness of the suggested idea, obviousness, and clarity of the situation, subject's attitudes, and interpretation of the task).[48] Cantril speaks about a favorable mental context as a condition of suggestibility.[49]

Suggestion may shape lower as well as higher feelings, without awareness. In reference to the lower feelings, we are reminded of how one or two generations ago, verses written on the fans which girls carried at dances shaped unwittingly the love feelings of thousands of educated dancers. Love novels are a powerful means of indirect suggestion of love feelings.[50] Similar is the influence of movies.[51] There is a general experience of having stronger love feelings for the sweetheart after a person sees or reads a good love story. The warmer emotional reaction to the paintings of an artist whose exhibition has been commented upon favorably by the newspapers is likewise a rather general experience. We may sometimes be aware of the changes in our emotional life induced by such indirect suggestion, but in most cases we do not think of them at all; in other cases, we may incorrectly explain the change by other causes: our sweetheart may seem more beautiful today because of a good rest or good mood, the pictures of the painter may seem to be more beautiful because we have discovered certain of their features we had not noticed previously, and so on.

2) By Imitation

Slight unconscious imitations which change our emotional states all day are probably very numerous. How often are we aroused into sharing the moral indignation of people with whom we work! How many impressions of the beauty of nature during a hike reflect the enthusiasm of our friends! How many resentments or sympathies do we experience because other people expressed them!

The extent of imitation of emotional states depends on the number of supporting conditions. Suppose we work in the same room with a man who becomes morally aroused about the dirty trick played on him by our superior. His resentment arouses similar, though weaker, feelings in ourselves. The strength of our imitated feelings depends on whether our moral values and his moral values are similar or different, whether our personal relation to the boss is similar to his, whether we are as sensitive as he is, and so on.

Also equally important is the similarity of outward conditions. Two employees in the same office who have the same salary, the same colleagues, the same type of work, who obey the same regulations, and so on, imitate easily the emotional states of each other as far as the office situation is concerned. When some of the common conditions disappear, the imitation is weaker. It operates fully as long as the employee works in the same office, but not after he leaves or even after he decides to leave. Being in the same situation as our friend is so important a factor that we may share his feelings even if we do not have the opportunity to see his emotional reaction. We imagine his reaction and imitate it. If we have the opportunity of seeing him, then our imitative reaction is due to the co-operation of three processes: first our empathy with his feelings as we perceive them, second, empathy with his feelings as we imagine them, and, third, our empathy with his situation.

Similarly, a retired man shares more fully the feelings of another retired man than does the person who never had such an experience. The mother whose child has been deathly ill is more upset about the fate of another mother with a very ill child. The more numerous or more emotionally charged are these special similar conditions, the stronger the empathy, identification, and imitation.

The most general factor that facilitates imitation is probably the structure of the body. Therefore, compassion with physical pains, needs, and efforts of another human being is easiest and most frequent. The skin color is not a serious obstacle unless a strong racial prejudice checks it.[52]

There is also physical compassion for animals, although other conditions being equal, it is lesser than with men. We hypothesize that it is relatively the strongest with mammals because it is based on similar features of warm blood, muscles, bones, skin, number of limbs, and so on. Most of these are less similar in birds and practically dissimilar in insects with whom we have much less physical compassion. Empathy with a running centipede is very hard.

The similarities in culture, values, attitudes, ideologies, convictions, and beliefs strongly support the imitation of emotional states, while their dissimilarities are obstacles to it. In some cases, the similarity in subcultural attributes has first to develop before similar emotional states appear. The newcomer at a football game[53] has to attend the game several times before he is ready to be carried away by the enthusiasm of the mass of people.

An especially favorable condition of imitation of emotional states is the need to solve a similar problem. Two men looking for a job share and easily imitate each other's emotional states. A student before the examination understands and shares the restlessness and apprehension of another student in the same situation better than a student who has already passed the examination or who is not taking any. They share the feelings of a man struggling with a similar problem more than other people do, although the similar conditions may not enter consciousness.

There is more inclination toward imitation based on empathy if

144

we are in presence of two or three persons expressing the same emotional states. The particular empathies summate (without awareness) into a stronger effect in the mind of the man than is that of a single influence. Stimulation by three persons is also stronger than stimulation by one. It mobilizes more energy which presses to be discharged and facilitates the imitation. Empathy with each particular individual, however, is somewhat weaker and more intermittent.

The weight of the feelings of three persons also is heavier than that of one single person. It is unconsciously understood that three minds agreeing about a certain issue are less bound to commit an error than is one mind.

3) Through Assimilation to the Emotional States of the Group

For the discussion of this topic, we may come back to our example of the new football fan (see Ch. X, footnote 53). Besides the imitation of emotional states of the neighbors and of the mass of other people, besides stimulation by them and weighing their large number, another similar process was going on — that of unconscious assimilation to the crowd's emotional states. A frame of reference established from the behavior of thousands of individuals has a strong attractive power and an intense normative coloring.

On the other hand, more of the details of behavior of particular individuals escape attention, and more impressions are of an impersonal, collective nature. There are fewer empathies with and less imitation of each individual member of the crowd; there are practically no empathies with the distant members of the mass of people. If the individual watches the crowd from the distance, empathy would not develop at all; and imitation probably would not occur. The behavior of the crowd would seem incomprehensible.

It is recognized that the processes of imitation and of assimilation to the crowd's emotional behavior often occur in a milder and more sophisticated form in many fields of social life, such as in political meetings, in the enjoyment of popular songs sung in group, in the activities of boys' gangs, or at a social gathering.[54]

B) UNCONSCIOUS ASPECTS OF IMITATION AND GROUP ASSIMILATION OF EMOTIONAL STATES

We now have to examine how often and how far these imitations and assimilations occur unconsciously. The emotional states observed in another person are perceived in part consciously, in part uncon-

145

sciously. The basic emotional state of the social model is generally (though not always) consciously perceived; the details may remain marginal or possibly subliminal. Whatever the proportion of the unconscious perceptions may be, the process of imitation and its result are mostly unconscious. The mother whose child had been deathly ill and who strongly sympathizes with another mother with a sick baby may not notice what is going on in her emotional life. The new visitor at a football game also often remains unaware of the imitation of the emotional reactions of his neighbors.

The imitation of the scientific enthusiasm of the professor often remains unnoticed. This applies, likewise, to the imitation of artistic feelings, even if we make a conscious effort to imitate. The violin teacher, for instance, who first plays the musical piece studied by the pupil requires the imitation of his musical performance with all the emotional expression, and the pupil has to become partly conscious of it. Yet even here, a large proportion of the imitated musical expression remains unconscious. The easier the imitation, the more of it will be performed unconsciously and will remain so. On the other hand, the possible difficulties in imitation will bring more of it into the consciousness.

It is understandable that much of the assimilation of the individual's emotional states to the emotional states of the group also escapes the attention of the imitating individual. The perceptions of the behavior of the members of the group, especially of a large one, are too numerous for anyone to be aware of all of them. Many of them remain marginal, and the excitement generated by the group pushes still others to the margin of attention. Sometimes, if the excitement is especially strong, almost all of these processes are unconscious. Some of the preparatory processes, such as the establishment of the emotional frame of reference, of the emotional ties toward the group (friendship, sympathy, group belongingness), as well as the pressure of the group toward a certain emotional behavior are often fully unconscious.

All these unconscious processes help to produce emotional conformity, which is of basic importance for the group. By adjustments of this type, the individual adheres more closely to the structure and to the goals of the group, society, and culture.

c) Unconscious Operation of Accepted Emotional States

The emotional states acquired by suggestion, imitation, or assimilation may induce action, without the individual's being aware that they had induced it or without his being aware of the action itself.

When, after a fiery speech (the influence of which on our emotions and feelings is clear to us) we have to decide how much money we will give for the purpose advocated by the speaker, we may unwittingly and without being aware of the real reason give a larger amount of money than we would have given otherwise. The state of our mind made the decision of itself; there was no conscious deliberation, no awareness of emotional reasons, even though naturally we knew the amount we gave.

In other similar cases, people may vote for a certain candidate without any clear awareness of the real reasons.[55] The feeling aroused by the speaker might have induced the decision directly, without passing through consciousness.

If we have to choose a new suit or hat and are inclined to make a certain decision, we may decide differently after we hear the opinion of an experienced person. The feeling of beauty, which has been changed by it, operated without our awareness. We may become less strict in our feelings about the misbehavior of our son after we heard how his homeroom teacher feels about it, and we unconsciously behave accordingly. We may feel less enthusiastic about a new musical piece after we heard a connoisseur express his feelings about it. We also may not attend the concert in which this piece was to be played and which we planned to hear, without having in mind our changed feelings.

The numerous, inconspicuous, emotional states suggested or imitated during the day by many social contacts often remain unconscious and so does their influence on our actions. After having gotten into a good mood through social stimulation, the whole matter before us looks different. This rosy mood might have been unconscious, as well as its operation.

In certain social situations such a case may not be purely of academic interest. The decisions taken on the stock market are sometimes the result of depressed mood which has been spread by suggestion, imitation, or assimilation.

The operation of the emotional states aroused in a crowd situation is often completely unconscious. People may not know what expressions of enthusiasm they uttered, what threatening gestures they used, or how they misbehaved under the influence of the induced emotional states.[56]

D) CREATION OF EMOTIONAL STATES

1) By Participation in Face-to-Face Groups

The group life may produce new unconscious emotional states which did not exist in any of the members of the group before.

If a piece of news comes to a face-to-face group, the group may react as a whole. The news reaches each individual, not separately, but as a member of a group who feels as such, who is stimulated by the group, who receives the news within the framework of the group, who reacts to the reactions of other members to the same stimulus and adjusts his own reaction to their reactions. That is one of the reasons why the ensuing feeling is generally more homogeneous, stronger, and has a different character than if the person received the news alone.

Let us take an example. Suppose, for instance, that a subordinate public servant commits gross negligence in the work he was entrusted with. The employee had never done anything like this before. In this case, he was supposed to work on a task as yet unknown to him; he had been asked to do it as quickly as possible; and in addition to that, he had had some troubles in his family. Each of the elements of this situation has different moral relevance and weight. When the top officials receive the news in an informal meeting and discuss the case, several moral feelings are expressed, each of them corresponding to the moral attitudes of the participants. Later on, some of the same persons may become members of the disciplinary committee and have to decide how to punish the man. At that moment, the influence of the discussion of which the participants were unaware appears fully. The new moral feelings which developed during the informal discussion may still be unconscious, but despite that, they are strong enough to make the officials decide differently from the way they would have done before.

The processes that create new emotional states by participation in a face-to-face group, without our awareness, are very frequent in our daily life. In each common meal, in each gossiping group, in a casual meeting of people in the street, or in the corridor of an office building, in a group of workers working on a common job, there may be creation of new emotional states.

The development, existence, and operation of the ensuing emotional states is often unconscious. The operation of such emotional states may occur simultaneously with the processes of participation in group life. This happens typically when the public applauds an actor or soloist. The emotional states which last longer may induce a certain behavior later. The gay disposition after we come home from a ball or from a gay dinner party, the enthusiastic state of mind after a brilliant concert or a successful political meeting, the pleasant mood after a party with one's intimate friends, may later on induce acts

148

without one's being aware of them (for instance, smiling, being more conciliatory, having new plans for the future, and so on).

2) By Transfer

Another unconscious way of developing an emotional state is transfer. After having reacted in a strongly emotional way to a person or object, we are inclined and sometimes do react in the same way to objects which are related to them. A boy, after having been punished in school and getting angry at his teacher, transfers his feelings to the teacher's son or dog. Agreeable experiences with two or three Spaniards may induce a sympathy for Spain, if we have no other experiences with this country.

The transfer of emotional states is more often unconscious than conscious, as are existence and operation of the transferred emotional states. We discover its existence mostly when we act under its influence. But certain types of transfer never become conscious; and if they do, we may not believe it. We may not believe that we are critical of the work of the disliked person partly because we dislike him.

The transfer may be very narrow; it may reach only such objects as are very close to the object of emotion or feeling. In other cases, it may be broader, even very broad. It may reach practically all the objects with which we come into contact. The rosy light of an excellent mood, caused by a very happy event, is unconsciously thrown on almost all the objects and persons we dealt with at the moment.

The transfer of emotional states shapes the social relations between people, groups, and institutions and is socially significant despite its mainly personal character. It is a source of new social behavior. It may be culture disrupting, culture creating, or culture maintaining, without being of cultural origin itself.

TENSION-FEELINGS

Although it is not possible to deal with all kinds of the socially relevant, unconscious emotions and feelings, we have to discuss at least one more kind: the feeling of tension which may arise 1) between two different ideas, norms, values, obligations, ties, or attitudes, 2) between an idea, norm, value, obligation, tie or attitude, and a reality, 3) between those and the tendencies, drives, and wishes of the personality.

These may arise if one of the tension producing factors is unconscious or if the person is not aware of the comparing process (see p. 118-120). As long as the tension-feeling is weak or mild, it generally is unconscious or operates unconsciously. But even strong tension-feelings

149

sometimes may remain unconscious or disguised. Unconscious tension-feelings are with us most of the time despite general inclination of the human personality to remove or reduce tensions.[57]

The tension-feelings often accept the form of feelings of right or wrong (the behavior of our friend toward us was right), of like or dislike (for a toy pleasing or not pleasing to a child), of sympathy or antipathy, of beauty or ugliness (good or bad proportions of a house or piece of furniture), of attraction or repulsion (our attention being drawn by the economically attainable motorcycle and repulsed by the expensive car) without having any more concrete content.

If one of the factors between which the tension arises (object, person, situation, or idea) is conscious, only the negative or positive character of the feeling generally enters consciousness. But sometimes even this may be unconscious.

The content of the feeling would not be conscious if, for instance, when choosing between two objects, we were able to say only that we like one of them better. It would be fully unconscious if we just decide in favor of an object and discard the other object without even knowing our feeling about it. This happens often when we buy a hat, a suit, a pair of shoes, or another item where personal liking is important. We choose one, but we may not know well why. In reality there is a tension-feeling between our attitudes and the rejected objects or similarity between the chosen object and an object of high prestige. The reason for the liking remains unconscious.

Similarly, we immediately feel that a certain proposition, plan, or decision is unfair or immoral without being clearly aware why. Our conviction is based on moral feelings instead of moral knowledge. The reason for it may be that two or more components of the situation have been taken into consideration only unconsciously. They were unconsciously compared and found to be morally incongruous.

Similar moral feelings may appear when an unrecollected moral rule is applied to the situation under consideration. Moral feelings replace moral knowledge also when the mutual relation of two unconscious moral norms, of a conscious and an unconscious norm, or an unconscious norm and the unconscious fact, arouse tension.

Esthetic feelings are very often tension-feelings between the esthetic norm and reality, or between the different parts of the object as compared with the correct relation or proportion. The feeling may be positive or negative without other conscious content. Here we may quote Miss G. P. who met another girl wearing a new outfit: "Upon my first impression, I know I do not like it; but I cannot understand why, at first; I study the outfit and study its newness, the design in the material, and perhaps even the style. After some minutes of further study, I finally discover that two of the colors . . . do not blend. . . ." The esthetic feeling aroused by the relation of two colors was there before its content became conscious. Still less conscious are esthetic feelings which produce only an esthetic undertone of our daily experiences.

Besides moral and esthetic tension-feelings in which a norm, ideal, value, or obligation are involved, there are other such tension-feelings, based on unconscious normative summations, derived from previous experiences. Because of them we may feel that a certain object belongs in a certain place, (although we cannot say why), or that certain behavior is not in good taste. Many of our esthetic judgments concerning new fashions are of the type of diffuse informal feelings, derived from vague unconscious normative summations, produced by previous experiences. Likewise, moral feelings, although probably less often than esthetic feelings, may be based on them. Nevertheless, being more closely connected with the basic structure of society, they are to a greater extent expressed in formulated norms.

Likewise, we may feel that the object we want to buy would not please a certain member of our family, although we are not able to formulate any reason for his expected dislike for it. Despite that, our feeling may be as strong and as clear as if we had good conscious reasons for it. It is based on unconscious summation of previous experiences with this person, which, compared with the object in mind, produced tension-feeling. We witnessed several times that he refused a certain thing and accepted another one, that he enjoyed looking at certain things, but never cared for others, that he recommended to his friends certain things, but never mentioned others; that he resented still others; and so on. We have naturally forgotten most of the cases and do not recall others at the moment of our judgment. Nor have we tried to put them together and compare them with the object.

In another case, we may know what the member of our family likes (for instance, bright colors); but we feel that he would not like the considered object although it is in his line. ("Yes, I know that he likes bright colors and rather ostentatious things, but I feel that he will not like that.") An unconscious summation corrects a conscious knowledge. The feeling guiding our decision is, then, the tension-feeling between the unconscious summation and the considered object.

Similarly, in our daily work we feel that the letter written by our correspondent is not really courteous; that the products of the factory where we work are not so attractive as they should be; that the novel we are reading is not so thrilling as we had expected; that a theatrical

151

piece will not be well accepted by the audience because it does not suit its taste. None of the standards which were the starting point of the tension-feeling between them and the reality was conscious and clear; all of them were unconsciously worked-out, normative summations of previous experiences.

Another very interesting example of this type of feeling, which is very helpful and which, despite all our scientific efforts, often remains without conscious reasons, is the above mentioned linguistic feeling. Linguistic feelings are tension-feelings between the unconscious normative summations of the ways certain words or phrases are used and the text we are considering.[58]

Tension-feelings are a powerful means of enabling the individual to observe the cultural patterns of behavior. With their help, we are able to keep our place in society, to function as socialized human beings, and to react as is expected of us in all the numerous social situations. We are able to perform satisfactorily our functions in the economic, artistic, or religious life, in family life, in the life of social organizations of any kind, in relations with our friends, with the members of our club, or in any other social position or relation. The tension-feelings are watchdogs of social norms and expectations.

Second, tension-feelings induce new adaptations and social norms. Often they are the only means available to achieve them. They enable satisfactory unconscious adaptations before we can get conscious information and before our intellect can consciously grasp the situation and cope with it. Thus, for instance, the requirements of our friendship toward a man change gradually with the changes of certain conditions in our or in his life. We may not be able to formulate the changes of our friendly feelings; we may not be able to give reasons why we no longer feel toward him as we had until recently. Yet our feelings express all these conditions well and guide us safely.

In the case of the two conflicting norms, tension-feelings help us behave according to the more relevant norm, without thinking of their relative importance. Tension-feelings help also to solve the conflict between our drives, motives and the existing norms in an equally unconscious and generally satisfactory way.

In group life, the tension-feelings safeguard our conformity with group norms. In conflicting or in new situations, we are helped by them to behave as is best for the group, as well as for us.

UNCONSCIOUS ENDURING EMOTIONAL CONFIGURATIONS (SENTIMENTS)

The line of demarcation between temporary emotional states and enduring emotional structures is neither clear nor sharp. Some temporary emotional states last for seconds, others for hours. There are emotional states which, although not with the original strength of the first outburst, last for days, months, or even years. The displeasure aroused by the bad behavior of our children may last only several minutes. Yet if somebody very close to us dies, our sorrow may last for years.

On the other hand, enduring emotional structures, in most cases, do not last for a whole lifetime. Some of them disappear after decades or years and are replaced by other sentiments. Admiration and love for a well-known writer may last for years before it is replaced (after new literary experiences and maturation) by a similar love for another writer.

Thus, from the point of view of durability, there is continuum between enduring and temporary feelings. There is another similar continuum if we consider the difference between both, from the point of view of the organization of the personality. Sentiments are part of the structure of the personality; the temporary emotional states do not seem to be. Patriotic feelings, for example, shape the personality in a permanent way and enable it to function as a well-adjusted member of the nation to which the individual belongs. Emotional states, on the other hand, may be more incidental and superficial.

Some enduring emotional configurations are often called emotional attitudes. These are ready to induce, consistently, a certain outward reaction whenever we enter into contact with the respective person, object, or situation. Sentiments sometimes do not induce any consistent reaction. Cognitive components in sentiments[59] generally play a less prominent role than in attitudes. Despite that, the borderline between both is not exact; the differences between them are gradual.

Sentiments generally remain an inactive part of the personality structure when there is no question as to their object. That is why several outstanding students of sentiments, like Stout,[60] Shand,[61] McDougall,[62] Murray,[63] Morgan, French,[64] consider them as dispositions. They are sources of emotions when we come across the object of the sentiment. But some other sentiments influence our behavior, even if there is no question of their object. People who fall in love may acquire new durable psychic characteristics. They smile more often, are more kind, and more enthusiastic, look fresh, and so on. A strong religious sentiment affects the entire behavior of a person.

Thus we can distinguish enduring emotional configurations which operate only when the object of the respective sentiment is reacted to (in fact or in imagination) and others which aside from such reac-

153

tions influence one's whole behavior, even when the emotional reaction is not aroused by the particular object.

The majority of sentiments are shaped or produced by culture. Social structure supposes their existence and requires them.[65] Every socialized individual is supposed to have certain sentiments and to behave as if guided by them. The society secures their development by social training, social pressure, and by enthusiasm produced by group membership and group participation. Despite the requirements of a relative conformity of sentiments, every culture tolerates limited deviations. Biological elements are often involved not only in the lower, but also in the higher sentiments. In religious feelings, for instance, anxiety may be involved. In esthetic sentiments, there may be sublimated love. Certain moral feelings may involve social ties developed from biological needs (sex).

On the other hand, cultural influences achieve surprising changes in some lower sentiments, too. In the warlike culture of Mundugumor in New Guinea, love feelings express themselves in fighting, while in the nearby Arapesh culture they take the form of play.[66] Likewise, aggressiveness is banned from some cultures (Hopi, Zuñi), while it is a general behavior pattern in others (Kwakiutl).

Yet some sentiments are based on the influence of certain personal experiences. Thus, an inferiority complex may develop in a child because he has a domineering mother or a much brighter brother. More general conditions may produce such sentiments separately in thousands of individuals, in a whole social class. Workers, for instance, each one in his personal position, may develop an inferiority feeling similar to other inferiority feelings of thousands of other workers. These originally were general in the workers' class, not because they were part of the accepted cultural patterns, but because they developed separately in thousands of cases; and only later on were they strengthened by interaction between workers, socialized, conceptualized, and shaped with the help of unions or of socialistic or communistic movements.

Whatever the main process of the establishment of a new sentiment, it is almost never the only source. Other factors generally are active. The configuration of a sentiment almost always includes some assumptions, some knowledge, some respect for certain values, frequently some reasoning, some learning, or some personal experiences.

Thus, sentiments are complex configurations, including not only emotional elements, but also numerous cognitive and conative components. Their composite nature was recognized long ago by R. Descartes and, again later, by Shand,[67] Pear, McDougall,[68] Murray,[69] Morgan, Asch,[70] G. Allport,[71] Dashiell,[72] Stagner,[73] Cattell,[74] Cole,[75] and

154

others (see p. 140). Burgess's[76] analysis of the components of love is a factual confirmation of this contention.

Both ways of shaping or acquiring enduring feelings (the social training and group influences, as well as the personal experiences) may be conscious or unconscious. The unconscious development of socialized sentiments was clearly recognized by Cooley although he did not give it more detailed analysis: "Feeling has an organic social growth which is, perhaps, still less likely than that of thought to be conscious."[77] Let us study now the particular processes by which such acquisition is achieved.

A) CONDITIONING AND LEARNING

So far as some of the basic emotional reactions can be considered as inborn, their conditioning is a source of new sentiments or rather of sentiments toward new objects. Children may be conditioned to fear white fur or dark places or ghosts. Some of our sentiments are conditioned several times in succession. Such, for instance, is the feeling for the comic which develops through a series of successive conditionings (from the original reflective reaction to tickling).

Some of these conditionings are taught by parents; and their children may be fully aware of it. But probably more of them are produced without the awareness of the child. Fear of snakes, of communism, disgust for Nazism may be developed without any real teaching. The child is conditioned by the behavior of adult people and may be completely unaware of it. He may be equally unaware of the product of such conditioning.

Conditioning is often complemented by other kinds of learning and by certain cognitive elements. Thus in adults, a sentiment is rarely only a conditioned behavior; it may be, though, a configuration in which conditioning is a prevailing component.

In the chapter on learning, it was found that sentiments, too, may be learned (often unconsciously). Some psychologists and social psychologists accept this fully.[78] Hartley and Hartley go so far as to consider the social learning of feelings as prior to the social learning of facts in the development of the child.[79] Unfortunately, many of the writers accept learning of sentiments without any further elaboration on the nature of this learning.

Those who are more explicit explain it often by transfer, generalization, or conditioning. In these explanations, there is a certain implicit assumption that the basic emotional reactions are inborn and that they can only be used toward new objects or in new situations, or possibly that they can be strengthened or weakened.

155

As for us, we are inclined to stress the novelty of certain learned sentiments. If we consider the enormous differences in sentiments in different cultures, we have good reason to believe that many of them have been learned as new kinds of behavior. Such would be, for instance, certain kinds of mystical excitement, of humility, or reverence, as produced by the respective cultures.

Let us pay attention, first, to the regular learning of sentiments, such as learning tender feelings toward flowers in school. Small children, as we know, do not show any such sentiments. On the contrary, they generally dispose of flowers mercilessly. Parents and the school attempt to change these feelings. The teacher may use a poem depicting the beauty of flowers in order to develop more tender feelings toward them. She first reads the poem with an appropriate emotional expression. Then, the pupils read it, imitating her expression. At the beginning, they read the poem like a dry, factual text. They are corrected and shown again how to read it. But first, they imitate only the outward expression of the feelings. The sentiment does not yet exist, and the recital of the poem sounds very artificial. Only slowly, through imitation and repetition, through reading, and other new experiences, and also through maturation does the desired sentiment develop.

All this seemingly conscious learning is in reality only partly conscious. There is a great deal of unconscious learning by imitation. The child does not perceive consciously all the inflections of voice, all the gestures, and other expressions of feeling which he imitates. Many of them are noticed marginally and imitated unconsciously. The more unconscious is the empathy, imitation, and identification with the teacher, the more successful the development of new feelings. Conscious imitation by the industrious and intelligent pupils does not always achieve the full development of the new sentiment and may even sound artificial. Good imitators always use a great deal of intuitive imitation.

Tender feelings may develop also without any formal teaching. Take, for instance, the informal development of such feelings toward animals. Inborn inclinations lead the child very often to very thoughtless behavior toward animals. Some small children like to pull off the legs of a spider or the wings of a fly. Some burn the whiskers of dogs and cats. The tender reaction may be developed by simply watching the tender behavior of adults. If they caress and fondle a kitten or a puppy, the child may gradually understand the feelings guiding this behavior. He easily identifies with the puppy because the parents behave similarly toward himself. He understands their feelings very well; and he understands (or thinks he understands) how the puppy feels, too. In identifying at this point with the puppy, he wants it to feel as he feels when fondled. In addition to that, the parents serve as social models, showing the way to do it.

Identification with the parents is supported also by the situational similarity. The parents, as well as the child, are much bigger and more powerful than the puppy and can handle it at their will. This similarity helps to induce similar behavior on the part of the child. Thus, transfer of tender emotional states gives the new configuration its emotional content, and empathy and identification with parents gives it the desirable form, as well as the rest of the emotional content. Repetition of such experiences induces learning.

This new configuration is an organization of a new emotional behavior, of one old emotional pattern (pleasure from tactile contacts with mother), of one transfer, of empathies and identifications, as well as of the grasping of the similarity of the relation of the child and of the parents in relation to the puppy. All these processes may be completely unconscious.

Nevertheless, the learning of socially desirable sentiments is most frequently of mixed nature, partly conscious, partly unconscious. Some unconscious processes are perhaps always involved. Yet a number of sentiments are acquired without our knowing anything about their acquisition. The culture of any occidental nation has developed sentiments about which nobody ever speaks or thinks and whose existence is practically unknown. Foreigners are able to notice some of them, often to the great surprise of local people.[80]

Sentiments which, during a rather long sojourn in a foreign country, have been unconsciously learned may be discovered often only after our return home. Having spent two years in France, I learned to a certain extent French gallantry toward ladies which is much stronger than that of my own country. I learned the feelings associated with it, without knowing anything about this change.

What I was clearly aware of was that after my arrival in Paris, I felt that my behavior toward ladies was less gallant than the behavior of Frenchmen. These impressions later became less frequent and less strong. That was all I realized during my stay in Paris, except for some rather unimportant changes which I introduced into my behavior on purpose. On the other hand, after my return home the behavior of my countrymen toward ladies seemed to me rather crude. I felt different from them. Evidently, I unconsciously acquired new sentiments; but I had no knowledge of how I acquired them and that I had done so.

Some social sentiments may develop even against the conscious plans and intentions of the individual. A youth, for instance, may be opposed to certain feelings of the older generation. I remember how opposed we were to the old-fashioned patriotic feelings of the older generation. Our parents lost all hope that we might ever become good patriots. But, later on, when we entered public life ourselves, we found our patriotic feelings ready to intervene in favor of our mother country. Especially when the first international meetings of students took place, we naturally felt that we had to defend the interests of our country. Of course, the spontaneous social ties toward our family, friends, town or village, toward our university, toward the capital of our country would probably appear in a certain form, even without the teaching of our parents. Yet this raw material appeared spontaneously in the characteristic form of the modern European nationalism, as we knew it from the older generation. We learned these patriotic sentiments unconsciously and against our will. The teaching of the older generation, as well as the unwitting imitation of their sentiments, induced learning processes which went ahead without our conscious knowledge and against our will.

Similar cases of an unconscious learning of sentiments to which the personality was opposed occur in religious, artistic, or moral conversions. There are famous historical cases, like those of the Apostle Paul, Ignatius de Loyola, Tolstoy, and more numerous cases of less famous people. Men who previously hated and persecuted Christians became ardent followers of Christ; men who led a life of dissipation became disciplined ascetics and experienced, all at once, the emotional states to which they were opposed for years. A traumatic experience or aging were not the only causes of the conversion; the new emotions had the exact cultural form of the feelings of the opposed group. They appeared in full strength after they had been unconsciously well-learned for years.

Similarly, painters or composers who have belonged to a certain school may experience a conversion, finding out suddenly that the school which they previously opposed was right. Naturally, the change might also be gradual. But sudden changes are more interesting for us. They show that there was a previous unconscious learning of sentiments of beauty which appear fully developed and well-shaped at the moment of conversion.

The acceptance of new sentiments may occur despite a vigilant and continuous striving to keep the old ones. French dressmakers, working for years in a foreign country, make the most resolute effort to keep their French esthetic feelings but, actually, slowly adjust to the taste of their country of residence. Awareness of the danger, maintenance of available French social contacts, regular reading of French fashion

158

journals, contempt for the crude esthetic feelings of the country of residence, and the determination not to accept them, do not prevent their acceptance.

Diplomats stationed in a foreign country fight perhaps less violently against the acceptance of the sentiments of the country of their residence; but they finally accept some of them, whatever was their original attitude toward them.

Another way of unconsciously learning sentiments is by play-acting them. G. W. Allport says that "the mask becomes the anima,"[81] and Lindesmith and Strauss say that ". . . play-acting . . . becomes instead a genuine expression of experienced emotions."[82] Thus, the brotherly behavior in a fraternal organization is at the beginning only play-acted but finally may become real. The development of the brotherly sentiments is generally unconscious.

Finally, a considerable amount of learning of sentiments is due to repeated emotional experiences [83] Consistent pleasant experiences with a person may teach us to like or love him. Repeated experiences of frustration or anger may develop a sentiment of hatred. Both may develop unconsciously. (See Chapter III.) If this happens to a number of people who communicate, a new cultural pattern may develop. Sentiments which were thus learned serve toward its maintenance and functioning.

B) TRANSFER

Enduring emotional configurations may be transferred in a way similar to that in which emotional states are transferred. Well-educated people, owing to their rational training, are often opposed to this transfer, as to an irrational way of behavior. But this opposition does not help much since it is difficult to fight something you do unconsciously.

Thus, the love for one's own country often imperceptibly makes all the conditions of the country more beautiful in the eyes of its countrymen. Popular maxims of the type "What is Czech is nice" may be found also in other national cultures.

Surprisingly enough, transfer of this kind may be found in regard to another nation too; or it may develop toward rather irrelevant things connected with the object of one's sentiment. A sports fan likes everything connected with his sport, such as the players, the colors of his team, and so on. Artistically-minded people have warm feelings for everything connected with their favorite art.

In most cases, the process transferring the sentiments goes on

159

without awareness, and the existence and operation of the transferred sentiments may be unconscious, too. Even highly educated people may be completely unaware of their transferred feelings.

Depth psychologists have described many cases of unconscious transfer, completely unknown to the respective persons. For instance, people generally do not know that their emotional attitudes toward their parents are transferred to their superiors, leaders, or to God.

Unconscious transfer of sentiments may lead to both maladjusted or well-adjusted behavior. It sometimes opposes the social values of equity or justice and corrupts logical thinking. But it may also help to enforce accepted values and behavior patterns like, for instance, turning the respect held for parents to superiors or to God. It may help in other ways, too. The biased feelings of an artist produced by transfer, may inspire artistic activity and produce beautiful creations.

The transfer of sentiments is often an inevitable unconscious component of our social adjustments. It also produces new cultural patterns if the individual transfers are general in a group or society. They become part of a permanent or changing social structure.

c) SUGGESTION

Suggestion is less important for the creation of durable feelings than it is for the arousing of temporary emotional states. There are three different ways in which suggestion may create enduring emotional structures: 1) by learning through suggestion, 2) by summation of the suggested emotional states, 3) by influence of the prestige, power, importance, or other supporting properties of the suggesting agent.

1) Learning Through Suggestion

Repeated suggestions of the same emotional states may produce learning of certain sentiments. In addition to what has been said above, we have to add the following: Mere suggestions rarely suffice to induce learning of any sentiment. If the suggested feelings do not suit the social and personal situation, if they are not supported by empathy with and imitation of the suggesting person, if there is no sympathy for the suggesting person, if the suggesting person is neither powerful nor important, if the suggesting group is not a membership or reference group, the learning of suggested enduring feelings will be difficult or impossible.

Let us take a concrete example where some of the supporting conditions are missing. The citizens of a state that has compulsory military service must serve in the army even if they belong to an oppressed nation, unwilling to defend the interests of its oppressors. I knew such conditions in old Austria-Hungary where the non-Germanic and non-Hungarian nations opposed their oppressor and his army. In these conditions the feelings suggested to the soldiers that they should be loyal toward the army ran a small chance of being accepted. Only suggestible, weak, or unintelligent persons learned some of them.[84] Several psychologists acknowledge that supporting conditions are necessary but do not give a detailed explanation of them.[85]

A sentiment may develop years after it has been (probably repeatedly) suggested to us. Its organization might have been delayed by lack of supporting conditions. As soon as these appear, the old suggestions may organize the new sentiment without our knowledge (we may even be convinced that our old resistance to the sentiment still exists). This is often the case of children whose teachers attempted unsuccessfully to inculate certain sentiments in them. Only after they marry, have their own children, and undergo more life experiences, do some of the suggested sentiments appear. The old traces of the suggestive words often are unconsciously organized into a new sentiment.

Even if unrecollected, forgotten, or marginally perceived, the supporting conditions may help the suggested sentiments to materialize. Sometimes both the suggestion and the supporting conditions may be unconscious. But even if both are conscious, the newly produced sentiment may be unconscious.

It is interesting that the necessity of supporting factors is intuitively known to practical people. A study of the endeavor of Christian and non-Christian churches in developing certain religious sentiments, or a study of propaganda and advertising techniques would show that the responsible agents are often unconsciously aware of the indispensability of supporting conditions.

The learning of sentiments through suggestion is more efficient with children. A school or youth organization may sometimes achieve good results, even if backed by a minimum of supporting conditions. Some children of sentenced anti-Nazis or anti-communists, educated in special institutions with a very intensive Nazi or communist training, might have finally acquired sentiments opposed to those of their parents. Continuous pressure, fear and terror, as well as assimilation to the group of peers, empathy with and imitation of the teachers, and a false cognitive frame of reference helped the suggested feelings to be accepted. But in the majority of cases, the suggested sentiments could not remove the disharmonious elements of the opposed parental attitudes and of the fact of the imprisonment or execution of the parents.

The process of learning sentiments by suggestion may escape our awareness, even if the suggested feelings are conscious.

2) Summation of Suggested Emotional States

Suggested emotional experiences may summate as other emotional experiences do. Yet the summation of merely suggested emotional states has less power to develop sentiments than does the summation of other emotional experiences. And this summation, too, needs certain supporting experiences.

Suppose that it is continually suggested to a young man to hate a foreign nation, race, or class (as was done in the "Hitlerjugend" and is done in the Comsomols). These suggestions alone are not sufficient to induce any strong hostile feelings. Yet if then, by chance, the young man had an unfavorable experience with the member of the foreign nation or another race or class the suggestions may suddenly summate into a real hatred.

The repeatedly suggested hatred of Jews in Nazi Germany was supported by invented unfavorable experiences with Jews. The hatred of the bourgeoisie suggested by communist teachings is similarly supported by certain unfavorable experiences with persons of bourgeois status (again overdone by propaganda); imposed religious feelings are supported by certain spontaneous religious experiences (or experiences defined as such).

3) Influence of Prestige, Power, Importance, and Similar Factors

Another way to change the short-lived suggested feelings into sentiments is through lasting prestige, power, or importance of the suggesting person, institution, or group. The Catholic village priest in a poor mountain valley has such prestige and importance in the eyes of the lowly peasants that the Christian feelings he suggests are really accepted. Typical are strong esthetic feelings toward famous artistic creations. Their recognition by the best specialists, by artistic institutions, and by governmental agencies has a strong suggestive influence. Several experiments proved that texts or pictures labeled by the name of great artists are considered as beautiful, although they were produced by unknown men. The influence of the indicated big name is generally unconscious (even if the emotional attitude toward it is conscious).

Sentiments produced by suggestion may operate just as unconsciously as other sentiments. Even many sentiments produced by suggestion of which we are aware may operate unconsciously. Here belong

162

certain imposed emotional biases, resentments, sympathies, desires for advertised goods, and other sentiments of this kind. Not only our smiles, gestures, posture, melody of voice, but also our decisions, our avoiding certain places, our coming to others, may be caused by these sentiments without our being aware of them.

D) SUMMATION

In the chapter concerning forgotten experiences, we gave several examples of summation of the emotional parts of the traces into an enduring emotional configuration. Such was the development of hatred toward Nazis in the occupied countries during World War II. Burgess and Locke point to similar accumulations of tensions in marriage.[86]

The real nature of such a configuration is not yet fully clear to psychologists. The recent studies of tensions aroused by repeated stimulation in animals, carried on by the Cornell Behavior Farm,[87] show how many questions are unanswered in this field. There is probably always some organization. In humans, the cognitive components are of great importance in the process of organization of sentiments.

Psychologists seem to agree that the emotional parts of the traces are longer and better preserved than other parts of the traces.[88] This long availability of the emotional part of the traces constitutes rich material for the summations of emotional experiences; and this material is continually used for creating new sentiments, for reshaping old ones, and for the maintenance or revival of existing ones. Despite that, the summations of the emotional experiences may grow weaker if new emotional experiences are not added. Churches, European political parties, organizations of artists, and other organizations have knowledge of this fact. They revive the desirable sentiments by regular meetings of their members, in which new emotional states are aroused and added to the fading emotional configurations.

Many summations are combined with learning by repetition. The theoretical line between them has been drawn in the chapter dealing with forgotten experiences (p. 19). The practical distinction between them is much harder.

The process of summating a number of emotional reactions into a sentiment is mostly unconscious, as, for the most part, are its results. Only on rare occasions are we aware of the strengthening effect of an additional emotional experience. This happens, sometimes, when our emotional reaction is opposed to our wishes or obligations or when it occurs soon after other similar experiences. For instance, a negative emotional reaction against a person with whom one is supposed to be

163

friendly (for instance, the marriage partner), which occurs after a succession of similar experiences, may arouse a conscious idea that this stronger reaction may lead to a deeper rift between the two. Emotional reactions which are not opposed to our wishes or obligations summate mostly without entering the consciousness. The summations of negative emotional experiences probably enter more easily into consciousness than the summations of the positive emotional states.

Many people whose religious feelings are strengthened through participation in religious services are not aware of the strengthening, while others are aware of the feeling of elevation and purification. Still less often are people aware of the strengthening of their love for music after having listened to a good concert. Later on the new feeling may be noticed suddenly in a new social situation. When a student graduates, or when one of his professors dies, he may show feelings of thankfulness to the teacher or love toward the deceased, which he was never conscious of having felt before, although such feelings undoubtedly already had existed (at least in a milder form).

The operation of sentiments produced by summation is often unconscious. It is probably more often unconscious than their existence. We may, for instance, remain completely unaware of our facial expression or gesture as caused by a certain sentiment produced by summation; we may remain equally unaware of having a bitter tone or of showing enthusiasm in the inflexion of our voice, or of making a biased decision.

Sentiments produced by summation shape our relations to the social environment. They have a mostly positive adaptive value which may be further increased by the influence of social models, values, norms, and group membership, all of which may enter the final emotional configuration.

Often the sentiments produced by summation support the existing cultural and subcultural patterns. In other instances, they prepare the development of the new ones. Besides adaptations of the personality to social life, they also induce certain adaptation of social life to the changing conditions.

e) EMOTIONAL ATTACHMENT

Very little is known about the nature of emotional attachment. It develops probably in four different ways. First is the development of an attachment for the person who satisfies the basic needs (the child's mother). The second appears at around eight years of age when the need for friendship and the capacity for love appear in children. It is no longer the egocentric need for help, security, and emotional reassurance, but an altruistic, emotional tie. Sullivan pointed to this quiet miracle of preadolescence;[89] Piaget found it by an empirical study.[90] A third source of emotional attachment is the attractiveness of certain physical or psychic traits; and the fourth one consists of repeated agreeable experiences with a person, such as contacts characterized by kindness, willingness to help, and so forth. Such attachments develop generally unconsciously. Usually, we become aware of them only after they induce a certain new kind of behavior.

Emotional attachments are important in the creation and maintenance of small groups even when they are unconscious. Similar attachments, however, may develop toward large groups, toward institutions, and toward cultural products (language, music, and others).

F) PSYCHOANALYTICAL MECHANISMS

Some of the dynamic mechanisms introduced by psychoanalysts give important, although not yet fully accepted, explanations of the establishment of certain emotional configurations. Some of them develop from socially prohibited feelings which are sublimated,[91] displaced, or otherwise changed into acceptable ones. Aggressive emotional impulses may be changed through sublimation into a love for a certain profession like that of a surgeon, butcher, or housewrecker. Prohibited hostile feelings may also be changed into their opposites through reaction formation.[92] A hostile person may be excessively sweet or obliging. Some other unconscious psychoanalytic mechanisms are mentioned on p. 140. The individual is generally unaware of his real feelings. It is recognized that all these mechanisms operate unconsciously.

Most of these unconscious mechanisms are in service of social norms and values. They enable the individual to satisfy their requirements, without any clear decision or intention of the individual. Certain other psychoanalytic mechanisms lead to modifications of cultural standards (see pp. 265-266).

EMOTIONAL STATES AND ENDURING
EMOTIONAL CONFIGURATIONS

The preceding analysis of the unconscious establishment, existence, and operation of temporary emotional states and of enduring emotional configurations did not clarify the demarcation line between them except in a few points.

If the repeated emotional states produce a sentiment, the sentiment, on the other hand, is expressed in emotional states. Some sentiments do not operate otherwise than through temporary emotional states; on the other hand, they are also revived by them.

AN EXAMPLE OF THE RELATION OF SENTIMENTS AND EMOTIONAL STATES

The artificial division of the unconscious emotional life in the preceding analysis into sentiments and emotional states yields a partly incomplete and distorted picture. In reality many of the processes of acquisition and creation of new sentiments go hand in hand with the operation of existing sentiments. New emotional states are also modified by existing sentiments, while these are reshaped by present emotional states. Emotional states produced by sentiments may integrate with other emotional states. All those mutual influences generally occur without awareness of the participating individual.

It is best to discuss the complexity of emotional life on a narrow concrete field — such as, for instance, the field of religion. Many of the previously analyzed processes will gain a more tangible profile and may be understood more fully. Religious feelings are taught in church, in school, and by parents, and are unconsciously learned by watching the latter's behavior. The outward expression of the feelings is mastered sooner than the inward emotional states.

Once the religious sentiments are developed and become a part of the personality structure, they have to be kept alive and strong. Despite the numerous differences between different Christian churches, the methods of reviving and maintaining them by Sunday worship are basically similar. The clergyman who conducts the service plays the double role of a suggesting personality and a social model. He urges the listeners to develop certain religious emotional states, and his prestige helps him to induce them. He often demonstrates strong emotional states, which are intended to be empathized with, identified with and imitated.

The whole church setting, including the building, pictures, organ, statues, altar, possibly the odors of incense, as well as other religious symbols, and the whole atmosphere support the influence of the social model and of his suggestive behavior.

Another means of suggestion is the reading of Holy Scripture with appropriate expression of face and voice, and with certain slow and impressive gestures expressing unmistakably the reverence for, seriousness, and importance of the subject matter. It also serves as an important conceptual framework for the development of religious feelings.

166

During this part of the church service, the congregation plays only a minor role and appears to be wholly inactive. Despite that, the impassive faces and motionless postures play a certain role in the ongoing processes. They unwittingly remind everybody of the character of the place and of the aim of the religious service. They quietly express the religious sentiments and revive them in most of those who perceive them. And, generally, they prevent many unbefitting feelings. The occasional standing up and sitting down is a good technique of bringing out what the immobile faces and bodies do not show fully while the congregation is seated. All the movements are slow, respectful, dignified, and reverential. Through suggestion, empathy, and imitation, they help to produce the expected religious emotional states.

Singing is perhaps the most important factor in reviving the existing religious sentiments and in creating new ones. It opens the opportunity for numerous group processes which produce emotional states. First, the slow, serious, and dignified movements of mouth and eyes give a fuller expression to religious feelings than did the quiet posture and standing up and sitting down. They strengthen similar feelings of members of the congregation by empathy and imitation. Secondly, further suggestions, empathies, and imitations occur through our participation in common singing. We empathize with the singing of several close neighbors and imitate their religious feelings as expressed by it. Third, sometimes we hear one of our neighbors singing a melody or phrase louder and with more gusto than other neighbors. We may find ourselves responding with an added warmth in our own singing. This warmer expression of our religious feelings has the same effect on other people, possibly also on the person we responded to. Stronger emotional states are produced in both individuals.

The fourth process is the establishment of a frame of reference from the variety of religious feelings of so many people, as communicated by their singing. This frame of reference impels the individual to assimilate his own feelings to those of the congregation. But the individual does not stay at such a quasi-average emotional level. He is also stimulated by the mass of voices and carried away by their impressive and continuous sound, by a convincing mass glorification of God (fifth process). The sixth one is certainly the emotional effects of the esthetic qualities of the hymns. The bringing back of the emotional content of similar, previous experiences from congregational singing, especially from childhood, is to be considered as the seventh factor.

Eighth, a strong process of participation in the group activity and of common creativity develops. The individual, when singing, par-

167

ticipates in creating new emotional states (composed of enthusiasm, devotion, and stimulation).

Adding the above mentioned objects (such as pictures, statues, etc.), we have in all fourteen different factors reviving and creating the religious cmotional states and sentiments. The summative effect of all the numerous emotional experiences is the fifteenth one. It is the same kind of effect we know from the walk through a blossoming orchard (see Ch. X, footnote 54).

The emotional states produced by all these processes leave strong traces, despite their partial fading soon after the religious service is over. They have also retaught and partly reorganized the old religious sentiments.

All this technique, which has been developed in part unconsciously in order to revive and keep up religious feelings, has been used through many centuries with rather good results. People again and again come on Sundays to go through this empirically established procedure, which usually produces the expected effects. The involved psychic processes being greatly unconscious, these effects may easily be ascribed to the influence of supernatural powers.

* * *

The role of the unconscious emotional states and sentiments as well as that of their unconscious operation in social life is enormous. Although Western culture is not especially an emotional one, they penetrate almost the whole of it.

The sentiments developed unconsciously in young people and in adults by individuals and by groups are powerful means of socialization. Teachers, priests, ministers, as well as gangs, boy scout troops, churches, and schools, arouse many emotional states (of admiration, enthusiasm, and so forth) which make the acquisition of the cultural heritage easier; they also form sentiments of strong adherence to it. Think of enthusiastic followers of great masters or influential teachers, ardent readers of good fiction, movie-goers, patrons of concerts and the legitimate stage, the influence of an organization of hobbyists; think of the admiration of lower classes for the cultural patterns of life of the upper classes in order to visualize the socializing power of the often unconscious or unconsciously operating sentiments and emotional states!

Sentiments and emotional states produced by group life support the maintenance and functioning of these groups. The assimilation of the individual members to the group is to a large extent carried on by them. They make it faster, smoother, and more efficient. The observance

168

of a group's subcultural patterns, the playing of different roles, as well as the adherence to the group, very often have a strong, frequently unconscious, emotional component. Sentiments toward the group, group symbols, group values, norms, and goals are cornerstones of its existence. And tension-feelings guide our participation in our countless reactions and adaptations to group life, especially when the necessary factual knowledge is missing. Often, they originate the development of new norms.

The unconscious or unconsciously operating socialized sentiments are major levers in the existence and functioning of culture. Adherence to culture, its defense, and the enforcement of its values and norms are to a large extent due to such sentiments. A very large number of our culturally shaped acts are guided by them. They enable the individual to behave with ease and pleasure according to many cultural requirements simultaneously. They enable consciousness to deal with other insistent problems and simultaneously to play other necessary social roles. Thus, the participation of the individual in cultural life may be much richer and more intense. The emotional equipment of the socialized human nature also secures the desirable rapidity of the given actions and reactions, often to the point of their being automatic.

Only the individual fully equipped with culturally desirable sentiments is well adjusted to the culture of his society. Most of the social values, many of the social attitudes, many norms of moral, esthetic, and religious life are connected with strong and dependable sentiments, which secure their existence and functioning mostly unconsciously.

The emotional equipment of an accultured individual includes emotional relations toward material products of culture and persons adhering to it, as well as toward the nonmaterial parts of the culture. The mass of the socialized daily behavior which sustains the bulk of our culture does not reveal to us the hidden emotional incentives of our actions.

The culturally formed sentiments are also mainly responsible for our feeling of belongingness to our society and culture. They make us its professors and protagonists, undoubting believers in its patterns and values.

Finally, temporary, unconscious, emotional states (especially the tension-feelings) and partly also sentiments, are basic factors to innovations and to cultural changes.

Social structure depends as strongly on sentiments as on moral and institutional supports. They are a necessary condition for its existence. The lack of strong appropriate sentiments may cause the breaking down of the social structure or one of its parts, despite strong legal and institutional supports. The dismemberment of Austria-Hungary (and of other states) is an example of a spontaneous breaking down of the political part of the social structure, chiefly owing to the lack of supporting sentiments on the part of the Austro-Hungarian nations. The breaking down of the feudal social structure was helped by the lack of support by appropriate sentiments. Most of our sentiments supporting the existing social structure are unconscious and also operate unconsciously. They maintain it on an almost completely automatic basis.

FOOTNOTES TO CHAPTER TEN

1. Ross Stagner, *Psychology of Personality,* McGraw-Hill, New York-London, 1937, p. 74 says: ". . . we feel justified in treating our discussion . . . in terms of feelings and emotions, making no distinction between the two." In the new edition of this book (1948) emotions are considered as more complex than feelings (p. 88). T. M. Newcomb says (in his *Social Psychology,* Dryden Press, New York, 1950, p. 103) the following: "We shall . . . use 'affect,' 'feeling state' and 'emotion' interchangeably." See also R. T. LaPierre and P. R. Farnsworth, *Social Psychology,* McGraw-Hill, New York, Toronto, London, 1949, p. 40. G. W. Allport, *Personality,* p. 408.
2. See for example, M. B. Arnold, *Emotion and Personality,* Vol. I, p. 19.
3. R. Stagner *op. cit.,* pp. 66, 69 and 73; M. B. Arnold, *op. cit.,* p. 21.
4. *Ibid.,* p. 69.
5. K. F. Muenzinger, *Psychology,* p. 155.
6. R. Stagner, *ibid.,* p. 72.
7. E. Freeman, *Principles of General Psychology,* H. Holt, New York, 1939, p. 204.
8. See F. Brown, "The Nature of Emotion and its Relation to Antisocial Behavior," *J. Abn. Soc. Psychology,* 28, 1934, pp. 446-458 (esp. 453). K. Koffka, *Principles of Gestalt Psychology,* p. 406 says that "there may be emotions arising with creation of tensions, with their working and with their relief."
9. K. Young, *Personality,* p. 68.
10. *Ibid.,* p. 74.
11. These are, for instance, K. M. Bridges, F. Brown, R. Stagner, A. H. Maslow, R. B. Cattell, R. F. Creegan, W. A. Hunt, N. L. Munn, H. Ludholm, etc.
12. W. Wundt recognized six original emotions, Stagner four, Watson three, Stratton and Bridges one.
13. E. L. Hartley and R. E. Hartley, *Fundamentals of Social Psychology,* p. 295; some, as S. E. Asch, have an opposite opinion (*Social Psychology,* p. 80).
14. W. McDougall, *Outline of Psychology,* C. Scribner's Sons, New York, Chicago, Boston, 1923, p. 418; K. Koffka, *op. cit.,* p. 402; E. W. Burgess and H. J. Locke, *The Family,* pp. 322-331; S. E. Asch, *ibid.,* p. 569.
15. R. B. Cattell, *Personality,* McGraw-Hill, New York, 1950, pp. 264-5.
16. V. V. French, "The Structure of Sentiments," *J. of Personality,* 15, 1947, p. 274.
17. R. Benedict, *Patterns of Culture,* Houghton Mifflin, Boston, New York, 1934, p. 49; O. Klineberg, *Social Psychology,* H. Holt, New York, 1954, pp. 172-174.
18. C. Blondel, *Introduction à la psychologie collective,* A. Collin, Paris, 1927, pp. 158-161.

19. C. H. Cooley, *Social Organization*, C. Scribner's Sons, New York, 1909, pp. 178, 179; K. Young, *op. cit.*, pp. 71; O. Klineberg, *op. cit.*, p. 178.
20. E. Durkheim, *Rules of Sociological Method*, p. 107; C. Blondel, *op. cit.*, p. 165.
21. C. Blondel, *ibid.*, pp. 156, 160, 161.
22. C. H. Cooley, *op. cit.*, pp. 28-30; E. Fromm, *op. cit.*, p. 13; G. Simmel, *Einleitung in die Moralwissenshaft*, W. Hertz, Berlin 1892-1893; H. Lundholm, *The Aesthetic Sentiment*, Sci-Art, Cambridge, Mass., 1941; J. Piaget, *The Moral Judgment of The Child.*
23. O. Klineberg, *op. cit.*, p. 174; C. Blondel, *ibid.*, pp. 156, 160, 180.
24. C. Blondel, *ibid.*, p. 163.
25. C. Blondel, *ibid.*, p. 163.
26. C. H. Cooley, *op. cit.*, p. 30; A. K. Cohen, *Delinquent Boys*, Free Press, Glencoe, Ill., 1957 pp. 57-58.
27. G. LeBon, *The Crowd*, esp. pp. 39-66; S. Sighele, *Psychologie des Sectes*, V. Giard and E. Brière, Paris, 1898; G. C. Homans, *The Human Group*, pp. 360-361.
28. N. Bayley, "A Study of Fear by Means of Psychogalvanic Technique," *Psychological Monographs*, 38, No. 176, Univ. of Iowa Studies in Psychology, No. XI.
29. R. B. Cattell, *General Psychology*, Sci-Art Publishers, Cambridge, 1941, pp. 169, 170, 171.
30. R. W. Husband, *General Psychology*, p. 189.
31. R. Stagner, *Psychology of Personality*, McGraw-Hill, New York, 1948, p. 83.
32. S. E. Asch, *op. cit.*, p. 570.
33. See J. G. Miller, "The Experimental Study of Unconscious Processes," in C. T. Morgan, ed., *Feelings and Emotions*, The Mooseheart Symposium, McGraw-Hill, New York, 1950, p. 263.
34. G. LeBon, *op. cit.*, p. 28.
35. A. L. Kroeber, *Anthropology*, p. 246.
36. H. A. Murray in his *Explorations of Personality*, p. 89, says: ". . . an emotion may occur without the subject's being aware of it (unconscious emotion)." Similarly, in C. Kluckhohn and H. A. Murray, *Personality in Nature, Society and Culture*, he speaks about "unconscious emotion" (p. 8).
37. E. L. Hartley and R. E. Hartley, *op. cit.*, pp. 299, 301.
38. J. G. Miller in *Feelings and Emotions*, p. 263.
39. R. B. Cattell, *Personality*, pp. 161, 265, 400.
40. V. V. French, *op. cit.*, p. 273.
41. R. B. Cattell, *op. cit.*, p. 400.
42. We use the term 'suggestion' although it is not psychologically well understood or even defined (see, for instance, G. W. Allport, *Personality*, p. 166 or S. E. Asch, *op. cit.*, p. 411).
43. E. Durkheim, *op. cit.*, p. 5.
44. D. Cartwright and A. Zander, *Group Dynamics*, Row, Peterson and Co., Evanston, Ill., 1960, p. 166.
45. E. L. Hartley and R. E. Hartley, *op. cit.*, p. 677.
46. In D. Cartwright and A. Zander, *op. cit.*, (ed. 1953), pp. 165-166.
47. M. Sherif, *The Psychology of Social Norms*, p. 108; "An Experimental Approach to the Study of Attitudes," *Sociometry*, I, 1937, p. 98. See also R. A. Schonbar, *Some Social Factors in Judgment*, Ph. D. Thesis, 1945,

Columbia University Library, quoted by M. Sherif and H. Cantril, *Psychology of Ego Involvements,* p. 57.

48. A. S. Luchins, "On Agreement with Another's Judgment," *J. Abn. Soc. Psychology,* 39, 1944, pp. 97-111.
49. H. Cantril, *The Psychology of Social Movements,* pp. 65, 66. See also his Attitudes and Opinions, in E. G. Boring, H. S. Langfeld and H. P. Weld, *Foundations,* p. 564.
50. Indirect suggestion of this kind is very close to imitation. As a matter of fact there is some imitation in it too.
51. H. Blumer, *Movies and Conduct,* Macmillan, New York, 1933.
52. The power of race or class prejudice may be considerable, though. Likewise, other social conditions may be obstacles to it. The Roman citizens did not seem to have any compassion for the gladiators dying for the pleasure of the onlookers.
53. The man who sees it for the first time does not imitate the enthusiasm of the crowd in the stadium. He must first develop the same emotional attitudes as the people in the crowd before he is able to imitate their emotional outbursts of joy, enthusiasm, disappointment, or resentment. The newcomer at a football contest resents the 'childish' behavior of the fans as incomprehensible. The mass of fans is not a reference group for him. See M. Sherif, *An Outline of Social Psychology* (1956), pp. 175-178. The only similarity between him and them is the general biological and psychic attributes and the general cultural background, all of which are not sufficient for sharing the emotional experiences of the fans.

I hypothesize that most often one's first empathy with the fans of the hitherto unknown game first develops not with the immense crowd but with one or two onlookers. It is helped by their attractive features or behavior. Suppose that your neighbor is an older good-hearted gentleman with an open and kind facial expression. He makes a remark about the well-known temperament and endeavors of one of the members of the local team. He expects him now to break through the defense of the opposing team. Soon afterwards the player succeeds after several unsuccessful attempts. During this time the older gentleman showed impatience, strong tension, and expectation. These generally human reactions (in the shape given to them by the local and national culture) bring the first slight empathy and identification, which generates empathy with the repeated attempts of the player to break through the defense of the opponent's team. The final success arouses stronger empathy with the high satisfaction of the old gentleman and imitation of his enthusiasm by the newcomer. The whole process may be supported by another simultaneous process of increasing empathy with another neighbor, say an attractive young girl. Thus, gradually, a new attitude toward the football game develops. The newly developed attitude enables the visitor to imitate the enthusiasm of people who are more distant physically, and of the crowd, too.

54. Before we end this discussion, we have to point to a process which may sometimes be mistaken for it. If we repeatedly experience pleasing stimulations in a continuous succession, we may, through summation, get into a state of strong enthusiasm or excitement. This happens, for instance, when we walk in a large cherry orchard in blossom, or when we watch thousands of gymnasts perform calisthenics. The thousands of summated impressions produce a strong emotional experience. A similar cumulative

173

effect of many mildly pleasant impressions is produced by the mass of tones coming from a large orchestra, by a number of different hues of a color movie picture, by a large display of beautiful old embroideries or of old china. These are mere summations without group assimilation (or empathies).

55. See p. 142.
56. It seems to us that this has been recognized already by G. LeBon in his study of crowd behavior, where he speaks about the unconscious personality of the members of the crowd whose feelings and ideas transform immediately into acts (*op. cit.*, p. 32).
57. See, for instance, C. Kluckhohn and H. A. Murray, *op. cit.*, pp. 35-36.
58. Certain psychologists consider tension-feelings as unpleasant. This certainly is often the case, but it seems to us that some of them may be without any unpleasant tone and that some others may be pleasant. After several harmonic chords, a disharmony, arousing normally an unpleasant tension-feeling, may bring forth a refreshing, pleasant feeling. After years of quiet, dull social life, a minor social scandal seems refreshing. (A prewar Viennese movie was based on this idea.) A rougher word is sometimes equally well accepted at the end of an elegant and polite speech.
59. See S. E. Asch, *op. cit.*, p. 570.
60. G. F. Stout, *The Groundwork of Psychology*, Hinds and Noble, New York, 1903, pp. 223-4.
61. A. F. Shand, *The Foundations of Character*, Macmillan, London, 1914, p 38.
62. W. McDougall, *An Introduction to Social Psychology*, J. W. Luce, Boston, 1921, p. 126.
63. H. A. Murray and C. D. Morgan, "A Clinical Study of Sentiments" I., *Genet. Psychol. Monogr.*, 32, 1945, p. 11.
64. V. V. French, *op. cit.*, p. 271.
65. Among the few modern social psychologists with a similar understanding of certain emotions are M. Sherif and C. W. Sherif: "There are established social norms in regard to emotions as well as other psychological functions, and certain situations are standardized to elicit characteristic emotional reactions and expressions." (*An Outline of Social Psychology*, p. 385). But thirty years ago, the sociologist Cooley wrote: "In this way sentiment, even passion, may have an institutional character." (*Social Process*, p. 25). As we know, the anthropologist Malinowski speaks about "standardized emotions, values, and loyalties specific to each culture" (*Dynamics of Culture Change*, Yale University Press, New Haven, 1945, p. 71).
66. Margaret Mead, *Sex and Temperament in Three Primitive Societies*, W. Morrow & Co., New York, 1935, pp. 105, 216.
67. A. F. Shand, *op. cit.*, p. 35.
68. W. McDougall, *op. cit.*, p. 125.
69. H. A. Murray and C. D. Morgan, *op. cit.*, I., pp. 17, 19.
70. S. E. Asch, *op. cit.*, pp. 133, 569.
71. G. W. Allport, *op. cit.*, p. 258.
72. J. F. Dashiell, *Fundamentals of General Psychology*, p. 160.
73. R. Stagner, *op. cit.*, 1948, p. 88.
74. R. B. Cattell, *Personality*, p. 159, see also pp. 229-232 of this book.
75. L. E. Cole, *General Psychology*, p. 250.
76. E. W. Burgess and H. J. Locke, *The Family*, pp. 322-26.

174

77. C. H. Cooley, *Social Process*, p. 25. See also his *Human Nature and the Social Order*, p. 625.
78. See, for instance: A. R. Lindesmith and A. L. Strauss, *Social Psychology*, p. 118, speak about "actual learning of emotional behavior," Stagner, *op. cit.*, 1937, p. 73 assumes "that emotions are learned," E. L. Hartley, and R. E. Hartley, *op. cit.*, p. 295 ("learning to feel as culture dictates"), K. Young, *op. cit.*, p. 71 ("Specific emotions are really learned"), as well as Husband (see pp. 141 and 171, footnote 30).
79. E. L. Hartley and R. E. Hartley, *ibid.*, p. 102.
80. A German official who came from occupied Poland in 1943 told me how surprisingly strong are the Polish family ties and what great sacrifices the Polish parents are willing to make for the sake of their children. The awareness of the existence of this cultural trait generally escapes the Poles almost completely. When thinking of the family life in Poland, they are rather inclined to see its deficiencies like divorces, unfaithfulness, the drunkenness of men, and so on.
81. G. W. Allport, *Personality*, p. 207.
82. A. R. Lindesmith and A. L. Strauss, *Social Psychology*, p. 119.
83. This standpoint seems to be supported by a short remark of R. B. Cattell that by a repeated satisfaction of a drive, an emotional habit structure is induced toward the particular object (*Personality*, p. 265).
84. E. Fromm makes a distinction between genuine feelings, which originate in ourselves and pseudofeelings which are not really our own, although we believe that they are (*op. cit.*, p. 195).
85. G. W. Allport, *Pattern and Growth in Personality*, p. 431; R. Stagner, *op. cit.* (1948), p. 85; Kurt Lewin, *Field Theory*, pp. 249-251.
86. E. W. Burgess and H. G. Locke, *op. cit.*, p. 517.
87. See H. S. Liddel, *Emotional Hazards in Animal and Man*, C. C. Thomas, Springfield, Ill., 1956, as well as "Conditioned Reflex Method and Experimental Neurosis" in J. McV. Hunt, ed., *Personality and the Behavior Disorders*, Ronald Press, New York, 1944, pp. 389-412.
88. E. Freeman, *op. cit.*, p. 195; see also E. L. Hartley and R. E. Hartley, *op. cit.*, p. 101.
89. H. S. Sullivan, *Conceptions of Modern Psychiatry*, pp. 19, 20.
90. Jean Piaget, *The Moral Judgment of the Child*, pp. 238, 250, 288, 308, 319.
91. Sigmund Freud, *A General Introduction to Psycho-Analysis*, Liveright Publ. Corp., New York, 1935, pp. 327, 332; S. Freud, *The Basic Writings*, pp. 18, 568.
92. S. Freud, *The Basic Writings*, pp. 584, 625-626; F. Alexander, *Fundamentals of Psychoanalysis*, W. W. Norton, New York, 1948, pp. 104-108.

XI

SOCIAL TIES, OBLIGATIONS AND NORMS

It is not usual to put together these three concepts, although as a matter of fact, all three have much in common, and often there is no sharp line of demarcation between them. The social ties gradually may take on more and more of the nature of social obligations, and social obligations often gradually become social norms. All three may be called social bonds.

UNCONSCIOUS ESTABLISHMENT AND EXISTENCE OF SOCIAL BONDS

A) SOCIAL TIES

We understand by social ties all the bonds of social, psychological, or biological nature which the individual feels are attracting him to or keeping him together with another individual (group of individuals) and/or make him act in his favor.

Lovers, friends, and people who have the same hobbies, or play music together, are bound by certain mutual ties. Similar ties originate also in the personal relations between some members of formal organizations like clubs, professional associations, military platoons, school classes, political parties (labeled often as a "clique"), etc.

1) One-Sided Social Ties

The simplest ties are the unilateral social ties without reciprocation by the other person. Here belong the enthusiastic admiration of bobby-soxers for a tenor or the devotion of a mother to her child. The movie stars, writers, political leaders, soloists in different fields of art, ignore the existence of the majority of their devotees.

Nobody knows yet how man is equipped by nature[1] in this respect. Nevertheless, it is well known that there are enormous differences between different animal species. The strong attachment of dogs to their masters is generally known. Siamese cats develop similar attachments, although other cats seem much more reserved and often do not show any attachment to their masters. There are also differences between individuals of the same animal species. The innate equipment of humans in this respect and differences between individuals are difficult to demonstrate because of varied social experiences of every one of them and because of strong subcultural and cultural training. These may mold the inborn inclination in many different ways. But there probably is some biological basis to certain differences in personal ties. There is probably some biological basis even in the attractiveness of a certain timbre of voice, of elegant movements, of beautiful physical features, of a certain kind of laugh, as well as in the attractiveness of the whole personality ("charm," "fascination," "magnetism," the elusive "it"),[2] or a psychic attribute of it. On the other hand, cultural values weaken, strengthen, modify, or produce social ties. The highly valued political or spiritual leaders are objects of devotion mainly because of their high social value. The religious person is more attracted by another religious person, while the irreligious person loses part of his charm in the eyes of the religious man. Love of a girl for a boy is strongly enhanced by his outstanding (socially valued) qualities.[3]

Many of the social ties of this kind develop without awareness. But the behavior of persons betrays their existence. We may hear them saying "I don't know why, but I have to do it for him," or "I cannot help it but I can't refuse him anything."

2) Mutual Social Ties

Let us now discuss two people with mutual personal ties. Such ties may develop through a single experience. Two people, who until yesterday did not feel anything like friendship for each other, now have mutual, friendly feelings. Since the common entertainment of the previous evening (dancing, drinking, singing, or a mere interesting discussion), new friendly relations between them have emerged, without being noticed at the beginning.

Their existence and strength appear from their operation, which starts spontaneously and automatically. When next morning we receive news which may interest our new friend, we feel impelled to phone him about it. We would not have felt that way the day before. Also, when by chance somebody mentions our new friend in an unfavorable way, we defend him. What happened to us to make us behave that way? We sometimes ask such questions ourselves because we are surprised to discover that some unknown force is pushing us into such unexpected acts. We may answer by usual social concepts of sympathy, interest, or friendship; but we do not really penetrate the puzzling reality. On the other hand, as scientists we know that the uncomprehended rise of new social ties must be explainable.

The rise of any friendship between two persons has a long cultural and personal prehistory. It is a complex social-psychological process involving cultural and subcultural (local, class, family) patterns plus appropriate training, personal experiences, social models, (and, of course, a certain bio-psychic background).

The first shaping of friendly reactions occurs in the first years of life by the relation toward one's own mother. In this relation, the basic ways of accepting personal nearness and of responding to it are formed.[4] There are large differences in this respect between different cultures[5] and even between local and class subcultures.[6] Another source is the interaction between siblings. Because of the nearness of age and the give-and-take character of the relations between siblings, a substantial part of the experiences is carried over into future friendships. In the family develop the personal needs for sharing emotional experiences; for close intimate contacts; for emotional interdependence, companionship, admiration, moral support; for sharing special interests, and other similar needs.[7] Also influential are the family-developed needs for certain personality traits (like warmth, firmness, restraint, sensitivity), for a certain kind of conversation (wise, witty, gay), preference for certain facial features, liking of elegant or athletic appearance or of an attractive personality.

These influences are partly supplanted by the first experiences of friendship in grade school. Here also the influence of certain cultural patterns is evident. I have been surprised by the ease with which the youngsters in the United States make new friends when they enter a new school after the family has moved to a different location. In Europe it takes much longer. In this, children naturally follow cultural patterns of their country, without any awareness of them.[8]

A very different kind of friendship developed between two young men in another occidental country, in ancient Greece. Real friendship was relatively rare, and those who became friends developed deep and far-reaching mutual relations. In friendship often homosexual overtones were involved. In the present occidental culture there is nothing like that any more. In Europe of today, people generally have several personal friends for years, sometimes for a lifetime. Their other friends are labeled rather as acquaintances, and there are no real intimate personal ties between them. Real friends develop their mutual relations slowly. Many emotional, intellectual, and social requirements are to be satisfied before a friendship is sealed. To both new friends it is clear in which things there is a possibility of real personal intimacy and in which there is not. Certain needs and wishes (ambitions, sexual desires) are often concealed even before very intimate friends. Dishonesty, certain types of hatred, mean motives, and unpleasant attributes are likewise not revealed. There is a difference between friendships of men and those of women. Friendships of men are more frank, sincere, and open. In friendly relations, the troubles and joys are to be mutually communicated. The more they are communicated, the firmer the friendship becomes. Thus, friendship is just an institution to gratify the need for sharing the emotional states.

Compared to the European, the American friendship is cemented much sooner and faster. Americans also have more friends than Europeans. The obligation to help is strong. But there is less emotional intimacy and effusion of feelings. The common personal interests, perhaps, are not so necessary as in Europe.

But in all these cultures, in classical Greece, in Europe, as well as in America, people know how to behave in relation to their friends, although they are not aware of any rules. They know how to talk to them, how to smile at them, how often to see them, what they can ask from them. The feeling of disillusionment will tell either of the parties when an unformulated and unknown expectation has not been fulfilled.

Youngsters mostly do not know anything about the existence of the cultural patterns of friendship they follow. They obey, most often unconsciously, some of the advice their mothers gave them years ago; equally unconsciously they may imitate certain social models, perhaps their fathers' friendships, the friendship of some local leaders, or of some of their peers. In some cases, fiction furnishes further, unconsciously followed, social models, especially to educated people.

Certain broader cultural patterns exercise their influence on friendship relations, too. Such patterns include culturally developed introversion or extroversion, certain cultural habits and customs for dealing with people in general, the rural or urban cultural conditions, and certain basic behavior patterns. There is no doubt that even the songs we have heard in childhood and the way they were sung (emotionally, excitedly, lyrically, devotedly, passionately, dramatically, and so on), the proverbs concerning relations among men, perhaps also biblical teachings, and other factors, exercise some unconscious influence. Personal attractiveness is enhanced by good appearance, cleanliness, and politeness (as defined by a given culture).

Now let us come back to the friendship developed after an evening spent in dancing, drinking, singing, or discussion. Imagine now how many

179

processes have occurred in the personalities of the two young new friends! Imagine how much advice from the mother, how many models of other friendships, how many personal experiences, cultural ideals of friendly behavior, cultural concepts of friendship, proverbs, social values, habits, and customs, shaped these new social ties. The unconscious organization of all these largely unconscious influences, with culturally (and family) shaped interests, likes, emotional needs, and desires to share them, produced our ready-made, culturally well-shaped behavior, suiting all the accepted norms.

In such a process, there is first the raw material of attractiveness and cordial impulses and the shaping of them in order to suit the requirements of the cultural norms. Then there is the adaptation of all these to the specific social situation, and third, adjustments to the desires and expectations of the new friend. Friendship, however, may start with any of these three factors.

Social ties may be enhanced by certain special conditions. If we live for several weeks in a common room with 10 or 15 soldiers, as is usual in military barracks, amazingly strong ties with two or three of the roommates often develop. The continuous need for mutual help and interaction, the immediate common interests, needs,[9] experiences, and the sharing of most of the intimate situations establish numerous strong personal and social ties. The countless mutual empathies and identifications,[10] with emotional reactions of the buddies (resentment of the common oppressing forces, joy from outsmarting them, and the like) are probably the most potent sources of the common ties which develop in culturally accepted forms. The frequent repetition[11] strengthens the effects of these processes.

These social ties have also been established unconsciously, and some remain unconscious. Only from time to time do exceptional circumstances reveal, gradually, the existence of more of them. When, for instance, a soldier is going to be punished or put in prison (which happens easily in military service), his comrades may be surprised at the sizable sacrifice they make to help him.

Similar, although much weaker, social ties develop in civilian life on such occasions as a weekend hike. Still weaker are the ties of a friendship arising from a railroad trip. If we sit for several hours in the same compartment of a European railroad car with two or more people and experience all the stations, cities, and views of the open country together, comment on them and react in a similar way, and render to each other small services, such as assistance with luggage or the offer of a cigarette, we establish new ties towards them. The common ties are further strengthened by common help to a lost and crying

180

child looking for his mother or by the resentment of the impolite behavior of the conductor. All the processes that develop such social ties are generally unconscious.

3) Group Ties

Social ties between two persons have to be distinguished from group ties. Unfortunately, the distinction has not been clear to some students of group life. In the studies of military life, as well as in the experimental studies of groups of boys, often no clear distinction is made between them.[12] In sociometric studies, for instance, the personal ties between two people who are members of the group are the measure of the group ties.

Group ties are not based primarily on personal attractiveness or empathy. Empathy, if there is any, is rather more cognitive (understanding of common interests, needs, problems) than emotional or physical (there is minimum empathy with emotional experiences of the group as a whole). The emotional and physical empathies, personal attraction, sharing of common experiences, and close physical contacts are limited to few immediate members of the group and are personal rather than group ties.

In the group, on the other hand, there is a group structure (including the name, goal, organization, insignia, norms, and duties of members) and adherence to it; there is group morale and atmosphere; there are frames of reference established from the behavior of members; there is feeling of belongingness, acceptance of common behavior patterns; there are group attitudes, values, ideals, and there is participation in group activities.

All these may be unconscious or may operate unconsciously. Sherif and Sherif recognize that identification (with a social class) may be unconscious.[13] Homans finds that part of the group structure, the scheme of interaction, may be produced unconsciously.[14] Being part of such a scheme is a social tie between the members of the group. Cartwright speaks of unconscious group goals[15] (which incite ties).

The feeling of belongingness may also exist unconsciously and may operate unconsciously. It even may develop unconsciously. The feeling of belongingness to a group of vacationists, for instance, may be established gradually and without awareness. It may exist for a certain time and operate without awareness, too. A revelation of the existence and of the strength of ties comes at the moment of departure for home.

Another revelation of a group belonging comes when we first use the pronoun "we" when speaking about a group. Such is the case of

181

immigrants to the U. S., who for years say "we" when speaking about their mother country and "they" when speaking of the U. S. But after a certain time, they unwittingly use the pronoun "we" to refer to America. At that moment, the feelings of belonging to the American nation have become so strong that they have changed the referents of the pronouns. But their gradual strengthening was unnoticed, often completely unconscious.

The feeling of belongingness to our mother country is revealed fully when we live in a foreign country. When at home, the strength of this feeling is hidden under the daily routine and also under the frictions and difficulties of daily life. Only unusual circumstances may partly reveal this feeling. Such are, for instance, political attacks of a powerful neighbor, loss in an important international contest, war, and so on.

Our attachment to the products of group life (values, ideals, norms, institutions), which can equally be considered as a social tie, may be just as unconscious as the ties toward the members of the group. One's attachment to cultural products, which are part of our daily life, may especially easily escape our consciousness. But as soon as we are deprived of them, we feel a strong attachment to them which, of course, existed before this experience. Such may be, for instance, the case of national folksongs we learned in school and perhaps resented because we were corrected by the teacher when singing them. Similarly, our own language might have been the object of trouble in school. But after having lived years in a foreign country, we may miss both terribly.

The development, as well as the strengthening or weakening of group ties, goes ahead automatically like a natural (chemical or physiological) process. It progresses whether it is conscious or unconscious. We do not mean, however, that awareness of some aspects of the process does not change anything in it. But it is no more than one of the components which, all together, produce the final result.

We may say in general that such processes often are not only unconscious but that in most cases they cannot be conscious. Only their product may later on become conscious, as well as its operation.

B) SOCIAL OBLIGATIONS

An obligation develops through similar processes. Suppose that a friend of ours who has a large vegetable garden has been sending us vegetables for years. Finally, he comes to feel that he cannot stop it without good reason. It would indicate something about our friendship. Similar obligations may develop in exchanging letters, fishing together, sending gifts for Christmas, visiting, and so on.

In a group of friends who hike together, similar obligations concerning group roles gradually develop. For instance, one of the members of the group always carries a can opener, knife, matches, strings, and other practical devices. After several hikes, it is expected that he will have all these again. If, unexpectedly, he does not, both he and the others would feel as if he were not meeting his obligations. Telling stories and jokes, leading group singing, leading philosophical discussions, and many other activities may involve a strong coloring of obligation for persons who have done it for a certain time.

Likewise, people who live together in a dormitory, in a summer resort, who meet regularly in a social club, or even our travelers in the compartment of a European train, easily develop a number of unconscious and unassigned obligations. If, in the train compartment, we help a lady put her luggage on the luggage carrier and later help her again when she wants to take her sandwich from her suitcase, and again when she looks for her book, she expects that we will help her again the next time. If we did not, and just looked at her struggling with her suitcase, we would feel very bad about it. The culturally accepted norm of helping ladies is not so strong as to make us feel such an obligation; our repeated help, however, is.

Let us discuss a similar case from a large group, an ad hoc committee meeting of which I was a member. We met in a meeting room with a round table and nine chairs. It was not clear which of the chairs was for the chairman, the round table being the same all around. After some hesitation, everybody was seated without any seating order. After four hours of common work, we had dinner together and went back to the meeting room. After a shorter hesitation, everybody took his previous place. Next morning after a very short hesitation, people took again their previous places, except one man who by mistake took the place of his neighbor. But he apologized and took his previous chair. The same happened after lunch, except that the wrongly seated man did not recognize his mistake. Upon arriving his neighbor said to him, "Pardon me, that's my place." At that time, it seems, everybody considered his place as firmly belonging to him. During one and a half days, people unconsciously developed certain increasingly stronger obligations.

The following facts are to be noticed. At first, the situation was completely unstructured. With gradual acceptance of the seating order, the hesitation at the beginning of each session became shorter and shorter. At the beginning of the third session, the order was so well-established that the wrongly seated man felt that he had acted against his obligation. At that time, probably no one would have yet asked for his chair, the mutual obligations not being strong enough. But at the beginning of the last session, the new order was so well-instituted that

183

one man felt the right to ask for his previous seat. Probably other members felt the same way although they were not aware of any clear obligation.

What were the components of these unconsciously developing obligations? First, there was probably the newly-established habit of looking at the chairman from a certain side, of expecting the reactions of the legal expert from another side, and the reactions of the reporter from a third direction. Such expectations make the participation of each member easier. Second, everyone could unconsciously presume that because of the developing habit each member liked to keep his place.

Besides these personal elements, there certainly was something like a freshly, and not very firmly-established, structure of the group. Certain spatial relations, as stabilized by chance, became part of this structure. It was for the sake of the group itself, for its smooth functioning that the established spatial relations had to be maintained. All these factors probably influenced the behavior of the members of the group unconsciously. Their influence was equally unconsciously combined.

It is perhaps significant that, despite my being a member of the group, I have certain doubts about the number of unconscious elements operating in the establishment of the accepted order. These doubts show most clearly how unconscious the process of establishing the social obligations may be. Perhaps there were one or two or more additional elements (for instance, the unconscious imitation of those who came first and took their previous place, or transfer of behavior patterns from other similar groups). If this is really so, then these additional components are still unconscious, despite all my efforts to discover them. Undoubtedly, no other member of the group was aware of any single component of the feeling of obligation.

Even in well-established organizations there is always some space left for creation of additional personal obligations. If the boss habitually offers his employee a cigarette, a chair, and asks about his family's health before talking business — all these may develop into obligations or at least expectations. Whenever he would omit some of them, the boss would feel that he should not have frustrated his employee this way; and the employee would feel the same.

Similarly, in a group of workers in a shop,[16] on the farm, or in an office, the officially enforced rules of behavior are complemented by spontaneously developed obligations of the members of the group toward one another.

c) Social Norms

We understand by social norms the formulated rules of behavior.[17]

They may be formulated in laws, proverbs, maxims, principles, or as recognized habits and customs. Part of these originate in consciously established rules while the majority are created by the group life itself with the same spontaneity as the obligations.

Sherif's boys in the experimental summer camp created a series of group norms in the time of less than two weeks. Such were, for instance, keeping secret the swimming hole of the group, not mingling with the members of the other group, punishing in a standardized manner; more general norms included solidarity and loyalty.

Naturally, group norms are more likely to be conscious than social ties or obligations because they have the tendency to be formulated and communicated. But as Sherif and Sherif say ". . . standardization of norms is a natural process in group interaction and need not be conscious. . . ."[18]

The unconscious development of social norms may follow two different ways. It may be a process leading directly to a new social norm as, for instance, when a new misdeed arouses general opposition, or it may be a process producing first a vague obligation, which finally is accepted as a social norm.

The unconscious processes leading to the direct establishment of a social norm again may be divided in two. The new misdeed may hit strong, general, and long existing attitudes and may arouse a general feeling that a severe sanction against its repetition is to be established. The lawmaker's role is only to give an appropriate expression to this feeling. Or the social structure of the group may have changed so much that the previously harmless deeds may arouse increasing opposition. These new feelings developed with the changing conditions without the awareness of the members of the group; only their existence and the formulation of the new norm were conscious.

The increased concern with children's health brought about a number of laws to protect children. Big disasters, thefts of large amounts of money, and unusual misuses of public power arouse a strong reaction which provokes new measures of protection. Numerous unconscious judgments evaluate the possibility of repetition of such a happening and consider the political danger, the danger to public property, and national security, and shape the attitudes of people favoring the new protective measures.

On the other hand, social norms may develop from unconsciously established obligations. Many norms of behavior, for instance, were felt as obligations before they were formulated as rules of etiquette, as written regulations, laws, articles of constitution, or bylaws. Many norms of solidarity, honor, and good behavior in business circles, in the army, or in professional organizations were originally only vague obligations.

UNCONSCIOUS ACCEPTANCE OF READY-MADE BONDS

Certain personality traits, emotional and practical needs, expected satisfactions or rewards, may be the psychological sources of the acceptance of culturally established bonds. Other sources include the assimilative tendency to the behavior patterns of a group, attractiveness of the group, and adherence to its behavior patterns, group membership, pressure, and prestige. Unconscious learning, conditioning, judgment, imitation, and suggestion are the psychic processes in unconscious acceptance of social bonds, which often use unconscious experiences.

The same processes help the teaching of the bonds. Children are taught them until the desired social bond finally appears. The conscious teaching may induce unconscious learning.

In other situations, we learn the bonds without conscious teaching. The solidarity of miners, smugglers, big game hunters, or crews on whaling ships is learned unconsciously by the newcomer very quickly. The degree to which people feel obliged to keep their word differs in different cultures and subcultures. The newcomer soon accepts the more or less strict norm in this respect and learns to behave accordingly.

Another way of learning ready-made social bonds without imitation is through disagreeable experiences. It is sufficient to forget about the birthday of a member of the family only once to learn never to forget it again. Likewise, for instance, the speedy answering of letters is learned through unpleasant reactions of the people concerned or possibly through more disagreeable experiences. The process of learning the social obligations of this kind may be completely unconscious.

Esthetic norms, too, may be learned unconsciously from pictures of great masters. Many moral norms and norms of etiquette are accepted without awareness by people who become members of a new group or social class. For instance, it is very interesting to watch a bank employee who has been promoted to an executive position. Although he probably consciously imitates the behavior of other executives, he also gradually learns some norms of behavior without noticing it. Such may include greater respect for the interests of the bank and less for those of the employees, stress on smooth relations with customers, and so forth. Even people who dislike some of these norms learn them unwittingly.

UNCONSCIOUS OPERATION OF SOCIAL BONDS

The weaker the influence of social bonds on our behavior and the

186

fewer obstacles our behavior encounters when guided by them, the greater is the probability that they will operate without our awareness.

A) SOCIAL TIES

Falling in love may be such a case. At the beginning, we may not notice the changes in our behavior, such as coming more often to places where she (or he) often comes, thinking of objects she (he) uses, reading books she (he) reads, and the like. Only when the changes are consistent or too conspicuous do we become aware of our love.

Teachers, heads of department, army officers, bosses of all kinds, often prefer some of their subordinates, trust some of them more, give them better grades, or judge their work more favorably without knowing about the existence of the tie between them and without noticing its operation.

The sport achievements of compatriots in international competitions are generally rated higher, even by otherwise correct judges. Some of them are convinced of their correctness despite their knowledge of the social ties toward their mother country. Their knowledge about the existence of the tie may not reveal its operation. The unconscious operation of a social tie is often helped by our unwillingness to acknowledge it. The mother may not want to know about and does not admit her preference for one of her children.

B) OBLIGATIONS

An obligation may function unconsciously in several ways. If we see the well-known beggar at our door, we just take a dime from our pocket and automatically hand it to him without being aware why we are doing it. In a certain situation we feel that we should send a friend of ours a picture postcard, in another that we have to help him. Similarly, we feel that we have to do a certain thing for our political party, for our village, for our family, and so on, without having any clear idea why. Following an internal impulse, we unconsciously fulfill our obligation without letting our consciousness throw any light on it.

Similarly, we feel that we "have to" write a letter to the editor about a current problem, that we "have to" appear at a party, or that we "have to" give more money for a certain purpose, and so on. Obligations which were formulated nowhere, which were proclaimed by nobody, whose source is often unknown to us, guide our behavior every day without our knowing it. They help us play our social roles in the family, among friends, in public life, and so on.

187

Let us consider now another type of obligation that was produced by a new situation. In Czechoslovakia I watched an applicant for a chauffeur's job who, after he presented himself to the new boss and after he agreed to the conditions of employment, immediately started to act as an employee, holding the boss' coat, opening the door for him, and so on. He did this before he actually entered the service. The new obligations started to operate automatically, without any conscious decision by the driver.

And what about moral obligation? When in 1948 the communists came into power in Czechoslovakia, many people felt that they had to continue to fight them. Some people who fled to the U. S. zone in Germany after the communist coup came back several times to bring news and to give necessary information to the leading people of the underground at home. They felt obliged to risk their lives, and some in fact perished. The moral obligation operated automatically after they got into a new situation.

The number of moral obligations functioning this way is large. All the fluid, changing moral forces emerging from a changing social life, which have never been formulated and expressed in the form of moral norms, guide our behavior toward the acceptance of certain new political ideas, toward supporting certain new institutions, toward helping the local symphony or an exhibition of modern paintings, toward sympathizing with a new literary movement, and so on.

Unconscious judgments concerning the present situation of persons and institutions in question, the attributes of persons (age, economic situation, ambitions, interests), objects and institutions, our previous reactions to them, values and attitudes involved in the situation — all these and other conditions set in motion the proper operation of certain moral obligations, generally unconsciously.

Originally conscious, repeated, obligatory behavior may become automatic and is then performed without any co-operation of consciousness. Reverent behavior toward the teacher or boss, as well as toward the national flag or hero, is a case in point. We automatically respect the interests and needs of others and automatically help them.

c) Norms

Also the norms of taste very often operate without awareness. Watch people judging ladies' hats, for instance. A girl feels that this particular one is the most beautiful. She may not know whether it is chiefly the color or chiefly the form, or both, or still something else which makes the hat beautiful. The unconscious norms of beauty were applied by her unconsciously and in many cases, immediately. If you ask her why the hat she chose is the more beautiful one, she perhaps will not be able to give the reasons. In another case, she may find, after a short hesitation, one reason or two. But, as a matter of fact, several other reasons which cannot be brought into her consciousness influenced her judgment, too. Nevertheless, at the moment of judging the hats, even the first two reasons, which later on entered her consciousness, were unconscious.

Also, certain moral and legal norms may operate in the same automatic, unconscious way. We automatically avoid use of objects belonging to other people, we automatically avoid conversing at length or in too lively a manner with the young wives of our friends; we automatically stop the car when seeing a red light. In a similar way, we side automatically with moral issues against immoral ones.

Obedience to orders becomes automatic for subordinates in any well-disciplined institution, such as the army, the monastery, or the Catholic clergy. Many of the norms of work in an office, shop, or factory are executed automatically. In the operation of most of these and other similar norms, there is no awareness or very little of it.

*　　*　　*

Unconsciously produced, existing, or operating social bonds are basic to the existence of groups, as well as of the larger society. They belong to the factors which create and maintain groups without the conscious effort of their members. Likewise, they unconsciously maintain certain cultural patterns: indirectly through attachment to people who adhere to them and directly through attachment to the cultural patterns themselves.

Social obligations and norms also have special importance for the existence of social structure. Through them we adhere to the social structure, and we act as part of it even without thinking of it.

It is not an overstatement to say that without the unconsciously established and unconsciously operating social bonds the major part of the group life, of the life of society, and of culture would be impossible.

FOOTNOTES TO CHAPTER ELEVEN

1. The biological and psychological nature of social ties is not well known. Besides identification (see, for instance, G. Murphy, L. B. Murphy and T. M. Newcomb, *Experimental Social Psychology,* Harper and Br., New York, 1937, p. 514; D. Cartwright and A. Zander, *Group Dynamics,* p. 660; S. Scheidlinger, *Psychoanalysis and Group Behavior,* Norton, New York, 1952) also attraction (physical and psychic), emotional response, Freudian libido, McDougall's gregarious instinct with the ensuing active sympathy or broader, inborn tendencies (like Sullivan's tendency or capacity for love or Horney's general reservoir of warm feelings) are indicated as bio-psychological sources of social ties. Nevertheless, none of them gives a fully satisfactory explanation of the subject.
2. See E. W. Burgess and H. J. Locke, *The Family,* pp. 323.
3. The attractiveness of animals is also partly due to cultural values the animals seem to express or gratify. The attractive elegance of a cat is certainly partly owing to the culturally established value of elegance. We love a dog because of his faithfulness, which we evaluate in terms of the social values of human faithfulness.
4. See E. W. Burgess and H. J. Locke, *op. cit.,* p. 369.
5. R. Linton quotes cultures where "the child is taught that its mother really is not a member of the family, and hostility between mother and child is encouraged" (*Study of Man,* Appleton Century, New York, 1936, p. 123). A. Kardiner says about the Alorese culture that "all factors conduce to the preponderance of hatred and aggression toward her (mother)" (*The Psychological Frontiers of Society,* Columbia University Press, 1945, p. 150).
6. W. A. Davis and R. J. Havighurst, *Father of the Man,* Houghton-Mifflin Co., Boston, 1947.
7. See E. W. Burgess and H. J. Locke, *op. cit.,* pp. 366-369.
8. It has been proved that hostile attitudes toward Negro children are implanted by mothers, but that later on, the children do not know anything about it (E. L. Hartley and R. E. Hartley, *Fundamentals,* p. 152). See also W. L. Warner, *Democracy in Jonesville,* Harper and Br., New York, 1949, pp. 77-88.
9. See S. Scheidlinger, *op. cit.,* in D. Cartwright and A. Zander, *Group Dynamics,* 1953, pp. 58, 59, 81, 82.
10. *Ibid.,* p. 58.
11. G. C. Homans says ". . . persons who interact frequently with one another tend to like one another," (*The Human Group,* p. 111) and ". . . the more frequently persons interact with one another, the stronger their sentiments of friendship for one another are apt to be." (*Ibid.,* p. 133). The decrease of interaction, on the other hand, brings a decrease of the interpersonal

190

sentiments (*ibid.,* p. 361). Such weakening of social ties occurs generally as unconsciously as their establishment.

12. This confusion has been in existence since E. Durkheim started to use the concept of social ties or bonds in his explanation of suicide in 1897. See the English translation: E. Durkheim, *Suicide,* Free Press, Glencoe Ill., 1951, especially pp. 171-216.

13. M. Sherif and C. W. Sherif, *Groups in Harmony and Tension,* p. 11.

14. G. C. Homans, *The Human Group,* p. 105.

15. D. Cartwright and A. Zander, *op. cit.,* p. 310.

16. This has been convincingly shown in an excellent study by F. J. Roethlisberger and W. J. Dickson, *Management and the Worker,* Harvard Univ. Press, 1939.

17. This is in disagreement with the broad understanding of social norms as introduced by M. Sherif and as accepted by many contemporary social psychologists, who include practically all social and cultural regulations of behavior.

18. See p. 102 and also Roethlisberger and Dickson, *op. cit.,* pp. 533-536.

XII

ATTITUDES

The concept of attitudes is one of the most controversial ones. At the present time, we may find some thirty different meanings for it.[1] Another difficulty lies in a large number of other similar concepts which are often confused with attitudes.[2]

The most penetrating approach to attitudes has been developed by Sherif and Cantril in their common book[3] (we are not referring to Cantril's original definition of attitude as determining tendency[4]). Sherif, later on, in his more recent study[5] formulates this approach in the following way: an attitude 1) is a functional state of readiness[6], 2) reacts in a characteristic way to certain stimuli. Further, it 3) implies a subject-object relationship and it 4) has an affective property. Both authors agree that attitudes are learned and formed (not inborn).[7]

We agree with this conception of attitudes. Only it seems to us that the role of the cognitive components is more important than indicated by these writers. An attitude consists not only of selective perceiving, judging, information, standards of values, assumptions,[8] but also of our conceptions about things as produced by thinking, imagination, by guesses, summations, computing service, insight, and other processes.

Thomas and Znaniecki's conception of an attitude,[9] as an individual counterpart of social value, does not seem correct. Some attitudes are established independently of any social value. They may be derived from personal values or may be independent of any value at all. The attitude may also be opposed to the respective value. We can recognize the high value of a famous picture; but personally, we may not like it.[10]

Attitudes certainly are not only conscious, as Thomas and Znaniecki believe.[11] There are also unconscious attitudes or attitudes with unconscious components. Sherif[12] found experimentally that subjects may be unaware of assimilating their norms (including attitudes) to other members of the group. Newcomb's study of changing attitudes of students established that some of these changes were unconscious.[13] Miller speaks about unconscious mechanisms,[14] which are the counterpart of conscious attitudes. F. H. Allport speaks about unconscious assuming[15] of an attitude; anthropologist Linton[16] claims that in all cultures there are attitudes lying ". . . deeply below the level of the individual consciousness . . ."; K. Young and Burnham speak about largely unconscious attitudes (habits) and K. Young[17] about unconscious building up of attitudes; similarly, Murphy[18] and Mead [19] speak about unconscious taking over of attitudes and Sullivan about unthinking acquiring of attitudes.[20] Munn[21] and Husband mention the unawareness of the basis of our attitudes. The unconscious operation of attitudes is mentioned, for instance, by Murphy[22] and Sherif,[23] but, on the whole, less often.

The lack of a satisfactory, theoretical knowledge of attitudes has been acknowledged by several writers. This makes our analysis rather difficult.[24]

In the discussion of the unconscious establishment of attitudes we will use some of the results of our previous analysis of emotions and feelings. Certain enduring emotional configurations, as we know, are hardly distinguishable from emotional attitudes. If the prevailing part of the content of an attitude is affective and its organizational elements are chiefly affective, too, we speak rather about sentiment than attitude. If there is a considerable cognitive component and a specific reaction, it is an attitude. If, for instance, the presence of a person makes us consistently uneasy and we resent it, without doing anything about it, it is a sentiment. But if we avoid the person, it is rather an attitude.

It is to be stressed that attitudes are formed (not inborn) and that they are configurations, organized of conative, cognitive and affective components. Some authors also add perception as another component (Cattell,[25] G. Allport,[26] Burnham,[27] Cantril, Sherif, Krech, Crutchfield,[28] and others). Cattell[29] and Krech and Crutchfield include also motivational elements. Asch is the most inclusive: ". . . attitude includes all psychological functions."[30] Any of the main components, cognitive or emotional, may be a chief organizer of the attitude.

UNCONSCIOUS ESTABLISHMENT OF PERSONAL ATTITUDES

Personal attitudes are interesting for us only in so far as they concern the life of society or in so far as they are the raw material of social attitudes.

a) Emotional Sources of Personal Attitudes

There are several emotional sources in the formation of personal attitudes. The first one is the traumatic experience. But although we know about such experiences, we do not know enough about the process by which they contribute to the formation of a new attitude. The second way is the repeated satisfaction or dissatisfaction of inborn and acquired drives,[31] needs or wants.[32] This may be strengthened by thinking processes of different kinds: expectations of similar future experiences; abstractions from certain properties of objects or persons causing the experience; generalizations and transfer on similar persons or objects; judgments; and establishment of certain policies and action-guiding principles (for instance, hedonistic, humanitarian, determination of achieving a career, and the like).

Since Freud's time special attention has been paid to the enduring effect of repeated frustrations which, for instance, may develop different anxieties, specific or general. Naturally, only specific anxieties[33] related to a certain object are interesting for our study. It seems that experimental and anthropological material supports this theory. For instance, the lack of sufficient food in infants (or in young rats[34]) is claimed to develop food anxiety and a strong tendency for hoarding. Nevertheless, it seems that in the case of infants, the lack of food was combined with a lack of fondling and mothering to produce this effect.[35] Although the corroboration of this theory[36] is far from complete, it is understood that the origin and development of attitudes of this kind in humans is unconscious.

Repeated frustrations may also cause an aggressive attitude toward the frustrating (or other) person or object. The aggressive individual often does not know the real cause of his aggressive attitude and seeks its explanation in false rationalizations.[37]

Another important source of attitude is the spontaneous development of strong emotional attachments.[38] Insofar as such emotional configurations induce the individual to react in a characteristic way and have a considerable cognitive content, they may be an attitude. Such may be the development of a strong interest in old china, of love for a poet or writer, for a foreign culture, or the development of a strong attachment to an animal pet. The causes of the development of such an attitude and the development itself are often concealed before the consciousness.

Empathy, too, may be a source of attitudes. Both may be strengthened by co-operation with the empathized individual. A hunter who used to hunt with his dog for years develops a deeper attachment to and empathy with him than does a mere lover of a pet. A boy empathizes more with another boy when they explore nature together, when they fish, or make fire together.

194

B) UNCONSCIOUS THINKING PROCESSES
IN ESTABLISHMENT OF PERSONAL ATTITUDES

Some students of attitudes stress the importance of perception for the establishment of attitudes. They point to the selective processes included in our perceptions, to the relational properties as perceived on the object, and to the organization of the percept.

In this respect, we have to stress that some attitudes (perhaps the majority of them) are not formed when we perceive the relevant object or happening, but much later, after we have "thought it over" (perhaps unconsciously).

The establishment of the point, scale, or frame of reference is another process stressed as important in the development of attitudes.[39] But simple summation of similar experiences and the computing service play an important role in the establishment of certain personal attitudes, too. Comparison and judgment are the most frequently mentioned thinking processes involved in the establishment of some personal attitudes. All of these may be unconscious.

Although judgment is considered as an important part of the formation of attitudes, not much has been said about the details of this process.[40] One of the simplest unconscious judgments that originates a new attitude is the drawing of conclusions from a new fact (see pp. 37-41). The man who lost his job, as well as the man who became suddenly very rich, or the man who was promoted, all of them unconsciously developed a large number of new attitudes by drawing conclusions from the changed situation.

Not only the development of such attitudes, but even the facts on which they were based may be completely unconscious.[41] Typical in this respect is the attitude of trust or distrust toward a person, without any knowledge of good reasons for it. We may even distrust a person who is kind to us and renders services to us.

Other unconscious judgments that produce attitudes are to be found in the application of certain ideas, principles or policies to persons, situations, or objects. People who are punctual may develop a strong aversion toward a person who is not. The idea of personal superiority, of a special personal mission, the principle of avoiding difficulties or of meeting them straightforwardly, the cautiousness toward women[42] (some of whom may be "insincere"), the dislike for clergymen (because some of them are not good Christians), all these and similar attitudes may often unjustly develop in an unconscious way.

Other personal attitudes may be unconsciously deduced from culturally established norms.[43] Thus, the discovery of microbes led some overanxious people to be suspicious of raw vegetables, fruits, restaurants, and other public places. They developed such extreme attitudes from the valid medical norm.

The transfer of the established attitudes to similar objects or persons may often be unconscious, too. Likewise, other thinking processes such as the understanding of a new situation, insight, computing service, and other thinking operations that lead to new attitudes may be unconscious.

c) Learning

Some psychologists consider learning, conditioning, or acquiring of a new habit as the main or only process responsible for the formation of a new attitude.[44] This is overdone. The cognitive and emotional content which is not learned plays an important role, too. The cognitive component allows the learned or habitual behavior pattern to go on, or it may check it or modify it. Attitudes vary with the social situation. Thus, our general politeness, which is learned, varies according to what we know about the age, sex, position, and social status of a person and according to the place where we meet him (funeral, church, football stadium, or formal reception).[45]

Of the different learned aspects of attitudes the most frequent are the connections of the emotional content with the object or situation and the linkings of the object or situation with the appropriate reaction.

We know that we may learn a sentiment through repeated emotional responses. It may become an attitude if there is a readiness to react in a characteristic way and considerable cognitive component is attached to it. Both the fact that we learned the new attitude and the result of the learning process may be unconscious.

The most frequently discussed kind of learning of attitudes is conditioning. It is more frequent in the development of personal attitudes than in any others. It is more often unconscious than conscious. This also applies to its product — the attitude.

ACQUISITION OF SOCIAL ATTITUDES

a) Acceptance of Ready-Made Attitudes

"The first and by far the most important and most common method is for the individual to accept an attitude whole from a culture before he has necessarily had any contact with the specific objects toward which the attitude is later directed," says Cantril.[46] We get hundreds of attitudes from our parents and teachers before we really know their

196

objects. Some of these are simply understood and accepted as such. In many cases, though, there is also suggestion, learning, and imitation. The mere fact of the existence and use of the attitude in adults having a rather high prestige is suggestive.

The intellectual organization of such accepted attitudes at the beginning is simple. In the eyes of the child, things belong or do not belong together, suit each other or are opposed to each other, approximately as the adults say. Later on, this simple and passive structure is strengthened by the subsequent perceptions which are selective and are organized, generally, as the attitudes of adult people want them to be. In this way new experience may seemingly "confirm" the original passive and weak structure of the attitude, often disregarding the real nature of the object.

Some of the ready-made attitudes are accepted consciously. The words are heard and understood. But often, the words are accompanied by a certain gesture or expression of voice, which is noticed marginally. On the other hand, attitudes may be presented only indirectly and even without any use of words. Turning a cold shoulder on a member of a different nationality or race is such an indirect presentation. When repeated, such experiences may unconsciously develop a similar attitude in the child. I remember a young man from a bourgeois family who became a member of a socialist party. His new friends noticed many of his bourgeois attitudes and occasionally pointed them out to him. He was surprised by it and became aware of some of them for the first time in his life. K. Mannheim indicates that a social class may become aware of its own attitudes after an attack by a political opponent.[47]

Every profession or occupation has special attitudes of its own, some of them belonging only to its unwritten ethos or atmosphere. There are unconsciously acquired church attitudes, office attitudes, political party attitudes, sport club attitudes, artistic group attitudes and so on.

Another group of accepted attitudes are those acquired in later years from new group[48] contacts or from campaigns of all kinds. Immigrants gradually accept a great many new attitudes without knowing it. It is not important whether at the beginning they were painfully aware of them or whether they did not notice them.

Campaigning of all kinds, including advertising, in many cases makes us aware of the new attitude which we are supposed to accept. Yet the processes of gradual acceptance of the new attitude may be fully unconscious. Unconscious empathies, identifications, imitations, learning, habit, and suggestive influence start the process of acceptance, perhaps hesitatingly and half-heartedly, until the induced selective perceptions confirm it. The process of building the new attitude is generally

197

concealed from us. But its outcome, the new attitude resulting from it, may be conscious. Sometimes a new attitude develops suddenly as, for instance, in conversion, although, as we know, the basic change often results from long, unconscious learning (see p. 158), and possibly insight.

Face-to-face participation in the life of the group increases the similarity of attitudes of its members. This occurs in several ways. First is the conscious acceptance of some group attitudes through commitments to the goals of the group. Second is the slow assimilation to the group attitudes through learning, habituation, and sometimes insight. To become a member of a fraternity, a service club, a religious order, a church, or to become a student at a college are cases in point. The special shades of reverence toward the symbols of the organization, toward the leader, toward certain customs or feelings, toward attitudes derived from the atmosphere of the group generally are acquired through participation in the life of the group. Not only the process of reception, but also the accepted attitudes may be unconscious.[49] The degree of the influence of the group depends on its congeniality.[50]

Besides these spontaneous processes, there is always pressure on the individual to accept the desirable attitudes. As long as the pressure is informal we often are not aware of it nor of its effects[51] (see pp. 142, 161-162).

b) Creation of Reshaped Personal or of New Attitudes by Group Participation

Personal attitudes are often basic to group attitudes. Nevertheless, as a rule, the life of the group reshapes them. As an example of reshaping let us consider the development of attitudes of the prewar domestic servants in Europe toward their employers. For decades they had low wages, very little free time, and their personal dignity suffered by the strong subserviency to their masters. A personal resentment necessarily developed. After certain political parties started to organize them and invited them to their meetings, however, new, common, and more radical attitudes were produced by interaction. The process, as well as some aspects of the resulting attitudes, was partly conscious and partly unconscious. Unconscious was, for instance, the part resulting from the group atmosphere, from group stimulation, from empathies and identifications with neighbors, and so forth.

A very good example of the development of new social attitudes through group interaction (previously existing neither in the individual nor in the group) is the above mentioned study by Sherif[52] of the two

198

newly constituted groups of boys. Twenty-four boys, who did not know each other, were put in a summer camp. After they developed new friendships, the group was split in two so that friends were placed as nearly as possible into opposite groups. The groups played competitive games, and the members of the winning group were rewarded attractively. In addition to that, several situations were arranged so that the behavior of one group caused the other group severe frustrations. New attitudes toward the ingroup (stronger adherence) as well as attitudes of hostility toward the outgroup developed. The original attitudes of friendship changed into hostility and the attitudes of indifference into friendship. New attitudes toward the group name, toward the leaders of the group, toward catchwords, activities, and buildings also developed. Although it was not stated in Sherif's study, undoubtedly the processes and a part of the attitudes were unconscious.[53]

UNCONSCIOUS OPERATION OF ATTITUDES

The unconscious operation of our attitudes shows up in almost all of our behavior. This is widely recognized, especially by psychiatrists, and partly verified by experimental studies. We know how enormous is the unconscious influence of our attitudes on our perceptions.[54] We know that an unfavorable attitude tends to obliterate recognition of individual differences (for instance, between Negroes[55]) and makes us see more characteristics of a race against which we are prejudiced.[56] Our attitude toward money is responsible for our overestimation of the size of coins. Coins of greater value are overestimated by children more than coins of lesser value, and poor children overestimate more than rich children.[57] Attitudes are one of the selective factors in our perceptions. Objects which according to our attitude are less important may not be perceived.[58]

In a similar way, our attitudes unconsciously distort recall. The Negroes on the same picture were incorrectly remembered by white children as engaged in some menial tasks. Psychoanalysts found that a certain attitude may suppress part or all of the memories concerning a subject. Ideas repressed by the unconscious operation of an attitude are not allowed to enter consciousness or are expelled from it. Learning appears to be affected by attitudes in a similar way. The majority of people show a superior recall for passages which are in agreement with their own attitudes.[59]

Many students have shown that attitudes affect also the interpretation of facts. The description of identical pictures by liberals and by conservatives (also by pro-labor and by anti-labor subjects) is different according to their basic attitudes.[60] Attitudes produced by hypnosis yield new interpretations of the same pictures.[61] People with different basic attitudes give a very different, sometimes opposite meaning to cartoons of Mr. Biggot.[62]

Aside from whether these and similar studies clearly point to the unconscious operation of the studied attitudes or not, there is no doubt that the operation of most of them is unconscious.

a) Unconscious Operation of Unconscious Attitudes

Increased self-confidence (after a successful achievement), stronger cautiousness (after a bad experience), development of sympathy toward somebody (because of his kind behavior toward a needy person), loss of sympathy (after the person has been cool and aloof), stronger love for a foreign nation (after a longer sojourn in the foreign country), all these and many other similar attitudes, of which we are not aware, may operate months or years without our being aware of them.

The behavior of a Czech who marries a German girl or who lives for years in Germany, thereby accepting certain German attitudes, may be guided by these without knowing it. Such men, for instance, were not as able to oppose the Germanization policy of the Austro-Hungarian empire as decisively as other Czechs generally were.

The unconscious operation of an attitude we do not know about is still easier if it can be labeled by the name of another acceptable attitude. Love for an artist may operate under the label of the love for art. Similarly love of showing off in good society may operate under the label of the love for opera, or interest in women under the love of ballet. I knew militant communists who honestly believed that their violent and bitter fight for social justice was their guiding attitude and thought that they did not seek personal advancement or property. Yet on being ousted from the communist party, they stopped fighting for social justice and looked for a rapid promotion in another field.

Another well known case in point is that male jurors are almost always more favorable to a beautiful young woman defendant than they should be. Many of them may believe that they are interested only in justice; and they do not admit their favorable attitude, which operates unconsciously,[63] toward the young woman.

Fiedler, Warrington and Blaisdell[64] found that unconscious attitudes make us consider fellow group members, whom we like better, as more similar to ourselves and as more similar to our ideal self than those we like less. The unconscious attitude may lead to very energetic activity only as long as it remains unconscious. When it becomes conscious, a moral or esthetic concern may not allow it any more.

B) UNCONSCIOUS INFLUENCE OF CONSCIOUS ATTITUDES

It is possible that members of a certain church or of a certain service club or members of a certain political party are often not able to fight successfully against the influence of their particular attitudes on their decision even if the attitudes are conscious. Their fight for correctness and impartiality is in vain, despite their best efforts. The unconscious influence of the conscious attitude in many cases cannot be overcome.

This applies even to people of extreme moral rectitude. The attitude provides the plausible rationalization, supporting factual information and good reasons which cannot be fully refuted because, surprisingly enough, the counter-arguments are somewhat unavailable. The effort to be strictly just and impartial does not arouse as many energies as the biased tendency. It does not bring as much material either. Thus, even an impartial mind unconsciously and almost necessarily sides with the case favored by the attitude.

Conscious attitudes also produce certain tensions in our muscles, certain movements, facial expressions, restlessness, walking around and other mainly physical behavior, of which we become aware only in some cases.[65]

* * *

The unconscious influence of conscious or unconscious social attitudes is interesting for us, especially as far as the cultural attitudes are concerned. They may skip our consciousness when operating. Owing to them the socialized personalities support, produce, and enforce culturally accepted behavior without our thinking of it. Of course, subcultural and group attitudes also often guide our behavior without our awareness. Unconscious and unconsciously operating attitudes are also an important element of social and group structure. They produce and maintain a considerable portion of it.

The unconscious and unconsciously operating attitudes surpass by their number and by their operation the capacity of consciousness. Conscious attitudes are probably less numerous than the unconscious ones. But the role of consciousness is further diminished by its small influence on the operation of the conscious attitudes. Thus, attitudes are one of the most unconscious tools of achieving and maintaining our well-adjusted social behavior.

FOOTNOTES TO CHAPTER TWELVE

1. See E. W. Nelson, "Attitudes: I. Their Nature and Development," *J. General Psych.*, 21, 1939, pp. 367-399.

2. Such are, for instance, set or set for verbal responses (MacKinnon), conditioned reflex, disposition (Wallas), acquired predisposition (Dewey), need (MacKinnon), desire, tendency, opinion, inclination, prejudice, conviction (Thurstone), habit, stereotypes, and others. Cattell defines attitudes as dynamic traits arising from some deeper sentiment or innate drive (*Personality*, p. 84).
   Certainly not all sets are attitudes. Only longer lasting sets comprising some emotional elements may be attitudes (W. E. Vinacke, *Psychology of Thinking*, p. 318). Conditioned reflexes are not attitudes because of the orientation of the attitudes to the world of objects (R. E. Park, "Human Nature, Attitudes and Mores," in K. Young (ed.), *Social Attitudes*, H. Holt, 1931, p. 31). Attitudes are not reflexes because they are communicable, while reflexes are not. They have a cognitive component which reflexes do not have. Habits are not communicable either (opposite opinion is held by C. I. Hovland, "Changes in Attitudes through Communication," *J. Abn. and Soc. Psychology*, 46, 1951, p. 427). We refuse to identify attitudes with sets for verbal responses because these may induce any kind of behavior. Not all inclinations and tendencies are attitudes either (such as, inclination to laziness or tendency to exaggerate) because they may lack the orientation toward certain specific objects. Attitudes are not needs. Respect or admiration, for instance, are not needs. Again, not all dispositions are attitudes. A disposition to outbursts and many others are not attitudes.
   Agreeing with R. E. Park that attitudes are connected with a certain tension, we refuse to identify them with opinions, stereotypes and convictions which often lack tension. Personality traits are not necessarily oriented to objects and therefore are different from attitudes.

3. M. Sherif and H. Cantril, *The Psychology of Ego Involvements*, p. 5.

4. H. Cantril, "General and Specific Attitudes," *Psychological Monographs*, 192, 1932, p. 11.

5. M. Sherif, *An Outline of Social Psychology*, pp. 202, 207.

6. This is accepted by several contemporary students of attitudes such as T. M. Newcomb, "Social Psychological Theory," in *Social Psychology at the Crossroads* (ed. by J. H. Rohrer and M. Sherif), Harper and Brothers, New York, 1951, p. 37; G. Murphy, *Personality*, p. 980, and others.

7. M. Sherif and C. W. Sherif, *An Outline of Social Psychology*, p. 494.

8. M. Sherif and H. Cantril, *op. cit.*, pp. 34, 43; H. Cantril, *Psychology of Social Movements*, pp. 19-21.

9. W. I. Thomas and F. Znaniecki, *The Polish Peasant in Europe and America*, p. 22.

10. D. Katz and E. Stotland seem to be opposed to this conception. An attitude for them is the "predisposition to evaluate;" see their "A Preliminary Statement to a Theory of Attitude Structure and Change" in S. Koch, ed., *Psychology: A Study of a Science*, McGraw-Hill, New York, 1959, vol. 3, p. 428.

11. W. I. Thomas and F. Znaniecki, *op. cit.*, p. 22.

12. M. Sherif, "An Experimental Approach to the Study of Attitudes," *Sociometry*, I., 1938, pp. 90-98.

13. T. M. Newcomb, *Personality and Social Change*, Dryden Press, New York, 1943, esp. pp. 116-117, 119-123, 125-132.

14. J. G. Miller, ed. *Experiments in Social Process*, McGraw-Hill, New York, 1950, p. 178.

15. F. H. Allport, *Social Psychology*, p. 277.

16. R. Linton, *Study of Man*, p. 339.

17. K. Young, *Personality*, p. 104; W. H. Burnham, *The Normal Mind*, Appleton Century, New York, 1924, p. 285.

18. G. Murphy, *op. cit.*, p. 291.

19. G. H. Mead, *Mind, Self, and Society*, pp. 68-69.

20. H. S. Sullivan, *Conceptions...*, p. 130.

21. N. L. Munn, *Psychology*, 1956, p. 106.

22. G. Murphy, *op. cit.*, p. 201.

23. M. Sherif and C. W. Sherif, *Groups in Harmony and Tension*, p. 171.

24. "There is no escape from the conclusion that we need a theory of attitudes . . ." says Asch, (*Social Psychology*, p. 559). Newcomb claims that "The exact process by which infants and children acquire attitudes has not been adequately studied . . ." (*Social Psychology*, p. 128). Sherif surmises that "There must be some basic principles governing any attitude;" but, evidently they are not known yet. (M. Sherif, *op. cit.*, 1948, p. 247) R. B. Cattell states that ". . . the nature and cause of . . . source traits in attitudes and interests . . . is not yet clear" (*Personality*, p. 83). C. I. Hovland complains about the lack of adequate experimentation in attitudes on a more basic level, *op. cit.*, p. 431.

25. R. B. Cattell, *Personality*, p. 445.

26. G. W. Allport, "Attitudes," in *The Nature of Personality, Selected Papers*, Addison-Wesley Press, Cambridge, Mass., 1950, p. 13.

27. W. H. Burnham, *op. cit.*, p. 285.

28. D. Krech and R. S. Crutchfield, *Theory and Problems of Social Psychology*, McGraw-Hill, New York, 1948, p. 152.

29. R. B. Cattell, *General Psychology*, p. 175.

30. S. E. Asch, *op. cit.*, p. 592.

31. T. M. Newcomb, *Social Psychology*, pp. 128-130.

32. D. Krech, R. S. Crutchfield and E. L. Ballachey, *Individual in Society*, McGraw-Hill, New York, 1962, pp. 180-186.

33. See K. Horney, *The Neurotic Personality of Our Time*, also, her *New Ways in Psychoanalysis*, W. W. Norton, New York, 1939, and *Our Inner Conflicts*, W. W. Norton & Co., Inc., New York, 1945.

34. J. McV. Hunt, "The Effects of Infant Feeding-Frustration upon Adult Hoarding in the Albino Rat," *J. Abn. and Soc. Psychol.*, 36, 1941, pp. 338-360.

35. Compare A. Kardiner, R. Linton, *The Individual and his Society*, Columbia

University Press, 1939, pp. 212, 216; A. Kardiner and assoc., *The Psychological Frontiers of Society*, pp. 26-27, 204, 246, 250, 253.

36. J. Dollard, "Hostility and Fear in Social Life," *Soc. Forces*, XVII, 1938, pp. 15-26; J. Dollard and others, *Frustration and Aggression*, Yale Univ. Press, New Haven, 1939.

37. B. Zawadski, "Limitations of the Scapegoat Theory of Prejudice," *J. Abn. and Soc. Psychology*, 43, 1948, pp. 127-141; G. Lindzey, "An Experimental Examination of the Scapegoat Theory of Prejudice," *J. Abn. and Soc. Psychol.*, 45, 1950, pp. 296-309; G. K. Morlan, "A Note on Frustration-Aggression Theories of Dollard and his Associates," *Psych. Review*, 56, 1948, pp. 1-9.

38. See pp. 164-165.

39. M. Sherif and H. Cantril say: ". . . . attitudes are referential affairs, consciously or unconsciously related to a framework" (*op. cit.*, p. 286).

40. See E. L. Hartley and R. E. Hartley, H. Cantril, M. Sherif, S. E. Asch, D. Krech and S. Crutchfield, and others.

41. L. Diller studied such establishment of unconscious self-attitudes ("Conscious and Unconscious Self-Attitudes after Success and Failure," *J. of Personality*, 23, 1954, pp. 11-12).

42. See A. Kardiner, *The Psychological Frontiers of Society*, p. 239.

43. M. Sherif and C. W. Sherif say: "The attitudes . . . of individual members . . . will henceforth be derived consciously or unconsciously from these norms standardized in the process of interaction" (*Groups in Harmony*, p. 233).

44. For instance, K. Young, *op. cit.*, p. 104; M. Sherif and H. Cantril, *op. cit.*, p. 20; M. Sherif, *An Outline of Social Psychology*, p. 212; J. J. Gibson, "The Implications of Learning Theory for Social Psychology," p. 161, in *Experiments in Social Process*, McGraw-Hill, New York, 1956.

45. T. M. Newcomb says that "norms concerning behavior are not merely standards of judgments . . . permanently interiorized by individuals. Rather they are subject to constant revision in the light of what other people are observed to be doing." ("Social Psychological Theory," in J. H. Rohrer and M. Sherif, *Social Psychology at the Crossroads*, p. 41). Also, Sherif himself seems to feel that he cannot consistently maintain his conviction that the permanence of the attitude is due to learning. In his book with Cantril (*The Psychology of Ego Involvements*, p. 22), he says: "An attitude becomes a more or less enduring state . . . because of the cognitive components in its formation."

46. H. Cantril, "Attitudes and Opinions," in E. G. Boring, H. S. Langfeld and H. P. Weld, *op. cit.*, p. 562.

47. K. Mannheim, *Ideology and Utopia*, p. 207.

48. See W. H. Whyte, *The Organization Man*, Doubleday Anchor Books, Garden City, New York, 1957, p. 332.

49. E. L. Hartley and R. E. Hartley say: "Once the individual is in a group, he is subject to its influence, often without any awareness of the range of changes being induced." (*Fundamentals*, p. 677). Similarly, D. Cartwright and A. Zander say: ". . . informal groups also exert an influence over their members, but often . . . without the awareness of the members that it is happening." (*Group Dynamics*, p. 138).

50. See S. E. Asch, "Studies in the Principles of Judgments and Attitudes, II.,

Determination of Judgments by Group and Ego Standards," *J. of Soc. Psych.*, 12, 1940, pp. 433-65.

51. L. M. Killian, speaking about the behavior of people during disasters, says that the "individuals . . . were not always conscious . . . of the existence of cross-pressures" (D. Cartwright and A. Zander, *op. cit.*, 1953, p. 250).

52. M. Sherif and C. W. Sherif, *Groups in Harmony* . . .; also, M. Sherif in J. H. Rohrer and M. Sherif, *Social Psychology at the Crossroads*, pp. 388-424.

53. G. C. Homans says that "Norms often arise from the diffuse interaction of the members . . . as if overnight. . . . One day they were followed though not consciously held . . ." (*The Human Group*, p. 417).

54. Basic in this respect is F. C. Bartlett's *Remembering*, see especially p. 191.

55. V. Seeleman, "The Influence of Attitude Upon the Remembering of Pictorial Material," *Arch. Psychol.*, 1940, No. 258.

56. G. W. Allport and B. M. Kramer, "Some Roots of Prejudice," *J. Psychol.*, 22, 1946, pp. 9-39.

57. J. S. Bruner, "Social Value and Need as Organizing Factors in Perception," *Am. Psychologist*, 1, 1946, p. 241.

58. E. L. Horowitz and R. E. Horowitz, "Development of Social Attitudes in Children," *Sociometry, I.*, 1938, pp. 301-338.

59. M. Henle *et al.*, "An Investigation of the Influence of Needs and Attitudes on Perception and Memory," unpubl., quoted by S. E. Asch, *op. cit.*, p. 615.

60. H. M. Proshansky, "A Projective Method for the Study of Attitude," *J. of Abn. Soc. Psychol.*, 38, 1943, pp. 393-95.

61. C. J. Leuba and C. Lucas, "The Effect of Attitudes on Description of Pictures," *J. of Exp. Psych.*, 35, 1945, pp. 517-24.

62. P. L. Kendall and K. M. Wolf, "The Analysis of Deviant Cases in Communications Research," in P. F. Lazarsfeld and F. N. Stanton, *Communications Research*, Harper and Brothers, New York, 1949, pp. 152-179.

63. J. G. Miller reports about the larger proportion of foreign-born defendants being found guilty even by judges who in all sincerity attempted to decide every case on its merits. See his *Unconsciousness*, p. 195 and also H. J. Rees and H. E. Israel, "An Investigation of the Establishment and Operation of Mental Sets," in "Studies in Psychology from Smith College," *Psychol. Monographs*, 46, 1935, No. 210, pp. 1-26.

64. F. E. Fiedler, W. G. Warrington and F. J. Blaisdell, "Unconscious Attitudes as Correlates of Sociometric Choice in a Social Group," *J. Abn. Soc. Psch.* 47, 1952, pp. 790-796.

65. M. H. Krout, "An Experimental Attempt to Produce Unconscious Manual Symbolic Movements" and "An Experimental Attempt to Determine the Significance of Unconscious Symbolic Manual Movements," *J. General Psych.*, 51, 1954, pp. 93-152.

XIII

VALUES

The different conceptions of values range from value being an idea,[1] belief,[2] criterion,[3] standard or norm[4] (and as such, part of the ego)[5] to value being an element capable of evoking a covert response.[6] Thus, value is considered as something that is in the mind of people, or, on the other hand, as something outside the human personality. But those who understand value as an idea generally add that it is an idea of an object so that the other non-personal part of the value comes into the picture; those who claim that value is an object add that it has a meaning or usefulness. Certainly ideas, on the one hand, and objects and persons, on the other, are never considered as unrelated to each other.

Thomas and Znaniecki expressed it by saying that value is any datum having an empirical content or meaning.[7] Yet "meaning" seems to us to be too broad. More adequate seems to be the definition by Gillin and Gillin stating that value is the desirability of a thing as compared with something else[8] or that of Morris as something preferred or preferable.[9] The element of comparison with other values is an important characteristic of the value.

Values are often defined as being derivative of, or otherwise, as basically related to the attitudes (Bonner,[10] Young,[11] Thomas and Znaniecki,[12] Sherif-Cantril,[13] Stagner[14]). The closeness and similarity of attitudes and values are evident. It remains to be seen what are the similar and dissimilar components of each.

Of the four characteristics of attitude as given by Sherif and Cantril, value has the subject-object relationship. Second, both generally have an affective quality and a cognitive content. Yet values are not always states of readiness to react in a characteristic way. On the other hand, attitudes are not always to be compared and preferred to other attitudes as values are. Further, values often are more objective, factual, and better founded. We may have a romantic attitude toward a girl; but considering all the conditions opposed to our marrying her, we feel that she has only a very low value for us. We have no attitudes toward many valued objects of our daily life (for instance, air).

Thus, values appear as configurations of cognitive, affective, and also conative components expressing a personally or socially important relation of the individual or group to objects (or to ideas, institutions, persons, or groups). They are arranged into a preferential order with other values.[15]

Relatively very few students of values took cognizance of their possibly unconscious establishment, existence, and operation. Murray and Kluckhohn say that the process of evaluation may operate without self-awareness.[16] Cantril claims that the sources of personal values are generally forgotten.[17] Woodruff found in values subconscious mental processes, especially the choosing processes and learning.[18] Stagner recognizes that some social values are unconscious.[19] The unconscious operation[20] and existence[21] of values is accepted also by Cantril. Hartley and Hartley say that the "freighting of emotional impact with social values"[22] may be unconscious. Rose claims that some values are sometimes unconscious,[23] Wolff speaks about unconscious evaluation.[24]

PERSONAL VALUES

The most widely accepted assumption is that personal values originate in basic human drives, needs, and wants,[25] which are inborn, reshaped,[26] or acquired by experience and cultural training. Values are considered as established by canalization (Murphy), by conditioning, or by other kinds of learning.[27] Habits[28] are also often considered as a component in certain values. Alexander sees the source of personal values in the necessity of working out a scale subordinating or even relinquishing certain desires if they are in conflict with some more important ones.[29] Cantril considers personal values as often derived from basic standards of judgment.[30] One of the few who pointed to the situational meaning of values is Asch.[31]

To these sources of personal values a few more should be added. Personal values can be established by drawing conclusion from one or several facts. Another source of personal values is the summation of certain similar experiences and emotional attachments. Finally, some values are established through transference. In most cases, several of the above mentioned processes co-operate in establishing and maintaining a personal value.

A) Unconscious Establishment and Existence of Personal Values

1) Through Summation, Organization, and Use of other Values

Each new favorable experience associated with a person or object

207

adds something to its value. The favorable experiences may be summated into a pretty high value of the person or object. The process of summating (as well as comparing its results with other values) and the value itself may be unconscious.

Let us take an example. Suppose that being on vacation we discover a pleasant and refreshing walk through the woods and along the shore of a clear pond. By enjoying this experience repeatedly, the walk becomes a value for us. The process of establishment of the value has been unconscious, and the value itself is partly so. It becomes fully conscious only after we speak about it with our friends and especially after the path has been made unavailable.

The process of summation of emotional experiences, chiefly responsible for the establishment of the value, has been supported by other secondary processes. Similar summated, pleasant experiences also induced some learning, while dissimilar experiences (like watching a hawk and, another day, an otter; seeing an old tree felled in a windstorm; occasionally finding large mushrooms) were organized. There also was a use of certain social values, such as the romantic value of nature as acquired in school, from novels, and other sources. There were still other components, such as the idea that walking is healthful, that the fragrant forest air is good for the lungs, that there is no dust along the grassy path, and so on. Unconscious anticipation of future walks was another support of the value of the path. Unrecollected, previous experiences with similar landscapes certainly gave it a certain charm. And some other conscious recollections of similar pleasant places helped to enhance the value, too.

After being (often unconsciously) established, the values of people and objects are ready to be used. A boss knows the value of each of his employees, even if he does not evaluate them consciously. He knows who would be the first fired if necessary, as well as who would be the last. It is interesting that the employees with tenure, who no longer have a strong interest in the matter, develop a similar evaluation of themselves and of their collaborators. The process of evaluation goes ahead practically all the time without any outspoken intention or plan. They may never think of it, but if asked, they would be able to give a good answer about the value of each one of the employees. Another example of the establishment of a value (of a fountain pen) has been given in a previous chapter (see p. 122).

2) By Drawing Conclusions and by Comparing

A value may be unconsciously established by drawing conclusions directly from an experience, from a fact, or from several of them. If we have been given a new ointment which heals our wound fast and well, it becomes a value to us. The evaluation process went ahead spontaneously, unwittingly, automatically, and unconsciously. In certain cases, such a value could be explained chiefly by conditioning or learning. Yet it is also supported by unconscious thinking processes, for instance, by general consideration of health and good appearance made salient by the necessity of finishing an important task or by the anticipation of delivering a public speech.

In certain situations, we make real discoveries about the values of certain objects. When we have to choose between love and a career or between scientific interests and a well remunerated job in industry, we discover for the first time in our life which one of them we value higher. When fleeing their country before Nazis or communists, people had to make a choice of what to take in their knapsack. The family photographs or letters of a sweetheart, in some cases, proved to have higher value than some other objects badly needed in daily life.

If the value is not ready at the moment of decision, we sometimes establish it in a split second. During the short time of hesitation, several unconscious processes may establish it. We "feel," from a given moment on, which objects to choose, which one of them is more valuable to us.

3) Through Learning, Habit and Emotional Attachment

Some of these processes are so similar to each other and so often overlap that it is better to discuss them together.

We may learn the value of our glasses after we mislaid them several times and ran into difficulties in delivering our lecture or a public speech. Similarly, we learn "subconsciously"[32] to value highly the person with whom we have had several favorable experiences. Naturally, unconscious summation also helps in the development of such a value (see p. 123).

A personal value may be learned through a single experience, too. For instance, one serious sickness may teach us the value of good health. Such a strong lesson generally makes the learning process, as well as the learned value, fully conscious. Yet if during another similar experience our attention is fully occupied by other happenings, it may be unconscious, too.

Habit is frequently another source of a personal value. Our fountain pen may have a special value for us because we are used to its size and point. After we occasionally use other pens, the unconscious comparisons may lead to the establishment of its real value for us. A given violin may have a similar value to a violinist.

An emotional attachment, which so often helps the unconscious formation of a value, may in some cases be the main cause of a value. The persons or objects to which we develop an emotional attachment may become a value for us. Naturally, comparison must supplement the emotional attachment to produce a value. The emotional components are further complemented by habits, concepts, judgments, expectations, assumptions, learning, automatic behavior, and perceptions of the changing environment. Some or all these components and processes, as well as their result, may be unconscious. Generally, the individual becomes conscious of the value later, at the moment of trial. We may be completely unaware of the value of a tree which we were used to seeing from the window of our study. We discover it after the tree has been felled.

Another way to discover a personal value is the willingness to spend a certain amount of time and energy for the sake of a valued object or person. A political leader who rendered an unusual service to his country, the physician who healed our child, the servant who proved loyal and attached to us — all these become values for us. Their place on the scale of our values may be discovered when we write an article or make a speech for the sake of the political leader, or defend our doctor against his opponents, or render a service to our servant. The amount of work we are willing to do for the sake of the valued person almost empirically reveals its place on the scale of our values.

The value itself may be hidden in a larger complex, and we discover it only after a changed situation differentiates the particular components from each other. Such a complex may be, for instance, the human personality. We may have high regard for a man without knowing whether the valued quality is the service he has rendered to us, or the general fine human traits of his personality which impelled him to it, or perhaps the likelihood of services he may render us in the future. Only when we know that his human traits are far from fine and he will no longer be able to help us in the future, and we still value him highly, do we know that the value consisted chiefly in his past service to us.

FORMATION OF SOCIAL VALUES

A) BY INTERACTION BETWEEN PERSONAL VALUES

Certain social values may be developed from personal values of people living in similar conditions and valuating certain persons or objects similarly. Personal values may be reshaped through interaction into more uniform patterns — and accepted as values of the group.

But before we turn our attention to these processes, let us look at the social elements comprised in a personal value before the interaction begins. One of them is the socialization of our needs and desires. Further social elements may be the influence of a certain social situation, of a certain social structure, and of certain social products. The mere presence of another person during the process of valuation stimulates the process and may change it. This presence may bring the valuation closer to the values of the other person and may create greater enthusiasm; or it may veer away from them, may become more determined, more independent, and so on. Another component of personal values is the influence of social values.

All these social elements of a personal value, however, are not sufficient to change a personal value into a social value. The personal value becomes a social one only by being accepted by a group. The first type of interaction that socializes personal values is

1) Discussion

Discussion confronts the personal values of a number of people. Suppose, for instance, that in the case of the value of the walk in the woods and along the shore of the pond, a number of summer guests independently formed a similar personal value of the walk. Although all of them were enthusiastic about it, the value of each of them varied from the values of other summer guests. Shortsighted people were more impressed by colors, others were more sensitive to the beauty of rocks, while fishermen, on the other hand, valued higher the beauty of water. Older people liked places where they could rest and contemplate the scenery; young people liked climbing over the rocks. Literary people gave their attention to the scenery which reminded them of certain great literary works; those interested in painting were inclined to compare certain views to outstanding pictures and to value such views higher than others. City people, country people, hunters, gardeners, and hikers perceive and love different aspects of nature.

Suppose, for instance, that the majority of summer guests, although each somewhat differently, highly valued the view of the lake from the cliff. Only two persons did not. They valued more highly some other aspects of the walk.

In the discussion, the minority people succeed in convincing the others that there is something to their minority value. On the other hand, they now see clearly that they were wrong in underestimating the view of the lake from the cliff. The values of both groups came close together.[33] The longer they discuss them, the more similar, generally, become the values of the two groups.

Also, the stronger the feeling of belongingness to the group, the faster is the development of conformity. The less structured the stimulus field,[34] the more accepted the group is as the reference group[35] and the stronger the development toward conformity.

The tendency toward conformity is caused at least by three (generally unconscious) factors. First, it is due to our learning as children to conform to adults.[36] Secondly, as long as the individual enjoys the group, he unconsciously tends to avoid differing from the values of the group. This shows up in different forms: as the need to be understood, to be accepted, as well as the striving for security, as the wish for support, the wish to be liked, or as the influence of the prestige of the group.[37] It may also be a vague fear of nonconformity.[38] Thirdly, the individual may notice during the discussion that certain facts escaped him; and he may correct his one-sided approach.[39]

Any reshaping of values through discussion in a group may have some unconscious elements or even be completely unconscious. Numerous discussions about small everyday values, as they occur in a family or in a group of friends or co-workers, shape the content of social values much more unconsciously than consciously. Often, even if we consciously keep our own original standpoint, unconsciously we may have already fallen away from it.

Such chiefly unconscious establishment of values through discussion produces a large part of the common values of any contest jury, hobby organization, artistic or scientific group. This also is true of the values which are not discussed directly and formally but only by remarks or gestures, without any clear arguments. In such a way, the value of certain foods is often established as well as the value of certain objects of daily use, friends, public personalities, and so on. The exchange of reactions often may not end with a clear, formal acceptance of the standpoints but rather stay open.

Actions and reactions often come from several people simultaneously. Sometimes the whole group is acting and reacting. Only a smaller part of these reactions can be perceived consciously; others are perceived marginally or subliminally. Some of them cannot be distinguished clearly from each other; and they converge into the impression of a certain atmosphere, mood or vague attitude. All the unconscious and conscious impressions enter the process of leveling off and influence its results.

The reshaping of a value goes on all the time during the discussion. There is a continuous flow of mostly unconscious thinking. Arguments are met by counter-arguments, by agreement or resentment, enthusiasm or dislike, by corrections and comparisons. The computing service and summation, as well as the drawing of conclusions, operate continuously;

the emotional reactions alternate and are combined with thinking processes. Other processes serve to indicate how far the value can be accepted without jeopardizing the personal interests, without hurting personal dignity, personal attitudes, sentiments, and so on.

In formally organized groups governed by previously established rules, more of the group processes are conscious. Also, certain unorganized groups (such as scholars) follow certain informal, customary, though conscious rules of discussion. For instance, the value of a certain medieval king may be discussed by a number of historians. They bring rational, scientifically shaped arguments and counterarguments indicating the higher or lower value of the king in the development of the country. But even here, certain unconscious judgments and emotional states of the debaters, likes and dislikes, democratic or autocratic convictions, a socialistic or conservative coloring, and other characteristics enter unconsciously as well into a seemingly purely rational, and conscious interaction. In artistic discussions, which may also follow an established pattern and use conscious arguments, the unconscious and emotional elements are more numerous.

The second important change a personal value undergoes through discussion is in its emotional content. Similar emotional states of other persons confirm and strengthen it; divergent emotional reactions discourage and weaken it. Strong emotional states strengthen it more than lukewarm ones do. Besides that, the interaction itself stimulates certain emotional reactions.[40] These are summated and organized.

Practically all the discussions combine intellectual and emotional elements. Everyday discussions and exchanges of views between ordinary people about current issues are usually more emotional than the discussions of educated people. In scientific discussions, the proportion of the intellectual elements is probably the highest. The discussions in mass meetings may have a chiefly emotional character.

The interaction between personal values brings still another important characteristic to the value. The mere knowledge that a number of people have similar or identical values adds firmness and stability to the value.[41] Personal or minority values are almost always subject to doubt.

All these processes of intellectual and emotional assimilation and of increased firmness are basic steps toward socialization of personal values. What still remains to be done is the recognition (which may be unconscious) of the new product as a value of the group, the identification of the group with the new value, and the replacement of the personal feeling about the value (expressed by "I recognize the value") by the collective one ("we recognize the value"). It is to be noted that

213

the group officially may not adhere to a value although its individual members do. A strict Protestant sect may not officially accept the more lenient attitudes of the majority of its members.

2) Other Types of Interaction

People may look or smile at each other in such a way that their opinion is expressed very clearly. Also, unverbalized sounds and acts are understood and reacted to. Being often finer and subtler, such interactions may be very important in the formation of certain values.

Another type of interaction develops from co-operation on a common task. The actions and reactions of the people express their valuation of the common conditions of work. Workers producing the same kind of goods in one shop interact frequently. As a result, they produce certain common values referring to the daily output, to the material worked on, to the reward for work, to the management, to their own group, solidarity of its members, other groups of workers, special cliques, to distinctions in dress, to different jobs in the factory, and so on.[42] Likewise, the co-operation between the subordinate and the superior (giving and executing orders, leading and being led) may shape certain values.

We are less aware of any of these value-producing interactions than of the interactions through discussion. They comprise more marginal and subliminal perceptions and more unconscious judgments. Also, the values they produce are more often unconscious.

b) By Social Acceptance of a Personal Value

The establishment of a social value often takes place by acceptance of a value proposed by an individual. It may be a really individual creation (music, novel, poem) or a proposal of a small group of individuals (possibly a committee).

Acceptance by a group is the only way of producing a social value and the only test of it. The greatest art becomes great art only when it is recognized as such and accepted by people. There is no other criterion for it.

During the creation of a value by the individual the interpersonal interactions are to a great extent replaced by similar interactions between the ideas in the mind of the creative individual himself. The concepts of different values and their intellectual and emotional content influence each other as they do in the group interaction. The lack of stimulation by other people is replaced by a warmer and more intense emotional internal life of the creative individual.

A musical work, for instance, expresses in an abstract, often emotional, way the everyday values of thousands of individuals of our society. They were assimilated to each other in the mind of the composer to yield a product which expresses the values of many people in a single and powerful form.

The processes of acceptance of an individual's value by other individuals and by a group are generally complex. Unconscious past experiences, judgments, comparisons, insights, learning processes, finding of proper relations to other values, perhaps other unrecollected social values, as well as interactions enter the valuation process. Its final product, the recognition of the value, is a result of a number of these components and processes.

When we hear a new musical composition for the first time, we rarely accept it wholeheartedly. A second or third hearing brings it closer to us until it may become a value to us. What happened between the first and the third hearing to produce the value?

First, a better understanding developed. We see more clearly the relations of different parts of the composition which satisfy our (culturally developed) taste. Later, we better grasp the whole structure as a well-organized unit (often without any clear awareness). We feel more clearly the agreeable effect of the alternation of the gay and fast movements with the slow and serious ones. Certain unconscious comparisons with other similar works put the new composition into a certain frame of reference and give it a certain more pronounced profile. Thus, the originality of the main motif as well as the depth and width of its variations are better understood.

Besides these intellectual processes, there are emotional processes, too. The composition is found to express an individual's mood or emotional needs. The new form of the composition, which was an obstacle in conveying such a feeling at the first audition, is more familiar and no longer stands in its way.

Better knowledge of the composition creates certain expectations which again produce esthetic pleasure after we hear the now familiar melodies. The processes producing this esthetic feeling, as well as the previously mentioned ones, are mostly unconscious. They help to produce the new configurations of acceptance of the new value by the individual. If similar processes develop in many people who interact, the composition may become a social value. The most usual interaction generally takes place among the members of the audience at a public performance.

A special case of acceptance of a personal value is produced by campaigning. Although we may be aware of the insistence to accept

215

the new value, we may be fully unaware of the processes of suggestion and imitation, of learning and habituation, as well as of the acceptance of the arguments and intellectual structures proposed by the campaigner. Our processes of organizing this material may likewise remain unconscious. Interaction with other readers or listeners exposed to the same experiences accomplishes the final step in the process of acceptance.

c) BY COLLECTIVE CREATION

If we keep in mind our example of the walk in the woods, we may imagine that our summer guest had his first walk with a group of friends. They discovered the beauty of different parts of the walk together and reacted to them simultaneously. Most of their reactions were produced under the influence of the reactions of others. The perceptions of the beautiful spots occurred in a more excited state of mind. Similar emotional reactions of others confirmed and strengthened our guest's own reactions. Numerous empathies with similar emotional reactions of others induced a number of imitative processes which, again, added something to the strength and conformity of his own emotional reactions. The appreciation of the points which were generally accepted as beautiful became more enthusiastic. Empathies into partly divergent, emotional reactions of other members induced alterations of his feelings, and changes in the evaluation of the walk. The set of processes was similar to those operating in the collective establishment of attitudes. Especially important was the stimulation by the group.

A very common example of the collective creation of social values is the acceptance of a new stage drama or of a new symphony by the audience. Each member has his own impression of the performance, strengthened by the expectant and attentive atmosphere of the audience. When, after the performance, he hears the expression of similar emotions by hundreds or thousands of people in the audience (applause, whistles, shouts, cheers, or other reactions), his own evaluation of the work of art is further strengthened. Some of his expressions of agreement or disagreement, enthusiasm or resentment are direct reactions to similar or dissimilar expressions of his neighbors and the rest of the audience. In the applause, the common evaluation is directly worked out by a special combination of individual reactions to the performance and to the reactions of others (see p. 148).

During the performance itself, when the audience remains quiet, there is a frequent combining of individual reactions to the piece performed with either very subdued noises coming from the audience or possibly with the complete lack of such noises. There is a con-

216

tinual, internal reacting under the influence of these perceptions, summated often in the impression of a general atmosphere (tense, friendly, enchanted, startled, interested, critical, uncertain, divided, and so on). All three sets of impressions (performance, noises, atmosphere) combine and influence each other. They are unconsciously organized, intellectually and emotionally, and unconsciously related to previous experiences and knowledge, and to the present personal and external situation (political, literary, and other).

More permanent groups also create some of their group values through collective creation. Each high school class has certain special values such as an actor, a particular joke, a signal, a special type of puzzle, or even particular regard for a frog in the classroom aquarium. Each family may have its own values, such as Sunday afternoon parties, the old family house, the old family cat, photographs of grandparents, the curls or first shoes of children, certain verbal expressions, certain modifications of moral norms, special meaning of certain words, and others. So do summer camps,[43] members of an orchestra, people working in the same shop or office, or soldiers of the same platoon.

The working out of a value in permanent groups takes a longer time and follows a different scheme. In the family, for instance, there often is first an impression and emotional reaction to an event such as a visitor, an illness in the family, or marriage of a friend, and some discussion. The impressions are re-discussed later in a more quiet mood. Then new impressions from the same source may come, and a new discussion may follow. There often is repeated alternation of the common impressions, the discussion and personal thinking. Thus, the first impression may be rather well checked-on and organized; the important components of the value may become apparent and the unimportant ones dropped.

The unconscious, above mentioned elements of collective value creation (unconscious emotions, impressions, and traces) often are accompanied by stimulation, summation, thinking, learning, imitation, group identification, pressure and organization. All these may be so far unconscious that the resulting value may be unconscious, too. More often it happens that the value is partly conscious. The person knows about the value but its depth and breadth will appear later in a new situation.

As we know, some writers are inclined to underrate the power and importance of social processes in creating social values and prefer to see the real basis of the value chiefly in the object itself. In reality, the valuation process may partly disregard the factual conditions; and value may be due more to social processes of interaction and to the belongingness to the group than to appropriateness of the object to the needs

217

of people. Evidently there is less freedom in creation of the value of material objects, the usefulness of which is obvious, than of non-material things such as personal relations, religious, moral and esthetic concepts, group attitudes, and so on, which yield more to the power of social definitions. Yet the power of the value-creating processes is so great that they may produce certain striking differences even in the values of material objects. It is surprising, for instance, how large are the differences in values of different kinds of meat in different countries. In most of Europe, the brains and sweetbreads are considered very tasty and are expensive. Americans do not like them, and many avoid them. Conversely beef, so highly valued in the U. S., is considered a commonplace meat in Europe. Veal is appreciated much more, while in America it is not. These differences of values cannot be explained by differences in supply, the relative proportion of all these kinds of meat being approximately steady. The divergent values are only a consequence of differences in the valuative processes.

These are also responsible for the contradicting valuation of certain kinds of fish. The carp, for instance, is highly valued in Central Europe, while it is refused by Americans. Europeans consider it tasteful; Americans, distasteful.

The varied appreciation of nature among different social classes and in different times (the pre-romantic and romantic era!) is an interesting example of differences in the value of the same material reality.

d) By Acceptance of a Foreign Social Value

Acceptance of a foreign social value is in many respects of the same nature as acceptance of foreign cultural traits, which will be discussed in Chapter XVI. Here we will point only to some specific characteristics pertaining to the acceptance of social values. We have in mind especially the acceptance of a social value by another nation, another class, or by the young generation after it has been worked out as a social value in a more developed nation, in another social class, or in the previous generation. The conscious and unconscious processes which precede the establishment of the value have already been realized by the creating group and need not be repeated by the receiving group. Their result — the social value — is known as such to the accepting group. It is not a proposed value but a functioning social value of another group which may be accepted (and probably readjusted). If it fits the needs and conditions of the other group, it may easily be accepted without important changes. In reality the acceptance is never without

218

some change. The value is always to be readjusted to the special conditions of the accepting group. Malinowski showed this convincingly in the case of European culture traits which were accepted by African natives.[44] The French etiquette, accepted by the Russian upper classes in the 18th and 19th centuries, changed into a warmer, less formal, and more neighborly one. The type of the English gentleman, accepted as an ideal by the upper and middle classes of many western nations, was reshaped to fit the national character of each of these nations. The same applies to imitations of French literature by writers of different European nations in the nineteenth century.

Powerful social realities reshape even "unchangeable" values and adjust them to the needs and characteristics of the new society. Take, for instance, a poem or a quartet. The work is executed as precisely as the notation indicates. Yet the change is introduced in another way. The same words may be understood differently, and the same music may be interpreted with many different shades of expression. For instance, the interpretation of Beethoven by German, Austrian, French, Italian, or Czech musicians is certainly considerably different. The German interpretation stresses the monumental quality and sentimentality of the musical work. The Italian interpretation stresses the melody of the work; the French interpretation stresses its architecture; and the Czech interpretation, the lyrical content of the work; the Austrian interpretation would be something between the Czech and the German one. These differences are differences in values.

The Marseillaise was one of the very impressive expressions of the value of freedom. However, the nations of Austria-Hungary understood it somewhat differently from the way the French did. For them it was much more the expression of the wish for national freedom than for the freedom of the middle and lower classes from exploitation by the upper classes.

Most of these modifications of values were probably realized altogether unconsciously. The Russian upper middle class certainly did not notice the changes they introduced into French manners. The imitators of the English gentleman or of French literature on the European continent did not notice the deviations in their interpretation of these values, and deviations that were due to their national character. The musicians of different nations honestly consider their own interpretations of music to be good and authentic.

Now let us give more attention to the unconscious nature of the acceptance of a new social value. The values of upper classes and of mighty nations are attractive to lower classes and less powerful nations. Yet their acceptance may be completely unconscious. Thus, it is an offense for a communist leader to hear that he wants to live as the bourgeois class. Similarly, the nations that border France and Germany have striven to preserve the national character of their own cultures without copying France or Germany. Despite this determination, the communists imitate the way of life of the bourgeois; and the prestige of French and German culture induces the small neighbors to accept (mostly unconsciously) many values of these two outstanding cultures. The bourgeois revolutions against the privileges of the nobles in \the 18th and 19th centuries spread many of the values of the nobility into the bourgeois class despite the bourgeois' rebuff of nobles.

Another example of unconscious reasons for acceptance of a foreign value is the imitation of French cultural values by Poles and Czechs because they were afraid of German cultural influence and ensuing Germanization. In certain cases, however, the German cultural values might possibly have better fitted their national needs. Despite that, the newly introduced values were honestly believed to be useful and appropriate to the conditions of national life. The influence of the real cause of the acceptance remained mostly unconscious.

Likewise, in other cases the reasons for acceptance remain unconscious. A translation of a new set of poems, for instance, may be welcomed by the public with unexpected enthusiasm. A new foreign fashion may be accepted as precisely just what was needed, without clear knowledge why.

About forty years ago, a new fashion was accepted, started by the Prince of Wales, of leaving the last, low buttonhole of the vest open. It somehow expressed a disinclination toward 19th century formalism and the wish for more freedom of the individual, and meant identification of the young generation with a young prince who opposed formal traditions and Victorian rigidity. There probably were more elements in the psychological field of the young generation supporting the acceptance of this new fashion which we do not know. Of course, the young people of the time were not aware of any of these reasons.

Unconscious thinking, empathy, imitation, learning, and possibly other unconscious processes also help acceptance under pressure, sometimes even against the interests and will of the individual. This happened, for instance, in Nazi concentration camps. Some inmates eagerly accepted certain values of their SS torturers.[45]

The acceptance of the values of adults by children may also happen without any awareness. The mere consistent high valuation of certain objects, persons, and groups by adults induces processes of unconscious learning, habituation, and imitation, supported by group belongingness, loyalty, solidarity, by emotional attachments and by group interactions.

DEGREE OF ACCEPTANCE OF A SOCIAL VALUE

The acceptance of a social value may be wholehearted and unconditional or halfhearted, hesitant, or partial. The reasons for it may be unconscious. Some people, for instance, are not able to formulate the reasons for their reluctance to accept certain artistic creations, generally considered as outstanding. The reasons, though unknown to them, are strong enough to work out the value.

Unconscious causes may likewise be responsible for a halfhearted acceptance of a value by the group. There may be lack of understanding of certain factual relations; there may be conflict between certain emotional components, there may be lasting ambivalence of certain emotional relations, and there may also be conflict between the intellectual components. The conflict may last for years or centuries without any improvement or knowledge of it. For instance, the conflict between the sacred character of the marital institution and the sinful character of sex, which is one of the foundations of marriage, escaped the consciousness of Christianity for almost two thousand years.

If one of the highest values of great church organizations could be undermined by such an unconscious conflict for so long, despite the intellectual work of thousands of the best theologians, we understand that there may be similar conflicts in many other values.

UNCONSCIOUS OPERATION OF VALUES

The operation of a social value from the point of view of the individual refers to the way and the degree to which his behavior is influenced by the value. The behavior of the person who accepts the value differs in four ways from that of a person who does not, in that he:

a) recognizes the value;
b) observes the value;
c) defends the value;
d) enforces the value and sees to it that it is observed by others.

As a matter of fact, the operation of a value does not always include all these elements of behavior. Not all the recognized values are always observed; not all recognized and observed values are always defended; not all recognized, observed, and defended values are always enforced. But, on the other hand, sometimes certain unrecognized values are observed. Some people who laugh at moral values do not really live immorally. In other cases, values which are not observed may be recognized, defended, and even enforced with reference to others. An alcoholic may recognize the value of temperance, may defend it and may enforce it with regard to his children. A gangster may recognize the value of an honest way of living and enforce it in the case of his children.

The operation of a fully accepted value may be limited at a given moment to only one or two of the four ways. We may recognize a certain value all the time, but we have no occasion to observe it. Or, we recognize and observe a value but we do not defend and enforce it if there are strong reasons against it, such as respect for the feelings of other people, inconvenience of place, other strong interests opposing it at a given place and moment, and so on. On the other hand, we may recognize and enforce a value without having any opportunity to observe and defend it.

The operation (partial or full) of a value of which we are aware is, in many cases, unconscious. The value generally creates a set, which often makes it function automatically. In some values there is also habit, routine, or learned behavior, which make them operate automatically. Take, for example, religious values. A man who has accepted them carries out many actions because of them, without thinking of them. For instance, he puts a tone of reverence into his voice when speaking about religion or religious questions, often without knowing that he does it. Similarly, we show respect when speaking about the president of our country, or about the flag. We also show admiration when speaking about Venus of Milo or about Beethoven. The accepted values unconsciously influence even our perception. A number of psychologists have shown this.[46]

Also, unconsciously accepted values may operate in a similar automatic way. We may speak with an expression of admiration about something which we have not yet consciously accepted as value. Yet our friends may recognize this sooner than we do; they see it in our behavior. I noticed several times that people who did not accept communism spoke about it with such an expression of voice and face that their friends surmised that soon they might become communists. At that moment, they sincerely denied it; but the unconsciously accepted value functioned already in an unconscious way.

Now let us examine how far the limited operation of a value is unconsciously set in motion. Before the value starts to operate, the social situation is generally automatically checked. One or more components of the acceptance of the value are set in motion according to how far the situation is suitable for the operation of the value. The checking of the situation and the ensuing behavior are generally done unconsciously, chiefly through perception (often marginal) and through unconscious judgment. For instance, we avoid defending and enforcing our religious convictions in the presence of a person belonging to a different denomination. We do not want to hurt his feelings. Later on, we knew that this was the reason for our restraint; but we behaved as we did without thinking of it.

The decision to set different aspects of the value in operation is not as simple as it looks at first glance. Often there is a complex interplay of a number of elements of our psychological field. Suppose that we have to discuss a certain value in a public lecture. How fully, openly, energetically we shall do it depends on certain assumptions (that, for example, our public is educated enough to hear a disagreeable truth, that most of it adheres to the opposite value); on certain expectations (that people might react favorably, that they would oppose certain portions of our statement); on certain knowledge of present conditions (that our promotion depends on the success of our lecture, and that, therefore, we have to be impressive but cautious); on certain limitations imposed by socially accepted patterns (general politeness, respect toward the opinion of others); and some other conditions. Of course, the needs, wishes, interests, likes, and dislikes of the speaker enter into the complicated interplay, too. Such are, for instance, the strong desire to be successful and impress people, the inclination to make startling and sweeping statements, a special interest in a girl in the audience and in her reaction to the lecture, and so on.

The recognition of a value is least subject to these processes. It is relatively stable and consistent. The observation of the value may be modified or interfered with much more often because it is more closely related to changing conditions of the present situation. The defense and enforcement of the value depends still more on changing conditions.

*　　*　　*

Social values are powerful means of socializing the individual and of keeping him socialized. They represent a large part of the adaptations and adjustments of the individual to the group as well as to the rest of society. Susceptible to being produced unconsciously, they help his unconscious adaptations and adjustments. Operating unconsciously, they enable the individual to participate in the life of society in a much richer way. Without their unconscious establishment and operation, the life of the individual, of the groups, and of the society would have been much poorer and in some ways impossible.

A number of social values back the social structure and help its existence. The operation of the structure would be impossible without such backing. Because so many values are needed to maintain the social structure, many of them have to work without awareness. The consciousness is not broad enough to achieve the necessary support without them.

FOOTNOTES TO CHAPTER THIRTEEN

1. A. L. Kroeber, *Anthropology*, p. 294.
2. J. F. Cuber, *Sociology*, Appleton-Century-Crofts, New York, 1955, p. 42.
3. D. Krech and R. S. Crutchfield, *Theory and Problems of Social Psychology*, p. 68.
4. M. Sherif, *An Outline of Soc. Psych.*, pp. 207, 249, 415.
5. M. Sherif and H. Cantril, *The Psychology of Ego Involvements*, p. 150; M. Sherif, *op. cit.*, pp. 261, 266, 269.
6. R. Linton, *The Cultural Background* . . . p. 111.
7. W. I. Thomas and F. Znaniecki, *The Polish Peasant* . . ., p. 21.
8. J. L. Gillin and J. P. Gillin, *Cultural Sociology*, Macmillan, New York, 1948, p. 157 and G. Murphy, *Personality*, p. 999. See also W. R. Catton, Jr., "A Theory of Value," *Am. J. Sociol.*, 24, 1959, p. 312.
9. C. W. Morris, *Varieties of Human Value*, Univ. of Chicago Press, Chicago, 1956, p. 12.
10. H. Bonner, *Social Psychology*, American Book Co., New York, 1953, p. 189.
11. K. Young, *Sociology*, Am. Book Co., New York, 1949, p. 110.
12. W. I. Thomas and F. Znaniecki, *op. cit.*, p. 22.
13. M. Sherif and H. Cantril, *op. cit.*, p. 24.
14. R. Stagner, *Psychology of Personality* (1937), p. 185.
15. See Robin M. Williams, *American Society*, A. A. Knopf, New York, 1960, p. 403.
16. C. Kluckhohn and H. A. Murray, *Personality*, (1950), pp. 9-10.
17. H. Cantril, *Social Movements*, p. 8.
18. A. D. Woodruff, "The Roles of Value in Human Behavior," *J. Soc. Psychol.*, 36, 1952, pp. 98, 101.
19. R. Stagner, *op. cit.*, (1937), p. 432.
20. H. Cantril, *op. cit.*, p. 23.
21. *Ibid.*, p. 26.
22. E. L. Hartley and R. E. Hartley, *Fundamentals*, p. 178.
23. A. M. Rose, "Sociology and the Study of Values," *Brit. J. of Soc.*, VII, 1956, p. 7.
24. W. Wolff, "New Concepts in Experimental Depth Psychology" in H. P. David and H. von Bracken, *Perspectives in Personality Theory*, Basic Books, Inc., New York, 1957, p. 309.
25. G. Murphy, *op. cit.*, p. 272; W. I. Thomas and F. Znaniecki, *op. cit.*, pp. 72, 73.
26. G. W. Allport, *Pattern and Growth in Personality*, pp. 226-229.
27. G. Murphy, *op. cit.*, p. 272; M. Sherif, *An Outline of Social Psychology*, p. 95; J. B. Watson, *Behaviorism*, W. W. Norton, New York, 1925, p. 82.

28. H. Cantril, *op. cit.*, p. 15.
29. F. Alexander, *Fundamentals of Psychoanalysis*, W. W. Norton, New York, 1948, p. 89.
30. H. Cantril, *op. cit.*, p. 15, 19, 20.
31. S. E. Asch, *Social Psychology*, pp. 375-378.
32. See A. D. Woodruff, *op. cit.*, p. 101.
33. A. K. Cohen, *Delinquent Boys*, p. 61.
34. M. Sherif, *op. cit.*, pp. 225-227; M. Sherif and H. Cantril, *op. cit.*, p. 47; A. S. Luchins, "On Agreement with Another's Judgment," *op. cit.*, p. 110.
35. T. M. Newcomb, "Attitude Development as a Function of Reference Groups," in M. Sherif, *An Outline of Social Psychology*, pp. 138-155; M. Sherif and H. Cantril, *op. cit.*, pp. 114-115.
36. E. L. Hartley and R. E. Hartley, *op. cit.*, p. 422.
37. See T. M. Newcomb, *Personality and Social Change*, pp. 107, 129, 131, 133, 136.
38. B. B. Gardner, *Human Relations in Industry*, R. D. Irwin, Chicago, 1950, pp. 187, 188.
39. Of course, there is no simple leveling off of the differences (see H. T. Moore, "The Comparative Influence of Majority and Expert Opinion," *Am. J. Psychol.*, XXXII, 1921, pp. 16 20). A strong and attractive personality, a specialist or an important person will probably influence the group more than will other members of the group. A special willingness to yield to values of other members may be shown by the so-called compulsive conformists. (M. L. Hoffman, "Some Psychodynamic Factors in Compulsive Conformity," *J. Abn. Soc. Psychol.*, 48, 1953, pp. 383-393).
40. Compare F. H. Allport, *Social Psychology*, pp. 261-70; J. F. Dashiell, "An Experimental Analysis of Some Group Effects," *J. Abn. and Soc. Psych.*, 25, 1930-31, pp. 190-199.
41. In this respect they are similar to sentiments. See p. 141, as well as C. Blondel, *Introduction* . . . pp. 154, 156 and C. H. Cooley, *Social Organization*, p. 30.
42. See F. J. Roethlisberger and W. J. Dickson, *Management and the Worker*, pp. 496-518.
43. See M. Sherif and C. W. Sherif, *Groups in Harmony and Tension*, pp. 182-307.
44. Bronislaw Malinowski, *The Dynamics of Culture Change;* see also pp. 256, 263.
45. See Bruno Bettelheim, "Individual and Mass Behavior in Extreme Situations," *J. of Abn. and Social Psychology*, 38, 1943, pp. 417-452.
46. From the more recent experimental studies see, for instance, L. Postman, J. S. Bruner and E. R. McGinnies, "Personal Values as Selective Factors in Perception," (*J. Abn. Soc. Psych.*, 43, 1948, pp. 142-154); G. V. Haigh and D. W. Fiske, "Corroboration of Personal Values as Selective Factors in Perception," (*J. Abn. Soc. Psychol.* 47, 1952, pp. 394-398); H. Fensterheim and M. E. Tresselt, "The Influence of Value Systems on Perception of People," (*J. Abn. Soc. Psychol.*, 48, 1953, pp. 93-98); J. C. Gilchrist, J. L. Ludeman and W. Lysak, "Values as Determinants of Word Recognition Thresholds" (*J. Abn. Soc. Psych.*, 49, 1954, pp. 423-426).

PART FOUR

PERSONALITY AND CULTURE

XIV

ABILITY TO ORGANIZE UNCONSCIOUSLY

The ability unconsciously to work out so many appropriate configurations which guide our behavior in an enormous number of different social situations is socially one of the most important properties of human nature. The ability to maintain the very rich psychological field (and to store traces of past experiences), much richer than was probably supposed by K. Lewin, and the ability to organize continually and mostly unconsciously so many of its conscious and unconscious elements in so many different ways, generally without delay, are the greatest gift for social life, as well as for the creation, maintenance and change of culture. Instead of the old saying that man is "homo faber," we could say that he is "producer of configurations." The Gestaltists were the first to enter this neglected area by discovering the organized nature of perceptions (Koffka, Köhler), of certain of our learning and thinking processes (Wertheimer, Koffka, and others), of recall and of emotions. Yet many other similar processes of unconscious organization are going on in our mind. The gestalts of this school are only a fraction of a wider kind of similar structures.

Other psychologists have pointed to other organizations similar to gestalts. As has been mentioned above, some of them stressed the organization of sentiments, others the organization of attitudes (Cattell, G. Allport, Burnham, Cantril, Sherif, Krech and Crutchfield, Asch, and others). We have pointed out above that judgments, habits, social ties, values, and others also are organized.

Burgess and Locke,[1] as well as Cattell,[2] have analyzed the components of different types of love. Halbwachs pointed to the composite nature of our memories. It seems to us, also, that G. W. Allport's functionally autonomous motives are a kind of configuration although they were not discussed as such in his book.[3]

These are only examples which point to the fact that the field of psychic configurations is very broad, much broader than it is generally conceived. Nevertheless, instead of trying to give a complete picture of the field let us take a closer look at the nature of psychic configurations.

First let us pay attention to the ability of configurations to incorporate new components under the influence of the changes in the situation. Take, for instance, love for our mother and its recent changes. It was derived from, among others, the satisfaction of our early physical and emotional needs and developed further through her continuous care and devotion, through her personal sacrifices in order to give us a college education and to prepare a happy life for us, and through her protecting us from our severe father.

But our love has some more recent components. It has been strengthened since our father died. We pity our mother for this irreparable loss, and we try to compensate for it by our increased attention and kindness. We are also moved by her gradual mental and physical decline. Another rather temporary increase in our love developed from the care our mother gave to our children during their recent illness. Still more temporary are certain situational components in the expression of our love. Suppose we want to buy her a birthday present. We may want it to be similar to the expensive present our friend bought for his own mother, who is acquainted with our mother. We would be ashamed to be outdone by him.

Thus, the configuration of love for our mother has been supplemented by additional, temporary or lasting components produced by the changing situation. Such changes of the configuration are practically automatic and occur mostly without the person's awareness. Nevertheless, they are not mechanical. The weight of the new and old components, their nature, and their relation to accepted norms and values find their proper place in the readjusted configuration.

Allport's autonomous motives point to another characteristic of configurations. They may comprise a number of more simple configurations such as values, attitudes, prestige and others. They may, perhaps, be labeled as superconfigurations in which generally all the configurations needed in a given lasting or repeated situation may be linked together into an organic whole. As examples of autonomous drive Allport gives a workman's compulsion to do a good job even though his security no longer depends upon high standards, and mentions a mother's care for her child even if the "parental instinct" is lacking. The fear of critical neighbors, of the law, and the hope that the child will provide security in her old age, may hold a mother to her work until it becomes a joy.

Both of these, as well as other examples given by Allport, point to the complex organization of the derived drives. In our judgment, a craftsman's internal impulses to produce high quality products may involve the habit of working that way; it may involve an acquired skill and the pleasure of using it, his devotion to his master who taught him to work well, his personal honor and dignity (a complicated social-psychological configuration in itself), the prestige he has in the eyes of specialists, his conviction of the bigger esthetic value of high quality products, and probably several other components. All of these components support one another. They are roughly in logical and factual harmony. They maintain the configuration even if the craftsman's need for security does not depend on it any more. This points to an important characteristic of configurations: that in some cases they may survive even if they lose some of their original components.

Another, though perhaps not so frequent, characteristic of configurations is that alternate preliminary structures may be built up before the final configuration develops. Love for a person of the opposite sex may provide us with a good example. Every culture accepts several types of love, each of them composed of different basic components. Burgess and Locke list the following components: sexual desire, physical attraction, attachment, emotional interdependence, idealization, companionship, stimulation, emotional reassurance and others. Various combinations of these produce different present (or historical) types of love such as lust, infatuation, romantic love, affection, comradely feelings, platonic love, and adolescent love. Now the question arises how it is that the individual, when he falls in love, picks out one of the culturally accepted types and not a type which his culture does not accept? How does he make a choice among the available types? How does the particular love configuration of the person who fell in love come into being?

It is well known that it is not a matter of choice. First there is the raw biological background of instinctive drive which is more stimulated by a certain person of the opposite sex than by another. But there are a number of other additional cultural components which unconsciously help to produce the particular culturally accepted configuration.

The discussion of the unconscious processes of the human mind points to some of these components. First of all we "feel" (mostly unclearly or unconsciously) which current types of love are generally accepted by our culture and subculture. We "know" about them, without being clearly aware of them, from novels, from movies, newspapers, perhaps from poems and certainly from the loves of our friends. We vicariously "know" from experiences of praise, blame, or of other value judgments, from proverbs, public discussions, songs, and court trials,

231

which of the types are available to the person we are, in the position we occupy, and which other types are less or not at all acceptable. A number of emotional experiences through empathy with real or literary cases of love, emotional experiences from operettas and sentimental music, as well as from all kinds of art, the embarrassing smiles, the understanding looks, and the warm expression of voice when people refer to a certain love affair, are relevant, too. From all these often forgotten or unrecollected experiences, we unconsciously produce generalizations and points of reference. The large majority of people are not aware of them at all.

Of course, other broader cultural and subcultural influences determine our love feelings, too. Our emotional life in general is shaped not only by the family and friends, but also by some general cultural patterns such as decency, good taste, dignity, respect toward other people, esthetic feelings and norms, levels of aspiration of our class, economic values, religious norms, obligations and some moral norms.

All these factors are selected according to personal needs and traits and adapted to them as well as to the behavior of the loved one and to other conditions, and are organized (often suddenly, without any conscious plan or intention) into one of the culturally accepted types (for instance platonic love). Yet we have to stress that before one type of love has been organized we were ready for several culturally accepted types, and that, as a matter or fact, later on, we may develop another one (for instance, romantic love). Thus, before a certain configuration develops, several prefabricated patterns of love might be waiting to be used. Whenever the opportunity arises, one of them is readily filled in by additional components, and the particular configuration of love comes into being. The fact that our personality carries several alternate prefabricated frames of possible configurations in its structure is an important ability worth mentioning.

Let us look now for another attribute of configurations. We may find it by analyzing a certain type of joke used in a given culture[4] and in a given situation. We have in mind a type of joke used in Central Europe. The joker (generally in a middle class group) produces a comic effect by pretending he is more stupid, clumsy, uncultured, and unrefined than the other people present. Yet the joke is not this simple. One acts as stupid and clumsy only when everybody understands that he is not. In certain situations it is sufficient if the majority of people understand and one or two do not. This may become an additional source of merriment.

This type of joke may consist of mispronunciation of a French

232

or English word, in misunderstanding generally-known, scientific expressions, in not grasping a simple situation which everybody else understands; in misspelling, in mixing up two similar but clearly different ideas; or in being unable to put together several parts of a very simple gadget. Although occasionally other persons may also be ridiculed this way, there are generally accepted limits. You can abase yourself, but not your mother; you can ridicule neither science nor art (especially music), your sexual potency (unless you are known as an extremely vigorous individual), nor important interests of your country.

I am not able to give a precise and exhaustive description of this type of joke. Only research would reveal all the relevant facts about this complex trait of Central European culture.[5]

The individual's unconscious configuration results from years of learning, imitation, use of unrecollected and forgotten experiences, insights and other components and of a number of organizational processes.

A thorough socialization from childhood is needed to make a joker use this type of joke well. Undoubtedly, a foreigner will never achieve the perfection of a native. Similarly, no foreigner will achieve the brilliance and refinement of Parisian jokes told by a Parisian nor will a Czech who spent his childhood outside Žižkov (a suburb of Prague) attain the flavor of typical Žižkov jokes.

The social-psychological configuration of the joke stretches over a very wide area of the psychic life of an individual. Many positive and negative values are involved in it, values of one's own self, of other persons according to their social status, sex, age, or occupation; values of many social institutions; attitudes toward individual persons, as well as toward the social institutions, cultural products (for instance, family, mother country, science, art) and social movements; concepts of friendship, of entertainment, of social obligations, of the role of host or guest, and others. The operation of the social-psychological configurations is influenced by momentary (mostly unconscious) judgments about the situation; by the unconscious assumptions concerning the members of the group; their interests and wishes (for instance, that they are waiting for a good joke of this special kind, that they will not be offended, that they will be pleased by an indirect attack against a certain person or institution, that no one else will probably be able to make a better joke and so on); by social ties toward the group or toward some members of the group listening to the jokes; by momentary personal conditions such as mood, fatigue, jealousy, excitement; and by a favorable reaction to or imitation of a recent

233

successful joke. Some of these momentarily reshape the configuration to a certain extent.[6]

Thus it seems that there is a general unconscious scheme on which the particular jokes are based in the mind of the joker, including the feeling of the comic, relevant values, attitudes, concepts and other components. This is the core of the configuration, which undergoes special adaptations to physical and social conditions as well as to momentary personal ones. Then there is the stimulus to make a joke which suits certain momentary goals like the wish to tease someone or to teach him a lesson.

This seems to be a general pattern of a number of configurations. They seem to have (a) a relatively permanent skeleton and (b) an additional filling in by momentary components. Although most of the momentary components are short-lived, some of them may leave changes of more enduring nature. If repeated, the short-lived supplements may become a permanent part of the configuration.

Some social configurations, especially those produced and maintained by accepted cultural patterns, are structures of much broader scope than those generally studied by psychologists, social psychologists, and sociologists (such as values, learned behavior patterns, attitudes and similar). They also generally are more complex. They are a new concept, a new category of social-psychological reality, so much needed for the understanding of cultural patterns and their changes.

The properties of configurations may be briefly described in the following way: (1) the ability to produce configurations certainly is *inborn* but it is greatly *developed* by personal *experiences*, and is *shaped by culture;* (2) configurations result from the meeting of a *considerable part of the personality* (including, for instance, memory, interests, values, sentiments) or of the *whole personality* with *all* the relevant *aspects of the situation;* (3) configurations are *flexible* and *adjustable;* (4) they *change* practically *all the time;* (5) they accept *temporary* components or (6) they may incorporate *new lasting* components; (7) they may *lose* some, sometimes *without disintegrating because of it;* (8) generally there is a *skeleton structure with* additional *fillings* according to the needs of the momentary situation; (9) some of the components of the possible future configuration are partly *organized long before* the configuration is needed and formed (see p. 241); (10) several *alternate preliminary structures* may be formed before the final configuration develops; (11) some of the configurations *comprise* a number of more *simple configurations* and may be considered as super-configurations; (12) configurations are produced by the human mind *continually* and *spontaneously* in a *large number,* more often unconsciously than consciously.

The forces which set the organizing processes in motion may be grouped into four basic categories: (1) vectors of chiefly organic nature (almost always shaped in some way by experience and social influences), (2) empathy, sympathy, personal ties, (3) vectors produced by membership in groups and devotion to them (feeling of belongingness, enthusiasm for a group and its goals), (4) pressure of physical and social forces. The last factor is close to the Freudian reality principle. Freud's pleasure principle covers the prevailing part of the first factor, though not all of it. The two other factors go beyond the Freudian principles, although the pleasure principle could be applied to a smaller part of perhaps both of them.

Although it seems that the impulse of the organizing process comes either from the individual or from the environment (social pressure, physical necessity), it is generally the result of the interaction between the former and the latter. Even the seemingly personal impulses are found to be shaped to a certain degree by previous contacts with the physical and social environment.

The ability of the personality to produce so many different kinds of configurations spontaneously and continually and to reshape them if needed is amazing because of their enormous number, because of the large number of components included in some configurations, because of their frequently unconscious establishment, and because of their generally good suitability to the external and internal situation, as well as because of their readiness to be used. Equally amazing is the personality's ability to unconsciously choose the appropriate configurations to be used in a given situation and to adjust and use them.

Our analysis points to the necessity of extending the concept of the organizing ability of the human personality. Configurations may tentatively be classified into four main categories. The psychological laws of organization are responsible for the first category. The second category includes the configurations produced by culture. Third, the personality may develop specific configurations of its own. Finally, specific configurations are also produced by unique conditions in which the group lives. The perception of an interrupted circular line as a circle is an example of the first category. Linguistic patterns or joke schemes are examples of the second category. Personal configurations comprise, for instance, the high valuation of a novelist who generally is not valued, a special ideal of one's own appearance, or new personal forms of artistic expression. Configurations developed by special

235

minority conditions which deviate from the accepted cultural patterns may serve as an example of the fourth category.

The most important configurations for the existence of culture are those of the second kind. They are basic for the maintenance and operation of culture. Personal and special group configurations, on the other hand, are basic to changes of culture. A number of culture changes are brought about by them.

The organizational activities of the human mind are supposed to make a situation more satisfactory for the individual or group; they have a meaning. Although the first kind of configurations has a strictly psychological meaning, the rest of them refer to the situation of the individual or group. The configurations are often, though not always, adaptive and adjustive in nature. Frequently they include both receptive and creative processes.

The original impulse and the meaning it gives to the future configuration most often takes the leading role in the process of organizing the new configuration and is the main agent in carrying it through. Generally, it is helped by a number of secondary factors (such as interests, prestige, or certain values). In addition to that, it may be reinforced by agents which were stimulated or released by the process. The inclination to generalize (developed through experiences and training) or the pleasure of reasoning or learning may help the organizing processes with their own energies. Nevertheless, they remain under the guidance of the main stimulus.

In the organization of some configurations other components may be as important as the main one. In most of the configurations of a devout Christian, religious convictions maintain an important place, even if the configuration aims at the satisfaction of other, non-religious interests.

As a rule, the components are held together by the continuing existence of the condition (or conditions) which initiated the process of organization and by the meaning the configuration has for the individual or group. There is a frequent, automatic, often unconscious checking of the existence of these conditions. But some of the components may develop their own reasons for existence and by this they may considerably support the whole structure. Such are, for instance, habits, concepts, learned behavior, sometimes sets, and possibly other components. Their power may be such that they may keep it functioning even when the configuration itself fails to suit the changing conditions. Cultural lags and survivals are due partly to these factors.

Another reason for the survival of a failing structure is social pressure which may not allow the individual to drop the configuration.

The devotion of an individual to his group may also be so strong that he clings to the failing configuration for the sake of maintaining group status.

The most important property of configurations is that each of them *operates as a whole* when conditions suitable for its operation arise, sometimes consciously but often unconsciously.

FOOTNOTES TO CHAPTER FOURTEEN

1. E. W. Burgess and H. J. Locke, *The Family,* pp. 322-326.
2. R. B. Cattell, *General Psychology,* p. 165. See also R. B. Cattell, *Personality,* pp. 151-162, 189-190.
3. G. W. Allport, *Pattern and Growth in Personality,* pp. 226-229.
4. See J. C. Flugel, "Humor and Laughter," in *Handbook of Social Psychology* (ed. by G. Lindzey), Addison-Wesley Publishing Co., Cambridge, 1954, p. 727.
5. S. Freud says that analytical investigation can determine why we are laughing, although we rarely know it before such investigation (S. Freud, *The Basic Writings,* p. 739).
6. A more simple conception of a joke as a configuration has been developed by Egner. Nevertheless, it involves certain doubtful typological and racial assumptions and does not emphasize enough its cultural aspects (See Fritz Egner, "Humor und Witz unter structurpsychologischem Standpunkt," *Archiv für die ges. Psychol.,* 84, 1932, pp. 330-371).

XV

SOCIALIZED PERSONALITY

Although our previous analysis has yielded more hypotheses than proved knowledge, it seems to us that a partly new light has been shed on certain aspects of the human personality in its social setting. Let us summarize its results from this point of view and draw the attention of the reader to some conclusions and to some problems resulting from them.

STRUCTURE

A) Unconscious Past Experiences

Personality structure appears to be much broader and richer than it generally is conceived of by the students of personality. The present conceptions do not, for instance, pay enough attention to the part of the personality structure consisting of unconscious past experiences. There is a certain place in personality structure[1] where the past unconscious experiences are kept as a provision to be used in all possible future situations. Whenever a change in the habitual situation occurs and the usual well-adjusted behavior patterns do not suit it any more, the provision of traces of past experiences is explored, mostly unconsciously, in order to secure material for the readapting or readjusting processes.

The provision of traces of past experiences is not dissimilar in certain respects to the provision of water in tropical plants. It is part of their permanent structure to keep a certain provision of water and to use it in the dry season as the situation demands. It is not functionally connected with the life of the plant as long as water is plentiful. The provision of traces plays a similar role in personality structure. The traces are not used as long as other parts of the structure secure the normal functioning of the personality. As soon as they cannot, the provision of traces is used to secure a satisfactory functioning.

From the point of view of the organization of the personality, it is very important that all these traces be, or may be linked, if needed, with its main interests, needs, attitudes, and traits in order to enable it to face a new situation. Although mostly at the periphery[2] of the personality structure, the unconscious past experiences may be connected with its central, basic parts. The relations between the past experiences and the leading motives are available for the possible connection. This makes them an important part of the personality structure. The personologists have not seen their place in the personality structure in this light as yet.

The stored traces of past experiences may become part of what Lewin[3] called the psychological field. They are its reserve material, spare parts (figuratively speaking) which may be drawn into the active section of it. As we see it, they may become the last of these four main sectors of the psychological field: perceptions, conscious recollections, internal psychic conditions of the personality (needs, wishes, tendencies, motives, knowledge, moods), and finally, the activated traces of the appropriate past experiences. According to Lewin, only the present psychological field is relevant, not the past and the future psychological fields. But the psychological field may be rapidly supplied with certain elements of the past (traces of past experiences) according to the needs of the situation. Lewin did not stress enough this ability of the personality to incorporate them in a split second into the active psychological field. These unconsciously used, past experiences are more important for the participation of normal individuals in social life than some unconscious forces of the psychoanalysts, which on the other hand play such a dominant role in the life of neurotic people. We are inclined to believe that basically this is not in disagreement with Lewin's views and that in reality, probably, Lewin himself indirectly took such unconscious experiences into account.[4]

Our analysis gives a new meaning to Lewin's claim that the past is part of the present psychological field. Of course, this does not apply to all the past but only to that part which has been preserved in traces and which has been drawn (consciously or unconsciously) from the storage of traces into the present psychological field.

We may suppose that it is in the most peripheral part of the personality structure that traces of the relatively isolated type are probably stored. They are not organized into meaningful, workable wholes with other traces and with other parts of the personality structure, but may eventually be used if needed.

The second less peripheral layer consists of traces which are linked with other traces by similarity, contiguity, frequency, and inseparability. These also may be used both ways, consciously or unconsciously.

The third layer is made up of unconscious experiences, organized partly into meaningful configurations, no longer according to the laws of association but according to their future use in certain possible situations. They are prefabricated structures, prepared for a more ready use than are the traces of the previous two types. They will receive a finishing touch when being used.

An example of such a partial unfinished organization was made known to me recently. A three-and-half-year old girl had to flee with her mother and sister from a communist country. The group spent a whole night walking through the deep woods of the borderline region. The night without home, without bed and sleep made a deep, shaking impression on the child. The unconsciously operating fear that she could again be exposed to such a bad experience made her especially sensitive to all news about other people spending a night without home and bed.[6] For two or three years she listened carefully to news about floods, night fires and earthquakes, which chased people from their homes as well as to stories about children who got lost in the woods, about friends of the family who were looking for hours for a hotel room in an overcrowded city, or of hunters who slept in woods.

This gathering of experiences, which were mostly forgotten, yielded certain prefabricated structures which would prove helpful to further action. With these at hand she would have faced a similar emergency better prepared, with more ready and better suited reactions.

Still more centrally located are the traces of past experiences unconsciously organized to be used directly in a situation we are sure to face in the future. Several years before retirement, a public servant unwittingly pays more attention to everything connected with retirement. He does not prepare for it consciously yet, say eight or ten years ahead, but he listens to such experiences with more interest; they impress him more, and he takes them more seriously. The pertinent experiences are unconsciously selected and organized. Most of them will come in handy when the man prepares for retirement and after he retires. The traces which are fully and consciously organized into a configuration are, of course, still closer to the main structure of the personality.

The storing of traces, their organization and reorganization, go on without interruption and generally unconsciously and unwittingly. Only the human personality is capable of such a rich, many-sided, spontaneous, and unconscious activity. This partly explains the unique

241

ability of humans to adapt to very complex physical conditions and to still more complex social conditions.

b) MENTAL SETS

The rich system of psychological sets, working continuously and mostly unconsciously as an important component of the socialized individual's dynamic structure, has not yet been put into full light by personologists either. These sets exist in very large numbers. Social values, ideals, attitudes, mores, roles, expectations, tastes, norms, laws, as well as the levels of aspiration, needs, sentiments, tensions, and other components of the psychic life are automatically put and kept in operation by appropriate sets whenever the situation calls for it. Such a system of sets is responsible for a considerable part of the person's social behavior. It is a substantial component of the personality's dynamic equipment, operating as an agent of the group or of culture as well as of the individual's socialized personality.

Likewise, sets are indispensable for a great deal of perceiving, as well as of storing and of the first organization of traces. They keep up a considerable part of the computing service, of reacting, and of producing creative ideas. Sets enable the personality to develop many of the social adaptations and adjustments during the socialization period as well as in the later years of life. Preservation of these adaptations is due even to a larger extent to different sets.

Owing to our complex culture and social structure, a number of sets have to operate simultaneously or in a rapid alternation. Personality structure is equipped so that it can meet this necessity. Nevertheless, we do not know how many sets the personality may have at a time and how many of them can operate simultaneously. The decision as to how many and which sets have to operate at a given time, and how many and which ones in the next moment, is generally made unconsciously.

c) ATTITUDES

Attitudes appear partly in a new light, too. They are much less rigid parts of the personality structure than they are generally conceived to be. Also, they exist and operate always in connection with many other relevant psychic factors. Certain cognitive and emotional elements of the psychological field such as unconscious judgments and assumptions, as well as sets, levels of aspiration, desires, and expectations are necessary conditions for the existence and operation of

242

any attitude. The attitude may change, disappear, or operate in a new way if any of these conditions change. It operates only in the frame of the whole situation as represented in the psychological field.

We may go so far as to regard stable and definitely formed attitudes as perhaps non-existing. All of them are continually, mostly unconsciously, readjusted, complemented, strengthened, weakened, or momentarily modified. Even such attitudes which appear as very firm, strong and clear, like our attitude toward a vital foe or toward somebody who saved our life, may vary under the influence of momentary conditions. The broad smile or frowning forehead of the foe or benefactor may momentarily change our attitude toward either one of them. As components of the personality structure they remind neither of the steel parts of a machine (which have a fixed form) nor of the organs of the body (which may change under the influence of illness or other factors, but have the tendency to regain the original form). Attitudes may change more thoroughly or even disappear or develop into the opposite of what they were. Also, they may continually oscillate around a relatively permanent basic shape.

The socialized personality living in society is equipped with a very large number of attitudes as required by the complex social structure and culture. How far can their number be increased with the increasing complexity of social and cultural life? Where are the psychological limits to such an increase? How many of the attitudes may be unconscious and operate unconsciously? These questions await to be answered by future research.

There is no doubt that some of the attitudes are more or less closely and logically organized together and constitute a considerable section of the personality structure. On the other hand, there are discrepancies and conflicts between certain attitudes. How large discrepancies can an attitude stand without breaking down? How many conflicts between attitudes, especially between the conscious and unconscious attitudes, may exist without wrecking the personality structure? How do the unconscious attitudes affect the conscious ones?

d) Values, Emotions, Social Ties

Much the same could be said about values, emotions, and social ties. Even these may be slowly readjusted or promptly modified or may possibly fluctuate around the basic form. The increasing number of values, sentiments, and social ties in modern complex society again raises the question of what their maximum number is for one personality. All of them operate within the continually and unconsciously

243

checked circumstances. They are, to some extent, in harmony with other parts of personality; and they have partly to be in harmony among themselves. Where are the limits to possible disharmonies, especially between the conscious and unconscious configurations of this kind? How much disharmony can a personality stand without harm and in what conditions? What is the mutual relation of the conscious and unconscious values, emotions and social ties? These are some questions for further research.

E) AUTOMATIC BEHAVIOR, ROUTINE, HABIT

The question of the maximum number in one personality applies here too. Their operation again depends on the unconscious checking of present conditions. Yet they are a less flexible part of the personality structure; their generally unconscious relation to other components of the personality, as well as to the situation, is less close.

PROCESSES

A) THINKING

Unconscious judging, reasoning, and other thinking processes, which go on practically all the time,[6] are set into motion automatically by the outward, physical, and social stimuli as well as by the internal generally socialized stimuli. Several thinking processes may possibly go on simultaneously or in rapid alternation; it remains to be found how many.

The computing mechanism is an invaluable equipment of the personality, necessary for its adaptations and adjustments to the social environment. How dependable is it and how many such services may a personality have at a time? The tendency to spontaneously establish frames of reference is another indispensable automatic adjustive mechanism.

B) LEARNING

Learning by the human individual in a normal social setting is stimulated, supported, directed, and hampered by often unconscious social concepts, norms and pressures, as well as by socially shaped, dynamic elements of personality which fructify, automatically, almost any useful experience for the sake of learning.

What is important from the point of view of the socialized personality is not so much that we have an enormous capacity to learn, but that we really learn all the time, often several new skills concurrently, willingly, or unwillingly. There is more unconscious than conscious learning. The full extent of this amazing property has not yet been properly noted nor has its social importance.

c) IMITATION

Imitativeness is another often unconsciously operating part of the personality's dynamic equipment. Imitative processes set in, often without our knowledge or will. Although they are not as continuous as thinking and not as frequent as learning, there are many more than we notice.

Imitating processes often co-operate with each other, as well as with thinking, learning, social ties, pressures and with emotional states and other psychic elements. Hence, the imitated behavior may be a complex configuration.

PERSONALITY IN ITS SOCIAL AND CULTURAL SETTING

Unconscious experiences and other unconscious factors and processes naturally start very early in the life of every one of us. The proportion of unconscious processes is probably much higher in children than in adults. With increasing age, more and more of them become conscious.

Personality needs the unconscious processes more often for using the equipment of sentiments, values, attitudes, concepts, and social skills than for their modification. Physical, social, and cultural conditions do not change so rapidly that a large proportion of our social-psychological configurations should be considerably changed in a short time. Yet there are always some changes.

A) CHANGES IN SOCIAL-PSYCHOLOGICAL CONFIGURATIONS OF THE MEMBERS OF A STABLE SOCIETY

1) As Produced by Social Environment

Let us first consider the social adaptations and adjustments of an individual living in a society with a relatively stable structure and culture. Besides the small structural and cultural changes, there are, for example, considerable changes in the roles played by individuals and changes in mutual relations between people. Individuals around us marry, divorce, become friends or enemies, business companions or competitors, bosses or subordinates, some of them become members of a certain group or leave another. In public life, likewise, many changes occur without any modifications in social structure or in culture. New governments step into power, new people are appointed to fill different positions in political, economic, or religious institutions. Some firms develop the production of articles produced previously by other firms, others develop new local branches, new firms are founded, prices go up and down, and so forth.

A modern man listening to the radio, watching television, and reading newspapers, magazines, and books is exposed every day to a great deal of such news concerning his locality, his nation, and other nations. He gets further news from his friends, from his collaborators, from the memos and rulings of his firm. Of much of this, he is fully aware; and he acts accordingly. Other items of news are registered, selected, and stored unconsciously. Some of them are linked with recent or with older traces, or are possibly incorporated into older emotional or intellectual configurations. Still others help to reshape these configurations.

Some of the news which was perceived clearly was soon forgotten because of lack of interest, or because of other reasons. When, for instance, we read our newspaper, we turn over the pages pretty fast; we spend hardly a fraction of a second with most of the headlines and advertisements, and we forget them. We would not be able to reproduce even their most general content two or three days later. But, our future actions may well be influenced by them. The news reshuffled something in our mind, and we act accordingly.

Whenever we take the most superficial cognizance of the extended powers of a political leader, of a new success of our friend, of more friendly behavior of a person toward us, or other similar changes, we simply act in the future according to them, often without recollecting them. Only exceptionally may the habit be stronger and our first reaction momentarily still reckon with the previous situation.

Every very small and momentary impression may produce restructuring of several configurations simultaneously. One single sight of our aging father, for instance, confirms our reconciliation with the unchangeable necessity of his decline. At the same time it enhances our independence from his influence, makes us more self-confident, and increases our responsibility in the family group; and it sheds a new light on our relations to our own children, and makes us understand better the meaning of the life cycle and our own position in it. How often similar, maybe marginal, unimportant impressions, overheard words or news start similar adaptive and creative processes, modifying certain configurations in our mind!

Such restructurings go on practically all the time. The social changes in a stable society simultaneously and mostly unconsciously induce corresponding changes in the psychic configurations of all the members of society concerned with them. Some of these readjusted configurations are satisfactory, others are only rough products needing refinement, finishing, or perhaps other modifications. We may, for instance, accept a new boss with all the consequences; but we may still resent the fact that he is boss. The emotional adjustment to him is to be worked out later. The main value of the unconsciously readjusted configurations consists in the very broad field they cover, in the rapidity with which they are produced, and in their readiness to be used.

All these changes are carried through with full respect for the personal status, dignity, goals, interests, likes and dislikes of the personality and in harmony with the existing social conditions, with membership in different groups, with the accepted cultural values and other cultural products. An individual can function in his position in different groups and in society only because he is supported by the continuous unconscious processes of receiving information, of selecting and classifying news, of linking them meaningfully together, and of creating and reshaping configurations suiting the new conditions. Only some of these adaptations are carried through fully or partly consciously.

2) As Produced by Personal Conditions

Other changes which occur in the life of individuals even in a relatively stable culture and society are due to variations in their personal conditions. We adjust to a higher position after a promotion or increase in property; we acquire military behavior if drafted in the army; we "learn" to be husbands and fathers, to be adults, to be old, and so on.

Let us pay closer attention to changes of this kind. Because of the revolutionary changes of the last years, a middle-aged scholar of my acquaintance was suddenly put into a rather high political position. Soon after he became a member of the executive committee of his party, he was often sent to make public political speeches and to represent the party at different official occasions. At the beginning, he was not able to behave as was expected in his new position. His speeches were factual, logical, dry, impersonal; his dealings with the members of the party were too correct, restrained, lacking warm cordiality and camaraderie. He was told about it by his political friends. Nevertheless, it did not help him more than if you tell somebody how to skate or swim. On the contrary, it was worse. Everybody saw in him a professor who tried to act as a politician. His best intentions, his intelligence, habits

247

of hard work, and logical thinking did not help much at first. Later on, however, they proved to be useful. They established basic, strong sets aiming at improvement. He told me that he systematically observed the behavior of experienced politicians, purposely maintained many contacts with the members of his party, especially with local, small dignitaries; read speeches of political leaders; listened to political speakers, and paid attention to popular political arguments (so different from the scientific arguments!). But more was given to him by unwitting unconscious experiences. The handshakes, the smiles, the convincing tone of voice, the conspicuous optimism, the self-confident facial expression, the well-pretended interest in personal problems of political followers, the pleasant and simple jokes, and many other elements of political behavior had to be experienced many times, very often unconsciously, before they were incorporated in the appropriate configurations. Innumerable processes aiming at the overcoming of old ways of behavior and striving for the organization of better suiting patterns produced surprising improvements. The continually and often unconsciously operating psychological sets brought about unwitting imitations, unconscious learning, unnoticed pressures, unconsciously established frames of reference, unconscious insight, and so on. It was rather surprising to our scholar when in a certain political discussion he unexpectedly used a new tone of voice, a new gesture and made several new jokes of a very popular kind.

New habits, new gestures, new attitudes, new kinds of judgment, new expressions of speech, new skills, and other new behavior patterns were partly unconsciously worked out. Only some were premeditated, planned, and consciously accepted. The imitated elements of new configurations were unconsciously chosen from several social models, according to the needs of the situation, and according to his personal attitudes and wishes. The unremembered advice given by his political friends and forgotten experiences with the successful use of some of the patterns helped to organize them together with personally developed skills.

Many less striking changes in the personal situation ask for such adaptations and adjustments during the whole life of the individual. We discussed some of them in previous chapters (for instance, the effects of promotion and of getting rich, change of religious faith, or of political convictions). Many changes in such configurations occur during maturation and in old age. They are difficult in either case. Young people lack the necessary experiences; old people adhere to old patterns. Other adaptations to personal changes are, as a rule, easier. In all of them, the unconscious processes do their best to produce the satisfactory configurations.

B) CHANGES OF CONFIGURATIONS IN A CHANGING SOCIETY

Modern western societies change rather rapidly. There are changes in production techniques, in political ideologies, in political parties and regimes, and in literary and artistic tastes; new styles in architecture develop, and new fashions appear regularly. Courting and marriage mores, methods of education, scientific knowledge, church life, and philosophies of life change, too.

Some changes, like new fashions, are accepted by older people only partly or in a limited way. They resist them; and therefore many of the changes of their behavior become conscious. Others, nevertheless, may remain unconscious. I knew old people who were very much opposed to the increasing informality in dress and manners and to the shrinking of the covered surface of the body in evening dresses and swimming suits. But their convictions did not prevent them from appearing more frequently than previously without a tie or with an open shirt collar, from sitting more comfortably, making more sweeping gestures, laughing more heartily, and tolerating moderately-fashionable dresses and swimming suits of their granddaughters. Similarly, an old writer who is opposed to the freedom of stylistic forms and to the use of slang expressions may unwittingly make, contrary to his convictions, certain concessions to the new taste. His style is no longer so ornate, careful, and punctual as previously. All these, mostly unconscious, changes which occur against the will of the changing individual show the power of the unconscious, reshaping processes and their basic importance for the structure of the personality.

Now what about changes accepted consciously and voluntarily? Are they fully conscious? We do not think so. The elements of change are usually so numerous that co-operation of the unconscious factors is unavoidable. Take, for instance, a painter who shifted from the style he adopted in his young years to a new style of painting. He knows the principles of the new style: the different quality of colors (perhaps softer and lighter), new subjects and their presentation, new values given to lines, new combinations of colors, a different brush technique. These principles were consciously accepted; and at the beginning, some were consciously applied. They were, however, unconsciously complemented by imitation of certain famous pictures, by picking out certain of their most appealing traits, by using them in a way to meet the creative tendencies of the painter, by unconsciously pursuing certain esthetic effects, by unconsciously seeking a specific artistic presentation, by expressing certain indefinable esthetic values, by unconsciously yielding to the influence of certain leading personalities, and so on.

Likewise, changes in production, in political work, in handling the labor problems, and many others are partly produced unconsciously. This applies equally to the predominantly passive as well as to the more original, more creative adaptations.

c) CREATIVE ACHIEVEMENTS

Although we know that there is a certain degree of creativity in every acceptance of a new pattern and that every creative activity uses older elements, creative achievements are, of course, more active, and more original. The work of imagination and of reasoning is superior; and generally, more elements are taken into consideration than in the mere reception of an only slightly modified, ready-made pattern.

Creative achievements are more numerous than we generally think they are. Probably most of them concern our relations with persons and in a lesser degree with groups, institutions, or things. Even in a casual meeting of people, we often have to solve a number of problems: we have to mention disagreeable things in an agreeable way, to make unsuccessful people appear as rather successful without telling a lie, to speak about dull children in a way acceptable to their parents, we have to mention the shortcomings of our friends kindly and without distorting the facts, and so forth. Likewise, we have to speak respectfully about a certain church, political party, or other institutions we disapprove of, without contradicting our own convictions. We have to find acceptable excuses if the real reasons are socially unacceptable.

Every building up of a business enterprise, of a personal career, of a position in local community, such as that of a minister, lawyer, or family doctor, needs many such creative acts. Some of them do not bring anything new to the culture but help the existing cultural patterns, institutions, and groups function effectively; others may contribute to cultural changes. Neither of them is necessarily conscious.

SOME MORE HINTS FOR RESEARCH

Our previous discussion points to certain problems concerning the human personality, which have to be taken into consideration by future research. We need very much to know better the nature and operation of the unconscious parts of the personality structure.

There is no doubt, for instance, that the unconscious parts of psychic life are much less modifiable[7] and less under the control of the will of the individual than the conscious ones. They are more spontaneous and independent.[8] How many other differences between conscious and unconscious parts of the personality are there, and what are their types?

We certainly need to know not only how many unconscious processes of the same kind may proceed simultaneously, but also how many *different* unconscious processes may go on simultaneously. We learn and imitate simultaneously, at the same time yielding to the suggestions of a person, selecting traces of past experiences, and organizing them with present experiences (conscious or unconscious). We unconsciously defend a value to which we adhere, adjusting at the same time to the changing situation, perceiving marginally a number of stimuli, and obeying at the same time a number of social and cultural norms.

Likewise, social scientists are in need of knowing more about the nature of configurations. More laws of organization must be established. More should be known about what kinds of elements may or may not be organized together, how many components a configuration may comprise, how complex it may be, what are the types of configuration, and what processes are involved. More should be known about the stimuli, the conditions, and the causes of the organizing process. What is the role of the meaning of the configuration for the individual? How far does it start the organizational process and how far does it organize the configuration itself? How does it co-operate with other causes of the process of organization? How far do the psychological laws of organization limit the influence of the meaning of the configuration? How are the psychological causes and laws of organization affected by social and cultural causes of organization? How do these two kinds co-operate?

A more specific question is what is the mutual relation of the conscious and unconscious configurations of personality? How do they influence each other? We know that they may be in serious conflict, which may be accepted and rationalized by the culture and may no longer be frustrating to the individual. Most often, nevertheless, the conscious and unconscious configurations co-operate and support each other.

A single configuration often comprises conscious and unconscious components. The richness, flavor, as well as the connotations of conscious configurations (for instance, of an attitude or value), consist chiefly of unconscious components incorporated in them. But what

251

is otherwise the mutual relation of conscious and unconscious components? Which conscious and unconscious components can work together and which ones cannot? If they co-operate, what is the nature of such co-operation? How much can they influence each other if they support each other or if they oppose each other?

We know, for instance, that we may consciously adhere to a certain value, but may interpret and enforce it in a partly divergent way because of the pressure of some other unconscious configurations. We need to know the extent of such influence, the conditions under which it occurs, and the different types of it.

The complexity of social situations and large number of cultural patterns depend on the ability of the human personality to develop a very large number of configurations and to let some of them operate simultaneously.

In some social situations, for instance, we have to use simultaneously (or almost simultaneously) a number of social bonds and norms. Thus, in a mixed party we have to be polite toward gentlemen and chivalrous toward ladies; we have to express our enjoyment of the company; we have to pay special respect to the hostess; we have to use correct language, make innocent jokes, pretend to be interested in the subject discussed, and so on. The limitations set by the nature of the personality, in this respect, set natural boundaries on the development of social life, as well as on the refinement of culture. What are these boundaries?

Of course, some of the bonds and norms do not operate simultaneously, but in a rapid succession. It seems that the rapidly alternating reactions are more frequent and more important than the really simultaneous processes. What is the mechanism of this rapid, dependable, and mostly unconscious shifting? How much of it may be achieved? Which of the shifts are possible, easy, difficult, impossible?

Answers to all these questions, exact knowledge of all these abilities of the personality and of their limits are basic to the progress of sociological, social-psychological, and anthropological studies. They have been almost untouched until now.

Another problem is how many simultaneous or rapidly alternating operations can be kept unconscious. Should we suppose that if their number passes a certain figure some of them must become conscious? Or, is there no pressure toward awareness if too many of them act at once?

All these psychological problems need to be solved in order to make our understanding of the role of the individual in society and in the life of culture more adequate. As soon as we turn our attention to culture itself, further problems confront us. Assuming that cultural traits consist of configurations which comprise both conscious and unconscious components, a number of questions arise: What is the typical proportion of the conscious and unconscious components in a configuration which maintains a cultural trait? How many types of configurations are in existence if we classify them according to the proportion of conscious and unconscious components? Are there any cultural traits consisting only of conscious or only of unconscious components?

* * *

The human personality appears as a continuous stream of numerous simultaneous, spontaneous, and reactive processes. During the waking hours, a minor part of these is conscious; and in sleep most of them are generally unconscious. The processes are either mainly automatic uses of accepted ways and patterns, or adaptive, adjustive, expressive, and partly even creative activities.

The continuous and rich nature of this stream of processes enables the personality to adjust to physical conditions, to meet the requirements of the society and culture, and to harmonize them with the satisfaction of its own needs, interests, and dignity. It enables the individual to be a full member of his group, of his society and of his culture by enjoying and shaping the life of all of these.

The stream of spontaneous unconscious processes operates as long as the personality is alive.[9] It can be compared to a never-stopping factory, producing without interruption the goods required by the market. The (personality) factory spontaneously adapts to the changing requirements of the market, for the large part without conscious plans and decisions. The variety of products is incomparably larger than in any existing factory, and the social situations to which these are to be adapted are often incomparably more complex than any market situation. The adaptations do not cover only one (economic) field but a number of different fields. They are not guided only by one motive (profit) but by a large number of motives, needs, pressures, cultural requirements, and by many of these often simultaneously. The production, as well as the appropriate distribution of products (use of configurations), is very often unconscious.

The picture of the total personality, acting and reacting amidst the totality of physical, social, and cultural conditions is what neither sociology, nor anthropology, social psychology, personology, or psychology has given to us yet. Yet we do not doubt that such a picture

253

is long overdue; and we hope that the future development of these sciences will produce it gradually. This will solve some of their basic problems and bring a more thorough understanding to social and cultural processes.

FOOTNOTES TO CHAPTER FIFTEEN

1. The personality structure is not meant literally, physically. We want to say only that the organization of personality is such that it comprises traces of past experiences. See Philipp Lersch, "The Levels of the Mind," in H. P. David and H. von Bracken, *Perspectives in Personality Theory*, Basic Books, Inc., New York, 1957, p. 213.
2. Periphery of the personality structure again is meant figuratively. By using it, we only want to say that there are other, more basic parts of the personality structure where the traces are probably not stored.
3. See K. Lewin, *Field Theory*, pp. 240, 241.
4. K. Lewin, *op. cit.*, p. 180-182.
5. G. A. Kelly says: "A person's processes are psychologically channelized by the ways in which he anticipates events." (*The Psychology of Personal Constructs*, W. W. Norton Co., Inc., New York, 1955, p. 46).
6. See W. E. Vinacke, *Psychology of Thinking*, p. 60.
7. R. B. Cattell, *Personality*, p. 345.
8. M. L. Hutt and R. G. Gibby find five basic differences between the conscious and the unconscious. The latter has: no awareness of time, no understanding of deprivation and absence of negation, no social, moral and ethical considerations; it is irrational and infantilistic (*Patterns of Abnormal Behavior*, Allyn and Bacon, Boston, 1957, p. 60). H. P. David and H. von Bracken, on the contrary, do not find basic differences between conscious and unconscious evaluation and self-judgment (*op. cit.*, pp. 308, 309).
9. G. A. Kelly says: ". . . the person is not an object which is temporarily in a moving state but is himself a form of motion" (*op. cit.*, p. 48).

XVI

PERSONALITY AND CULTURE PROCESS

The previous discussion led us to certain conclusions concerning the mutual relations between the personality and culture, as well as the nature of the culture process itself. Let us now discuss these more systematically. We shall examine the unconscious adjustments of the personality to culture as well as the changes in culture resulting from personality's behavior, especially from adaptations and creative activities.

However, there is no clear line of demarcation between these two processes. In the life of culture there always is a combination of both acceptance[1] and creativity.

Let us first discuss the acceptance of an innovation by the individual, without making any distinction between the borrowed cultural traits and the local invention. There is novelty in each case and the individual (or group) must decide to receive or reject it.

ACCEPTANCE OF AN INNOVATION

a) Acceptance by the Individual Alone

Any innovation is a disturbing element to the present organization of an individual's psychic life. Often, it initiates a number of rather confused reactions of a shifting, unsystematic, sometimes playful nature. For a split second the individual imagines himself accepting the new pattern, then again refusing it, grasping some advantages[2] of its acceptance, guessing what he would miss by rejecting it, or feeling its suitability or unsuitability to his social environment, and so forth. But the relation of the innovation toward the respective social values, attitudes, norms, obligations, group membership, customs and other conditions, as well as toward the individual's interests, tastes, convictions and desires is soon grasped more seriously. This is done partly unconsciously. The individual may unconsciously feel that the innovation is not morally unobjectionable or that it is not in good taste. If asked about the reasons for his feelings, he may be unable to verbalize them.

All these processes use certain unconscious experiences and take place under a number of unconscious assumptions. These unconscious assumptions are later incorporated into a final configuration of acceptance or rejection. Likewise, many other elements involved in the process, such as emotional attachments, learning, habits, social ties, dislikes, relevant values, the general need for change, feeling of belongingness to a group, and others may be partly or fully unconscious.[3]

The initial process of checking the relations of the innovation with other relevant factors may be later extended to more remote situations and persons. The results of the initial, as well as of the extended, checks may penetrate into consciousness more often than the process of checking itself. They may either become fully conscious or may add only a slight favorable or unfavorable coloring to the attitude toward the new pattern.

The organizing processes often continue even if seemingly interrupted by another more important activity. They may continue even during sleep. Unconscious judgments exclude certain elements, assign the proper value to others, and organize those which were accepted according to the interests of the individual and the requirements of the situation. The tentative relations toward the new trait are unconsciously reshaped, and the emotional attachments and the social ties are modified or transferred to related objects or persons.

When positive elements predominate, a configuration of acceptance generally appears. The new trait gets its right of domicile and receives its place among similar or otherwise relevant configurations as well as in the organization of the personality.

We sometimes feel that the unconsciously arrived at results do not equal the consciously produced ones, and we consciously check on every item of the configuration of acceptance. In most cases, however, we have a convincing feeling that the result is good; and we frequently accept it 'as is'. There is neither time nor serious reason for checking.

This kind of acceptance of a new cultural pattern, although typical, is not general. In some cases, we may be enchanted by the new pattern and accept it at first glance. Then some of the above mentioned processes come into play later and may modify the initial configuration of acceptance.

Both schemes have an important limitation; they apply only to the reception of the "non-material" innovations. The acceptance of new material products is different. Their fitness is tested, and their material advantages and disadvantages are checked. Nevertheless, here non-rational factors may also play a part in acceptance. The elegant appearance of a kitchen appliance, for instance, may attract some buyers more than its mechanical qualities.

In some cases, the resulting configuration of reception or rejection may be far from perfect; there may be reservation or ambivalence toward it. Some elements of the psychological field may be permanently opposed to the newly accepted cultural trait. Nevertheless, a *modus vivendi* between the conflicting elements often is worked out. Strong social pressures or refined rationalizations may anesthetize the individual to the painfulness of the conflict, blind him to its existence, and solidify the coherence of the configuration. It is possible, for instance, to develop a special insensitivity to some conflicts between scientific convictions and religious beliefs.

The crucial question which remains to be answered is what are the factors that induce a decision to accept the new cultural trait. Let us first see what the students of culture tell us about it.

b) Conceptions of the Students of Culture

The most frequently listed favorable conditions or factors in the reception of a new cultural trait by the individual are psychological need, utility, interest, prestige, reward, dissatisfaction, discomfort, maladjustment, and imperfection. Some writers add compatibility, receptivity, communicability (Linton),[4] mood, functional relations of traits or common psychic dispositions (Goldenweiser),[5] alteration of acquired drives, similarities in culture (Gillin and Gillin),[6] teachability of the innovation (Gillin),[7] internal logic, pre-existing culture, changing emphasis, greater receptivity (Herskovits),[8] mental content (Spier),[9] drives (Hallowell),[10] restlessness (Ogburn, Kroeber), play impulses, strivings, surplus of energy, desire for change, boredom, fatigue, repugnances (Kroeber),[11] basic personality (Kardiner), curiosity (Ogburn),[12] dissidence, disillusionment, indifference, disaffection, resentfulness (Barnett)[13] and some others.

Naturally, these factors in the reception of a new trait were conceived from different standpoints and overlap greatly. A more serious shortcoming is that each of the students lists only a few of them, leaving the rest of them aside. Practically all of the factors are social-psychological in nature. Only some of them (prestige, similarities in culture, imperfection, and compatibility) are chiefly cultural and social. The writers who indicate several factors as relevant to reception of a cultural innovation generally do not say whether in a concrete case several or only one of them was in operation.

Only a few writers conceive of the necessity of co-operation of sev-

258

eral factors in the acceptance of a new cultural trait. Goldenweiser[14] and Gillin[15] each list three psychological factors; the former includes liking, need and habit, and the latter, unsatisfied drive or need, teachability of the new pattern, and expectation of reward. Only recently, Barnett has noted fully that several elements co-operate in producing a configuration of acceptance.[16] We think that there are generally a number of such elements.

Let us now see how much support the writings of the students of culture give to our conception of the role of unconscious factors and processes in the life of culture. A number of writers speak about them although none elaborate on them. Linton,[17] for instance, speaks about the unconscious automatic responses, and registry of the situation, about the individual turning his mind unconsciously in the same direction in which the minds of other members of society turn. Kroeber[18] acknowledges unconscious learning, imitation, want to conform, adaptations, unconscious compensation of adolescent generation and the not quite conscious acceptance of culture. Herskovits[19] uses the concepts of unconscious imitation, learning, and conditioning of culture and refers to unconscious acceptance of customs. Sapir and Benedict[20] speak about unconscious selections, Kluckhohn and Murray[21] about unconscious perceptions, intellection, expectations, needs, valuations, and resentments, and are convinced that all integrative processes do not have the property of consciousness. Warner[22] uses unconscious tendencies, Barnett[23] unconscious projection and assimilation, unconscious desire to assert, stabilize, and maintain the ego, and unconscious modifications of patterns. Kardiner's[24] conception of culture uses unconscious projections, unconscious projective systems, and unconscious patterns of perception. Benedict speaks about unconscious recasting of cultural traits and about unconscious canons of choice.[25]

All these writers (except Kardiner) felt somehow inhibited to discuss the unconscious factors in detail and limited themselves to brief remarks. In concluding this discussion, it seems to us that the process of reception-rejection by the individual may be conceived as follows:

1) as a rule, the factors and processes involved in rejection-reception are many; they generally include all the elements of the psychological field relevant to the given situation;
2) often a substantial part of the personality or perhaps the personality as a whole is involved in the reception of the new trait;
3) some unconscious elements operate perhaps in most processes of rejection or reception;
4) the final product is a more or less harmonious organization of the relevant components;

5) the new configuration includes information and assumptions about the present situation; and it may immediately be unconsciously changed if these change or seem to change;
6) one or several factors may be leading in the organization of the new configuration; other components may play a secondary role.

Opinions about the relative importance of particular factors in reception-rejection vary substantially. There is no doubt that some of the factors are completely missing in certain cases of acceptance, while they may have the most responsible role in other cases. This seems to follow from the viewpoints of a number of authors, especially from the detailed analysis of acceptance of innovations by Barnett.

c) Role of Psychological, Social-Psychological, and Social Factors in Acceptance and Rejection

Until now, the individual's reaction to the innovation has been discussed as if the individual were making the decision almost alone; and this, for the most part, is the way anthropologists have treated the subject — moving directly from the level of the individual to the level of culture. But the individual always participates in a group (groups), society, and culture. Let us examine a case of acceptance of an innovation and give full attention not only to the psychological and social-psychological factors, but also to the social and cultural influences as well.

Suppose a young lady has just received a spring issue of her fashion journal. As her eyes slip over the pages, numerous unconscious factors influence her mind. These include a number of unrecollected previous experiences with fashions and dresses; the unrecollected assumption that fashions have to change in spring and the desire to have a new dress (both shaped by our culture); unrecollected ideas about her own stature, about what becomes her; the unconscious need to enhance her self-confidence and half-conscious ideal of womanly beauty, and what shape of dress may improve her deficiencies so as to approach it (she should not look as tall, slim, or narrow, as she really is); numerous chiefly unconscious habits concerning the shape of sleeves, length of skirts, height of shoulders; unconscious physical feelings of having worn a similarly designed dress years ago; half-conscious comparisons of her body features with the shapes of new fashions; unrecollected wishes to please, to be admired, and envied; prevailingly unconscious attitudes toward certain materials; an unrecollected (culturally induced) set to avoid colors she had last season; unconscious thinking processes classifying the dresses into "reasonably" priced, too expensive, and too cheap (including the negative reaction toward the last two); a strong interest in a certain type of dresses and dislike for certain others; and perhaps some other factors. All these factors and perhaps others enter into the vivid play of prevailingly unconscious processes of the momentarily isolated individual. Despite her isolation, certain strong cultural and also social influences are to be found in her wishes, tastes, feelings, and judgments.

Her adherence to middle class norms limits her choice to the models appropriate to this class. Other similar limitations and obligations are "felt" by virtue of her belonging to a certain church and family, out of respect to the occupation of her father who is a minister, and so on. Her age group with its requirements of more vivid colors and more youthful appearance also exercises its influence. There were assumptions about the probable reactions of some of her best friends, as well as unrecollected wishes to please certain females and especially certain males, to make a good impression in the Easter parade, to outdo her feminine rivals, to please one man especially, and perhaps to induce him to propose, and to give pleasure perhaps also to her parents who like so much to see her looking beautiful. Some other similar, social considerations make still more animated the interplay of numerous spontaneous and lively processes.

After the mother of the young lady and later her sisters come back and discuss the new fashions with her, now direct social influences affect the process of reception-rejection. Further direct social interactions will take place when the last issue of the fashionable journal is gone over with friends and the new dresses in the show windows are discussed with her dressmaker. Likewise, the judgments, attitudes, logical reasons, and opinions of people who understand, reports and criticism in the daily papers, as well as reactions of certain strong personalities among her acquaintances, influence (often unconsciously) the provisional results of the previous processes. New elements are added, some parts of the provisional configuration are dropped, and some others are strengthened. Strong enthusiasm may be created by a common admiration for certain features of a certain model.

Of course, later on, broader social interactions also enter the picture. The young lady is anxious to know how the new fashions are accepted by the general public. Her computing service helps to establish the appropriate frame of reference. She may be especially sensitive to the attitudes of her own class ("girls from better families"), as well as to those of the upper class (reference group). She is inclined to imitate socially-leading people, especially actresses. The mere idea that a certain part of the public or some of the leading personalities oppose some new fashions may be decisive and may reorganize the configuration in the making. Every rejection is registered, and the proportion and weight of acceptances and rejections is kept in unconscious evidence.

Thus many subsequent social influences reshape the provisional configuration of acceptance. However, the social interactions continue, and social influences keep affecting it. The configuration almost floats on the changing waves of the attitudes of the relevant individuals, membership and reference groups, as well as of the public. Without the continued support of the undiminishing number of adherents, the configuration would weaken, and the cultural pattern would decline or perish.

Thus, the acceptance of a cultural innovation appears as a rather complex structure. From the beginning, at least seventeen socialized wishes[26] or clusters of wishes were active in organizing the configuration of acceptance. These were partly supported and partly limited by a number of unrecollected experiences and mostly unconscious habits, physical feelings, sets, attitudes, likes, and assumptions. A number of social norms and values and direct and indirect social influences entered into the processes of formation of the new configuration of acceptance.

Of course, fashions, which are very susceptible to change, represent only one kind of cultural patterns. Other, more stable patterns, are generally equipped with some additional components. Customs and mores, for instance, find a firmer and more formal support in proverbs, in teachings of parents and teachers, in stronger social pressures, and in tradition. Still firmer are the moral and esthetic norms with strong traditional supports in principles expressed in books, in programs of different artistic groups, in philosophical concepts, in organized movements.

The firmest cultural patterns have further supports in institutions such as churches, political parties and firms, in laws, constitutions, formal rules, and in the organs of power backing them.

The typical successive steps in the change from a personal configuration into a socially shaped and supported configuration of acceptance seem to be:

1) reshaping of the personal configuration through interaction with close people;
2) strengthening of the configuration through group stimulation and group enthusiasm;
3) assimilation of the configuration to the frame of reference established from behavior of members of membership and reference groups;

4) imitation of real or expected attitudes of leading people (actresses, prominent persons, leaders in fashion);
5) support of the configuration by public opinion;
6) continuous checking on possible changes in the attitudes of leading individuals, as well as of membership groups, reference groups, and public opinion and assimilation to them;
7) in the case of more formal patterns, further supports are secured by formal definition and institutional backing. Most of these steps often are unconscious.

Thus the configuration of acceptance of a new cultural trait results from the organization of the conscious and unconscious components of the individual's psychological field relevant to the innovation with the help of social interaction, group stimulation, social norms, and social approval.

D) CHANGE OF THE PATTERN THROUGH ACCEPTANCE

The accepting group selects some and modifies or refuses other attributes of the accepted trait (Goldenweiser, Herskovits, Spier and others). The terms of "selective borrowing" and "differential borrowing" were coined. Barnett goes even so far as to consider all acceptors as innovators.[27] We mentioned the changes of accepted values in Chapter XIII.

Malinowski[28] goes further and doubts the validity of the concept of diffusion of cultural traits in general. As we know (p. 219), he claims that there is no mere diffusion of European cultural traits in African colonies; there is even no mere mixture or fusion of the European and African cultural traits. There is a dynamic interplay of specific forces (such as race prejudices, political and economic imperialism, the demand for segregation, for safeguarding of the European standard of living, and the African reaction to all that), yielding new products. For instance, an African coal mine is a new type of enterprise having some new elements, such as the color-bar legislation and practice, the discriminative remuneration of labor, unilateral criminal sanctions included in the contract, the inducement to sign it, and so on. The mutual interaction of the two cultures produced a new drink "skokian," which is neither European nor native.

Malinowski's conception of cultural contacts supports our claim that acceptance of a foreign culture trait involves a number of factors. It indirectly points to the fact that these factors are organized into configurations and that the process of organization cannot be fully conscious. Nevertheless Malinowski did not say it this way.

263

We saw that even such values as the accepting culture wants to accept without change are modified, and that "unchangeable" values are at least interpreted differently (see p. 219).

Even when an unchangeable material object is accepted, the way it is used, how it is incorporated into other activities, its cultural frame and meaning, its emotional background and support, and the skills which are used to operate it may be different. The car has a different meaning in contemporary Russian culture (high prestige, official function, great power, connection with the Communist party) from that in American culture (utility, time saving, pleasure, business efficiency, mark of higher or lower social status). French wine used at a French table is a very different cultural element from French wine used at an American table.

All the local conditions close to the newly accepted trait are (often unconsciously) [29] incorporated into the configuration of acceptance. This configuration, then, is different from the original configurations of the members of the donor culture, who live in different physical and social conditions.

E) OBSTACLES TO THE RECEPTION OF A NEW CULTURAL TRAIT

It is interesting to note that the above-quoted students of culture, who indicate chiefly psychological factors as causes of the acceptance of a new cultural pattern, tend to give cultural grounds for their rejection. Psychological obstacles are listed only by a few, such as: Chapin[30] (reluctance, hostility), Gillin[31] (lack of motivation), Herskovits[32] (devotion to status quo, interests). Goldenweiser[33] and Ogburn[34] also list habits and Chapin[35] and Ogburn[36] fear.

The most frequently listed cultural obstacles to acceptance of a cultural innovation are competition[37] or conflict[38] with the traits of the borrowing culture, tradition or opposition to the whole cultural context (Kroeber, Gillin).[39] The isolated cultural trait is more readily accepted than social systems and schemes (Kroeber, Goldenweiser). Kroeber stresses the general character of culture as a cause of rejection of new traits. Herskovits[40] thinks that the focal aspect of culture is more hospitable to new elements, and Gillin[41] stresses that the ethos of the cultural system may be inhibitory to them.

Why do students of culture give predominantly psychological factors as causes for acceptance of a new culture trait and chiefly cultural forces as causes of resistance to accepting it? The main reason probably is that the accepted traits produce institutions and material objects which are evidently cultural, while wishes, interests, needs that favor the new trait,

264

generally are not backed by any institution or product and thus are easily conceived as psychological despite their social and cultural components. But the accultured needs, wishes, or interests, are social factors, too. Thus the conflict between the inclination to accept the innovation and the opposing culture context generally is a conflict between two social forces (often operating unconsciously).

On the other hand, there may be one really psychological obstacle to the acceptance of the new cultural trait which seems to escape the attention of the students of culture. This is the internal conflict produced by the new trait in the psychic life of the individual. The new trait may not be acceptable to the individual because of time or factual collision of which he may or may not be aware and which causes repeated internal conflicts.[42]

OTHER EXPLANATIONS OF ACCEPTANCE

a) Psychoanalytic Explanations

Psychoanalysts generally try to explain the acceptance of a cultural trait through the influence of only one unconscious psychic factor. We may take as a good example Fromm's explanation of the Reformation and of the Nazi movement.

In his *Escape from Freedom*,[43] Fromm notes that the end of the Middle Ages brought impoverishment to the poor in the cities, that the economic pressure on peasants increased, and that the lower nobility faced ruin. Even the prosperous segments of the population felt insecure. Luther's and Calvin's religious ideas gave expression to these feelings, brought them to the surface, and offered a solution.

The success of the appeal of Luther and Calvin was due to the psychic mechanism called the mechanism of escape. The insecure, powerless, anxious, isolated, blocked individual tends to give up his independence and in such circumstances one may want to "fuse one's self with somebody outside of one's self in order to acquire strength."[44] There is simultaneous striving for submission and domination, a masochistic and sadistic tendency.

These sado-masochistic tendencies led Luther and his followers (as well as those of Calvin and Hitler) to the complete submission to the high authority of God (or *Führer*) in order to eliminate feelings of insecurity, insignificance, and powerlessness.

In our judgment, the sado-masochistic tendencies were certainly not the only factor in the acceptance of Luther's and Calvin's teaching. Dissatisfaction with the church, the interest of high priests in power and luxury, the often low moral standard of the clergy, and the contradiction between these and the Christian ideals of poverty, humility, and love certainly played an important additional role in the success of the movement. We hypothesize that the configuration of acceptance was helped by conscious and unconscious reasoning, imitation, group assimilation, learning, and other processes which we have discussed above. It is known that in other similar religious movements of the time the sado-masochistic tendencies did not play any role. Luther's predecessor, John Huss, from whom Luther took a great deal of inspiration, was a mild-natured man who stressed love more than other parts of Christian teaching. In the Hussite movement, which was very successful, no sado-masochistic tendencies were in evidence; but all the above mentioned factors (opposition to the luxury of high priests, etc.) were. Love and brotherhood were stressed by another successful contemporary movement, the Union of Czech Brethren, which was opposed to the same shortcomings of the church.

According to Kardiner, the basic personality is inducive to the reception or rejection of a cultural innovation. It consists chiefly of the basic constellations[45] produced by early childhood experiences (for instance, frustrations). An especially important part of the basic personality structure is the projective systems, of which the subject may be completely unaware. The secondary institutions (such as religion, and folklore) must satisfy the needs of the basic personality. The basic personality structure accepts only such cultural innovations as are compatible with it.[46] Later changes of the personality and its experiences do not seem to play any role. The concept of basic personality represents another attempt to explain the acceptance of culture traits through a single unconscious mechanism. As in the case of Fromm's theory, other components of the configuration of acceptance of certain cultural traits are to be taken into account so as to make the explanation complete.

Linton's basic personality[47] consists chiefly in highly generalized value-attitude systems (some of them unconscious), formed in the first few years of the individual's life. The complex configurations of the child-training patterns produce complex personality configurations in the adult. Apparently, not only frustrations or satisfactions of inborn drives, but also other processes are responsible for the formation of the basic personality. Although Linton does not indicate how many of the first years are important for the formation of the basic personality, he does not argue against the importance of later years, which now seems to be more and more evident.[48]

Although Linton's standpoint is basically very close to our own, we consider also other social-psychological configurations (besides values and attitudes) as well as some other factors and processes as relevant to the acceptance of cultural innovations; and we stress that many of them are unconscious.

Still more social influences are recognized by Schaffner.[49] The son of the authoritarian father looks forward to being freed from his dependent position and to being able to assume the same role as his father. He is custom-tailored for an authoritarian family and for an authoritarian society.

Schaffner stresses also the child's family experiences after five years of age and recognizes the strong influence of school, work, military service, friends, and foreign travel.[50] He explains the authoritarian behavior of German men not only through psychoanalytic mechanisms, but also through imitation of social models such as father and mother.[51]

It seems to us that in addition to this, the individual's conception of the social structure and of his role within it are to be stressed. The Germans generally conceive of the structure of a group or institution as one where one person gives orders and others obediently execute them. They do not conceive of any other possible way. Every individual has one or the other of these two roles. Of course, this scheme is modified by a number of values and other norms, such as the special German thoroughness, manliness, industriousness, by special German sentimentality, by the concept of Gemeinschaft, by Christian ideals, and by some other parts of German culture.

The real configuration of adherence to a culture pattern is certainly more complex than is indicated by any of the three authors. It certainly involves a number of factors, many of them unconscious. All these explanations are both too narrow and too all-embracing.

B) BIOLOGICAL EXPLANATIONS

A recent biological view is Malinowski's[52] functionalism, which is founded on the satisfaction of physiological needs (such as the need for food, shelter, reproduction, and others), as well as of derived needs. Naturally, he is fully aware of the strong impact of social influences on these; and in opposition to older similar conceptions, he is aware that they do not operate as pure biological forces. Thus, his biological explanation of culture is only partial.

Despite his moderation, Malinowski's approach shares with the older biological explanations a common shortcoming, the inability to cope with the diversity of cultures when the biological nature of organic needs is the same. As for the rest, Malinowski himself seems to relegate the organic needs to a secondary role (although he claims them basic) by declaring the culture a "reality *sui generis.*" Subsequent to his earlier statements he acknowledged that the function satisfying the biological needs is neither the "first" nor the "true" cause. It remains for him primarily a heuristic device.[53] Thus, biological needs may be considered only as one of the explanatory principles of the reception or rejection of a new cultural pattern, which, as we claim, remains a product of a chiefly unconscious interplay of many biopsychic and social-cultural forces.

c) Cultural Explanations

Probably the mildest of the recent cultural explanations is the conception of cultural drift as formulated by Sapir and developed later by Eggan and Herskovits. Sapir[54] pointed to the fact that out of a great number of individual variations in language only few are accepted as durable changes and the rest are dropped. The selection is not haphazard; it has a certain direction — a trend, a drift. The drift induces the majority of people to make certain limited selections and to accept them. Eggan's[55] study of cultural drift among the Tinguian of the Northern Philippines comes to the same conclusion.

By analysing the drift in the past, according to Herskovits, we could possibly plot the future development of culture.[56] Another similar concept used by Herskovits is the "internal logic" of culture. Both serve to indicate which new cultural patterns will be accepted or refused.

Unfortunately, the attempt to give a more precise meaning to the concept of drift was not fully successful. Sapir refuses to attach any mystical connotations to the concept, and all three authors want to remain on the level of facts.

To us, cultural drift appears simply to be an expression of certain generally accepted social attitudes, values, and other social-psychological configurations, which may be unconscious and/or which may operate unconsciously. Let us check this contention on the example given by Herskovits — the trend in contemporary American culture to drop the wearing of neckties.

First, we would stress that this is a part of a broader tendency toward informality which involves several components. One is that the old ideal of a formally perfect gentleman has been abandoned and has been replaced by a new ideal, that of a successful entrepreneur. The old-fashioned gentleman lived under conditions that allowed him the time and leisure to be always formally perfect. Formal perfection was a sign of his status and dignity. In modern times, status and dignity are based more on success and money, both resulting chiefly from hard work. And hard work is opposed to formality, which inhibits the working man and cannot be easily maintained during work.

The second factor is the higher respect for human needs, well-being, and comfort, which is opposed to the uncomfortable requirements of formalities. The third one has been brought about by the increase of sport activities, which publicly present many people in informal attire. Thus, the public becomes accustomed to an informal appearance, which may be transferred easily to some other social situations. The fourth factor probably consists of more frequent and informal contacts between men and women which exclude formality, such as at work, school, and sports. Equalitarian values of Western societies undoubtedly contribute, too.

All five (and several other) factors support each other and are organized (prevailingly unconsciously) in the minds of people into a new configuration. With the help of social interaction and group stimulation, a new cultural tendency has been produced — the tendency toward informality. Thus, cultural drift appears to be a social and a social-psychological phenomenon which can and should be understood in terms of our analysis of unconscious structuring processes of the human mind, as well as through social interaction and other social processes. It is not a specific, different factor which alone explains the acceptance of foreign or new cultural traits.

Thus, all three explanations (psychoanalytic, biological, cultural) of the acceptance of a new cultural trait need to be complemented by other factors and processes, especially by the unconscious ones, some of which are not in fact used by psychoanalysts.

SOME COROLLARIES OF OUR STANDPOINT

Suppose that a "caveman" came to a big modern city. What would this man be able to accept and internalize from the modern culture? Certainly very little. He would probably be interested in and be able to accept some very simple tools and commodities; but despite his normal psychological equipment, he would not be able to understand and accept the more complex products of our religious, artistic, scientific, technical, administrative, military, or moral culture. His inborn psychological abilities alone would help him little.

A psychologically healthy adult, with a very limited cultural background, is practically immune to the acceptance of any new cultural trait. Only a socialized individual[57] whose culture has some similarities (Gillin and Gillin) to the donor culture (see also Golden-weiser's similar "moods" and "dispositions") and who seeks solution

269

to the same (often culturally produced) problems will be interested in and able to receive a foreign cultural trait.

The degree of similarity (whether conceived clearly or "felt" without clear awareness) which is necessary for the reception of a foreign cultural trait varies according to the field of culture, as well as according to the general character of the borrowing culture (its flexibility or rigidity, for instance). It varies also with the amount of the prevailingly cultural components of the foreign trait. If the biological relevance of the new trait is prevalent, less similarity is necessary for its acceptance. Thus, modern contraceptives may be more readily accepted by people of a different culture, than, for instance, modern music or philosophy. Nevertheless, even in this case, there must be at least some minimum of cultural similarity. At least, it must be known to the people of the borrowing culture that sexual intercourse is the cause of conception, a notion which some primitive people seem not to believe in.[58] Likewise, the receiving culture must not cherish any religious or moral convictions opposed to birth control or must not overemphasize the sexual pleasures which may be hampered by the use of contraceptives. The wish to have as many sons as possible, so general in the Chinese culture, may be another serious obstacle.

Let us discuss now certain difficulties in producing new cultural traits through interaction between people with similar favorable personal attitudes toward the innovation.

Some of these processes may not even be allowed to start. Favorable personal, psychic configurations may remain only personal if there is opposition to them, if they are morally prohibited, or if they are objects of shame. Then people cannot or are not in the position to express them and to know that they exist with other people. This may, for instance, be the case of certain illicit sexual practices, of atheistic ideas in a strongly religious society (for instance, in the Middle Ages), or of a new physical conception of the world in a society in which a different conception is exclusively valid (G. Bruno's heliocentric conception in the 16th century). If the opposition to such personal conceptions is strong and is backed by the political organization of society, the few people having them cannot even know about each other, the new personal configurations cannot become objects of social interaction, and they cannot produce a new cultural or subcultural trait.

Satisfaction of sexual desires with animals is a case in point. Shame is a strong obstacle to any communication of such experiences. Men who have experienced them practice concealment as much as possible. Although according to Kinsey's[59] report there are eight percent of such men in the U. S., a subculture having such a cultural trait

270

cannot develop. On the other hand, homosexuality which is opposed by law and by mores, may become a real subcultural trait because homosexuals have the opportunity to meet in sizeable, face-to-face groups.

The strictly personal configurations are rarely strong and remain doubtful if opposed by a conflicting cultural trait. Only in exceptional cases, especially if supported by a convincing factual knowledge, are they strong enough to endure (like Giordano Bruno's heliocentric conception).

A sufficient number of (often unconscious) experiences and traces similar to those of the donor group constitute an important condition for acceptance of a new trait by the members of the borrowing group. If this is the case, the differences of the two cultures become a less serious obstacle to the reception of the innovation. On the other hand, people with a number of different stored traces have great difficulty in accepting certain cultural traits from each other despite a relative similarity of the cultures. The unconscious processes producing the new configuration use different building material and, therefore, cannot arrive at the same results (see pp. 124-125).

OTHER CULTURE CHANGES

A) THE INVENTOR AND THE CULTURE

The inventor may seek a solution of a personal unsatisfactory situation, or he may seek to remedy the situation of a group or society. He may be led by his own needs, wishes, and interests, or, from the beginning, he may be preoccupied with the needs, wishes, and problems of a group or of his society. In this case he acts as an agent of society, whether he is formally entrusted to do his work or whether he does it as a volunteer. He keenly feels the problems produced by recent changes of the social and physical conditions of society. The culture which penetrated deeply into all parts of his personality has become a vital part of his life, a vigorous and animating, although partly unconscious part. The individual feels it as a precious substance of his own ego, which he lives for, which he defends and furthers.

This may be achieved only after many experiences and after a rich provision of relevant traces has been stored. Of course, only highly sensitive individuals with strong interests in the respective field of culture can achieve it. In young people, generally, the provision of conscious and unconscious building material is not yet sufficient. The inventor interested in his own problems generally produces inventions

271

of rather limited scope and generally is not so deeply involved in the culture in which he lives.

Basically, we should divide the different ways of producing new cultural patterns into three groups: 1) where the individual does not aim to create a new cultural pattern but feels the unsatisfactory present conditions until unexpectedly a new pattern appears in his mind; 2) where the individual is looking for a new cultural pattern, but the conscious efforts do not bring it; the parallel unconscious processes during some other activity suddenly present a new solution; 3) where the conscious seeking of a new pattern leads by conscious steps to the expected result with the help of some unconscious processes.[60]

The first type of creative activity often starts when a number of unpleasant experiences have generated tensions, resentment, or opposition to the present conditions. These are often blind; they do not aim to achieve any clear positive goal but unconsciously produce an attitude and a set which unwittingly focus the attention to certain experiences. The attitude and the set also secure better availability of the selected experiences and start the process of organization of the new configuration. Nevertheless, these preliminary structures may be abandoned because they prove unsuiting. In some cases, the abandoned half-finished structures are not necessarily lost. They may be reshaped or used again, later on, for the solution of the problem or other similar problems.

The last step in the creative process sometimes needs a new stimulus. It may be a new strong experience or a new inconspicuous event: an automobile accident, enjoyment of a good stage performance, a trip to a foreign country, or only a chat with small children, a good rest, or a vacation. A reaction to any of these experiences may produce the last, often unconscious, processes leading to a new configuration.

The inspiration of poets and creative artists is often of this kind. New political ideas often may be born this way. Founders of new religious sects sometimes arrive at their new conception of religious truth in a similar, unexpected, sudden flash, stimulated by a new experience. None of them might have been wanted, planned, or worked-toward intentionally.[61]

In the second type of creation of new cultural patterns, the product is planned and worked on consciously. It may be, for instance, the solution of a mathematical problem, which after unsuccessful conscious trials, may be solved by unconscious processes (see p. 130)

The third type of creativity may be represented by another mathematician who made all his operations carefully on paper and finally, found the solution. He has the impression that he has done all his work consciously. Nevertheless, this is only partly correct. As we saw in Chapter IX, in most such operations, unconscious factors and processes help the conscious ones. The conscious thoughts are complemented or even led by unconsciously operating habits, unconscious assumptions, unconscious insights and judgments, unconscious experiences with similar operations, with unconscious selections and organizational processes. Without these and perhaps some other unconscious processes (such as skipping some steps) [62] and factors, the mathematician would only be capable of mechanical operations, not dissimilar to the operations of the calculating machine. Thus, even the conscious creative achievements are very often brought about partly unconsciously.

B) SMALL INVENTIONS AND CHANGES WITHOUT INVENTION

From the peripheral types of inventions listed by Barnett (footnote 60, Ch. XVI) only two are to be mentioned here: the impulsive acts on the one hand and probing, doodling, and fingering (because some of them involve unconscious rudimentary inventive processes) on the other.

Linton gave attention to small, not very original inventions which follow the basic inventions and improve them. Kroeber was interested in small inconspicuous changes without real invention. He says that "in culture, too, there are a great many happenings, such as the growth of swing music, of informal manners and casual greetings, of sitting with legs crossed, which are undoubted changes of recent decades and yet would be hard to fit with sense into any rigid scheme of invention — persistence — loss. Nor are such changes all trifling: drifts toward or away from totalitarianism or democracy, or fundamentalism or liberalism, or industrialism or laissez-faire, are of the same order as these examples, in that they are gradual and growthlike instead of happening in jumps or steps."[63]

It seems to us that this consequential statement puts together two things which have to be discussed separately. The drift toward totalitarianism, democracy, or other political world views is the spreading of a definite existing cultural pattern. It is chiefly an internal diffusion and is to be understood as such (see p. 256-263). The growing informality, on the other hand, is a gradual development toward an unknown future type of behavior. Changes have not yet come to their end, and it is not clear what will be their final product.

Culture changes of this last type may be classified into four groups:

1) spontaneous, simple changes conceived as necessities;

273

2) similar changes due to free, similar reactions of a number of people;

3) changes produced by interaction and collective creativity;

4) a combination of processes 2 and 3.

1) People who were shaped by the same culture often react to new conditions only in one new way, which seems necessary and unavoidable. Everyone understands that the new condition requires such a change. No invention is needed. Disappearance of a certain raw material leads to the acceptance of the next best raw material. Drunkenness as frequent cause of automobile accidents arouses a public claim for rules forbidding drunken people to drive. Increased value of education brings about obligatory school attendance.

The development of modern bureaucracy is another case in point. Certainly a great deal of it stems from generally understood necessities (besides inventions by gifted individuals). For instance, increased criminality, smuggling, tax evasion, and similar unlawful practices necessarily lead officers to be more severe, and to use more drastic methods. Such and similar changes were incorporated in the bureaucratic system, without anyone consciously having invented them.

The series of gradual changes of this kind may extend over centuries and may be partly unnoticed by contemporaries, although later on, a historian can see the trend very clearly. Only in special conditions (wars, revolutions) may changes of this kind be more rapid and more noticeable. Such were, for instance, the changes in the Nazi or communist bureaucracy and in the organization of the anti-Nazi underground movements. The Nazi and communist bureaucracies, under the pressure of critical situations, introduced a series of new checkings, reports, verifications, identity cards, and other controls appearing to all involved as necessary in order to meet the heavy responsibilities.

Spontaneous changes in the organization of the underground movement in the countries occupied by Nazis were still more rapid. At the beginning the underground followed the well-established western organizational pattern. An organizational scheme was worked out, written down, and people were assigned to different functions. But when the first members of the underground organization were arrested by the Gestapo and the list of officers and members seized, all were put in jail.

Without any invention, everybody agreed that nothing should be put in writing. People memorized a number of names and functions. But again, disaster came. Thorough torturing produced some names of the members of the organization, and new arrests followed.

The underground limited the number of members known to every individual to a minimum. Finally, the rule was accepted that an individual might know only one other member from whom he would receive orders. But even this was not satisfactory. Sometimes the Gestapo succeeded in following through the line, to be stopped only by coming across an unusually resistant person. In response, the members of the underground accepted code names. The two persons in contact knew each other only by the code name.

This new, workable pattern of adjustment was found without invention. The necessities of the situation were clear to everyone who participated in the movement.

Certainly many changes in military tactics, in the methods of modern political parties, in the adjustment of churches to new social conditions, in the principles of advertising, in commercial methods in general, and in many other aspects of modern culture have occurred in a similar way. No particular individuals can be credited with them. Of course, other changes in these fields were due to personal inventions and still others to diffusion from other cultural areas.

All cultural changes of the type discussed occur by direct modification of configurations under the pressure of certain new conditions. The new conditions enter the psychic fields of a number of individuals shaped by the same culture and with many similar past experiences. People from another culture or subculture or people with different past experiences would react differently. These processes producing new patterns may be unconscious while the need for change and the new patterns are generally conscious.

2) The second type of spontaneous cultural change is produced by similar, though free, reactions of individuals who have been similarly shaped by the same culture. There is no doubt that certain mores change in this way. As extreme prudery at the end of the 19th century slowly disappeared, necking and petting became more and more widely accepted. Here also belongs the drift toward informality (see pp. 268-269). Certain formalities may seem more and more superfluous, embarrassing, funny, or outmoded. People may not know why but they now feel differently. Their new feelings developed as a reaction to certain changes in the social or physical environment which often were not consciously taken into consideration (see pp. 121-124). The new configurations in the individual's psychic life are later modified through imitation and interaction and may be strengthened by group adherence, stimulation, and pressure.

Similar changes occur in certain values, in the interpretation of certain principles (like freedom), in the authority of the government, in the prestige of the army and bureaucracy, in the (decreasing) attractiveness of the old ideals of beauty, and others.

3) Certain cultural changes are produced by common collective reactions to the new common situation (see pp. 216, 217). The behavior of football fans is a good example. Their shouting, yelling, encouraging their team, their gestures, and other "childish" behavior patterns, which were unknown to our forefathers, are not an individual invention. They have been created by the mass of football spectators through mutual stimulation. There is no doubt that, likewise, many religious, political, artistic, and other behavior patterns of modern culture were created in a similar way in meetings of participants in these activities.

This also applies to smaller and longer lasting groups, such as football teams, gangs, people working in a shop, office, artistic studio, a married couple, family, clique, or groups of friends. Some socially required mannerisms and rules of etiquette have been worked out in small groups of upper class people (often the nobility or the king's court). Typical in this respect were the French "salons" of the 18th century. The way of handling the fork and knife, of greeting, of bowing, smiling, speaking and the art of conversation in general were developed in 'the social parties given by the socially leading ladies. Probably some of them were not invented by any particular person.

Gangs of boys, as we know, create their own elaborate codes of conduct (especially with respect to loyalty, solidarity, fair play, justice, chivalry, kindness, brotherhood, not squealing, not lying to each other, protecting property of widows and blind individuals), their own greetings, roles, obligations, epithets, nicknames, argot, songs, attitudes, values, norms and sentiments.[64] Nobody can be credited for the invention of some of them. Soldiers, students, or inmates of different institutions also create their own special values, attitudes, mores, mannerisms, social habits, and so on. Some of these are a direct outgrowth of the group life of small groups. The new configurations were a) stimulated by the group, b) shaped by it, c) accepted by it. All three steps might have been unconscious.

4) The free slow change of individuals' configurations and collective creativity are often combined together. What was disapproved of as opposed to good manners, taste, mores, or decency may be less strongly and less often frowned upon because the changes which caused such transgressions have occurred also in the psychological fields of people who previously objected to them. Then also, the group reaction to the deviant behavior changes in the same way, and is now more lenient.

An example of such a change is a steady decrease of family prayers, of reading the Bible aloud, of saying grace.[65] Such changes occur spontaneously and separately in a number of individuals in many families. Everybody somehow feels, without knowing why, less inclined to observe the old ways as strictly as previously. Then children discuss their personal feelings with their siblings and other children who feel the same way. Similar interaction may occur between adults. The unconscious change of individual configurations gets social support and becomes a social change.

Together, all four processes of culture modification produce an enormous amount of cultural change. They occur continuously, more often gradually and slowly than at a fast pace. All of us take part in such changes without knowing that we do. All the daily events in political, religious, and social life continuously furnish quantities of raw material for unconscious changes in configurations.

c) CHANGES PRODUCED BY CULTURAL LAG

Any change in one part of culture requires adaptive changes in other correlated parts of the culture.[66] The question arises: what produces the adaptive changes after the cultural lag develops? Does the lag produce the adaptive processes by itself or through the members of society? Does a cultural force impose the changes on individuals, or is it individuals who are the source of a cultural movement toward change? As we see it, neither of these is the only cause. The maladjustment must be first noticed consciously, or felt unconsciously.[67] Thus a tension and an attitude favorable to change develop. They may possibly remain only in the form of a vague feeling, of a general idea, or a set drawing more attention to the objects and happenings around the critical spot. Similar psychic states develop simultaneously in the minds of a number of people, often quite independently. The interaction between them turns into a drift or social movement, producing new social-psychological configurations. Many of these processes may be unconscious. If the new configurations are accepted by the group, a new cultural trait is established and may be imposed on other individuals.

d) CHANGES PRODUCED BY INTEGRATIVE TENDENCY

In accordance with the old idea of Comte[68] that there is consensus between different parts ("series") of social life, modern anthropologists assert that culture has a tendency toward integration.[69] Discrepancies tend to be removed.

If we consider the continuous (mostly unconscious) attention given by the personality to all the relevant happenings in the environment, we easily understand how the development toward integration

277

starts. In the psychological field of the individual, two conflicting elements (such as norms or values) appear. This causes discomfort or frustration. If repeated, such experiences may develop a set aimed at the removal of the conflict; and then 'the processes similar to those removing cultural lag follow.

E) IMMANENT CULTURAL CHANGE

Let us limit ourselves to a discussion of a recent theory of this kind, formulated by Sorokin, and to the revised evolutionist theories. Sorokin is convinced that every culture bears the seeds of its change in itself.[70] The change consists mainly in the unfolding of the immanent potentialities of the system. The influence of the environment, although not negligible, consists essentially in retarding or accelerating the change. It cannot change fundamentally the immanent potentialities of the system and its normal destiny. The role of the individual is equally very limited.

Sorokin deduced from rich historical material that the sensate and the ideational (possibly also the intermediary idealistic) systems alternate in the development of culture. The most important question is wherein lies the powerful dynamic agent setting these alternations into motion? In our understanding it can only lie in individuals, both alone and in groups. Similar past and present experiences (some of them unconscious) develop similar tendencies shaped into conformity by empathy, imitation, group membership, interaction and stimulation, and organized into configurations.

The question arises how to explain that a certain system lasts for centuries and then starts to change. Why do the changes occur at a certain moment of historical development and not earlier or later? Are not the social-psychological equipment, the training, and the experiences of individuals during the long existence of one of the three systems (sensate, idealistic, or ideational) basically the same? Perhaps not completely. It seems to us that the experiences of some individuals are different. The refinement and exaggeration of sensuality at the end of a sensate era, for instance, differs considerably from the fresh and vigorous sensual enjoyments of the people at its beginning. And these, evidently, constitute a building material for the social-psychological configurations different from the experiences of the highly refined, complex, and sophisticated patterns of life at the end of the era.

The new individual configurations naturally tend to become social and cultural patterns because of their generality and their mutual assimilation through interaction, as well as because of the recognition given them by the majority. The changes are mostly unconscious.

278

A different idea of a necessary succession of different stages in the development of culture has been brought up by the recent partial revival of some evolutionary principles. It is claimed that the answers to the problems the evolutionists broached have not yet been found; and some writers such as Lesser[71] and White[72] accept again certain elements of the evolutionary principles, although with necessary limitations: hunting and gathering developed before herding, and agriculture or the use of metals everywhere succeeded the stone age. This again must be explainable by the above discussed psychological, social-psychological, and social processes. We do not see any reason to have recourse to any other principles of explanation. It may be that psychic (mostly unconscious) configurations, necessary for a successful use of metals, must be preceded by those developed by the use of stone. It would seem that stone was used first because certain stones found in number in nature had the size and shape that could be used for hammers, first in the hand and later on a handle, while metal did not. Metal could have been shaped as a hammer only after the concept of "hammer" and the possibility and desirability of its use became established as the result of experiences with stone. Thus the necessity of successive stages in the development of culture does not lie so much in the nature of culture but rather in the nature of *experiences* of individuals and the ensuing (mostly unconscious) *development of configurations* and in the appropriate social processes.

f) Changes Caused by Physical Environment

The physical environment certainly is a part (conscious or unconscious) of the psychological field of the individuals. Given certain inborn and acquired abilities, attitudes, values, and tendencies of the individual, given certain social attitudes, norms, and other social realities, the psychological field under the pressure of changes in the physical environment stimulates the establishment of certain new configurations, changed into a new cultural pattern by the above mentioned social processes. Yet the individuals and their groups are the only active agents producing changes, not the environment.

In order to see this point clearly, let us imagine a society whose members were all feeble-minded or neurotic. Would that make a difference in the development and changes of culture? It certainly would. It would equally make an enormous difference if all the members of society lost the ability of having and storing unconscious experiences, of having unconscious perceptions, or of using unconscious judgments. Likewise, if the members of a society lost only the ability to unconsciously organize their experiences into configurations, the culture would necessarily be very different and much poorer, even in the same environment. The environment does not produce any culture; it may be used by it, or it may inspire it (but the active part is played by the inspired person). It may wreck it, curtail it; and this is all. Nevertheless, given stable constitutional and social-psychological properties of people and similar social and physical conditions, we may expect certain effects of the environment on culture by means of appropriate psychological, social-psychological, and social processes.

g) Understanding the Variety of Explanations

Without discussing other conceptions of culture development and change, let us try to answer the question of how it is possible for so many contradictory conceptions to exist simultaneously, without any of them being in the position to prove its correctness. The missing link in all these explanations of the cultural change (except in changes planned or invented by leading individuals) is just the unconscious material of the past and present experiences and the unconscious processes that use these to work out social-psychological configurations. When this powerful link is missing in the chain of explanatory steps, the human mind feels impelled to fill the gap by a hypothetical factor which varies according to the inclinations of the author.

Theories which tried to fill the gap by psychological or biological factors could not account for the diversity of cultures. The environmentalists tried to remedy this by explaining the variety of cultures through differences in the physical environment. Unfortunately, the same physical environment may sustain different cultures in succession. Hence, the idea that culture has its own immanent laws of development. Yet the problem of what is the force behind these immanent laws remains open. More satisfactory seem, at first approach, the theories of cultural lag and of the integrative tendency of culture. But even if we disregard their narrowness (only a part of cultural changes can be so explained), their conception of the acting force inducing these cultural changes is far from satisfactory. It is evident that many changes of this kind are not achieved consciously; and thus the explanation through unconscious factors appears necessary.

A promising insight led psychoanalysts and some anthropologists in this direction. Unfortunately, this direction has not been followed far enough. Generally one or a few unconscious (sometimes unwarranted) psychic forces have been held responsible for cultural change. Psychoanalysts did not see the importance of a number of other unconscious factors, especially of the unconscious organizing processes and

280

of unconscious judgments, imitations, learning, computing service, sets, frames of reference, unconscious past and present experiences, unconscious attitudes, values, and so on. The ability of the human mind to organize unconsciously, using these unconscious factors to produce configurations, is the fantastic workshop where so many cultural changes are produced. Here, with the help of group interactions and other social processes, the new cultural patterns are formed and kept alive. Here also, they may be reshaped or discarded, if necessary. This unconscious personality workshop constitutes the long-sought-after link between personality and culture.

Unfortunately, we are not in a position to indicate the laws of the operation of this workshop. These are to be discovered by empirical research. All we wanted to achieve was to point out its importance and the need for research in this unexplored area, as well as to denote its direction.

FLEXIBILITY OF CULTURE TRAITS

In the conception of the students of culture, socialized individuals often appear as rather stable elements of the culture. Of course, the students of culture are aware of tendencies toward change; but these are understood to be limited rather to certain parts of the culture at a time. The rest of the culture seems to be firmly imbedded in the personalities of the members of the society. It appears, at least indirectly, that in the conception of certain anthropologists like Herskovits,[73] Linton,[74] and others, culture is learned. In Murdock's conception culture consists mainly of learned behavior and of habits.[75] Some others consider at least certain parts of the culture as habits. For Gillin and Gillin,[76] for instance, the customs are habits, and for Malinowski,[77] speech is bodily habit. Kroeber[78] speaks about habit adjustments.

In our opinion, the learned and habitual components of the social-psychological configurations maintaining a cultural trait are not the only ones responsible for it. We know that generally many other flexible components are incorporated in such configurations.[79] Besides that, we again have to stress the constant sensitivity of the personality to the existence of the social and physical conditions of the environment and the readiness to drop or change configurations no longer supported by the existing conditions.

The honorific title of "gracious lady," given in the Central European countries to upper and middle class married women, took on more and more a coloring of comic emptiness in the last two decades before World War II. Similarly, the honorific titles of "court coun-sellor" and of "counsellor to the emperor," which were awarded to outstanding citizens in old Austria-Hungary in the last decades of its existence, seemed empty and rather funny. Most of the "counsellors" never appeared in the court and never met the emperor. The strong habits of using these titles (also when addressing people) ceased work-ing as smoothly and automatically as they had in the past. People used them hesitatingly and pronounced them with a touch of irony. Similarly, the strong discipline of the army, supported by many learned behavior patterns and by strong habits and habitual ideas may sud-denly break down when hope of victory fades.

In all these cases, habits, generally learned behavior, and perhaps some other static elements of the social-psychological configurations, are not strong enough to keep the cultural trait in existence if some of the conditions on which it was built disappear. The configuration breaks down spontaneously, without conscious intention or decision.[80]

Let us take other examples from a more controllable field of cultural life such as table manners. These consist chiefly of habits and overlearned behavior. When eating, we sit properly at a set table; we use several plates, a glass, a cup, two or three spoons, a fork, knife and a napkin. We handle all these in a well-defined way. We use only the fork to carry the piece of food to our mouth, and we do it slowly and quietly. When sipping soup or masticating, we avoid making noise. We do not eat in a hurry, and we remain seated at the table without standing up or leaving our seat before the dinner is finished. We do not smoke when eating, we do not play with objects on the table, and so forth. All this is so overlearned that it has become automatic.

However, when isolated we are inclined to drop our life-long habits of good table manners. People living alone and eating alone generally substantially simplify their table manners. But if isolation is complete, the deterioration results in atrocious manners. Admiral Byrd reports this after one and a half months of isolation at the Antarctic.[81]

Why do we drop our life-long habits and learned behavior pat-terns with such surprising rapidity? Obviously, under normal condi-tions, habits and learned behavior do not work alone. They need the help of certain conditions which are missing in isolation. One of the conditions is other people and the other condition is the broader cul-tural setting around us. When eating at a table with others, we use our table manners out of respect for our table companions and for ourselves, although most people do not know it. Dropping them would be an offense to them as well as a humiliation to ourselves. Even when alone at home, we would feel inferior to millions of people living around us. We would appear to ourselves as uncultured; we would feel ashamed, and we would not feel members of the "good society," of our own class or profession. Yet when we are alone and very far from all these people, and when practically all our conditions of life are basically different from theirs, then we not only drop our usual table manners without any such feelings, but, on the contrary, we also feel that in such conditions we can behave differently.

Linguistic habits, as such, mentioned by Malinowski, generally are not used alone either. There are, however, a few cases of purely habitual word reactions (such as the greeting "hello"). Such a habitual word may exceptionally be used without any further connotation, meaning, or coloring; but generally, several other non-habitual meanings are added to it through different qualities of voice, through a different rhythm, melody, facial expression, or gesture. All these richly express our psychic states, our conception of the present situation, our relation to the other person, some of our pertinent judgments, ideas, attitudes, values, and so forth, which are not habitual but specific to the situation and sometimes even unique. The additional components of our one word greeting may express, for instance, self-assurance, respect toward the greeted person, doubts or hesitation about how we feel about him, a desire to please, a desire not to start the conversation, a wish to dominate, or an attempt to escape from an embarrassing situation, an attempt to hide one's own real thoughts, and so on. Words as bodily habits are rarely used by themselves. Generally, they are used as parts of broader social-psychological configurations comprising permanent and temporary components.

The use of a word alone, not as part of a phrase or sentence, is rare. The sentence (including the word) conveys a special or unique meaning. Even if the habitual nature of handling words cannot be denied, they generally are rather a building material of our sentences, organized by our momentary reasoning, judgments, emotional reactions, by our values, attitudes, and so forth. More than any other cultural behavior, speech emphasizes our concern with the present, often changing situation. It also involves more creativity and is more often a unique expression of the personality.

Now let us come back to the remark of Kroeber that the causes of the maintenance of culture are also the habit adjustments we make. This may be right or wrong according to the meaning we give to it. If Kroeber means certain habits alone, it is not a sufficient explanation for the maintenance of culture. If he means habit adjustments with the appropriate conscious and unconscious components of a configuration (knowledge, assumptions, ideas, sets, automatic behavior, routine) and all the above mentioned conditions, then he is correct.

Our analysis of the role of habit and learned behavior in culture confirms again that psychic factors maintaining cultural traits never consist of one static psychic component only. Generally, several components contribute to establishing such a complex configuration. Neither habit alone, nor learned behavior alone, constitute a psychic factor that maintains a cultural trait. For this reason such a trait is a flexible configuration of several psychic components, of which some may be conscious, others unconscious.

THE RELATION BETWEEN PERSONAL CONFIGURATIONS AND CULTURAL TRAITS

What is the mutual relation of the social-psychological configurations and cultural traits? Are they part of the same reality, two sides of a coin, or is there a considerable difference in their content?[82]

Under normal conditions, cultural traits and psychic (or rather social-psychological) configurations closely correspond to each other. At least most psychic configurations of most members of society correspond to accepted cultural traits. Otherwise, cultural traits would not exist as such. This does not mean, however, that there is a one to one relationship between the two. There are deviations, irregularities, shortcomings, and even conflicts which make the mutual correspondence far from perfect. First of all, the existing cultural traits (at least, those which are relevant for the individual) are part of the psychological field of the individual and are the raw material for his psychic (or rather social-psychological) configurations. Excepting special cases (feeble-mindedness, neurotic condition, lack of education, of information, strong personal or social biases, and so forth), psychic configurations cannot omit this building material. Of course, the personality may use it fully or partly, may modify[83] it, or even reject it.[84]

Even in cases of conforming individuals, the psychic configurations never fully correspond to the cultural traits. Every individual has his own emphases and de-emphases on different parts of each culture trait and his own, slightly unique interpretations of it. The psychic configurations of an individual often include only a part (mostly the major part) of the cultural trait and this part sometimes has a special personal coloring.

Despite this, it would be erroneous to consider psychic configurations as only incomplete derivatives of the cultural traits. In some instances (such as in the case of cultural change), psychic configurations appear first and are instrumental in establishing new cultural traits.

284

Generally, both psychic configurations and cultural traits are composed of psychic and social factors. Besides psychic components, the psychic configurations comprise the reckoning with laws, governmental policies, group memberships, social values, social movements, social situation, material cultural products, physical environment, and so forth. On the other hand, culture traits need for their existence the organized cognitive, affective and conative elements of the human personality.

In cultural traits, as well as in psychic configurations, we find two different kinds of components: the factual and the ideological ones.[85] The facts press on our psychological field and impose themselves on the cultural traits directly or are taken into consideration through concepts.

In process, both cultural traits and psychic configurations are led by wishes, needs, emotional stimuli, and other dynamic tendencies of the individuals and/or by the group goals, group adherences, enthusiasm, group pressures, group approval, social movements and norms. Both the individual and the social components find strong limitations in material and social facts, as well as in the psychic properties of humans.

Cultural traits are maintained, first, by the conscious or unconscious knowing of the existence of these facts; second, by their meaning for the individual and the group; third, by conservative elements of human nature (habits, learned behavior, and adjustments, for example); fourth, by the emotional and intellectual adherence to them; fifth, by the necessity of generally using tested and well-accepted behavior patterns (to achieve security and spare energy); sixth, by the need to understand others and to be understood; and seventh, by the need to be accepted. Further, they are maintained by social-psychological forces like group belongingness and by formal organizations (like churches and governments), by the functional interdependence of different cultural elements, as well as by the existence of cultural products (such as books, buildings, or machines).

Psychic configurations are maintained by practically all these forces plus mental abilities and emotional properties of individuals, by the functional interdependence of the psychic components, by special personal conditions of life, and by special personal experiences. (A patriotic man will develop a stronger patriotism if living in a sensitive outpost; unfortunate experiences resulting from an unhappy marriage of parents may lead the son to adhere strongly to the ideal of lifelong, happy marriage).

b) Conflict Between Individual's Configurations and Cultural Traits

The discrepancy between the culture traits and the individual's configurations may develop into a conflict. Even when originally in complete harmony, they may diverge and develop a conflict. Let us take an example of a patriotic citizen living in a nation with strongly developed patriotic feelings. His related configurations are very powerful. He is willing to defend the national interest at any cost and to make the highest personal sacrifices for it, even that of his own life.

If such an individual becomes aware of any danger to his nation, his related configurations start to operate immediately. The individual's psychic configurations and the developing social force still go hand in hand. The strengthening of the original patriotic configuration through social interaction is willingly and enthusiastically accepted.

The individual may voluntarily enlist in the civil defense, in military service, or in former Nazi S. A. or S. S. troops. Such a formal organization corresponds fully to his attitudes and carries through more effectively what his own feelings sought. But differences between his personal psychic configurations and the organizational requirements may appear. The organization supported or created by individual psychic configurations controls him and may do violence to his feelings. In some cases, the individual may be forcibly induced to act against his own conviction. Such was the case of the members of the Nazi movement in Germany. Thousands of people aiming toward new cultural forms got organized into a strong movement which dominated them more and more and finally terrorized some of them in order to impel them to behave in a way to which they were opposed.

The question now is: do the individual's pertinent configurations change because of the conflict, or do they stay as they originally were? Needless to say, they change. The fact of imposition of certain ways of behavior enters as an important element into the psychological field of the individual and is taken into account. It may arouse resistance, even increasing resistance; but more often, it produces a new psychic configuration of partial or almost full acceptance of the imposed cultural trait.

c) Influence of Imposed Cultural Traits

A much clearer incidence of such a conflict occurs in the case of imposition of foreign cultural traits on an indigenous culture. Let us discuss a concrete case which has been mentioned previously.

Such a powerful and sudden imposition in recent history occurred

286

during the German occupation of a number of nations in World War II. The Nazis attempted to introduce Nazi culture in greetings, in Nazi or pro-Nazi names of streets, squares, and national organizations, in Nazi institutions, and so forth. They replaced the previous democratic elective system by the "leader system," the labor unions by the *"Arbeits-front,"* and the system of democratic political parties by one political pro-German party with an appointed leader and subleaders. Resistance to these new cultural traits was strong and general, although rather inefficient. Open opposition was punished by confinement in concentration camps and executions and tacit non-co-operation by lighter sentences. But even the concealed non-co-operation resulted in serious personal hardships. A worker who refused to be a member of the official pro-German *Arbeitsfront* would lose additional rations of food, of warm underwear, of clothing, and of cigarettes (easily exchangeable for food), as well as medical treatment in spas, the right to go to summer resorts, and so forth. In the severe shortage of all goods, few people were able to stay out of *Arbeitsfront*. Resistance even to the new (pro-German) names of streets had to be dropped. A correct address was needed to insure delivery.

Connections of the new cultural traits with daily life were numerous and unavoidable. The pressing need for basic necessities of life secured strong supports for them. Despite that only a small number of opportunists accepted them really. In addition to these, a small number of honest people with certain special psychological characteristics adhered to them. They were either more susceptible to fear, or perhaps their personality was accustomed to yielding more easily to force. Some of them were more oriented toward the present situation than the average individual; or finally, the practical values of some people were perhaps stronger than those of others and their adherence to their own culture weaker. Interestingly enough, many of them still considered themselves as good Czechs, as loving their country, and not being disloyal to it. They were sincerely surprised by the critical remarks of other people concerning their new attitudes. They were honestly unaware of some of these changes. The new social-psychological configurations were organized unconsciously and seemingly without any basic change in their patriotic feelings. All happened by itself, without any conscious decision. I am certain that even most of the rationalizations of the new orientation developed unconsciously. It seems that it was just a normal, unconscious organization of the relevant parts of the psychological field.

The process of acceptance of an imposed cultural pattern against one's conscious convictions starts with the special psychic disposition we have already mentioned, which sets the process of organization of the new configuration in motion. This disposition (whatever its kind and nature) makes the person more aware of the reality of the imposed pattern. It makes it appear as unavoidable, as a fact to be reckoned with. It distorts individuals' perceptions and judgments; it induces an over-estimation of the expected satisfactions from the acceptance of the new trait, and it secures faster and stronger mental connections of the new trait with everyday life. All this helps to organize the new structure of acceptance automatically and without awareness of the individual. It also pushes aside some adverse conditions and/or minimizes them. Thus, the unconsciously operating processes build up not only a configuration of acceptance, but also its protection against the impact of loyalties toward one's own country, friends, groups, and conscience.

The automatic nature of the acceptance of a foreign, enemy pattern under pressure may be partly illustrated by the above-quoted case of the inmates of the concentration camps in Nazi Germany, who accepted certain values and outward signs of the Nazi culture from their SS guards (see p. 220) as well as the case of American prisoners, who accepted the viewpoint of their communist captors, especially that of the Associated Press correspondent Oatis (in jail in Czechoslovakia in 1951-1953),[86] and Colonel Schwable[87] (prisoner in Northern Korea, returned in 1953). Of course, their personal situation was considerably worse because of the fact that they were alone against a large number of policemen, guards, and interrogators. Schwable's resistance was also lowered by a very long solitary confinement and by severe physical privations[88] (cold, dirt, impossibility of using a latrine, and others). Nevertheless, it is striking that in both cases, their untrue confessions were not willful acts. The continuous pressure and privations were unconsciously connected in such a strong configuration with the imposed ideas that a certain kind of behavior, revolting to the victims since they were freed, developed by itself. It was not as in some other such cases a matter of shrewdness or of falsehood in order to save oneself from the excruciating situation. It was rather an automatic, spontaneous product of the present outward and inward situation.

We noticed something very similar in several milder previously discussed cases, such as those of French dressmakers adjusting against their will to the taste of the country of residence and of hostile neighboring nations imitating, against their will, the behavior patterns of their unloved neighbors. Less strongly opposed was Faris' acceptance of the French shrugging of shoulders and of the Negroes' pointing by lips, as well as the acceptance by men who lived in a foreign country of values, attitudes and other behavior patterns of the foreign culture. There was

288

some social pressure in all these cases which helped to produce the new configuration.

The human mind appears as a sensitive receiver, using all kinds of information for an unrelenting, often unconscious, establishment of new psychological configurations so basically relevant to the existence and changes of culture. The production of a new configuration may be set and kept in motion often without any intention or sometimes even against it. These processes are the bloodstream of the life of every culture, both in its changing as well as in its unchanging (or rather very slowly changing) aspects.

THE UNCONSCIOUS ASPECTS OF CULTURE
IN THE WRITINGS OF THE STUDENTS OF CULTURE

We have already discussed the views of the students of culture on some unconscious aspects of culture (see pp. XIX and 259). Their treatments of the unconscious in culture as a whole is no more elaborate.[89] Nevertheless, they seem unable to dispose of the concept; in fact, it appears even from their writings that the proportion of unconscious parts of culture is large, and that from whatever angle we study culture, we come to the unconscious areas. The impression we get from the respective passages is as striking as that from the foregoing quotations by writers who list particular unconscious aspects of the life of culture. In both cases, only a few authors are followers of the psychoanalytic or other psychological school based on the unconscious (such as Kardiner, Linton, Kluckhohn and Murray). None of the others seem to follow any school of unconscious or to have any theoretical reason for using this concept. The feeling that certain cultural phenomena have to be ascribed to the unconscious part of the psychic life was apparently so strong that the concept was used even without any special theoretical grounds. This enhances the importance of their statements. These were, as it seems to us, made only when the authors felt it unavoidable. This also explains their incidental, brief, and unsystematic use of the concept.

Thinking of this rather surprising phenomenon, we find it difficult not to have the impression that it is not due to chance. The authors seem to be shy of the concept of unconscious and certainly appear to abstain from its systematic use. Undoubtedly, they were influenced by the violent criticism of psychoanalysis by modern psychologists and probably were afraid of being called unscientific. Yet feeling that the unconscious processes and factors do play a certain role in the life of culture, they limit the use of the concept to the bare minimum.

*   *   *

289

If we look at the role that the human mind plays in the existence and change of culture, we have before our eyes a rather amazing picture. The role of a normal individual (or group of individuals), in this respect, is richer than has generally been thought. It is not only the creativity of the leading individuals, which so amazed social philosophers of the 19th century. It is not only the conscious acquisition of knowledge and of the rest of the cultural heritage by masses of people. It is also the rich activity of the unconscious maintenance and development of culture (the numerous acts of using, accepting, reshaping, adjusting, producing and rejecting existing or new patterns) operating continually in the individual's mind and often in several fields of culture or aspects of the situation simultaneously.

It is time that this complex, unconscious role of the human personality in the life of culture were recognized and studied more systematically. The unconscious and/or unconsciously operating past experiences, sets, automatic behavior, habits, routine acts, learned behavior, thoughts, sentiments, attitudes, values, as well as unconscious knowing that the conditions of life have or have not changed, are components of the psychic configurations which maintain the existence and operation of culture. The rich and continuous succession of simultaneous, often unconscious, experiences, their storing and selecting, followed by immediate unconscious comparing, reasoning, computing operations, as well as the creative and organizational processes, play a basic role in the changes of culture. The unconscious empathy, imitation, assimilation, and modification of the psychic configurations through social interaction and group membership are another source of such changes.

All the listed unconscious processes are a continuous, practically uninterrupted flow. Amazingly enough, all the activities of maintaining, reshaping, accepting, and producing culture traits go hand in hand, often simultaneously. The old cultural traits are maintained only with continuous unconscious checking; it can almost be said that they are always accepted anew whenever they are supposed to operate. The existing cultural traits are at least slightly modified all the time, and the new cultural traits are invented and accepted. Thus, the maintenance and change of culture appear as two aspects of the same stream of activities. Culture, itself, is a continuous process of reaccepting and reshaping the old patterns as well as creating and accepting new ones.

For the maintenance of the existing culture, as well as for the development of new culture traits, both the storage of common past experiences and a common perceptive basis are necessary. The mass of common past experiences represents the first uniformities of the future culture. These are the gold mine of the raw material from which culture is built. Socialized individuals with all their unconscious psychic processes are the miners; and the interactions between individuals are the production processes of new cultural patterns and of changes of the existing ones.

*   *   *

The study of unconscious factors and processes in social life, as well as of the unconscious establishment and the changes of social-psychological configurations which are basic to the existence of social behavior and culture, has a broader bearing than would appear at first glance. It may be one of the approaches which will enable us to grasp certain aspects of the laws governing social reality, and may bridge part of the gap between sociology and psychology.

Despite the rather general conviction that social life is governed by laws, the attempts to discover them have been, until now, extremely difficult and often fruitless. That is why many sociologists preferred to speak about regularities of social life rather than of laws. Certainly, there are regularities — that is happenings which recur with a certain rather limited degree of consistency. Such regularities may also be found in nature: four seasons of the year, blossoming of the trees and flowers, mating season of different animal species, erosion, and others. Yet in natural sciences we are not satisfied with regularities; we know that behind them strict laws are in operation.

The regularity in recurrence of natural or social events is the result of the simultaneous operation of several laws. In every recurrence, the combination of the forces obeying the natural laws is slightly different; hence, the final result of their operation is necessarily more or less irregular.

Thus the law of gravity does not mean that falling objects fall with the same velocity and acceleration. The fall of different objects is, as a matter of fact, different. It is to be explained by the differences in the shapes of the objects and in the density of the air at the given place and time. Thus, although the law of gravity operates strictly in every case of any falling body, each fall is different.

Behind the regularities of the birth rate, marriage rate, incidence of crime, observance of cultural norms and others, there are likewise strict laws. We cannot conceive of any other possibility. Mere regularity (with certain variations in each recurrence) cannot be understood as incomplete legality with a certain degree of freedom. There are strictly operating laws behind all regularities.

Unfortunately, it is very hard to discover them. One of the ways of discovering some of them probably is the study of unconscious processes, factors, and of their configurations.

291

Of course it is not the only way; and it cannot lead to the discovery of more than a certain number of laws. Social laws are more numerous than those governing the unconscious (or unconsciously established) configurations. But whatever their number, the study of unconscious factors, processes, and configurations will help considerably in the discovery of certain of them.

There is another aspect in which our approach can help the understanding of social life. Until now, most attempts at understanding social life through psychological laws have failed. Inborn imitativeness, wishes, desires, and needs proved to be useless tools. On the other hand, there is no doubt that psychological laws operate in social life. When both sociology and psychology have become more advanced, psychological laws will be a natural basis on which sociological explanations will be built. The laws governing the unconscious psychic and social-psychological processes, factors and configurations will be part of this long awaited basis. They will help to achieve the absolutely indispensable co-operation of the psychological and sociological approaches in the understanding of human behavior.

FOOTNOTES TO CHAPTER SIXTEEN

1. See, for instance, B. Malinowski, *The Dynamics of Culture Change,* esp. pp. 23-26; H. G. Barnett, *Innovation,* esp. pp. 329-334; R. Linton, *Study of Man,* pp. 339, 347.
2. See the discussion of acceptance of values, pp. 218-221.
3. C. W. King says that the ". . . . motives leading an individual to accept or reject any innovation are not always clear to the person himself." (*Social Movements in the United States,* Random House, New York, 1956, p. 60).
4. R. Linton, *Study of Man,* pp. 331, 341, 337.
5. A. A. Goldenweiser, *Anthropology,* F. S. Crofts and Co., New York, 1945, pp. 482, 486.
6. J. L. Gillin and J. P. Gillin, *Cultural Sociology,* pp. 563, 529.
7. J. Gillin, *The Ways of Men,* Appleton-Century-Crofts, New York, 1948, p. 543.
8. M. J. Herskovits, *Man and His Works,* pp. 558, 539, 543, 551.
9. L. Spier, "The Sun Dance of the Plains Indians: Its Development and Diffusion," *Anthrop. Papers, Am. Museum of Nat. History, XVI.,* part 7, pp. 504, 511.
10. A. I. Hallowell, "Sociopsychological Aspects of Acculturation" in R. Linton (ed.) *Science of Man in World Crisis,* Columbia U. P., New York, 1945, pp. 183-186.
11. A. L. Kroeber, *Anthropology,* pp. 387, 391.
12. W. F. Ogburn, *Social Change,* The Viking Press, New York, 1922, p. 191.
13. H. G. Barnett, *op. cit.,* pp. 378-410.
14. A. A. Goldenweiser, *op. cit.,* p. 484.
15. J. Gillin, *op. cit.,* p. 543.
16. H. G. Barnett, *Innovation,* pp. 337, 426, 432. See also, A. K. Cohen, *Delinquent Boys,* p. 149.
17. R. Linton, *The Cultural Background of Personality,* pp. 94, 95, 87, *Study of Man,* p. 320.
18. A. L. Kroeber, *op. cit.,* pp. 347, 275, 288, 577.
19. M. J. Herskovits, *op. cit.,* pp. 26, 625, 633.
20. R. Benedict, *Patterns of Culture,* p. 47.
21. C. Kluckhohn and H. A. Murray, *Personality* (1950), pp. 9, 10, 30, 25.
22. W. L. Warner, *Democracy in Jonesville,* p. 147.
23. H. G. Barnett, *op. cit.,* pp. 210, 122, 115, 76.
24. A. Kardiner, *The Psychological Frontiers of Society,* pp. 20, 19, 29.
25. R. Benedict, *op. cit.,* pp. 47, 48.
26. 1) The strongly socialized desire for having a new dress in the spring; 2) the wish to have a dress of different shape and color; 3) the wish to enhance one's ego; 4) wish to near the cultural ideal of womanly beauty;

5) wish to please men in general; 6) to please several good friends among them; 7) especially to please one; 8) and to make him propose; 9) to please parents; 10) to please some women; 11) to out-do rivals; 12) to excel in the Easter parade; 13) to be admired; 14) envied; 15) to impress people in general; 16) to conform to middle-class standards and 17) to the occupation of her father and probably more components, most of which operated half consciously or unconsciously. These could be grouped under the following headings: enhancing one's ego, erotic motives, meeting social expectations, and influences of primary group ties. Compare A. K. Cohen, *Delinquent Boys,* p. 152.

27. H. G. Barnett, *op. cit.,* pp. 49, 54, 255, 330-331.
28. B. Malinowski, *op. cit.,* pp. 18, 19.
29. See R. Linton, *Study of Man,* p. 403-4, who explains the meaning of a trait complex by associations attached to it, which are frequently unconscious.
30. See F. S. Chapin, *Cultural Change,* Appleton-Century Co., New York, 1928, p. 386.
31. See J. Gillin, *op. cit.,* p. 542.
32. M. J. Herskovits, *op. cit.,* p. 487.
33. A. A. Goldenweiser, *op. cit.,* p. 484.
34. W. F. Ogburn, *op. cit.,* pp. 173-180.
35. F. S. Chapin, *op. cit.,* p. 386.
36. W. S. Ogburn, *op. cit.,* p. 172.
37. J. L. Gillin and J. P. Gillin, *op. cit.,* p. 181.
38. R. Linton, *op. cit.,* p. 343.
39. J. Gillin, *op. cit.,* p. 549.
40. M. J. Herskovits, *op. cit.,* p. 550.
41. J. Gillin, *op. cit.,* p. 542.
42. The concept of internal conflict is broader than the similar concept of internal incompatibility by Barnett, which is based on the impossibility of substituting the old pattern by the innovation. It is also different from Kardiner's incompatibility. Many incompatibilities are harmless if so defined by the culture.
43. E. Fromm, *Escape from Freedom,* pp. 59-60, 66-68, 75, 81, 185.
44. *Ibid.,* p. 141; see also pp. 142, 164, 181, 185.
45. A. Kardiner, *The Individual and his Society,* pp. 21, 484.
46. *Ibid.,* pp. X, 476, 484-485; A. Kardiner, *The Psychological Frontiers of Society,* especially pp. 449, 454.
47. R. Linton, *Cultural Background of Personality,* especially pp. 111-113, 129, 131, 141-143.
48. H. Orlansky, "Infant Care and Personality," *Psychol. Bulletin,* 46, 1949, pp. 1-48.
49. B. Schaffner, *Father Land,* Columbia University Press, New York, 1948.
50. *Ibid.,* pp. 74, 44, 7.
51. *Ibid.,* p. 51.
52. B. Malinowski, "Culture," in *Encyclopedia of the Social Sciences, IV,* p. 627.
53. B. Malinowski, *A Scientific Theory of Culture,* Univ. of N. Carolina Press, Chapel Hill, 1944, pp. 117, 170.
54. E. Sapir, *Language: An Introduction to the Study of Speech,* Harcourt, Brace, New York, 1921, pp. 157-182.

55. F. Eggan, "Some Aspects of Culture Change in the Northern Philippines," *American Anthropologist*, XLIII, 1941, pp. 11-18.
56. M. J. Herskovits, *op. cit.*, pp. 585, 593.
57. See A. A. Goldenweiser, *op. cit.*, p. 495, and J. L. Gillin and J. P. Gillin, *op. cit.*, p. 529.
58. See literature cited by E. Durkheim, *The Elementary Forms of the Religious Life*, The Free Press, Glencoe, Ill., 1947, pp. 274-275.
59. A. C. Kinsey, *Sexual Behavior in the Human Male*, W. B. Saunders, Philadelphia, 1948, p. 670.
60. The students of inventiveness know about certain other types such as invention by chance, by random activity, by idle manipulation of objects, by impulsive acts, by probing, doodling, etc. Nevertheless, these do not involve organizational processes (see H. G. Barnett, *op. cit.*, 107-113) which generally start after the new pattern appears.
61. Some writers speak even about unconscious inventions and unconscious inventors (R. Linton, *The Study of Man*, pp. 313, 317). J. Gillin says that the individual may be unconscious of the fact that he originated something (*op. cit.*, p. 533).
62. See pp. 131-132.
63. A. L. Kroeber, *op. cit.*, p. 386.
64. See F. M. Thrasher, *The Gang*, Univ. of Chicago Press, Chicago, 1927, pp. 284-291, 294, 267, 269, 298; W. F. Whyte, *Street Corner Society*, Univ. of Chicago Press, Chicago, 1943, esp. pp. 12, 256-259; M. Sherif and C. W. Sherif, *Groups in Harmony and Tension*, pp. 192, 196, 202, 233, 237, 260, 269; H. A. Bloch and A. Niederhoffer, *The Gang, A Study in Adolescent Behavior*, Philosophical Library, New York, 1958, pp. 163-164; A. K. Cohen, *op. cit.*, pp. 34, 35.
65. J. Dollard, *The Changing Function of the American Family*, The University of Chicago Libraries, Chicago, 1931, pp. 204-206 (quoted by Burgess-Locke, *The Family*, p. 469).
66. W. F. Ogburn, *Social Change*, pp. 200-213; 256-268.
67. We know that this does not happen always whenever the cultural lag develops. The conflict may be concealed by an appropriate ideology or definition.
68. A. Comte, *Cours de Philosophie Positive*, Vol. IV, Bachelier, Paris, 1839, pp. 325-341.
69. See, for instance, G. P. Murdock, "The Cross-Cultural Survey," *American Soc. Review*, V., 1940, pp. 361-70, or R. Linton, *The Study of Man*, pp. 348, 363.
70. Pitirim A. Sorokin, *Social and Cultural Dynamics*, esp. *IV*, 1941, pp. 587-620, also *Society, Culture and Personality*, Harper and Bros., New York, 1947, pp. 537-713.
71. A. Lesser, *The Pawnee Ghost Dance Hand Game*, Columbia University, Contributions to Anthropology, 16, 1933, pp. 333-337.
72. L. A. White, "Diffusion versus Evolution: An Antievolutionist Fallacy," *Am. Anthropologist*, XLVII 1945, pp. 339-56.
73. M. J. Herskovits, *op. cit.*, pp. 236, 625.
74. R. Linton, *Cultural Background of Personality*, p. 32.
75. G. P. Murdock "The Common Denominator of Cultures," in *The Science of Man and the World Crisis* (R. Linton, ed.), pp. 126, 130-134, 137.
76. J. L. Gillin and J. P. Gillin, *op. cit.*, pp. 84, 563.

77. B. Malinowski, "Culture," in *Encycl. of the Soc. Sc., vol. IV.,* p. 622.
78. A. L. Kroeber, *op. cit.,* pp. 346-348.
79. Close to our standpoint is K. Lewin, who says: "Neither group 'habits' nor individual habits can be understood sufficiently by a theory which . . . conceives of the 'habit' as a kind of frozen linkage . . . Instead, habits will have to be conceived of as a result of forces in the organism and its life space, in the group and its setting. The structure of the organism, of the group of the setting . . . has to be represented . . . if the processes are to be understood scientifically." (*Field Theory,* p. 173).
80. Already W. I. Thomas and F. Znaniecki have noted the problems of such a sudden breaking down of the military discipline (*Polish Peasant . . .,* vol. I, p. 11).
81. R. E. Byrd, *Alone,* G. P. Putnam's Sons, 1938.
82. C. Kluckhohn uses similar, though different, concepts: "To phenomena of patterning in the covert culture it is proposed to apply the term *configuration* as a master concept comparable to 'pattern' in the overt culture" ("Patterning as exemplified by Navaho Culture," in *Language, Culture and Personality,* essays in memory of E. Sapir, Menasha, Wisconsin, 1941, p. 124). He says also that configurations ". . . are Sapir's unconscious systems of meanings, Benedict's unconscious canons of choice" and that they are 'motivations' for the culture carriers (*ibid.,* pp. 125, 128). To us, the overt, as well as the covert culture, is based on relevant configurations.
83. R. B. Cattell speaks about these kinds of unconscious adjustments. The unconscious superego especially plays an important role in them. (See his *Personality,* p. 395).
84. See H. G. Barnett, *op. cit.,* p. 395.
85. The borderline between facts and ideas of course is not clear. Ideas are facts, too; and some of them are generally considered as such. Others are not. Most of the non-material social phenomena, such as laws or mores are now undoubtedly considered as facts. The formulated individuals' wishes, plans, levels of aspiration, frustrations, concepts, and so on, are generally considered as ideas. But we gladly count them as facts if they belong to other people or to a group. The main reason for our considering our psychic states as ideas is that we may, though not always, change them if we wish. Sometimes we feel that the ideas of other people may also change. In such a case, we are inclined to handle them as ideas rather than as facts. But more endurable ideas of other people, and especially those of groups, are generally handled as facts.
86. See *Life,* Sept. 21, 1953, pp. 131-142.
87. See *The New York Times,* March 12, 1954, pp. 1, 5.
88. I. E. Farber, H. F. Harlow and L. J. West explain such cases by DDD (debility, dependency and dread), possibly by learning and conditioning. These (as well as empathy and some other factors), of course, only set the processes of organization in motion (see "Brainwashing, Conditioning and DDD," in *Sociometry,* 20, 1957, pp. 271-285).
89. Owing to the influence of Sapir, language leads in this respect. Thus, Gillin (*op. cit.,* p. 315) considers grammatical rules as generally not conscious. So does Herskovits (*op. cit.,* pp. 214, 543), who discusses the unconscious rules of grammar, as well as the dormant linguistic resources of people. Kroeber (*op. cit.,* pp. 11, 245, 246, 248, 427, 580) stresses the

unconscious structure of language. He also speaks about unconscious ethno-centrism, unconscious social structure, unconscious activity, and changes of culture (especially of its linguistic and esthetic components), and about the unconsciousness of culture. Herskovits (*op. cit.*, pp. 585, 223) mentions sanctions of culture beneath the level of consciousness. Kluckhohn ("Patterning as Exemplified by Navaho Culture," pp. 125-128) and Herskovits (*op. cit.*, p. 224) speak about unconscious configurations. Kroeber (*op. cit.*, pp. 249, 417) and Gillin (*op. cit.*, p. 477) consider some patterns as unconscious or not conscious. Gillin and Gillin (*op. cit.*, p. 315) say that culture is composed of customs, folkways, mores . . . organized consciously or unconsciously. Linton speaks about unconscious attitudes and values (*op. cit.*, pp. 112, 142). Barnett (*op. cit.*, pp. 262, 119) mentions unconscious prototypes and unconscious reworking of a myth. And the sociologist Ogburn (*op. cit.*, p. 180) states that conformity to customs seems to be insisted upon consciously or unconsciously.

INDEX OF NAMES

299

172, 174, 175, 225
Coover, J. E., 6
Cottrell, L. S., XIX, XXIII
Cournot, A., 83
Creegan, R. F., 171
Crespi, L. P., 71, 83
Crutchfield, R. S., 203, 204, 224, 229
Cuber, J. F., 224

Dashiell, J. F., 14, 71, 83, 100, 133, 136, 154, 174, 225
David, H. P., 224, 255
Davis, W. A., 190
Dewey, J., 116, 133, 135, 136
Dickson, W. J., 191, 225
Diller, L., 204
Dollard, J., 71, 83, 85, 99, 100, 204, 295
Dummer, E. S., 29
Dunlap, K., 1
Durkheim, E., XVIII, XXIII, 142, 172, 191, 295

Eckermann, J. P., 129
Edison, T. A., 50
Edwards, A. L., 13, 133
Eggan, F., 268, 295
Egner, F., 238
Eindhoven, J. E., 136
Ellwood, C. A., 83
Eriksen, C. W., 86, 100
Estes, S. G., 8

Farber, I. E., 296
Faris, E., XIX, XXIII, 70, 74, 83, 94, 100, 288
Faris, R. E. L., 86, 94, 99, 100, 134
Farnsworth, P. R., 171
Fensterheim, H., 225
Fiedler, F. E., 200, 205
Field, A., 71
Fiske, D. W., 225
Flugel, J. C., 238

Folsom, J. K., 71
Fredericksen, N., 74
Freeman, E., 171, 175
French, V. V., 141, 153, 171, 172, 174
Freud, S., 16, 17, 18, 28, 30, 101, 102, 133, 194, 238
Fromm, E., 15, 172, 175, 265, 266, 294

Gardner, B. B., 225
Gauss, C. F., 130
Gibby, R. G., 255
Gibson, J. J., 204
Gilchrist, J. C., 225
Gillin, J. L., 206, 224, 258, 269, 281, 293, 294, 295, 296
Gillin, J. P., 206, 224, 258, 259, 264, 269, 281, 293, 294, 295, 296
Gluck, W., 129
Goethe, J. W., 49, 129
Goffman, E., 51
Goldenweiser, A. A., 258, 259, 263, 264, 269, 293, 294, 295
Goldiamond, I., 1, 4
Goodnow, J. J., 136
Gorden, R. L., 142
Greenwood, E., XIX, XXIII
Guetzkow, H., 29
Guratzsch, W., 6, 13
Guthrie, E. R., 13, 85, 133

Hadamard, J. S., 102, 129, 133
Haigh, G. V., 225
Halbwachs, M., 87, 100, 229
Hallowell, A. I., 258, 293
Hamilton, W. R., 130
Hankin, H., 14, 106
Hansen, F. C. C., 1
Harlow, H. F., 296
Hart, B., 141
Hart, C. W., 74, 83
Hartley, E. L., 19, 29, 51, 72, 83, 84, 141, 142, 155, 171, 172, 175, 190, 204, 207, 224, 225

300

302

303

White, L. A., 279, 295
Whyte, W. F., 295
Whyte, W. H., 74, 84, 204
Wickens, D. D., 70
Wilamowitz-Moellendorf, U., 116
Williams, R. M., 224
Wissler, C., 83
Wolf, K. M., 205
Wolff, K. H., XXIII
Wolff, W., 207, 224
Woodruff, A. D., 207, 224, 225
Woodworth, R. S., 83
Wundt, W., 171

Young, K., 13, 14, 71, 83, 86, 100, 134, 171, 172, 175, 193, 202, 203, 204, 206, 224

Zander, A. F., 142, 172, 190, 191, 204, 205
Zawadski, B., 204
Zener, K. E., 23, 119, 136
Znaniecki, F., XVIII, XXIII, 192, 202, 206, 224, 296

INDEX OF SUBJECTS

306

307

308

311

312

Levels of aspiration, 56, 232, 242
Linguistic achievements, 92
Linguistic experiences, 25
Linguistic feelings, 152
Linguistic habits, 283
Linguistic patterns, 25, 90, 91
Literary style, 25
Loss of position, 39-41
Love, 76-77
  components of, 231
  culturally accepted types of, 231
  feelings, 232
  of science, 76, 77
Loyalty, 276, 288
  development of, xvii, 185, 220
Lust, 231

Majority patterns, 24
Mannerisms, 276
Marginal experiences, 5-15, 123, 146
Marginal grasping of character, 9-10
Marginal impressions, 5, 246
Marginal perceptions, 12, 94, 212, 214, 251
  incidental, 10, 12
Masochistic tendencies, 265
Mass meetings, 213
Masses, 9, 47, 110
Maturation, 85
Maze, 87
Meaning, given to a configuration, 236, 251
Meaningful configurations, 241
Mechanism of escape, 265
Mechanists, 101
Medical doctors, 14, 107
Memory, 43
Memory traces, 6, 16, 17, 96
  inactive, 45
  individual, 18
  original, 18
  provision of, 239
  storehouse of, 17, 42, 240
  unchanged, 18
Method, xxi
  scientific, 125

Mimicking, 75
Models, social, 41-42, 43-49, 164, 248
  combination of, 48
  historical, 50
  imitation of, 42, 43-49, 79
  literary, 49
  unrecollected, 41-43
  well-accepted, 47
Mood, 5, 12, 212, 233, 258
Moral feelings, 125, 148, 150, 151
Moral norms, 119, 150, 186, 188
Moral obligations, 188
Moral rectitude, 201
Mores, 242, 262, 276
Motivation, xix, 193, 264
Motives, 240, 253
  autonomous, 230-231
  hidden, 115
Mystical excitement, 156

Nazis (Nazism), xvii, 20, 155, 161, 162, 163, 209, 220, 274, 286, 287, 288
Need, 42, 62, 207, 223, 240, 242, 253, 258, 264, 266, 271, 285
  acquired, 62
  derived, 267
  for change, 257
  inborn, 62
  unconscious, 259, 260
Neurograms, 17, 115
Nonconformity, 212
Normalizing, 18
Normative coloring, 24, 124
Normative elements, 24
Normative summations, 126, 151, 152
Normativity, 23, 24
Norms, 3, 11, 12, 24, 47, 94, 97, 103, 105, 106, 116, 118, 120, 121, 127, 149, 151, 152, 164, 165, 184-186, 242, 244, 256, 262, 267
  change of, 126
  cultural, 81, 132, 251
  development of, xvii
  esthetic, 186
  legal, 189

313

moral, 119, 150, 186, 232
of beauty, 188
religious, 232
social (*See* Social norms)
standardization of, 102
validity of, 126

Obligations, 94, 121, 124, 149, 233, 256
moral, 188
unconscious operation of, 186
unconsciously established, 185
Opinion, 12, 16, 40
public, 11, 263
Organization, 106, 208, 217, 235
continuous, 229
laws of, 251
of attitudes, 243
of configurations, 229-238
of experiences, 232
of marginal impressions, 5
of perceptual traces (activities), 105
of traces, 18, 241, 242
unconscious, 2, 5, 10, 217, 287, 290
Organizational activities,
of human mind, 236
Organizational processes, 257, 290
Outward behavior, 25-26

Painters, 158, 249
Paralysis, 18
Participation in social life, 12, 103
Patriotic feelings, 97, 153, 158, 285, 286, 287
Patriotism, xvii
Patterns, 290
acceptance of, 253
artistic, 276
change of, 263, 264
cultural, 27, 60, 98, 152, 159, 164, 234
enemy, 288
group, 98
linguistic, 25
of behavior, 24, 46, 60, 80, 131, 276

political, 276
prefabricated, 232, 234
reacceptance of, 290
religious, 276
reshaping of, 290
subcultural, 98, 164
Perception, 106, 192, 193, 199, 210, 242, 288
direct, 8
incidental, 12
marginal, 12, 94, 212, 214, 251
of concealed thoughts, 7-8
selective, 197, 290
subliminal, 2, 94, 212, 214
unconscious, 95, 259, 290
Peripheral part of personality structure, 240
Peripheral vision, 6
Personality, 287
and culture, 229-238
and culture process, 256-297
basic, 258, 266
fictitious, 49
in cultural setting, 245-250
in social setting, 245-250
literary, 49-50
organization of, 42, 240
periphery of structure of, 240
socialized, 239-255
stage, 48
structure, 153, 239-244
workshop, 281
Play-acting, 159
Pleasantness, 139
Point of reference, 23, 24, 232
establishment of, 25
unconscious establishment of, 126
Politicians, 9, 89, 247-248
Prefabricated patterns, 232,
Prefabricated structures, 241
Pressure, 217, 245, 248, 253
inconspicuous, 78
of physical forces, 235
social, 142, 161, 235, 244
to solve a problem, 46
yielding to, 47

314

315

316

317

318

319

320

Unconscious striving, XIX
Unconscious structure of language, 297
Unconscious summation, 123, 125, 151, 209
of emotional reactions, 163
Unconscious tendencies, 259
Unconscious thinking, 41, 102, 195, 196, 212, 260
creative, 131
processes, 102, 196
Unconscious values, 281, 290, 297
Unconscious viewpoints, 36
Unconsciously established concepts, 127
Unconsciously established frames of reference, 122, 248
Unconsciously operating set, 55
Unconsciously organized impressions, 5, 217
Union of Czech Brethren, 266
Unpleasantness, 139
Unrecollected experiences, 21, 30-51, 123, 232, 233, 260, 262
Unrecollected factors, 34
Unrecollected idea, 260
of a role, 49
Unrecollected knowledge, 31

Valuation, 259
Value-attitude system, 266
Values, 11, 87, 94, 95, 97, 103, 106, 116, 118, 119, 121, 127, 149, 164, 165, 177, 188, 192, 206-225, 230, 233, 242, 243, 244, 245, 249, 251, 256, 257, 262, 264, 267, 276, 279, 281, 283, 290
development of, XVII
Values, personal, 11, 87, 94, 95, 207-210

establishment of, 207-210
Values, social, 12, 18, 35, 60, 81, 87, 94, 95, 160, 210-223
acceptance of, 221
assimilation of, 215
collective creation of, 216-218
creating processes, 218
defense of, 221-223
definition of, 206-207
enforcement of, 221-223
esthetic, 231
formation of, 210-220
through acceptance of personal value, 214-216
through discussion, 211-214
through interaction, 210-214
imitation of, 220
minority, 211, 213
observation of, 221-223
recognition of, 221-223
religious, 222
special, 217
unchangeable, 219
unconscious acceptance of, 219, 220
unconscious creating of, 217
unconscious defense of, 251
unconscious imitation of, 220
unconscious modification of, 219
unconscious operation of, 222-223
validity of, 3, 11
Vasomotor disturbances, 18
Vectors, 127, 235
"Verstehen," 105
Vocabulary, 16

Wishes, 149, 223, 233, 240, 248, 260, 261, 264, 265, 271, 285

Zuni, 154

ACKNOWLEDGMENTS

Acknowledgment is gratefully made to the publishers of the following works for permission to reprint selected passages:

B. Blanshard, *The Nature of Thought,* George Allen & Unwin, Ltd., London, 1948.

J. G. Miller, *Unconsciousness,* John Wiley & Sons, Inc., New York, 1950.